W9-CXV-008

automotive
SUSPENSIONS · STEERING
ALIGNMENT and BRAKES

FIFTH EDITION

WALTER E. BILLIET

WALTER ALLEY

AMERICAN TECHNICAL PUBLISHERS, INC.
HOMEWOOD, ILLINOIS 60430

Copyright ©, 1951, 1955, 1962, 1969, 1974, by
AMERICAN TECHNICAL PUBLISHERS, INC.

Library of Congress Card Catalog No.: 73-80444
ISBN: 0-8269-0122-0

56789–74–1514131211

The first two editions appeared under the title:
AUTOMOTIVE SUSPENSIONS, STEERING,
AND WHEEL ALIGNMENT.

PRINTED IN THE UNITED STATES OF AMERICA

Part One
Automotive
Suspensions
Steering
and
Alignment

CONTENTS

Part One

PREFACE TO THE FIFTH EDITION

This new FIFTH EDITION of *AUTOMOTIVE SUSPENSIONS, STEERING, ALIGNMENT AND BRAKES* has been revised and updated to include the most current information on Frames, Suspension Systems, Springs and Shock Absorbers, Steering Systems, Wheels and Tires, and the various methods of correction and repair.

When the automobile was first developed, steering, suspensions and brakes were relatively simple mechanisms. For the lightweight, low speed automobiles of that era they were adequate for the purpose. However, as the automobile developed in complexity these simple mechanisms were no longer adequate to provide the steering and braking control necessary to handle the higher speeds and heavier weights of the modern vehicle.

The ever-increasing demands made upon the entire suspension system (the axle, springs, steering gear and linkages) made necessary a series of almost constant refinements which have resulted in the entire suspension system evolving into a complex arrangement of parts requiring precision measurement and adjustment. The complex suspensions and steering linkages of today's automobiles demand precision measurement and adjustment for safe, efficient operation. For this reason, the mechanic who desires to become an expert needs to thoroughly understand the construction, mainte-

nance and repair of automotive suspensions and steering systems, and the knowledge of how to measure, interpret, and correct whatever causes faulty operation of any of the systems.

Involved with wheel alignment is the need for checking and correcting any frame damage or misalignment which may be present, since the frame is the foundation on which the suspension, and steering linkages are mounted. The newer type of unitized body construction calls for different procedures and techniques that require a full knowledge on the part of the mechanic who services them. This Fifth Edition supplies the practical information necessary to the understanding and development of those procedures. A special chapter on "Customized Vehicle Alignment" gives additional information necessary to the efficient use of latest equipment and procedures of precision alignment.

The development of the brake system has paralleled the other improvements in the automobile. As refinements and increased performance have taken place, the demands on the brake system have also increased. The complexity of the modern brake system and the need for more exacting service requires a thorough understanding of the operating principles and construction of brakes.

Since frame, wheel alignment, and brakes are generally unrelated to other aspects of service, the student can concentrate on becoming a specialist in this field without knowledge or experience in other kinds of automotive service.

A new appendix has also been added to provide a review of math including metric operations.

This FIFTH EDITION of AUTO-MOTIVE SUSPENSIONS, STEER-ING, ALIGNMENT AND BRAKES thoroughly covers frame designs and methods of correcting frame damage. Likewise, the subject of suspension sys-tems, steering control, tire wear, vehicle alignment and brakes and brake service are presented completely and logically in easy-to-understand language. AUTO-SUSPENSIONS, STEERING, ALIGN-MENT AND BRAKES is intended not only to teach the beginner but also to serve as an invaluable reference book for the accomplished mechanic.

The Publisher

Vehicle Positioned on Diagnostic/Service Alignment Rack. (*Hunter Engineering Corp.*)

CHAPTER 1

THE FRAME

For all practical purposes the frame of an automotive vehicle is the foundation upon which the car is built. The purpose of the frame is to provide a strong and rigid structure which will support the engine, transmission, drive shaft, springs, axles, wheels, tires, and the body which is mounted on the frame or is an integral part of the frame.

Proper alignment of the frame must be maintained at all times. Should misalignment result due to a collision, it is almost certain to affect alignment of doors, place undue strain on other body parts, and, generally, promote rapid body deterioration. If, for example, one side of the frame should be forced back farther than the other side as a result of a collision, the wheels of the vehicle would no longer be in alignment. The vehicle would then be unsafe for operation.

This chapter explains the practices and procedures applied in correcting and removing misalignment from an automotive vehicle frame. To achieve full understanding of frame correction and alignment it is necessary to become familiar with the various types of automotive vehicle frames and the differences in construction.

General Description of Frame

Frame side members, which are the basis of frame construction, are usually made of U-shaped channel sections as shown in Fig. 1-1, or box-shaped sections. Cross members of the same material reinforce the frame and provide support for the engine, wheels, and suspension systems. Various brackets and openings are provided to permit installation of the many parts which make up the automotive chassis.

The box channel type of construction is composed of two U-shaped channel sections fitted as shown in Fig. 1-1. The box construction is obtained by overlapping the free edges of two U channel sections and welding them together.

The various brackets, cross members, and braces are welded, riveted, or both, to the frame side rails.

Most frames are wide at the rear and narrow at the front. The narrow front

1

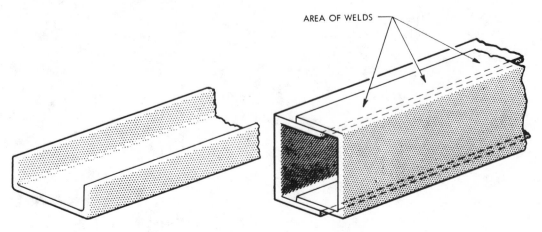

Fig. 1-1. U-channel frame section (left); box channel frame section (right).

construction enables the vehicle to make a shorter turn. A wide frame at the rear provides better support of the body.

Types of Frames

X-Type Frames

Frames vary in size and shape to accommodate the particular units they are intended to receive. Figure 1-2 illustrates an X-type frame construction. The side members or rails are of the box channel type construction. A heavy front cross member is used to support the upper and lower suspension control arms and coil springs. The "kick-up" at the rear (that portion of the frame raised above the center section) is to accommodate the rear axle assembly and permit flexing of the rear springs. With the center or main part of the frame dropped down between the front and rear wheels a lower center

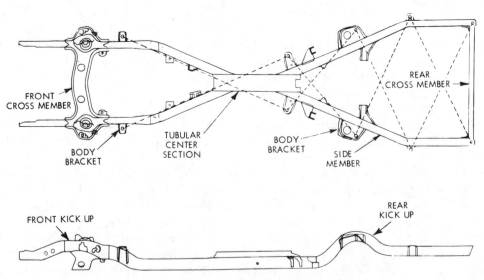

Fig. 1-2. X frame. (Chevrolet Motor Div., General Motors Corp.)

of gravity results for greater safety. Extended brackets welded to the frame side members provide for the mounting of the body.

Ladder-Type Frames

A ladder-type frame is illustrated in Fig. 1-3. No center bracing is provided in this frame. However, additional cross members provide the necessary bracing for rigidity. The side members are of the box channel type construction.

Perimeter-Type Frames

The perimeter-type frame as illustrated in Fig. 1-4 is similar in construction to the ladder frame. The full length side rails support the body at its greatest width which provides more protection to the passengers in case of a side impact to the body. The bend in the frame side rail just behind the front suspension cross member is sometimes referred to as a torque box section.

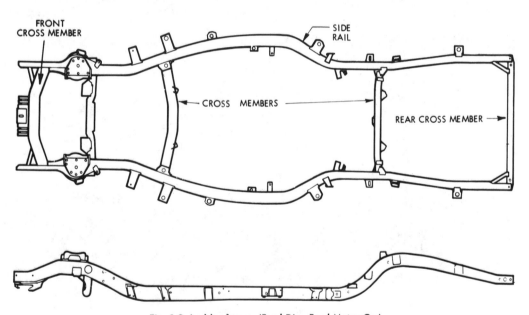

FRONT CROSS MEMBER

SIDE RAIL

CROSS MEMBERS

REAR CROSS MEMBER

Fig. 1-3. Ladder frame. (Ford Div., Ford Motor Co.)

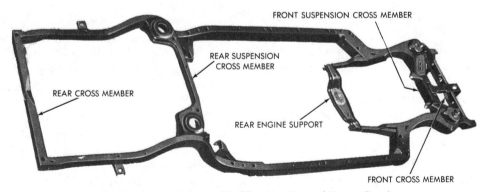

FRONT SUSPENSION CROSS MEMBER

REAR SUSPENSION CROSS MEMBER

REAR CROSS MEMBER

REAR ENGINE SUPPORT

FRONT CROSS MEMBER

Fig. 1-4. Perimeter frame. (Cadillac Div., General Motors Corp.)

Stub Frame

The frame used on a number of vehicles consists of a half frame (stub frame) and half unibody construction. The frame consists of short frame side members extending from behind the front doors to the front of the vehicle joined laterally by cross members. This provides support for the engine, front suspension assembly, steering mechanism, and transmission. The rear section has the frame as an integral part of the body, Fig. 1-5.

blies, which include the rocker panels form the underbody area, incorporate attachment provisions for the power plant, power train, and suspension systems. The side rails, sometimes referred to as body sills on this type of construction, and the various cross members are of heavy box type sections which distribute the load over broad areas of the body structure.

The front suspension member assembly which supports the engine and front suspension is structurally similar to the front end of a conventional frame. The rear suspension member assembly which

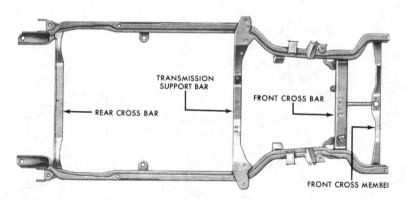

TRANSMISSION SUPPORT BAR

FRONT CROSS BAR

REAR CROSS BAR

FRONT CROSS MEMBEI

Fig. 1-5. Stub Frame. (*Chevrolet Div., General Motors Corp.*)

Unitized Body and Frame Construction

Some manufacturers combine the body and frame into a single unitized section. All of the metal parts which make up the body shell and supports for the driving, braking, and suspension loads are welded into a single unit, thus creating an integral body and frame of all steel welded construction. Figure 1-6 illustrates a typical unitized body and frame with the various components.

The floor pans and side rail assem-

supports the rear suspension is also similar to the rear end of a conventional frame; however, the assemblies are integrated into the rest of the body assembly.

Above the side rails the body structure is comparable to that of a vehicle with a separate body and frame construction.

Care must be exercised when using a jack or hoist to lift a vehicle with this type of construction. Unless the jack or hoist makes contact on rigid members, damage to the underbody may result.

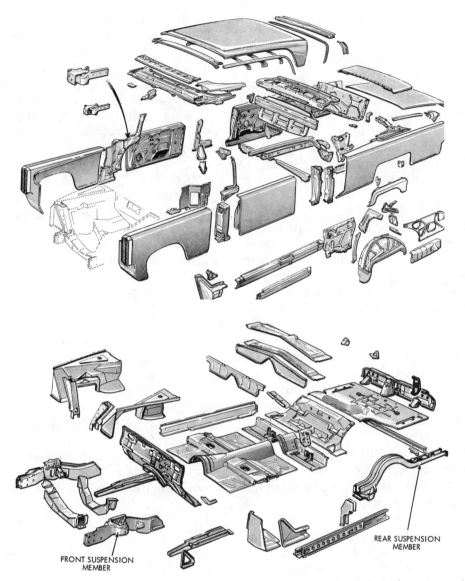

Fig. 1-6. Unitized type of body and frame construction, upper body (*top*) and underbody (*bottom*) assembly. In this type of construction the frame structure is built into the body. (*Lincoln Mercury Div., Ford Motor Co.*)

General Principles of Frame Repair

Ordinarily the only service required on frames is the result of an accident which has twisted, bent, or broken the frame. Generally it is possible to repair such damage by straightening the twisted or bent member. Those parts that cannot be repaired must be replaced. Each year more and more car manufacturers are employing unitized body and frame constructions. With unitized design becoming increasingly popular, body and frame repair are no longer distinct and separate operations.

Importance of Correct Alignment

As body damage corrections are made, it is absolutely essential that underbody alignment also be corrected as part of the entire operation. Correct frame alignment is very important in order to maintain correct steering, wheel alignment, and proper tire wear patterns.

Three Basic Steps

In frame straightening, the principles of reversing the forces of the original impact are used to restore the damaged frame and body sections. Frame repair can be made without the removal of the body, engine, or drive train. Three basic steps to follow are:

Analysis. Make a complete analysis to determine the amount of body-frame damage and misalignment.

Correction Sequence. Reverse the forces of impact in the proper sequence through the correct usage of essential tools and hook-ups.

Gaging. Check all dimensional planes with the correct gages to make certain measurements are within the manufacturer's specifications.

In the following discussion of these three basic points *analysis* and *correction* sequence will be treated as separate operations. *Gaging* will be explained as it applies to each separate operation.

Analysis of Kinds of Frame Damage

Frame damage usually results from a collision. However, a collision does not always produce frame damage. The direction of impact usually indicates the type of frame damage to look for. Over a period of years, the manufacturers of body straightening equipment, shop owners, and collision experts, have established a fundamental approach or collision pattern for estimating frame damage. Generally speaking, an average collision pattern would be 50% of the collision (damage) to the front of the vehicle, 40% to the rear of the vehicle, and 10% to the center of the vehicle.

Center Section Damage

Since the center of the vehicle frame is the least likely to be damaged in a collision, it is logical that the center section is the first to be checked. If the center section of the frame proves to be undamaged, it will then serve as a starting point so as to analyze the remainder of the frame.

Two types of damage may exist in the center section of the frame although the side rails may not be damaged; these are the *diamond* and the *twist*.

Diamond. Diamond damage is a misalignment that has occurred when the impact of a collision has forced one side member of the frame further back than the other, causing the body to shift on the frame. As a result of an impact on either front corner of the car, a diamond frame will be noticed by an unequal spacing between the rear bumper and the rear end of the body. Looking underneath the car, a diamond frame will be evidenced by the body bolts having been wrenched (shifted) on the body brackets on one side of the damaged car. Also note that the road film (dirt, etc.) will be cracked at the junction of the cross-members and side rails. Usually the box type frame is more susceptible to diamond damage than other types of frames.

Look at Fig. 1-7 and note that dimension A should be equal to dimension B if the frame is free from diamond damage. If dimension B were one inch longer than dimension A, the right rail would

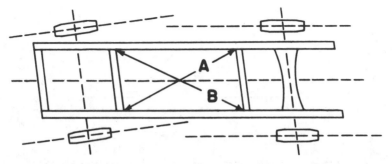

Fig. 1-7. Diamond type of frame damage which is usually the result of a front collision. (*John Bean Corp.*)

then be ½ inch behind the left rail. The frame would, therefore, have a one inch diamond. If the difference between the right and left rail were ½ inch or less, then this condition would not normally warrant straightening, since one rail would be only ¼ inch behind the other. The bumper bracket holes are slotted on the frame to make up for this difference.

The simplest way to determine the exact amount of diamond damage would be to cross check (measurements A and B, Fig. 1-7) with a tape measure. These measurements should be taken between the jig holes in the frame rails, since jig holes found in one rail have matching holes in the other rail. Rivets may be used to measure from, but recognize the fact that the rivet head may not be directly over the center of the hole and could cause an error in measurement. If the muffler is in the way, a two point tram (gage used for aligning) may be used to make the measurements as shown in Fig. 1-8. The use of a diamond sight gage is another method that reveals a dia-

Fig. 1-8. Cross checking a vehicle by means of a two-point tram or gage. (*John Bean Corp.*)

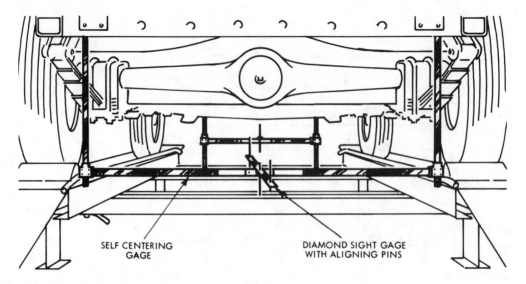

Fig. 1-9. Diamond sight gage. Note that the vertical aligning pins of each sight gage must be in direct alignment if the vehicle is free of diamond damage. See Fig. 1-11. (*John Bean Corp.*)

SELF CENTERING GAGE

DIAMOND SIGHT GAGE WITH ALIGNING PINS

mond frame very quickly. This gage is mounted 90 degrees to a self-centering gage and the pins of all the gages should align if the frame is free from diamond damage. See Fig. 1-9.

Twist. A twist in the frame is usually the result of a collision in which a vehicle that is carrying a heavy load has been overturned. This action raises one rail of the frame higher than the opposite rail, as shown in Fig. 1-10.

A vehicle that has a twisted frame will not set level to the ground. However, this may not be true in all cars that do not set level to the ground, since a weak or broken spring will give the same effect. One way of determining if the frame is twisted is to jack up the frame between the front wheels and observe if the car sets level. If the car sets level, then jack up the rear of the frame with the front wheels on the ground (jack in center of

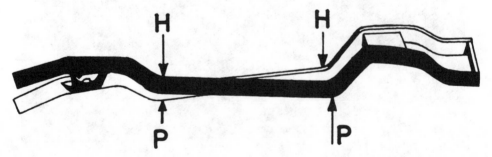

Fig. 1-10. A twisted frame as the result of a collision. The points marked H denote where the frame is to be held during the straightening process while the points marked P denote where the correcting force or *pull* is to be applied. (*John Bean Corp.*)

Fig. 1-11. Two self-centering gages mounted under a unitized body and frame construction to determine whether the body and frame are twisted. If the gage bars are not parallel when mounted, the body and frame then has a twisted condition which is referred to as twist damage. (*John Bean Corp.*)

frame) and observe if the car then sets level. If at both ends of the car, the car sets level, the uneven trim height when all four wheels are on the ground is due to a twisted frame and not to bad springs. The body may also be twisted and usually the glass in front or rear will not remain in the body intact.

Two self-centering gages mounted on the frame at the extremities of the center section will show the exact amount of twist in the frame. Sight the gage bars from front to rear. The gage bars, as shown in Fig. 1-11, must be parallel if the frame is free from twist.

The gage is called self-centering because the pin in the center of the gage always remains in the center regardless of how wide the gage is expanded. The gages are held in place by small pins which fit into the jig holes in the side rails of the frame. On a unitized body, however, the gages are mounted by means of C clamps, magnetic adaptors, or special studs screwed into the bottom of the body. A mounted self-centering gage is shown in Fig. 1-12.

Sag and Raise. Diamond and twist are the only types of damage that may exist in the center section of the frame in which the frame side rails have not been deformed.

The bottom edges of most side rails are flat underneath the body of the car. Sag is misalignment of the frame when one or both rails are bent downward upon impact. Raise frame damage occurs when one or both side rails are bent upward.

Visually, sag or raise damage to the side rails may be determined by a poor fit of the doors and a buckle in the roof. The rail itself will be buckled on top if the misalignment condition is sag, whereas a rail that has raise damage will be buckled on the bottom. Buckles in the rail, as shown in Fig. 1-13, are the result of one side of the rail shortening while the opposite side of the same rail stretches.

Sag or raise in the center frame section can be determined by the use of three self-centering gages, as shown in Fig. 1-14. If all three gages sight level, the center frame section is free from sag or raise. If the middle gage, which is placed at the cowl area, is higher at one end than at the other, one rail may have a sag condi-

Fig. 1-12. A self-centering gage mounted under a vehicle to determine the extent and type of vehicle damage due to a collision. The gage is called self-centering because no matter where the gage is placed, the center pointer will always be in the center of the gage. (*John Bean Corp.*)

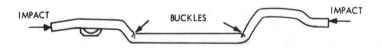

Fig. 1-13. A sag in the center section of a frame side rail. During a front or rear collision, the force of impact will cause one or both side rails to bend at its lowest point of construction, that is, the dip in the center area. This condition, if the buckles are on top of the frame side rail, is known as sag. (*John Bean Corp.*)

tion while the opposite rail may have a raise condition.

Since most side rails in the center section of the frame are level on the bottom, a straight edge may be used across the bottom of both rails to determine which rail is damaged. Usually a side rail will sag downward rather than raise upward as the result of a collision.

Sway. Sway occurs when one or both side rails are bent either inward or outward, depending upon the direction of

Fig. 1-14. Using three self-centering gages to check for frame sag. Note that all three gages must be in horizontal alignment if the frame is free from sag damage. (*John Bean Corp.*)

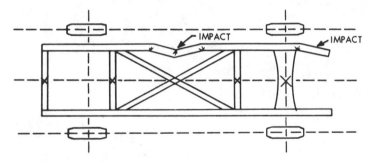

Fig. 1-15. A frame with center sway. When the force of impact during a collision forces one frame side rail inward toward the center of the vehicle, this condition is known as *sway*. The vehicle will lean *away* from the point of damage. (*John Bean Corp.*)

impact. Sway is a lateral misalignment of the frame due to a collision. The side rails of the frame will show evidence of sway by being buckled. The buckles will appear in the side of the rail, as shown in Fig. 1-15. An X-type frame with tubular center will usually bend at either end of the tubular center should sway damage occur.

Three self-centering gages placed in the center section of the frame will determine the amount and direction of misalignment. If the pins of all three gages as sighted from front to rear are in exact alignment, the center section is then free from sway. Refer to Fig. 1-14.

Rear Section Damage

If the tests made on the center section of the frame indicate that it is undamaged, then either the front or rear section should be checked. If the front of the vehicle obviously has been damaged then the rear section should be checked first. This may easily be done by taking the middle self-centering gage from under the center of the frame and placing it on the rear of the frame. The bars of all three gages will be parallel in the absence of sag or raise in the rear section of the frame. However, both rails may have the same amount of sag or raise damage. To determine the extent of rear frame damage, if any, a set of three side rail height gages may also be used. A manufacturer's dimension manual for each make of car

TRU–WAY GAGES

Fig. 1-16. Tru-way gages are installed on the frame, one at the front of the center section, one at the rear of the center section, and one at the rear of the vehicle side rail, to determine whether sag or raise damage is present in the frame. The two center gages are set as sighting pins to determine the location of the rear pin. If the rear pin is above the sight level, the frame rail is too high (raise damage). If the rear pin is below the sight level, the frame rail is too low (sag damage). (John Bean Corp.)

will give the height of the side rail at various points of the frame.

Usually the rear section buckles at the top of the rail in front of the rear kick-up and under the rail over the rear axle housing.

The height or tru-way gages, as shown in Fig. 1-16, will determine which side rail is out of alignment and which rail is the correct height.

The pin of the rear-self-centering gage will, when it is sighted with the pins of the other two self-centering gages, reveal any sway damage that may exist in the rear section of the frame. See Fig. 1-14.

Front Section Damage

The front section of the vehicle may now be checked for damage and repairs. Follow the same general procedure that was used to diagnose the damage to the rear section. A self-centering gage is placed on the front part of the frame, as shown in Fig. 1-14, to determine the extent and nature of damage. If the bar of the self-centering gage does not align with the two gages underneath the center section of the vehicle, the front frame section probably has a sag at the cowl area (in line with the windshield). A buckle will be visible at the top of the damaged rail underneath the cowl area and there will be a raise at the front suspension pocket. The front suspension pocket will be egg shaped - rather than round. Place the height gages on the side rail having the least amount of damage and check it out for height. The rail should meet height specifications within a tolerance of $\frac{1}{8}$ inch. If it does, the self-centering gages can then be used to determine when the other rail is straightened to the correct height. A complete analysis of the frame must take place before the frame straightening procedure begins.

Correction Sequence of Frame Repair

In general, the basic principle to follow when straightening a frame is to reverse the force that caused the damage, both in direction and amount. If heat is applied properly, the amount of force needed will be considerably less than the initial impact force. The energy that was consumed by the collision must be expended to straighten the frame and body back to its original condition.

The usual procedure that is followed is to straighten the side rails to their correct height and length. The side rails and frame can then be corrected for sway. After the sway misalignment has been corrected, the twist and diamond conditions are removed from the frame. As these corrections are made, the body must be brought along with the frame. Therefore, unitized body and frame construction will still entail the same basic frame straightening procedures as have been used for conventional frame straightening. Equipment used to straighten conventional type frames may be used on unitized body and frame construction if this equipment is brought up to date with modern body tools and gages. After the frame and body have been straightened, the front and rear suspensions must be completely repaired and aligned. Then the body shop may finish and paint the vehicle.

Using Straightening Equipment

The most simple tool used in straightening a damaged frame is the hydraulic ram, which is shown in Fig. 1-17. This tool can often be used directly against the frame to reverse the impact force of a collision. However, the ram is sometimes limited in its use since it can not always be brought against the work at the cor-

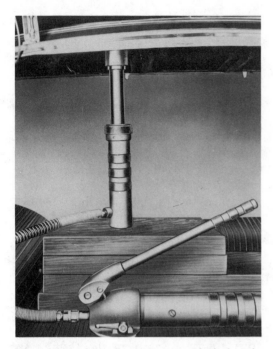

Fig. 1-17. The hydraulic ram is one method of applying the push which is necessary in frame and body straightening to correct damage inflicted on the vehicle as the result of a collision. (*Ford Div., Ford Motor Co.*)

rect angle. Often other vehicle parts such as the engine, exhaust pipe, etc., interfere with its use.

A body and frame aligner of the type shown in Fig. 1-18, uses the same type hydraulic ram as shown in Fig. 1-17. However, this ram is designed to apply the correcting force at any angle on all sections of the body or frame.

A frame straightener and body press, as shown in Fig. 1-19, is a more complete tool than the body and frame aligner. It often proves a faster method because more than one hook-up or correction may be made at the same time.

Repairing Frames

An analysis of the damage to a frame must be made before the condition can be corrected. The method used to straighten a frame usually depends upon the equipment available. In general, the body and frame aligner will use the same general method of hook-ups that the frame and body press would employ.

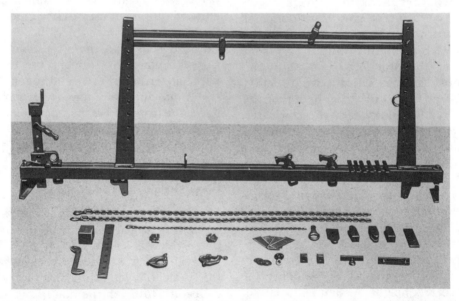

Fig. 1-18. The portable type of frame and body aligner, with its various clamps, chains and pull plates shown in the foreground. (*John Bean Corp.*)

Fig. 1-19. The frame and body press on which wheel aligning as well as frame and body straightening may be done. This type of construction is known as the *Visualiner*. (*John Bean Corp.*)

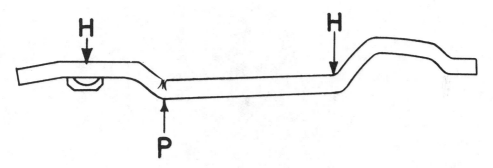

Fig. 1-20. A minor type of sag damage which exists in the frame side rail. Note that the buckle is on the top of the rail, causing the rail to sag downward. The points marked H indicate where the rail is to be held, while the points marked P indicate where the push or correcting force is to be applied. (*John Bean Corp.*)

Sag and Stretch Hook-ups. These are the most common hook-ups used and usually the first hook-ups made on a frame. A side rail that has a slight buckle at the top, as shown in Fig. 1-20, may be straightened by means of a chain hook-up attached to an aligner at the H positions. A corrective force in the form of a lift or push is applied by a hydraulic jack at the P position. This will straighten the side rail if the buckle is slight.

If the buckle is quite severe, a stretch and pull method must also be applied to the side rail. Figure 1-21 illustrates this

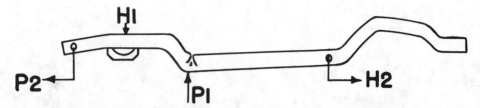

Fig. 1-21. The points marked H-1 and H-2 indicate where the frame side rail is to be held while the points marked P-1 and P-2 indicate where the correcting force is to be applied. This type of damage is similar to a compound fracture in a human bone, since the buckle is severe and more than one break may exist at that point. Therefore, this type of damage is known as a major sag. (*John Bean Corp.*)

method. The position marked P2, as shown in Fig. 1-21, is the point of applied pressure or pull and the H2 position the point of rear hook-up or hold. The buckle must be heated while pressure is applied to the rail or the buckle will tear.

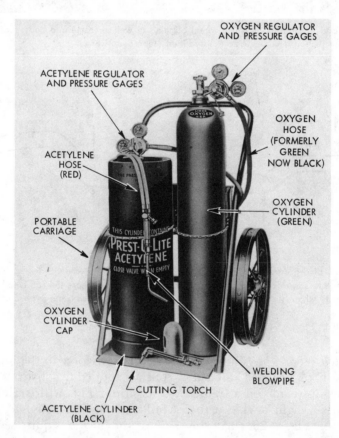

Fig. 1-22. Oxygen-acetylene welding unit. Note that each part of the unit is color coded for easy identification. (*Linde Air Products Co.*)

An oxygen-acetylene welding unit, as shown in Fig. 1-22, is used to provide the heat. During correction height gages are used to determine when the side rail has been straightened to its correct shape.

Figures 1-23 and 1-24 illustrate the

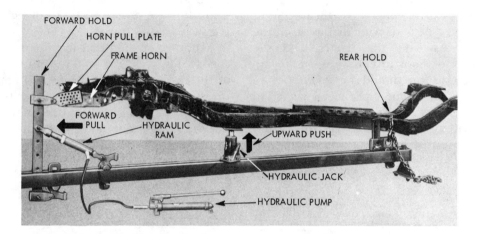

Fig. 1-23. The body and frame aligner in the process of correcting a sagged frame side rail. Pressure is supplied to the hydraulic rams by the hydraulic pump, the hydraulic rams applying an upward push at the center section of the rail and at the same time, a forward pull on the front section of the rail, thereby pushing and pulling the damaged rail into alignment. Note the position of the rear hold which allows only the damaged section to be moved. (*John Bean Corp.*)

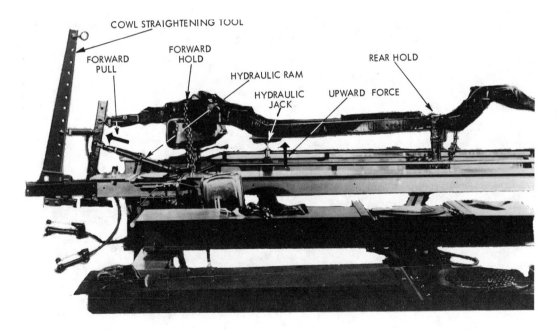

Fig. 1-24. The frame straightener and body press in the process of correcting a sagged frame side rail. Note the various hook-ups for applying the correcting force plus the body upright tool for correcting damage in the cowl area of the body. Note also the position of the forward and rear holds. (*John Bean Corp.*)

methods of hook-up for the body and frame aligner and the frame straightener and body press, which are used to correct a major sag condition.

Sway Correction. Sway is the next most common type of damage that exists in the frame. As with the stretch and sag method of hook-ups, heat must be applied. Caution should be taken not to overheat the frame, since metal heated to a dull cherry red color is hot enough for straightening purposes. If the metal should tear because heat was not applied

at the right place, immediately *stop the pulling action.* Then weld the tear with either an oxygen-acetylene welding torch or an arc welder. Figures 1-25 through 1-29 illustrate several methods of removing sway from a frame.

Another method that may be used to correct side sway is to hold the outer ends of the rail at the H positions and apply pressure on both rails at the P position. See Fig. 1-27. This will straighten the buckles in both rails and correct the sway in the frame.

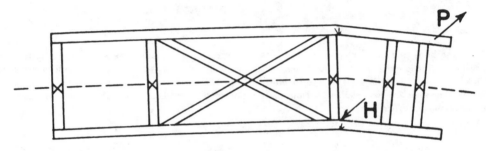

Fig. 1-25. A vehicle frame having side sway damage. The letter H is the point of hold, either against a frame crossmember, or if desired, a chain may be wrapped around the side rail at that point. The letter P indicates where the pull is to be applied. (*John Bean Corp.*)

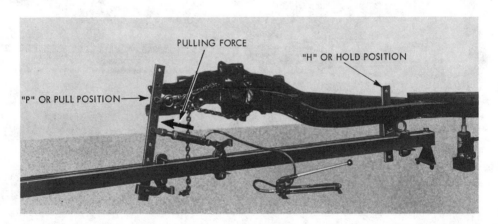

Fig. 1-26. The body and frame aligner correcting a frame side rail for sway. A chain is wrapped around the rail at point P and a tool bar is placed against the tube of the X member frame to provide the H or hold position. (*John Bean Corp.*)

On a frame straightener, a method known as a "sliding beam" setup is used to apply pressure at points P as illustrated in Fig. 1-27. A beam which is moved by means of a hydraulic ram is free to slide under the run-ways of the frame, applying pressure to the frame, Fig. 1-28. The sliding beam method is illus-

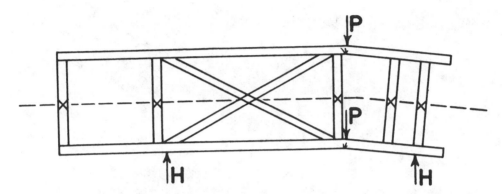

Fig. 1-27. Vehicle side sway in which the correcting force should be applied to both side rails, H marking the points of hold and P the points of push. (*John Bean Corp.*)

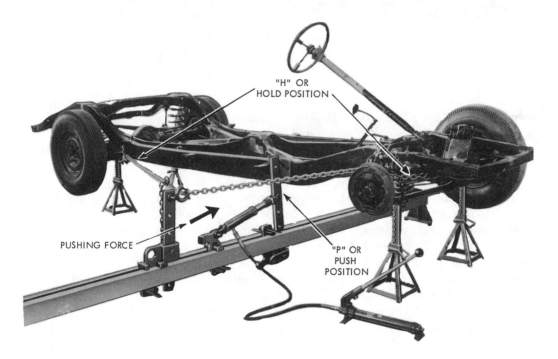

Fig. 1-28. The body and frame aligner in the process of correcting vehicle side sway. This method of alignment is often referred to as the bow string method. Push is applied against only one frame side rail and the vehicle body transmits the force of this push to the other rail. Therefore, the correcting force is applied to both rails through only one hook-up. (*John Bean Corp.*)

Fig. 1-29. The sliding beam method as used with the frame straightener and body press. The tool bars and carriage are in position to correct a vehicle frame with sway damage. (*John Bean Corp.*)

trated in Fig. 1-29. The hold or H positions are uprights (tool bars) which are locked to beams. These beams (called carriage beams) run crosswise or 90 degrees to the run-ways. The carriage beams are locked to the run-ways, as shown in Fig. 1-30. Therefore they provide the H or hold position against which the pressure or push may be applied so as to restore the frame to its original shape.

Twist Correction. After the sway condition has been corrected, any twist misalignment that may exist should next be removed from the frame. The side rails must be straight, and have the correct height, otherwise, the self-centering gages will not align after the twist condition has been removed. Figures 1-31 and 1-32 illustrate the hook-up methods and the pressures that are to be applied in removing a twist from the frame.

Diamond Correction. A diamond is the last major type of damage removed from the frame. There are two methods by which a diamond may be removed from the frame.

A diagonal push may be used as shown in Fig. 1-33.

A straight pull may be used to correct the diamond condition as shown in Fig. 1-34.

The portable frame and body aligner may be used to apply pressures to diagonally opposite corners of the frame, as shown in Fig. 1-33. The straight pull method of correcting a diamond frame, as shown in Fig. 1-34, is used only on a frame straightener.

Fig. 1-30. H or hold positions used to anchor the sliding beams to the runway of the frame straightener and body press. (*John Bean Corp.*)

Other Frame Hook-ups. At times a frame may be too narrow or too wide at various places for conventional hook-up methods. Figure 1-35 illustrates a squeezing action that may be applied to a frame to decrease the width. Figure 1-36 illustrates a spreading action that may be applied to a frame to increase its width.

In order to correct the front suspension cross members after a collision, it is necessary to apply pressure to the cross member from its center with the outer ends chained down. A cross member that sags causes the top of the wheels to lean inward, often to the extent that the normal adjusting procedures will not correct

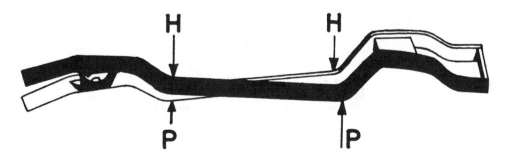

Fig. 1-31. The hold and push positions for correcting a vehicle with a twisted frame. The H positions are on the high points of the vehicle frame while the correcting force will be applied at the low points of the damaged frame area. (*John Bean Corp.*)

Fig. 1-32. Correcting a twisted frame with the frame straightener and body aligner. Chains are used to hold the carriage beams at the H position while the hydraulic jacks apply a pushing force at the P position. The hydraulic jacks are used to lift the frame until all the self-centering gages are in parallel alignment. Usually, the frame must be corrected past the misalignment, and in the opposite direction of the damage, in order to bring the frame to the correct position when the pressure is released. (*John Bean Corp.*)

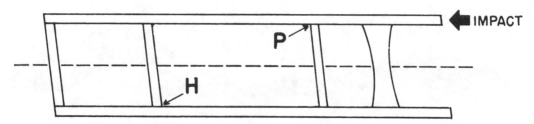

Fig. 1-33. The force of impact has forced one of the vehicle frame side rails slightly ahead of the other. This condition is known as diamond damage and can be removed from the frame by holding the side rail at point H while applying push in the direction opposite to that of the damage at point P. When the frame is cross measured at the center section and the distance is equal, the diamond damage has been removed. (*John Bean Corp.*)

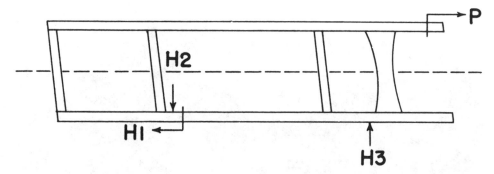

Fig. 1-34. The straight pull method for removing diamond frame damage. H-1 is the hold position to keep the frame from moving forward when the pull is applied at point P. H-2 and H-3 are the holds which are used to keep the frame from shifting off of the frame rack. Note that all of the hold positions are on the vehicle frame side rail opposite that to which the pulling force is applied. (*John Bean Corp.*)

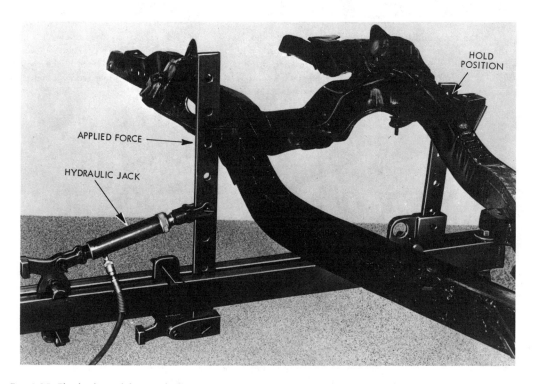

Fig. 1-35. The body and frame aligner being used to force the two frame side rails inward toward the vehicle center. The tool bar on the right frame rail provides the hold position, while the tool bar on the left frame rail provides the squeezing action when the hydraulic ram is expanded. (*John Bean Corp.*)

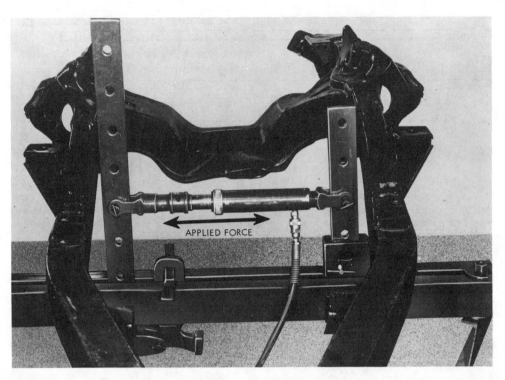

Fig. 1-36. The body and frame aligner being used to force the two frame side rails away from the vehicle center. The hydraulic ram is placed between the hold and the push positions, and when the ram is expanded, equal pressure is applied to both frame side rails, spreading the damaged portion of the frame back to the correct position. If the front end of the frame has been damaged so that the side rails are squeezed together, this hook-up may be used without removing the engine. (*John Bean Corp.*)

Fig. 1-37. Correcting a front crossmember for sag. Chains are used to hold the ends of the crossmember from moving upward as the hydraulic jack pushes upward against a plate which distributes the correcting force evenly to the bottom of the crossmember. (*John Bean Corp.*)

wheel camber to specifications. Figure 1-37 shows how this operation may be performed on a frame straightener.

In some types of collision the front cross member may be pushed rearward at the bottom. This causes a condition known as a rolled cross member which affects the caster of the front wheels. To straighten the cross member back to a satisfactory position, the method shown in Fig. 1-38 would be applied.

Good Hold Positions. In order that a pulling force may be applied to a side rail, the hold position must be strong, secure, and not cause further damage to the frame through slippage at the point of pull. One type of frame clamp that can be attached to a box type of frame side rail is shown in Fig. 1-39.

When it is necessary to apply a pulling action to the front of the frame, a horn pull plate may be bolted to the frame horn by using the bumper bracket bolt holes as shown in Fig. 1-23.

If the horn pull plate cannot be bolted to the frame, another tool, the horn pull clamp, may be used instead. This clamp employs a short piece of rasp which enables it to bite into the side rail. The horn pull clamp, as illustrated in

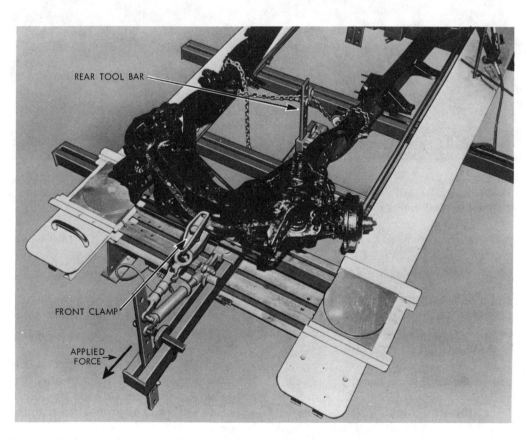

Fig. 1-38. Hook-up used to correct the crossmember for roll damage. A frame clamp is attached to the front of the crossmember to provide the pulling force needed to straighten the crossmember. A chain is mounted between the two frame side rails, the tool bar resting against the chain provides the hold position as the crossmember is pulled forward. (*John Bean Corp.*)

Fig. 1-39. Box frame clamp. This clamp, through the use of rasps which dig into the frame side rail, forms an excellent hold on the boxed inside rail. However, care must be taken since damage to the rail will result if the clamp is not installed correctly. (*John Bean Corp.*)

Fig. 1-40, is attached to a tool bar by means of a clevis. Since chains are not used in this type of hook-up, the connection is considered to be trouble free.

Repairing the Body and Frame

A frame straightening device should have provisions so that body and frame correction can be made at the same time. Figure 1-41 illustrates two uprights mounted to a beam on the frame straight-ener. The uprights support a beam which is used as a support for jacks or rams to correct body damage.

Figure 1-42 illustrates a multiple pull set-up utilizing a base unit that is set into the floor. Four air-hydraulic pumps connected to 10 ton rams provide the power source to pull out collision damage to the frame and body at the same time.

A portable frame aligner can be utilized as shown in Fig. 1-43 to perform frame and body correction.

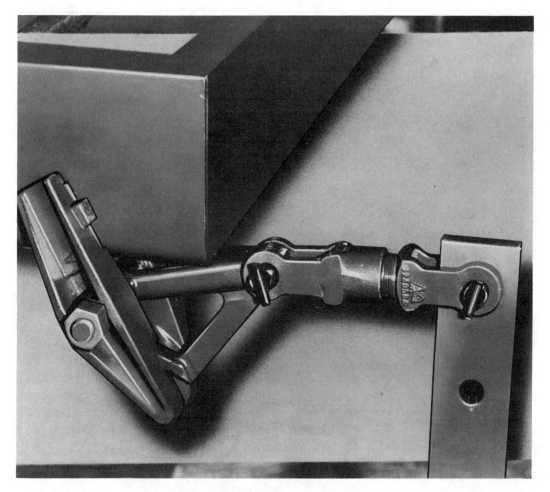

Fig. 1-40. The horn pull clamp is used for the same purpose as the horn pull plate and may be used in conjunction with the horn pull plate. (*John Bean Corp.*)

Frame and Body Estimating

The methods used to estimate the cost of body and frame repair would depend largely upon the extent of the damage and the equipment available to make such repairs. In some localities, repairmen charge a flat fee when a car is placed on their rack regardless of the extent of the frame damage.

The lack of frame straightening equipment and the production of more cars with unitized body and frame construction emphasizes the need for the portable type of frame and body equipment. This has also changed to a certain extent the method by which the cost of frame work is estimated. The hourly rate system now seems to be used in some frame and body shops.

The hourly rate system sets up a certain time in which to make a correction.

Fig. 1-41. Body tools mounted on the frame straightener. The lateral beam, which is supported on two uprights, may go through either the car door openings or through the window openings to provide the correcting force necessary to bring the body and frame into alignment. (*John Bean Corp.*)

Fig. 1-42. Body/frame repair system. (*Blackhawk Mfg. Company*)

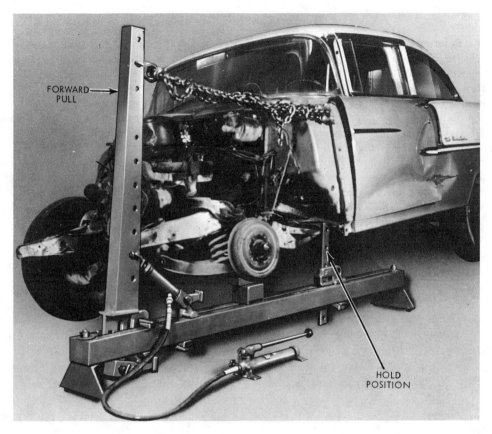

Fig. 1-43. Body and frame aligner in the process of pulling a damaged cowl into alignment. Clamps are used to provide the hook-up to the cowl. Note the hold position as provided by the tool bar against the frame body bracket. (*John Bean Corp.*)

A twist, for instance, may take three hours to be removed from the frame. The current average rate is about $20.00 per hour for work done on the frame machine. An average correction, such as side rail sag, would involve 3 hours on a frame machine and would cost $60.00. The body and frame aligner is popular with body shops since it allows repairmen to do frame work in their own shops.

In some localities, when a vehicle is estimated for the cost of the repair, the frame repair estimate is left open, and the cost is determined after the frame is straightened. Of course, this practice is frowned upon by the customer since he likes to know in advance what the job will cost him.

The ability of the frame repair man to know his equipment and estimate the time needed to do a certain repair is a matter of experience. It is hoped that this chapter has given the beginning frame man an insight into the problems of frame straightening and a knowledge of the methods and equipment used in the trade.

TRADE COMPETENCY TEST

1. What are the purposes of a frame?
2. What are the most common results of a mis-aligned frame?
3. How does a unitized body and frame construction differ from the conventional body and frame?
4. What are the basic steps in frame repair?
5. Why is the center section of the frame usually checked first when analyzing frame damage?
6. How can you recognize diamond damage to a frame without using special tools?
7. What are the usual results of a twisted frame?
8. How do the effects of a sagging frame show up?
9. What is the general basic principle to follow in straightening a frame?
10. What is the sequence that is usually followed in frame straightening?
11. What is probably the most essential tool needed for frame straightening?
12. What type of alignment equipment is needed for unitized body and frame straightening?

CHAPTER 2

FRONT SUSPENSION SYSTEMS

An automotive suspension system consists of the arrangement of springs, shock absorbers, and long and short arm linkages which connect the wheels to the vehicle frame.

The front suspension system carries the weight of the forward part of the vehicle, including the weight of the parts that go to make up the system. In addition, it must be so designed that the front wheels are free to pivot at various angles to permit steering and to move up and down to allow for springing.

Each wheel in a front suspension system is supported on a spindle which is part of the steering knuckle assembly. This arrangement permits the wheels to swing from side to side and enables the vehicle operator to steer. Leaf springs, coil springs, or torsion bars, absorb road shock and permit the wheels to move up and down.

This chapter deals with the construction, identification, location, and functioning of suspension parts, so that the reader can intelligently analyze failures and plan necessary repairs. This chapter also discusses the repairs required to re-store clearances, caused by wear, back to their original specifications. Other chapters will deal in detail with the adjustments and repairs required to restore proper alignment.

Independent Front Wheel Suspension Systems

The term independent suspension refers to the system of springing a vehicle so that each wheel is free to move up and down without directly affecting the other. No axle as such is used in the independent suspension system; the wheels are attached to a cross member of the frame of the vehicle by individual linkages.

All present passenger vehicles use the independent type of front end suspension in which each front wheel is independently supported by a coil spring or torsion bar. The coil spring arrangement is the most common; however, all forms of springs can be made to behave similarly.

The linkages used in the construction of the front end unit comprise the basic features of the suspension. All independent front suspensions used on passenger vehicles are of the short-long arm type with spherical type ball joints connecting the control arms and steering knuckles. Previous models used kingpins to attach the steering knuckles to the control arms.

Independent Suspension System with Ball Joints

On the short-long arm type of independent front end suspension two control arms are used on each side of the vehicle, an upper control arm (short) and a lower control arm (long). The arms are usually shaped like a chicken wishbone, or like the letter V. The arms are attached to the vehicle frame cross member by the open ends, extend sidewise from the mounting points and have the closed ends out beyond the frame side members. One arm is

mounted under the frame (lower control arm), while the other (upper control arm) is mounted above. Both arms are attached to the frame by means of pivot shafts which permit free movement of the linkage in the up-and-down directions. The other ends of the arms are spaced by the steering knuckle assembly which connects them. This steering knuckle assembly is attached to the control arms by means of ball joints. Figure 2-1 shows a typical short-long arm suspension system using ball joints.

A coil spring is generally located between the frame and the lower control arm (Fig. 2-1). On some front suspension systems the coil spring is located above the upper control arm (Fig. 2-2). The operating principles and basic components are the same as if the coil spring were located between the lower control

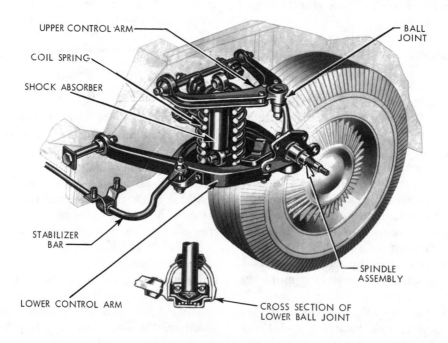

UPPER CONTROL ARM

COIL SPRING

SHOCK ABSORBER

BALL JOINT

STABILIZER BAR

LOWER CONTROL ARM

SPINDLE ASSEMBLY

CROSS SECTION OF LOWER BALL JOINT

Fig. 2-1. Independent front suspension system. This is a typical type of front suspension employing a direct acting shock absorber mounted between the lower control arm and the vehicle frame. The shock absorber is mounted inside a coil spring, the spring and the shock absorber working together to reduce road shocks. (Lincoln Div., Ford Motor Co.)

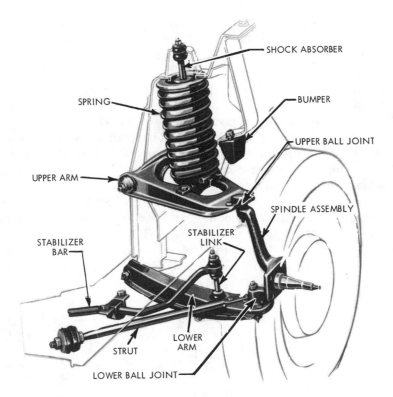

Fig. 2-2. An independent front suspension with the coil spring mounted between the upper control arm and the vehicle frame. The coil spring and the shock absorber still operate in the same manner no matter where they are mounted or whether they are mounted together or not. (*Ford Div., Ford Motor Co.*)

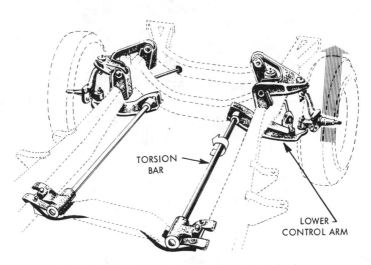

Fig. 2-3. Typical front end construction using torsion bars.

arm and frame cross member. When the front end is suspended by torsion bars rather than coil springs the basic construction remains the same (Fig. 2-3). The torsion bar replaces the pivot shaft of the lower control arm.

When the vehicle is in a normal position the frame rests on the spring and the spring rests on either the lower control arm, Fig. 2-1, or the upper control arm (Fig. 2-2). When the wheel goes up due to a change in the surface of the road, the control arms swing up at the outer end and the spring is compressed. The spring then proceeds to rebound and raise the weight of the vehicle. The same reaction

takes place on torsion bar suspension with the twisting of the bar.

Component Parts of the Suspension

The same general types of parts are used in all short-long arm suspensions regardless of whether coil springs, or torsion bars, are used to suspend the weight. Figure 2-4 gives the names of the component parts of a disassembled front suspension unit.

Control Arms. The control arms are attached to the vehicle frame cross member. They extend sidewise from the frame and are attached at the outer end to the steering knuckle assembly. Two

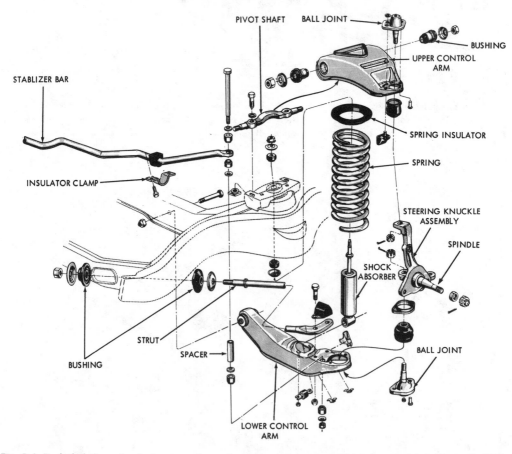

Fig. 2-4. Exploded view of a front suspension unit using a coil spring. (*Ford Customer Service Div., Ford Motor Co.*)

control arms are used on each side of the vehicle. These are called the upper and lower control arms. The upper control arm is always shorter than the lower control arm. Control arms are sometimes called wishbones or A frames.

Pivot Shafts. The inner end of the control arm is mounted on the frame cross member by means of the pivot shaft. Some manufacturers refer to this as the pivot bar or control arm shaft. The control arm is free to move up and down on the outer ends of the pivot bar. Shims may be located between the pivot shaft and frame cross member to permit caster and camber adjustment. On torsion bar suspension the torsion bar replaces the lower inner pivot shaft.

steering knuckle also consists of a spindle for mounting the wheel. A steering knuckle arm is incorporated for holding the knuckle in any desired position in its swing or travel. The arm is a part of the knuckle forging.

Short-Long Arm Suspensions

Maurice Olley is credited for designing the original short-long arm suspension for the Cadillac Motor Car Co. in the early 1930's. The short-long arm suspension design, Fig. 2-5, results in a constant tread width which keeps tire wear and scuff at a minimum. This condition is maintained as the short upper arm travels in an arc which is smaller than the lower control.

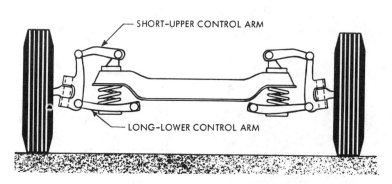

Fig. 2-5. The short-long arm suspension system.

Ball Joints. Ball joints attach the outer ends of the control arms to the steering knuckle assembly. Ball joints permit the knuckle to be turned for steering and also permit up and down movement when the wheel goes over an irregularity in the road surface.

Steering Knuckle. The steering knuckle has an elongated yoke which is attached directly to the upper and lower control arms by means of ball joints. The

Independent Suspension System with Kingpins

Previous designs of front suspension systems used an additional linkage member to attach the outer ends of the control arms. This additional member is known as a steering knuckle support and is attached to the steering knuckle assembly by means of a kingpin. Figure 2-6 illustrates a typical independent suspension using kingpins. Basically the suspension

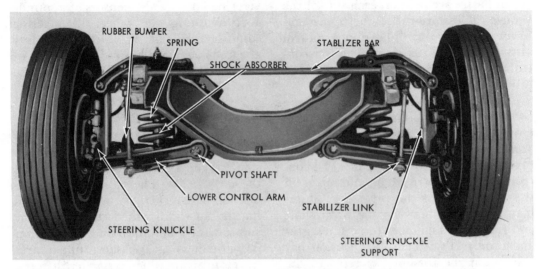

Fig. 2-6. Front suspension consisting of the steering knuckle and support assembly mounted together by means of the kingpin.

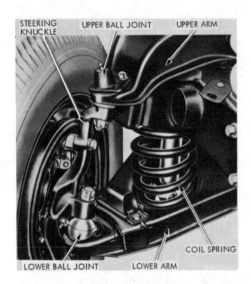

Fig. 2-7. A typical ball joint suspension. (Ford Div., Ford Motor Co.)

Ball Joint Suspensions

In the middle 1950's ball joints replaced the upper and lower outer pins, the steering knuckle support, the kingpin, and the bushings, Fig. 2-7.

The upper ball joint is spring loaded either with an enclosed coil spring or a pad of rubber compressed between the ball stud and the top of the ball joint socket, Fig. 2-8.

The lower ball joint was designed two different ways. One design has the ball end of the stud hanging downward. The weight of the car tends to pull the ball

construction is very similar whether ball joints or kingpins are used.

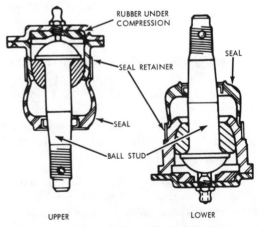

Fig. 2-8. Ball joint assembly.

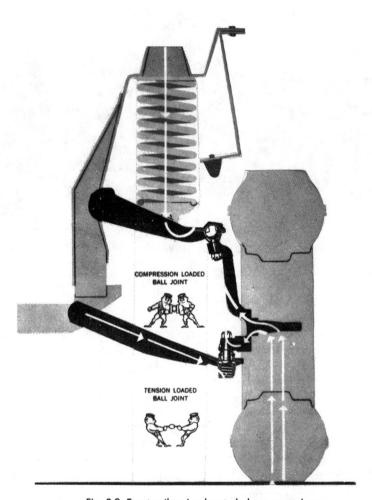

Fig. 2-9. Front coil spring located above control arm.

out of its socket. This design is often referred to as a tension loaded ball joint,
Fig. 2-8.

The other design of ball joint has the
socket resting on top of the ball stud.
This design is often referred to as a
compression loaded ball joint, Fig. 2-9.

Front Suspension Spring
on Upper Control Arm

On some installations the weight of
the vehicle is carried on a coil spring located between the upper control arm and
a spring housing located in the fender
well, Fig. 2-9. The ball joints in these designs are different than the ball joints
used in conjunction with a conventional
frame, Fig. 2-7.

Axle Suspension With
Leaf Springs

The front axle consists of a beam
which extends across the underside of the
vehicle for almost the entire width of the

Fig. 2-10. Axle type of front suspension using parallel leaf springs. This type of installation, no longer used on present automobiles, has been replaced by independent front suspensions using coil springs.

tread. Swiveling devices are attached to both ends of this beam. The axle beam is attached to the vehicle frame by means of leaf springs, either of the transverse type (crosswise to the frame) or of the type parallel to the frame. (Fig. 2-10).

Front Suspension Service

Other than periodic lubrication, the front suspension system of a vehicle usually requires little attention. The suspension parts should be lubricated in accordance with the manufacturer's specifications. If tire wear is uniform on the front wheels of a vehicle, the suspension is probably in good condition. Erratic tire wear, on the other hand, usually indicates the suspension system has been damaged either from lack of lubrication or as the result of a collision.

Locating Excessive Play in Suspension

The front suspension system should be checked for wear when the vehicle is being lubricated or the front end aligned.

Place a jack under the lower control arm below the spring and raise the wheel until it is completely off the floor. Then grasp the wheel at the top and bottom, as shown in Fig. 2-11, and shake it by pushing the wheel inward with one hand while pulling the wheel outward with the other. There should be no excessive loose-

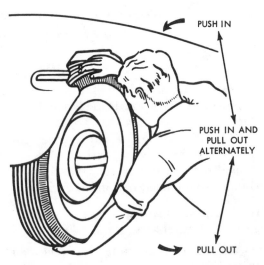

PUSH IN

PUSH IN AND
PULL OUT
ALTERNATELY

PULL OUT

Fig. 2-11. Locating excessive play in suspension during lubrication. (Ford Div., Ford Motor Co.)

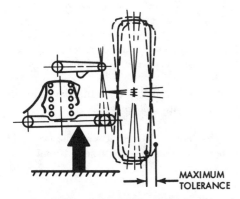

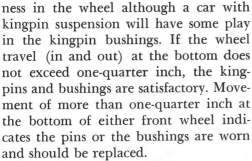

Fig. 2-12. Checking lower ball joint maximum tolerance (max. tol. ¼″).

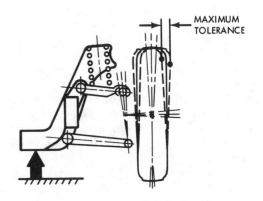

Fig. 2-13. Checking upper ball joint (max. tol. ¼″).

ness in the wheel although a car with kingpin suspension will have some play in the kingpin bushings. If the wheel travel (in and out) at the bottom does not exceed one-quarter inch, the kingpins and bushings are satisfactory. Movement of more than one-quarter inch at the bottom of either front wheel indicates the pins or the bushings are worn and should be replaced.

A vehicle with ball joint suspension will have about one-quarter inch of play in the load-bearing (lower) ball joint as the wheel is shaken, Fig. 2-12.

On most automobiles equipped with ball joints the lower ball joint supports almost the entire weight of the vehicle. Some cars have the coil spring bearing against the upper control arm, and therefore the upper ball joint will show some looseness when the vehicle weight is removed from the ball joint, Fig. 2-13.

A safe rule to follow is that any play in excess of one-quarter inch—regardless of the type of front suspension used on the vehicle—is cause for further investigation and probable replacement of worn parts.

Some of the conditions to check for excessive movement or play not caused by the ball joints are listed below:

1. Loosened bolts holding the upper and lower control arm shafts to the front cross member.

2. Worn pivot points such as the bushing and shafts holding the upper and lower control arms to the frame.

3. Worn pivot pins and bushings which connect the steering knuckle support to the upper and lower control arms.

4. Rubber bushings holding the control arms to their respective shafts. (Looseness at a rubber bushing may be due to a worn bushing or to a loose cap screw which permits the inner shell of the bushing to slip on the shaft.)

5. Wheel bearings which need adjustment. (Refer to manufacturer's specifications on wheel bearing adjustments.)

If you locate looseness or play at any of these points, replace bushings or shafts that have become worn and, when required, ream them to achieve the desired fit. Replace parts when necessary if the desired tolerance cannot otherwise be obtained.

TRADE COMPETENCY TEST

1. What is the purpose of an independent front-end suspension system?

2. What units are common to most independent suspension systems?

3. What is the difference in construction between the suspension system using kingpins and the one using ball joints?

4. What is the reason for having the upper control arm shorter than the lower control arm?

5. How does the torsion bar suspension differ from the coil spring suspension?

6. What will the wear condition of the front tires show relative to the front suspension system?

7. How do you check for excessive looseness in the front suspension system?

8. What are some of the conditions to check for excessive movement in the front end?

9. What is the difference in the two suspension systems with coil springs?

10. What are the differences in the ball joints being used in the suspension system?

CHAPTER 3

REAR SUSPENSION SYSTEMS

The rear suspension system carries the weight of the rear part of the vehicle which includes the weight of the components that make up the unit. The rear wheels must be able to move up and down with respect to the body and frame for spring action and also to assist in keeping the vehicle as near level at all times as possible.

Leaf springs or coil springs absorb road shocks and permit the wheels to flex when the vehicle encounters road irregularities.

The rear axle housing, which is designed to carry the rear vehicle weight, also serves as a means of propelling the vehicle on most installations. The springs, which make up a considerable part of the suspension system and suspend the vehicle weight, are located between the rear axle housing and the frame or body. Therefore, either the springs or some form of struts or braces must be designed to transmit the functions of the rear axle to the rest of the vehicle.

In order to overcome a fundamental law of nature which states that for every action there is an equal and opposite reaction, an additional function must be performed by the suspension system. That is, whenever power is transmitted through the power train to propel the rear wheels (driving the vehicle) the rear axle housing tries to rotate in a direction opposite to that of tire rotation. Thus, wheel rotation in one direction and the attempt of the rear axle housing to rotate in the opposite direction result in a twisting action which is called *rear-end torque*. Two different designs have been used to offset this opposing torque and to transmit the wheel torque from the rear wheels to the chassis. These are the Hotchkiss type of drive and the torque-tube type of drive. The torque-tube type of drive is no longer being installed as original equipment; however, there are still a number of vehicles in use with this type of driving axle assembly.

Hotchkiss Drive

With a Hotchkiss type of drive using parallel leaf springs, the driving torque is transmitted by the springs. The front end of the leaf spring is mounted in a hanger so that it can pivot. The rear end of the spring is mounted by means of

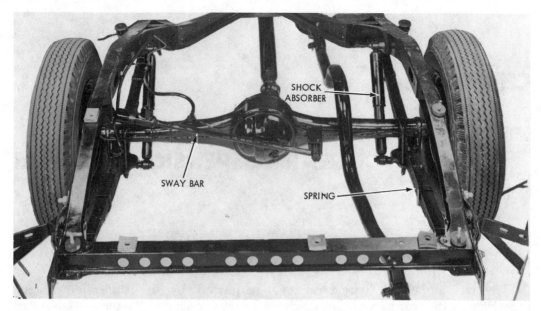

Fig. 3-1. Hotchkiss drive with leaf spring rear suspension. In this type of drive the rear axle torque is taken up by the leaf springs.

a shackle. This method of mounting permits the spring to lengthen and shorten as it flexes without causing a fore and aft movement of the axle housing. The center of the spring is firmly attached to the axle housing, as shown in Fig. 3-1.

No additional bracing is needed in this type of installation since the springs absorb both the rear-end torque and the driving torque.

When coil springs are used between the rear axle housing and the frame or body, some form of bracing must also be used to transmit torque. Generally, a support arm, a radius rod, or a strut is attached to each outer end of the rear axle housing between the housing and the frame or body, as shown in Fig. 3-2. The rear end of the support arm is attached rigidly to the axle housing while the front end of the support arm is attached to a hanger. This hanger permits the axle housing to move up and down when the springs flex but prevents forward and

backward movement of the axle housing. A track bar (sway bar) may be attached between one side of the frame or body and the axle housing in order to reduce the rolling action of the vehicle body on turns. Some installations will also use a stabilizing bar to increase body stability.

In addition to support arms at the outer ends of the axle housing, some vehicles use upper control arms. One end of the arm is attached to the center of the rear axle housing by means of a flexible connection, while the outer ends of the control arm are attached to a frame cross member by means of pivot pins. The coil spring type of installation using a control arm is illustrated in Fig. 3-3.

Regardless of the type of spring employed or method used in transmitting torque, shock absorbers are always used in conjunction with the springs. Shock absorbers are located between the axle housing and the frame or body. A rubber spring bumper is fastened to the axle

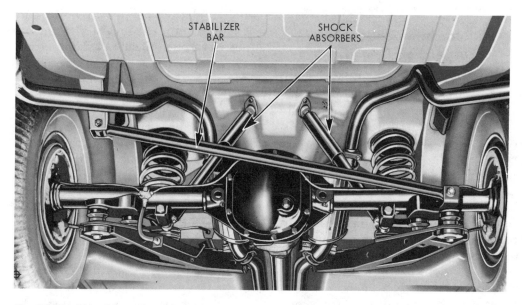

Fig. 3-2. Hotchkiss drive with coil spring rear suspension. Note the use of a stabilizer bar in this type of installation to provide a minimum of body roll as the vehicle makes a turn. Note support arms attached to outer ends of rear axle. (Lincoln Div., Ford Motor Co.)

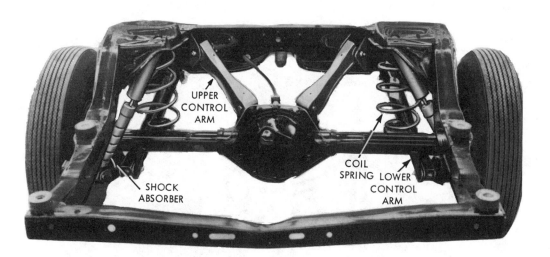

Fig. 3-3. Coil spring type of rear suspension using control arms. The control arms are a means of preventing the rear axle housing from falling away from the suspension system when the vehicle encounters road irregularities. (Chevrolet Div., General Motors Corp.)

housing, the frame, or the body to prevent bottoming.

Bottoming: Bottoming is a term used to *define the condition when the spring is* *compressed to its limit of travel and the* *spring bumper is engaged.*

Rear Independent Suspension System

Independent rear suspension is used by one American manufacturer at the present time. This type of suspension employs two axle shafts, each of which is driven through a universal joint so as to permit the axle shaft to move up and down when the vehicle encounters road irregularities.

The system is made up of a fixed differential carrier mounted on the frame at three points. Strut rods, drive shafts and torque control arms form three links at each wheel along with a transversely mounted leaf spring, Fig. 3-4.

One end of each trailing torque control arm is mounted into a frame side member through a pivot bolt and rubber bushing and extends rearward to connect to the transverse leaf spring. The wheel spindle and spindle support is bolted into each torque arm. The rear toe-in angle is adjusted through the use of shims located between the control arm and frame side member web at the forward pivoting joint.

The rear wheel spindles are driven through tubular drive shafts with universal joints at each end. The outboard universal joint is attached to the spindle through a flange and the inboard joint is bolted to the differential side gear yoke.

The spindle supports incorporate a mounting bracket to attach the rubber-bushed strut rods. The strut rods are mounted laterally from the spindle support to the lower surface of the axle carrier. At this point, the connection has an eccentric cam arrangement to provide for rear wheel camber adjustment.

Direct double-acting shock absorbers are located between the frame and the strut rod mounting shaft.

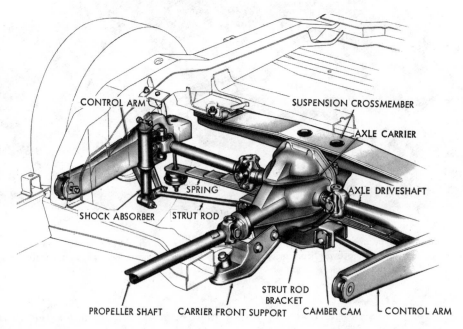

Fig. 3-4. Rear independent suspension system including driveline components. (*Chevrolet Div., General Motors Corp.*)

The center of the transverse leaf spring is clamped to the differential carrier cover. The outer ends of the spring are bolted to each torque control arm.

Rear Suspension Alignment

The rear suspension of an automobile must be properly aligned if it is to track properly. The body of a vehicle that is not parallel to the direction of vehicle travel is the result of the rear suspension being out of track. There are a number of conditions which will cause the rear suspension of a vehicle to be out of track. A rear suspension of the Hotchkiss design (a solid rear axle suspended by leaf springs) may go out of track as the result of the rear axle's slipping either forward or backward on one or both of the leaf springs which support the axle. The center tie bolt which ties the leaves of each leaf spring assembly together is used to determine the position of the rear axle housing in relation to the leaf springs. If the U bolts which hold the rear axle housing to the leaf spring become loose and the rear wheel hits an obstruction, the head of the spring center bolt mounting the loosened spring assembly may be sheared off. Should the bolt head shear off, the axle housing will move in relation to the spring causing the vehicle to be out of track. Failure of the vehicle to track properly will cause excessive tire wear.

The rear axle housing may be deflected downward at the center which would cause the top of the rear wheels to move inward. This inward movement of the top of each rear wheel would result in negative camber and cause the inside edges of the rear tires to wear. This downward bending of the axle housing at the center may result from overloading the vehicle or from imposing too much engine torque upon the rear axle during acceleration.

The rear axle housing is generally designed as a straight member and as such would have no camber, no toe-in or toe-out. However, a rear axle housing which is bent in a horizontal plane will cause the rear wheels to either toe-in or toe-out.

Should the vehicle become involved in a head-on collision, the rear axle housing may be so bent as to produce a toe-in effect in the rear wheels. The force of impact in such a collision would move the engine, drive line, and the center of the rear axle housing somewhat rearward, thereby causing the rear wheels to toe-in. Some vehicles are so designed that the rear axle produces a slight positive camber and a small amount of toe-in or toe-out on the rear tires so as to reduce tire wear.

Check Vehicle Track

A three-point gage called a track bar is used to determine the track of the rear suspension, as shown in Fig. 3-5. Before using this gage, amount of rear wheel run-out should be determined. The rear axle housing is lifted from the floor by means of a jack or alignment rack until the rear wheels are free to revolve. Place a runout gage against the rim of the wheel as the tire is rotated, marking with chalk the position on the rim where the runout gage touched the rim wheel. Then, lower the rear wheels to the floor, with the chalk mark at the bottom. Follow this procedure for both rear wheels. Sight along the sides of both front wheels, moving the wheels by hand until they are directly in front of or in line with the rear wheels. This represents the relation of all four wheels when the vehicle is traveling along a straight road. Next, place the three-point track bar against one front and one rear wheel of the vehicle. Place the single point of the track

Fig. 3-5. Checking the track of the rear suspension with a track bar. The bar consists of three pointers, one at the front and two at the rear. The two pointers are placed against the rim of the rear wheel while the front pointer is placed against the front wheel spindle (hub cap removed). The bar must be in alignment with all three pointers in position in order to determine the vehicle's track. (*John Bean Corp.*)

bar against the end of the spindle of the front wheel. Then, place the two pointers of the gage against the rim of the rear wheel. Adjust the relation to the bar, carry the bar over to the other side of the vehicle, and check the track of front and rear wheels.

The front pointer will now indicate whether the vehicle is out of track and whether the distance between the front and rear wheels on both sides of the vehicle is the same.

With the two pointers of the track bar on the rim of the rear wheel, the front pointer should rest on the spindle of the front wheel (hub cap removed) . If the front pointer is away from the spindle, the rear wheel on which the pointers are resting has a toe-out condition and the rear wheel on the other side of the vehicle has a toe-in condition. The front pointer also shows if the vehicle's wheel base is

either too long or too short. However, realize that the front suspension may also alter the wheel base. If the front suspension lower control arm has been driven backward due to the vehicle's being in a collision, the wheel base will be too short.

Check Rear Suspension for Camber, Toe-in or Toe-out

The camber and toe-out or toe-in of the rear wheels may be determined in the same fashion as camber and toe-in of the front wheels. Camber is the tilting of the wheel from the vertical.

The vehicle is backed on an alignment rack and the readings taken. Notice that since the vehicle has been backed on the alignment rack a reading of toe-in on an alignment machine actually represents a condition in which the wheels are toed out. The Visualiner, as shown in Fig. 3-6, may be used to check the track and the

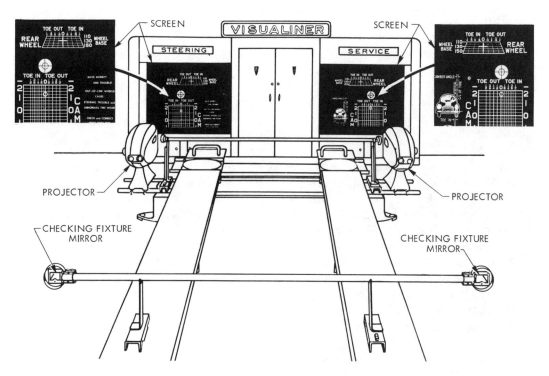

Fig. 3-6. The Visualiner with calibrating fixtures in position to determine the calibration of the machine. The alignment machine must be checked for calibration before it can be used to check the track of the vehicle. Always remove the error from any alignment equipment before its use on a vehicle. (*John Bean Corp.*)

rear wheels without backing the vehicle on to the rack. If the vehicle has abnormal rear wheel tire wear, the wheel alignment operator can determine the cause of this tire wear while checking front wheel alignment.

Check Rear Suspension with the Visualiner

To determine the condition of the rear suspension, first place a mirror like the one shown in Fig. 3-7 on each rear wheel. Then jack up each rear wheel and check the wheel for run-out. This is done by rotating the wheel and holding the rear wheel mirror to keep the illuminated cross on the rear wheel toe chart. As the wheel rotates, determine the maximum travel that the illuminated cross makes from side to side on the rear wheel toe chart. Stop rotating the wheel when

Fig. 3-7. Rear mirror as mounted on the vehicle's rear wheel. Two mirrors, calibrated in degrees of plus or minus, are used, one for each rear wheel. The arrow shows the adjusting screw by which the mirror may be locked in any given position. (*John Bean Corp.*)

the illuminated cross on the rear wheel toe chart is in the center of its travel. Lower the wheel to the machine.

This same procedure is used on the other rear wheel. Caution must be taken so that the wheel whose run-out has been determined does not rotate when the opposite wheel's run-out is determined.

Figure 3-7 illustrates the mirror as mounted on a rear wheel showing the lower cross on the numbered spaces of the mirror chart. The rear of the vehicle must be centered until both crosses fall on the same position on the lower portion of the rear wheel mirror. Most alignment racks have runways on roller chains that allow the car to be pushed at either the front or rear to center the crosses on the rear mirror chart. Then pivot the mirror about its shaft until the cross (projected forward to the screen) falls on the rear wheel toe chart on the projector screen.

The set up of the Visualiner can be seen in Fig. 3-6. The cross will now indicate the toe-in or toe-out of that rear wheel. The other wheel's rear mirror will tell the condition of the toe of the other rear wheel.

If both rear wheels read zero toe on the rear wheel chart, then the vehicle is in perfect track and the rear axle is straight as far as toe is concerned. If the left rear wheel has a ¼ inch of toe-in, the rear axle would then be out of track. However, if the right wheel has a ½ inch of toe-in and the left wheel has a ¼ inch of toe out not only would the rear axle be out of track but the axle housing would also have a ¼ inch of toe-in.

Vehicles with independent rear wheel suspensions must now have the rear suspension checked for toe and tracking. Refer to the manufacturer's specifications before making any corrections.

TRADE COMPETENCY TEST

1. What is the purpose of the rear suspension?
2. What is rear-end torque and what problems does it create?
3. What is meant by a Hotchkiss drive?
4. What must be added to the rear suspension if coil springs are used rather than leaf springs?
5. What is the purpose of a track bar?
6. What will cause a rear suspension to be out of track?
7. If the U bolts which clamp the rear springs to the axle housing are loose what may happen?
8. What design changes must be incorporated when an independent rear suspension system is employed?

CHAPTER 4

SPRINGS AND SHOCK ABSORBERS

The purpose of the springs and the shock absorbers in the automotive vehicle suspension system is to support the weight of the vehicle and to reduce or eliminate the effect of jarring or shocks which are transferred to the frame, the body, and to the passengers as the wheels of the vehicle move up and down due to irregularities in the road surface.

This chapter discusses the types and locations of the various springs now in use, how they are mounted and how to service and replace them.

Information regarding shock absorbers is contained in the last part of the chapter.

Springs

A spring is an elastic device that yields under stress, or pressure, but returns to its original state or position when the stress or pressure is removed.

Types of Springs

Four types of springs are in use in automotive suspensions. These are multiple leaf springs, single leaf springs, coil springs, and torsion bars. Multiple leaf springs and coil springs are characteristic of most automobiles manufactured in the United States. Single leaf springs may be found on a few models of passenger cars and some passenger cars will use torsion bars in front rather than coil springs.

An air suspension system for passenger vehicles was available on a limited basis for a few passenger cars in the past. Today its use is confined strictly to trucks and buses.

Leaf springs absorb shocks by bending, coil springs by compressing, and torsion bars by twisting.

Multiple Leaf Springs. These springs are made up of long, flat strips of spring steel. Each strip is called a leaf. Several leaves, four to eight, are placed one upon the other and are held together by clamps and a bolt. The one leaf that extends the full length of the spring is known as the main leaf. The ends of the main leaf are formed into loops which are called eyes. The front of each spring is secured to a bracket on the frame by means of a spring bolt which is placed through the front

49

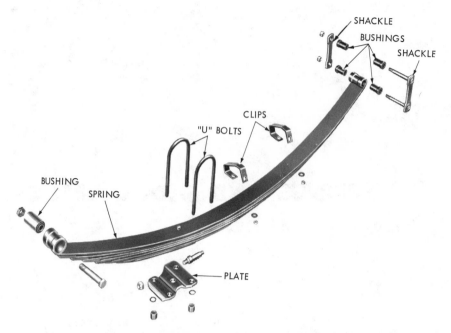

Fig. 4-1. Leaf spring construction and attaching parts. The leaf spring may consist of two or more leaves depending upon the design of the suspension. (*Plymouth Div., Chrysler Corp.*)

eye. The rear of the spring is attached to the frame by means of a shackle. The leaf spring is assembled as shown in Fig. 4-1, each succeeding leaf being shorter than the preceding one. In some springs the leaves are tapered to ends thinner than the middle position.

Each leaf has a hole in the center through which a bolt—called the tie bolt —passes to hold the leaves together. Starting with the main leaf, each succeeding leaf has greater spring camber (more arch). If the leaves were placed one on top of the other, they would not touch at the center until the tie bolt was tightened. The tie bolt serves to hold the leaves together at the center under stress, preventing normal arch of the individual leaves. Spring leaf clamps (also called clips) are used to hold the outer ends of the leaves in line with each other.

When a leaf spring bends or flexes, the leaves rub on each other. This rub-

bing produces frictional resistance to flexing. Interleaf friction is carefully computed as part of spring design, dependent upon the load the spring is to carry.

If interleaf friction is high due to the absence of lubrication, the spring will stiffen considerably. The riding qualities and load-carrying ability of the vehicle decrease under such conditions.

Most springs are built with interleaves or liners between the spring leaves. A typical interleaf consists of a paper-like material impregnated with wax or a similar lubricant. The wax is not soluble in water; consequently it does not wash away. Zinc interleaves are used between the spring leaves of some springs. Interleaf springs do not require attention unless a leaf breaks or an interleaf insert fails. Interleaf inserts should never be lubricated.

Instead of interleaves, some leaf springs may be fitted with inserts at the

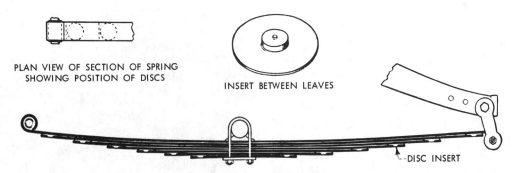

Fig. 4-2. Leaf spring insert of the disc type. These inserts are fitted between each leaf, thereby reducing the friction between the leaves as the springs flex.

ends of each leaf—except the main leaf—as shown in Fig. 4-2. The inserts may be of rubber, waxed cloth, or oil-bronze discs (porous metal discs made of powdered metal and impregnated with oil). The spring insert eases the rubbing action between the leaves, thus aiding in retaining correct interleaf friction to insure desired spring action.

Single Leaf Springs. A single leaf spring which is used on a few models of

passsenger vehicles, as the name implies, is one uniformly stressed leaf spring (main leaf) which is thicker than a normal spring leaf. The one leaf is designed to perform in the same manner as a multiple leaf spring. The single-leaf spring assumes uniformity of performance by eliminating the interleaf elements which frequently deteriorate unevenly and are subject to unfavorable weather conditions. The single leaf is always in action

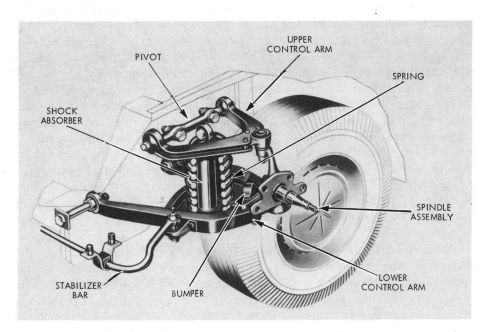

Fig. 4-3. Independent front suspension system employing a coil spring between the lower control arm and frame. (*Lincoln Div., Ford Motor Co.*)

while conventional leaf systems lose their efficiency when the interleaf elements become worn.

Coil Springs. Coil springs used in automotive suspension systems consist of helical coils made from spring steel rods. Such springs are made from round rods between one-half and seven-eighths of an inch in thickness and from 10 to 15 feet in length. The rod is heated to a high temperature, wound on a special form, and heat-treated to obtain the desired spring resiliency. The finished coil spring has an inside diameter of from three to six inches, is about one foot high, and has ten to twelve uniform turns or loops. In most constructions the ends of the coil are flattened to provide a better seat on the supporting framework of the vehicle. Figure 4-3 illustrates a typical coil spring installation. Coil springs used on rear suspension systems generally have one or two turns at the end of the spring wound smaller than the others to provide a means of attaching the spring to the rear axle housing (Fig. 4-3).

Torsion Bars. Some automotive vehicles use torsion bars in front rather than coil springs. The torsion bar (Fig. 4-4) is a straight bar made from round spring steel. The torsion bar is used in place of the lower control arm pivot and is so arranged that movement of the wheel upward or downward causes the torsion bar to twist from its normal position. As the wheel resumes the normal position, the bar untwists. It is the resistance of the torsion bar to twisting which provides the spring action. The torsion bar is a true spring.

Two torsion bars are used, one for each front wheel, the bars being mounted lengthwise along the frame (Fig. 4-4).

These bars take the place of coil springs. The suspension unit is constructed in the same manner as that used on a front suspension system using coil

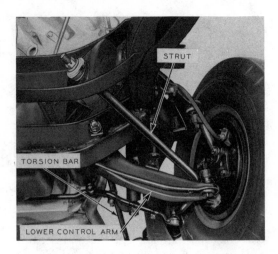

Fig. 4-4. Front suspension system using torsion bars. As the wheels flex, due to bumps in the road, the up and down movement of the wheels twists and untwists the torsion bars. This twisting action absorbs the road shock, thereby producing a smooth ride. (*Plymouth Div., Chrysler Corp.*)

springs. The front ends of the torsion bars engage the lower control arms at the inner pivot points (Fig. 4-5). The rear ends of the bars engage adjustable anchor assemblies, which are supported by brackets welded to the frame side rails located about two feet to the rear of the front wheels. A brace (strut) attached to the front frame cross member and to the outer end of the lower control arm gives rigidity to the front end assembly and prevents fore and aft movement. As the torsion bar has a hex on each end and fits solidly into hex sockets the bar must twist and untwist as the lower arm moves up and down with the movement of the wheel. This twisting action gives the same effect as a coil or leaf spring.

An adjusting bolt on the torsion bar rear support assembly is used to increase or decrease tension on the bar. The reason for changing tension is to bring the front end to a predetermined height should it be lower or higher than specified.

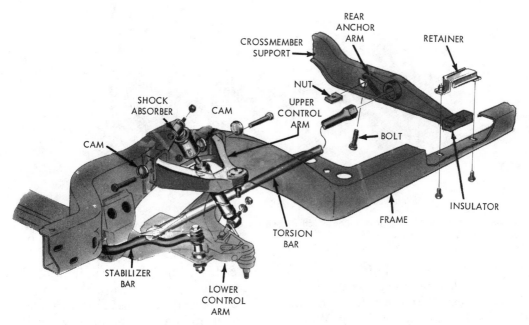

Fig. 4-5. Exploded view of torsion bar front suspension. (*Oldsmobile Div., General Motors Corp.*)

Spring Mountings

The method used to mount the spring on the frame depends on whether leaf or coil springs are used.

Leaf Springs. Leaf springs are used to suspend the rear end of many passenger vehicles. The springs are mounted lengthwise along the frame. Two spring units are employed, one on either side of the vehicle. Leaf springs may be parallel to each other or they may be farther apart either at the front end or at the rear, depending on the frame design.

The ends of the main leaf are secured to the frame of the vehicle; the center of the spring unit is attached to the axle on flanges (spring pads) by means of U-bolts (spring clips). The center of the spring may either rest on the axle or pass underneath it. Figure 4-6 illustrates a typical leaf spring installation. In all leaf spring mountings provision is made to prevent the center portion of the spring from sliding out of position if the U-bolt should loosen. The head of the tie bolt fits into a hole in the spring pad, preventing the spring from shifting even though the U-bolts might become loose. The fitting of the tie bolt head into the recess in the spring pad also serves as a means of properly locating the spring when installing it.

The front end of the spring is attached to the frame by means of a bracket or hanger which is riveted to the frame. The spring bolt, which fastens the spring to the bracket, is used with a rubber bushing which tightly surrounds the bolt and is pressed against the inside of the spring eye when the bolt is tightened. The rubber bushing provides insulation against noise and eliminates the need for lubrication.

The rear end of the spring is attached to the frame by means of a swinging sup-

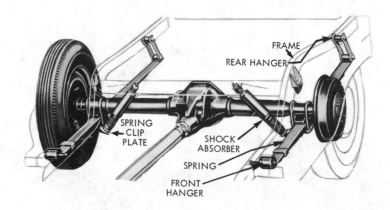

Fig. 4-6. A typical leaf spring installation which is used on a number of automotive rear suspension systems. (*Ford Div., Ford Motor Co.*)

port called a shackle. This arrangement is necessary because the distance between the spring eyes varies in accordance with the load the vehicle is carrying. When a vehicle is at curb weight (stationary and unloaded), the normal weight of the body and chassis rests upon the springs. Under these conditions most springs have a slight arch, and a specified distance is maintained between the spring eyes.

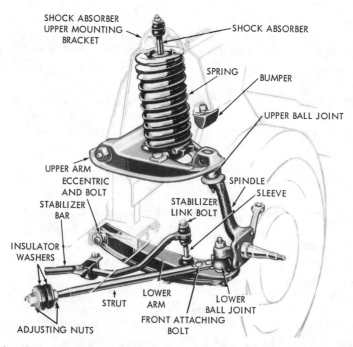

Fig. 4-7. Independent front suspension system employing coil springs between the upper control arm and frame. (*Ford Customer Service Div., Ford Motor Co.*)

When the vehicle is bearing a load, however, the springs flatten and the distance between the eyes increases. Some springs will have little or no arch under very light loads. When a load is placed on the rear suspension there will be a small amount of reverse arch.

When the vehicle is in motion, the springs alternately flatten and arch as the wheels move up and down in passing over irregularities in the road surface. This flattening and arching action causes constant variation in the distance between the spring eyes. To make this action possible shackles are used.

Coil Springs. Coil springs are mounted in either of two ways, depending on whether they are used on an independent front suspension system or on the rear axle.

In the independent front suspension, as shown in Fig. 4-3, the spring is held between the lower control arm and the frame. Circular recesses are provided at the upper and lower spring seats to receive the ends of the springs, and, once in place, the springs cannot slip. On some vehicles the spring is located between the upper control arm and the frame, but the principle remains the same, Fig. 4-7.

The upper and lower control arms swing up and down on their pivots. This action causes the coil spring to compress and expand, but it is always under load even when the control arms are at the lowest point in their swing. In other words, the spring is so constructed that its free height (unloaded or natural length) is greater than the greatest possible distance between the frame and the control arm. The spring is held in place by the load placed upon it and by the recesses into which the ends fit. A rubber insulator is generally installed in the recess between the spring and the frame.

When coil suspension springs are used on the rear axle, one or two turns at each end of the spring are smaller than the rest of the spring. The spring is secured to the frame and the rear axle by means of washers machined to fit the loops at both ends of the spring. A rear end coil spring assembly is shown in Fig. 4-8.

It is not necessary in this type of installation to secure the coil spring at both ends because there is a device to limit the downward movement of the suspension. On extreme rebound the axle could fall away from the vehicle if it were not secured by the shock absorbers' control arms. Radius rods or supports (sometimes called struts) are used to attach the rear axle housing to the frame, thus preventing forward and backward movement of the axle while the vehicle is in motion. In a suspension of this type the spring is subjected to compression only.

Spring Bumpers. On any type of suspension rubber bumpers are used to cushion the impact should the spring "bottom." The bumper is located on the frame above the rear axle housing on rear suspensions, or, in the case of front suspensions, on the lower control arm, as shown in Fig. 4-3.

Front End Stabilizers. All independent front end suspension systems include a stabilizer. It is another form of spring used to inter-connect the individual suspension units, either directly or by linkage. The stabilizer is a steel bar mounted transversely on (across) the frame. Arms on both ends of the stabilizer extend backward and are connected to the lower control arms. A typical stabilizer installation is shown in Figs. 4-3 and 4-7.

The stabilizer arms move up and down together when both coil springs deflect an equal amount. Under these conditions the stabilizer bar pivots in the rubber bushings by which it is mounted to the frame; hence, no spring action is in

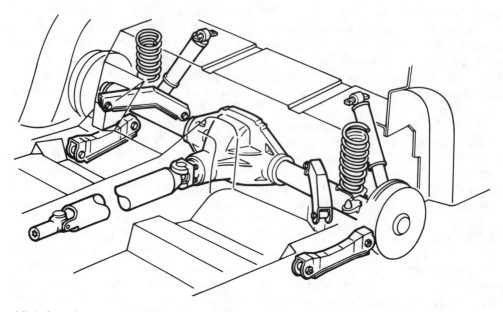

Fig. 4-8. Independent rear suspension system employing the use of coil springs and a control arm arrangement. (Chevrolet Div., General Motors Corp.)

effect. When only one wheel encounters a bump, however, only the spring suspending that wheel deflects, imparting a twisting action to the stabilizer bar. Then, as the twisting force is removed, the stabilizer returns to its original state. From this explanation it is clear that the stabilizer bar is a spring resistance, in the form of a torsion bar, to the independent action of independently suspended front wheels.

The stabilizer serves to reduce heeling or tipping of the vehicle on curves. During a turn the spring on the outside tends to compress while the spring on the inside of the turn tends to expand due to centrifugal forces involved. One stabilizer arm swings downward while the other end swings upward, imparting a twist to the stabilizer bar. It is the resistance to this twist that helps to hold the vehicle level and stable.

Rear End Stabilizers. To provide correct tracking and proper stability of the rear axle when the rear end is mounted on coil springs, a stabilizing device of some sort must be used. (Tracking means the following of the rear wheels directly behind, or in the tracks of, the front wheels.) A stabilizer bar, sometimes called a sway bar or track bar, is used on some installations. Other installations use a control arm arrangement for this purpose. See Fig. 4-9.

The stabilizer or sway bar is designed to control lateral (sidewise) movement of the rear axle. The bar extends from the axle housing on one side to the vehicle frame on the other, as shown in Fig. 4-9. Rubber bushings are used at both ends to insulate the bar from the frame and the axle and thereby to reduce noise. On a severe turn the vehicle frame has a tendency to swing out on the rear wheels. This tendency is overcome by the sway bar.

Characteristics of Springs

Leaf springs, coil springs, and torsion

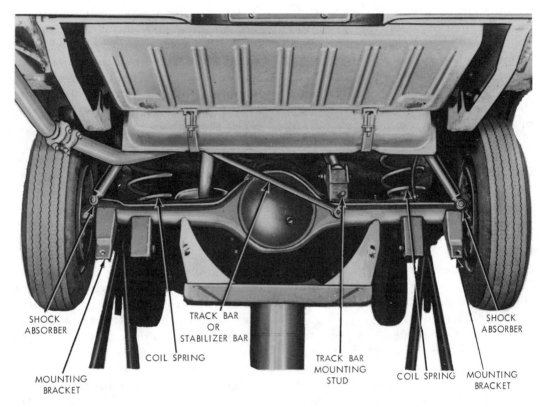

SHOCK
ABSORBER

TRACK BAR
OR
STABILIZER BAR

COIL SPRING

TRACK BAR
MOUNTING
STUD

SHOCK
ABSORBER

COIL SPRING

MOUNTING
BRACKET

MOUNTING
BRACKET

Fig. 4-9. The rear end stabilizer bar, also known as a track bar or sway bar reduces body roll when the vehicle makes a turn. (Vehicle on hoist while removing rear springs.) (*Ford Customer Service Div., Ford Motor Co.*)

bars all possess a number of characteristics which affect their operation. Usually taken into account are the deflection rate, the recoil frequency, and the fatigue point. Springs used in automotive suspension systems behave in the same manner under load, regardless of their design or type. The similarity of behavior is due to the fact that all springs are made of steel. To a certain degree steel is elastic. This means that if it is deformed (bent, squeezed, stretched, twisted) within certain limits, it will, when released, resume its original state.

Deflection Rate. Deflection rate is the amount a spring will bend under the influence of a given weight. Deflection rate

is specified in terms of pounds per inch; that is, pounds of weight applied per inch of deflection. If a load of 100 pounds will deflect a spring one inch, each additional 100 pounds will deflect it another inch. For each 100 pounds removed from the load the spring will return one inch toward its original state. The spring may be loaded at the rate of 100 pounds per inch until it is deflected beyond its capacity. This means the spring will become damaged and will not resume its original characteristics when the load is removed. This point is called the elastic limit. A spring loaded beyond the elastic limit is deformed permanently.

Deflection rate is also known as spring

weight. Spring weight is given as the force required to deflect the spring to a predetermined dimension. The term spring weight is usually applied to coil springs. Deflection rate is used in connection with leaf springs. It should be noted that spring weight and deflection rate apply only within the elastic limit of any given spring.

In a leaf spring the thicker and/or wider the spring, the higher the deflection rate; that is, the greater the force required to bend the spring a given distance. The longer the spring, the lower the deflection rate. In a coil spring thickness means the diameter of the steel rod from which the spring was made, not the size of the loops. Similarly, length means the length of the rod used, not the height of the finished coil.

Frequency. Frequency is the term used to describe the number of oscillations (bounces) per minute made by a spring when it is actuated. An automotive spring, when deflected by a bump in the road bed, always tends to return to its original state. This means that a spring under a load tends to return that load to the extent that will enable the spring to rebound to its original height. But the inertia of the load as the spring flexes carries the spring beyond this point and allows it to deflect in the opposite direction. Regardless of the load or type of spring, the return motion always occupies the same amount of time for any given spring, because each spring has its own frequency. That frequency for an individual spring depends on its length, breadth, and thickness—just as these factors control the deflection rate, as well. The distance through which a spring flexes is determined by the weight of the load and the severity of the shock encountered. Distance and severity have no bearing, however, on frequency; it is a constant factor.

In selecting springs to meet specific problems frequency and its effect on the relationship between sprung weight and unsprung weight must be considered. Sprung weight is the weight of everything supported by the springs. Unsprung weight is the weight of everything between the springs and the road. In general, unsprung weight should be kept as low as possible to assure a comfortable ride. Roughness in the ride increases when unsprung weight increases.

Fatigue and Spring Breakage. The most common causes of spring breakage are fatigue and overloading. Fatigue is the term used to describe spring breakage after the spring has worn out due to repeated flexings. Just as a wire or piece of metal will break after having been bent back and forth repeatedly, so will a spring break after many thousands of flexings. When fatigue sets in, the spring suddenly becomes weak and then breaks. Fatigue can even occur when the spring has never been deflected beyond its elastic limit. Nicks on the spring surface can hasten spring fatigue.

Overload, if extreme, results in spring failure and breakage. If the spring is heavily loaded and subjected to severe shocks, it will bend beyond its elastic limit and be permanently damaged.

A spring that is deformed or has broken leaves should be replaced. If the spring inserts are no longer effective, resulting in a spring squeak, the inserts can be replaced without removing the spring.

Spring Service

Servicing the springs on an automobile means periodic inspection of the springs and all spring components. Coil springs seldom require attention. If a coil spring becomes weak or fatigued, it should be replaced. A single spring is never replaced alone. Both springs must be replaced in pairs. One new and one old spring would cause the vehicle to have an uneven curb height.

Leaf springs are subject to breakage—usually one leaf at a time—with the result that the car will sag on the side that has the broken leaf. In normal use leaf springs often become fatigued, causing the vehicle to ride too close to the ground. In such circumstances either the fatigued leaf springs are replaced or the spring unit is sent to a repair shop to be rebuilt. Leaf springs require no lubrication since they are fitted with antisqueak inserts between the leaves. These inserts must be replaced when they become worn, and care must be taken to make sure the spring leaves are dry and free from oil and dirt before the new inserts are installed.

As previously described the rear leaf springs are attached to the frame by a hanger at one end and a shackle at the other by means of a spring bolt and a rubber bushing. In operating the motion between the spring bolt and the bushing is twisting. If the bushing becomes loose, a metal-to-metal contact can result, and it can cause a squeak. Under these conditions the spring bolt should be tightened to force the bushing more firmly into the eye and around the bolt. Under no circumstances should the rubber bushing be lubricated. Not only do petroleum-base lubricants cause rubber to deteriorate, but lubricants of any sort allow the rubber to slide on the metal and cause wear. If the squeak persists the bushing must be replaced.

U-bolts should be tightened periodically to prevent the axle from slipping on the spring. This condition causes the vehicle to "dog track," which means, to be out of track when driven on the straightaway.

Spring Replacement

Springs must be replaced when

broken or weak. The vehicle must be supported on jack stands placed under the body or frame during the operation. Be sure the correct lifting points are used on vehicles having unitized body construction.

Coil Spring Replacement. One method for removing a coil spring from a vehicle is stated in the following sequence of operations. First, remove the shock absorber from the inside of the spring. Place a chain over the top of the coil spring recess in the frame and tie the chain to the axle of a hydraulic floor jack. This procedure anchors the vehicle and prevents it from rising when the jack is raised. Since the vehicle cannot rise despite the pressure of the jack from beneath, the spring is compressed. With the jack in position lift the lower control arm until the upper control arm is clear of the rebound bumper. Either the lower pin or the lower ball joint may now be removed from the lower control arm. Once they are removed, the steering knuckle, hub, drum, and upper control arm may be lifted out of the way. Spring removal is shown in Fig. 4-10.

A rod approximately one-half inch in diameter and at least two feet long should now be placed in the hole formerly occupied by the shock absorber. This rod will act as a safety device so that, with the chain removed, the spring will not fly out of position as the jack is lowered.

Caution: Lower the jack very slowly!

To install a new spring simply reverse the removal procedure.

Leaf Spring Replacement. With the car up on jack stands, the rear axle will hang down from the frame, supported only by the rear springs. To remove the springs, place a jack under the center of the rear axle housing and lift the axle just high enough to support its weight. Remove the nuts from the U-bolts. Then remove the U-bolts themselves and the

Fig. 4-10. Position of jack under lower suspension arm while coil spring is being compressed prior to removal. (*Ford Motor Company*)

spring pads. Jack stands should be used to hold the axle in position before the springs are removed. A spring jack or hydraulic ram should now be used to spread the springs between the spring eyes as shown in Fig. 4-11.

Expand the spring jack or hydraulic ram until the spring is in its normal posi-

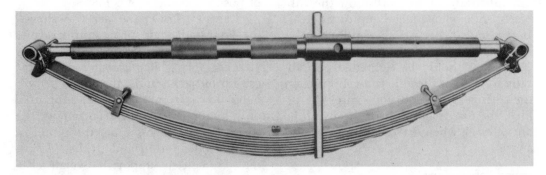

Fig. 4-11. In order to remove or install a leaf spring, it is necessary to spread the ends of the leaf by means of a spring jack. The above illustration shows the spring jack in use.

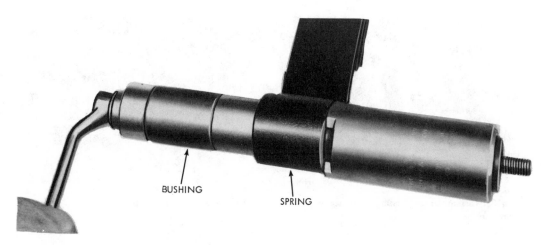

BUSHING

SPRING

Fig. 4-12. Installing rear spring front bushing. (*Plymouth Div., Chrysler Corp.*)

tion. Remove the bushing bolts at the hanger and shackle ends of the spring and take the spring from under the car. Replace it with a new or reconditioned spring by reversing the disassembly procedure. Whenever a spring is replaced new rubber bushings should be inserted between the spring bolt and hanger or shackle, Fig. 4-12.

Stabilizer Bar Service

The stabilizer bar requires no servicing except where it attaches to the frame and suspension parts. The attaching parts are usually made of rubber and as such should be periodically lubricated with rubber lubricant to prevent deterioration. New bushings are available for replacement in kit form called a stabilizer-link kit. Worn stabilizer links will cause erratic handling of the vehicle on the road.

Torsion Bar Service and Replacement

Front suspension torsion bars function in the same way as coil springs. To compensate for torsion bar fatigue, which permits the vehicle to sag, the torsion bar suspension system is adjustable. The front end of the torsion bar is attached to the lower control arm. The rear end of the torsion bar is attached to the frame by an adjustable anchoring device. Adjusting this anchor will reestablish the correct height of the vehicle. When adjustment is necessary, be sure to adjust both torsion bars to equal heights. A number of manufacturers make height gages and provide specifications so that these suspensions can be easily adjusted.

To remove and replace torsion bars the vehicle frame must be supported on jack stands at a height which enables the front wheels to clear the floor. When the front suspension is resting on the upper rebound bumper, the torsion bar anchor at the rear can be loosened. When the adjusting device is completely released, the torsion bar and rear hanger may be removed. Be sure that the torsion bars are not nicked, scratched, or marred in any manner during removal or replacement.

When re-installing a torsion bar notice that the ends of the bar are marked to indicate whether the bar is for the right or left side of the suspension. The ends of the torsion bars are retained in sockets which, like the end of the bars them-

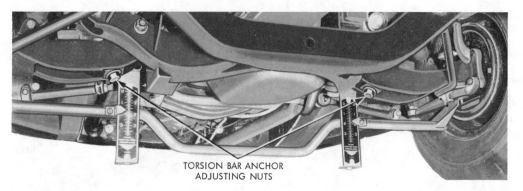

Fig. 4-13. Torsion bar adjusting nuts shown in position to measure front suspension height. (*Chrysler Corporation*)

selves, must be thoroughly lubricated, perferably with a heavy, wheel-bearing type of grease.

After the torsion bars are installed in their sockets, tighten the adjustment part way. Then lower the vehicle to its wheels and drive it on an alignment rack or some other level surface where the torsion bars may be adjusted until the vehicle attains the proper height, Fig. 4-13.

Shock Absorbers

A shock absorber is the assembly which checks excessively rapid spring movement and oscillation.

The ideal spring for automotive use would be one to absorb shock rapidly but return it to its original position slowly. A soft spring is too flexible and allows too much movement; at the same time, a hard spring is too stiff to provide a comfortable ride. Satisfactory riding qualities can be obtained by using a fairly soft spring in combination with a shock absorber.

It is the nature of a spring to oscillate; therefore springs absorb very little energy. A load supported on springs, when displaced, continues to rise and fall as the springs deflect and rebound until the spring action dies down. The load drops until resisted by the spring, stops, and then starts to rise as the spring rebound effort comes into play. The rebound action begins slowly, increases in velocity as the spring follows its oscillation pattern,

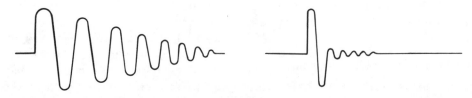

Fig. 4-14. Spring oscillations. The nature of a spring is to flex, and as shown in the left hand view, if the flexing of a spring or its oscillations are not controlled, the spring will not return at once to the released position. As shown in the right hand view, when the spring action is controlled by the shock absorber, it will return quickly to its released or at rest position.

then slows down and stops due to the influence of gravity on the load. Once again, the load changes direction and begins to drop. This complete cycle repeats until the spring action ceases, each succeeding cycle being reduced in the amount of deflection. Figure 4-14 illustrates controlled and uncontrolled spring oscillation.

Shock absorbers operate by absorbing the energy of vertical and lateral motion, converting the energy into heat and dissipating the heat into the air. The shock absorber takes in this energy and, in doing so, keeps spring oscillation to a minimum.

Shock absorbers are attached to the vehicle between the frame and the wheels. In this position they are able to control and to regulate spring action. Shock absorber mounting is shown in Fig. 4-15.

In many installations shock absorbers in the rear suspension are mounted on a frame cross member or floor pan. When installed in this manner both shock absorbers will lean inward at the top. This type of installation (Fig. 4-9) helps reduce body sway.

Types of Shock Absorbers

Several types of shock absorbers have been used over a period of years. The shock absorbers used today on both front and rear suspensions are of direct acting, double acting, telescope design. The principle of operation is the same for all hydraulic shock absorbers regardless of the type. Spring oscillations are retarded by alternately forcing fluid through small orifices from one chamber to another.

Direct Acting Double Acting, Telescope Type. Double acting shock absorbers restrict spring movement in both directions. They reduce spring deflection on compression as well as on rebound. The double acting shock absorber makes it possible to employ a softer spring in suspension design. Since the shock absorber assists the spring in resisting up and down motion, the spring can be designed to support only the vehicle load while the vehicle is at rest. In most double acting shock absorbers the rebound stroke offers more resistance than the compression stroke.

Basically, shock absorber operation consists of forcing a fluid within a cylinder through a restricted opening. This action is accomplished by a piston whenever the vehicle springs flex. The presence of the small opening causes fluid friction which converts the absorbed energy into heat. The heat is then taken up by the shock absorber fluid and dissipated into the atmosphere.

Understanding shock absorber construction aids in understanding operating principles. Generally, the shock absorber

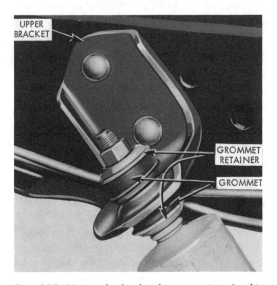

Fig. 4-15. Upper shock absorber mounting. In this installation the upper portion of the shock absorber is mounted to the frame side rail. (*Buick Div., General Motors Corp.*)

consists of an inner cylinder filled with hydraulic fluid and divided into an upper and a lower chamber by a double acting piston. When the fluid is under pressure, it passes through a restricted orifice (opening) or bleeder contained in a spring-loaded valve. If fluid displacement is rapid, the valve opens against the spring and permits a faster flow. Double acting shock absorbers contain two such valves: a compression valve and a rebound valve. The valves are located on the under side of the piston (to avoid forcing fluid under pressure against the piston rod seal) and are operated by vac-

uum on rebound and by piston pressure on compression.

The double acting piston is moved up and down within the cylinder by means of a piston push rod. The cylinder is joined to a reservoir of hydraulic fluid at one end by a reservoir check valve. The piston rod is attached to the frame while the reservoir end of the assembly is attached to the spring plate at the rear axle housing (rear suspension) and to the lower control arm (front suspension). A typical shock absorber is illustrated in Fig. 4-16.

A dust cover is sometimes affixed to the top of the piston rod around the reservoir, so that it moves up and down with the piston rod. Other shock absorbers of this type do not use dust covers but are constructed in the same manner and operate in the same way.

When the vehicle spring rebounds, the piston is drawn upward. The fluid above the piston passes through the rebound valve (and through the rebound relief valve if the action is severe) to the lower part of the cylinder. Because of the volume occupied by the piston rod, there is not enough fluid above the piston to fill the lower chamber. Therefore, the lower part of the chamber becomes a partial vacuum, and additional fluid is sucked into the cylinder from the reservoir.

When the piston is forced downward on the compression stroke, the fluid below the piston passes through the piston intake valve to the upper part of the cylinder. As the piston rod enters the cylinder, however, it displaces its own volume in fluid. The fluid thus displaced is forced out of the cylinder through the compression valve, located between the bottom of the cylinder and the reservoir.

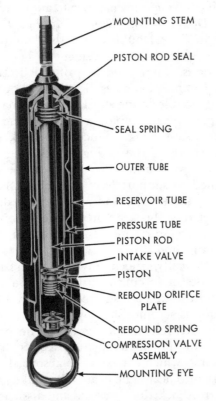

Fig. 4-16. Cutaway view of a typical direct acting type of shock absorber. This type of shock absorber may be mounted either between the upper and lower control arm or between the lower control arm and the vehicle frame. (*Buick Div., General Motors Corp.*)

MOUNTING STEM

PISTON ROD SEAL

SEAL SPRING

OUTER TUBE

RESERVOIR TUBE

PRESSURE TUBE

PISTON ROD

INTAKE VALVE

PISTON

REBOUND ORIFICE PLATE

REBOUND SPRING

COMPRESSION VALVE ASSEMBLY

MOUNTING EYE

Air Lift Shock Absorbers

Some manufacturers make available

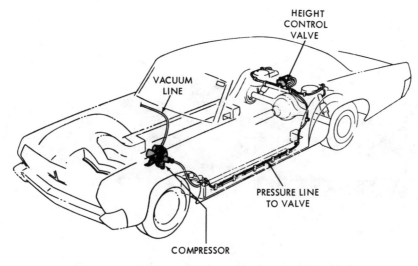

Fig. 4-17. Air lift automatic load leveling system. (*Ford Customer Service Div., Ford Motor Co.*)

a level control system in conjunction with the rear shock absorbers. The purpose of the system is to supplement the rear springs so as to keep the vehicle level whenever a load is placed on the vehicle.

Two different systems may be used, a manually inflated system or an automatically inflated system.

The manual system consists of two rear air lift shock absorbers interconnected by air lines to an inflation valve (similar to a tire valve) located at the rear of the vehicle. When the vehicle is carrying more than a normal load, the rear shock absorbers may be inflated from an outside compressed air source (air hose at a service station) to bring the rear of the vehicle up to normal height.

The automatic system is designed to function when a load equivalent to approximately three passengers is added to the vehicle. As the load is added, the air lift shock absorbers are automatically inflated, bringing the rear of the vehicle to a level position. As the load is removed, the shock absorber deflates, lowering the vehicle to the normal position.

The system consists of a vacuum operated air compressor (on some installations a reservoir is used), a height control valve and link, two air sleeve shock absorbers and the necessary connecting lines, Fig. 4-17.

The vacuum operated compressor, which is used to supply air to the system, is of the stage type receiving vacuum from the intake manifold. Incorporated in the compressor or reservoir is a regulator valve and a one-way check valve. The regulator valve maintains an operating pressure of approximately 125 psi. The check valve prevents air from bleeding back into the compressor or reservoir when the compressor is not operating. The height control valve and operating lever is mounted on the vehicle frame with a link connecting the lever to the upper control arm where it attaches to the rear axle housing or directly to the axle housing. When a load is placed on the vehicle, the frame lowers. As the axle housing and control arm, where it is attached to the axle housing, remains stationary the link will move the control

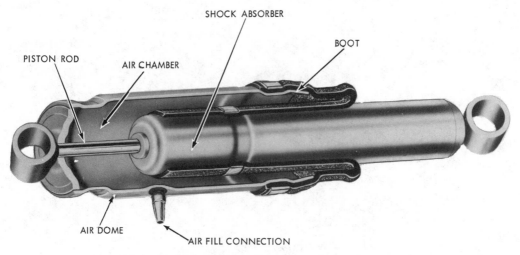

Fig. 4-18. Air lift shock absorber. (*Chevrolet Div., General Motors Corp.*)

valve lever, this opens the air passage to the shock absorbers. When the load is removed, an exhaust valve in the control valve opens, permitting the air to be exhausted from the shock absorber. This allows the vehicle body to return to normal height. A time delay feature of 4-18 seconds is incorporated in the control valve which permits normal road operation without actuating the lift system.

The air lift shock absorber is essentially a conventional direct acting shock absorber unit with a flexible nylon reinforced neoprene boot acting as an air chamber, Fig. 4-18.

Shock Absorber Service

The service garage does not repair or rebuild shock absorbers; therefore, a direct acting shock absorber must be replaced when it fails.

To install a direct acting shock absorber on the front suspension, remove the nuts or bolts that hold the shock absorber to the cross member. Remove the bolts that secure the shock absorber to the lower control arm. Usually, the shock absorber can now be removed by pulling it out through the lower control arm.

Some designs, however, make it necessary to remove the shock absorbers from the top. Always install new rubber grommetts (bushing) when replacing shock absorbers.

Shock absorber operation may be checked on some vehicles by grasping the bumper of the vehicle and bouncing the car up and down. Almost instantly upon release of the bumper the vehicle should stop bouncing. If it does not, the shock absorbers need replacing.

If the suspension system has the shock absorber connected to the upper control arm, this test will not work. The vehicle must be road tested and the shock absorbers removed if the ride indicates the shock absorber may not be functioning properly.

Another method is to check each shock absorber by itself after removing from the vehicle. Hold the shock absorber in its normal operating position; then extend the shock absorber and note its resistance. Compare this resistance to that of a new shock absorber of the same height and action. Compress the shock absorber and make the comparison in the same manner. If the shock absorber is serviceable, no difference will be noted. Moisture around the push rod of the shock absorber usually means it is leaking hydraulic fluid, and it may need to be replaced. Noise coming from the front or rear suspension is often due to shock absorber mountings that are loose or worn out.

TRADE COMPETENCY TEST

1. What is the purpose of automotive springs?
2. Name the types of springs in use on automotive suspension systems.
3. What is commonly used between the ends of leaf springs to prevent squeaking?
4. Upon what principle does a torsion bar work?
5. What is the purpose of a shackle used on one end of a leaf spring?
6. What is the difference in construction between a front coil spring and a rear coil spring?
7. How does a front end stabilizer operate?
8. What are the characteristics of all springs?
9. Why does a spring break?
10. What can be done to a coil spring if it becomes weak or fatigued?
11. Why shouldn't the rubber bushing and spring bolt be lubricated?
12. What is done to compensate for vehicle sag when a torsion bar system is used on the front end?
13. What is the purpose of shock absorbers?
14. Where are shock absorbers attached to the vehicle?
15. Can you describe how a double acting telescoping type of shock absorber operates?
16. How does an automatic air lift system operate?

CHAPTER 5

STEERING GEARS AND LINKAGES

The steering gear is a device which converts the rotary motion of the steering wheel into side to side movement of the front wheels, permitting the driver to control the direction of vehicle travel. Various types of linkage are used to connect the steering gear to the front wheels.

The steering gear also provides the mechanical advantage necessary for the driver to maintain steering control of the vehicle. The *mechanical advantage* of a machine is the ratio of the moving force to the applied force. If a five-pound force is applied to a machine to move a twenty-pound weight, the mechanical advantage is four. The driver need only exert a small amount of physical effort at the steering wheel to change the direction of travel. This mechanical advantage is particularly helpful when the vehicle is at rest, in which case the driver must overcome the frictional resistance of the tires on the road surface in turning the wheels. When the vehicle is in motion and the front wheels strike an obstacle, only a small part of the road shock is transmitted to the steering wheel. This is due to the mechanical advantage provided by the steering gear. Manual steering gear

mechanical advantages may vary from 10:1 to 28:1 depending upon the vehicle manufacturer. Power steering ratios will also vary according to manufacturer's specifications. The ratio in each case is selected to suit the needs of a particular vehicle.

Manual Steering Gear Construction and Types

The steering gear is bolted to a frame member of the vehicle. The steering column extends at an angle through the fire wall or floor pan and into the driver's compartment where the steering wheel is attached. A pitman arm (which swings back and forth as the steering wheel is turned) is attached to the lower end of the steering gear assembly and to the steering arm at each front wheel spindle assembly by means of linkages. As the steering wheel is turned the pitman arm and its connecting linkages cause the front wheels to swing back and forth for steering purposes. Figure 5-1 illustrates a typical steering gear arrangement.

Fig. 5-1. Typical steering gear arrangement showing the various linkages of the steering system such as the pitman arm, the idler arm, the tie rods and the tie rod ends. (*Pontiac Div., General Motors Corp.*)

Steering Gear Construction

All steering gears are enclosed in and supported by a housing. The steering gear consists of a worm gear of some type which is contained within the housing, this wormlike device being at the lower end of the steering shaft. The steering shaft and worm gear are an integral assembly. Ball bearings or roller bearings support the worm in the steering gear housing. See Fig. 5-2. An adjustment in

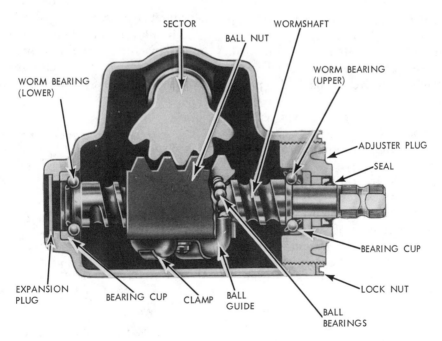

Fig. 5-2. Sectional view of a recirculating ball type steering gear assembly. (*Chevrolet Div., General Motors Corp.*)

the form of shims located between the housing end plate and housing or a threaded bearing adjuster nut permits the maintaining of the correct bearing pre-load on the worm. The steering wheel is mounted on the upper end of the shaft by serrations (saw edge formations) and a nut. The steering gear shaft assembly is located inside a tube known as the steering column jacket.

The cross shaft is located in the housing, at right angles to the steering column and supported on bushings. The steering gear cross shaft or pitman shaft incorporates a sector gear, a roller, or a lever, which meshes with the worm on the steering shaft. The outer end of the cross shaft extends through the housing, at which location the pitman arm is attached by means of serrations and held in place by a nut. An adjusting screw permits adjustment of steering gear lash or end play of the cross shaft.

Types of Steering Gears

Steering gears are classified according to the device used for engaging the cross shaft to the worm shaft assembly. All present American passenger vehicles use the worm and recirculating ball type of steering gear assembly, sometimes referred to as the ball and nut type, except for one model of passenger vehicle which uses the rack and pinion type of manual steering gear assembly.

In the past, in addition to the recirculating ball type of steering gear assembly, a worm and roller steering gear and a cam and lever type of steering gear assembly were used. As. these different types of steering gear assemblies are still being used, it is well to have an understanding of all types.

Recirculating Ball. The most widely used manual steering gear is the recirculating ball type. The worm used in the recirculating ball steering gear consists of

a straight cylinder with a round groove machined around the surface for the full length of the cylinder, like the thread on a bolt. A nut fits over the worm but does not mesh with it. A groove corresponding with the groove of the worm is machined on the inside of the nut. Engagement between the worm and the nut is obtained by filling the matching groove spaces with small steel balls. When the worm turns, the balls roll in the groove against the nut and cause the nut to move up or down along the worm. Each ball travels one complete loop around the worm, after which it enters a ball return guide and is pushed through the guide by the succeeding balls, over to the opposite side of the worm where it again enters the grooves. Figure 5-3 shows the complete circuit. Two complete circuits or loops are needed to actuate the worm and nut.

The worm and nut are mounted on ball bearings. An adjusting nut located at either the top or bottom of the housing provides a means of maintaining bearing pre-load.

The bottom outside face of the worm nut is machined in the shape of teeth forming a gear rack. A sector gear on the cross shaft acts as a pinion, meshing with

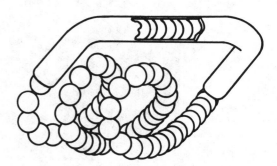

NOTE: THERE ARE TWO SEPARATE CIRCUITS OF BALLS CARRYING THE LOAD.

Fig. 5-3. Recirculating ball circuit as used in the recirculating ball type of steering gear. (*Buick Div., General Motors Corp.*)

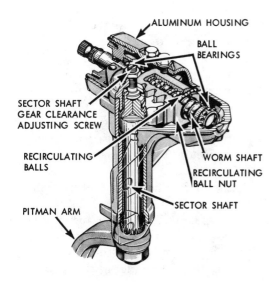

Fig. 5-4. Recirculating ball type steering gear. Each ball travels one complete loop around the worm, after which it enters the ball return guide and is pushed through the guide by the succeeding balls, over to the opposite side of the worm where it again enters the grooves. There are two complete circuits or loops which are used to actuate the worm and nut assembly when the steering wheel is turned. (*Plymouth Div., Chrysler Corp.*)

the rack, thereby actuating the cross shaft when the worm nut is moved. The cross shaft is mounted within replaceable bushings. Figure 5-4 illustrates the circulating ball type steering gear. An adjusting screw located in the housing side cover (covering the cross shaft) is used to remove end play in the cross shaft.

The worm shaft used with present recirculating ball type steering gear assemblies is short with serrations or splines on the upper end. The worm gear shaft is attached to the steering column shaft by means of a sliding coupling or a flexible connection. This design permits using a flexible joint in the steering column shaft for tilting purposes for ease of entering the vehicle, moving the steering column up or down for height adjustment and to permit the steering wheel and column to move downward (collapse) in the event of an accident.

Worm and Roller. The worm and roller steering gear consists of a concave

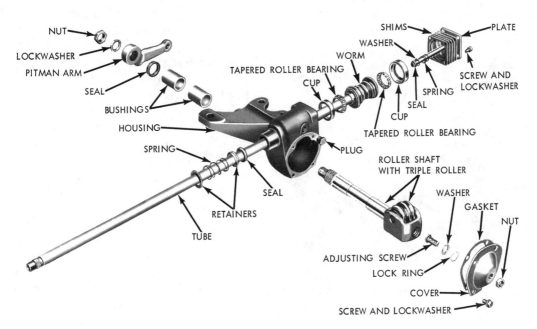

Fig. 5-5. Exploded view of the worm and roller type steering gear. Note that in this type of unit, the roller shaft has a triple roller. (*Plymouth Div., Chrysler Corp.*)

(hour glass design) worm mounted on the steering column. The cross shaft is fitted with a roller which may have one or more grooves, as shown in Fig. 5-5. The roller fits into the worm teeth, which have the same contour as the roller, the worm being supported in the housing by tapered roller bearings. Shims located between the housing end plate and the housing provide a means of adjusting the bearing pre-load. When the worm turns, the roller threads along the worm, rolling with it and turning the cross shaft. The cross shaft is mounted within the housing by replaceable bushings, the shaft extending through the bushings which support it. The lash between the worm and roller can be reduced by turning an adjusting screw located in the housing cover. Rollers may be of the single, double, or triple type depending upon the design of the worm.

Cam and Lever. In the cam and lever steering gear, the worm is shaped in the form of a cylindrical cam, (Fig. 5-6).

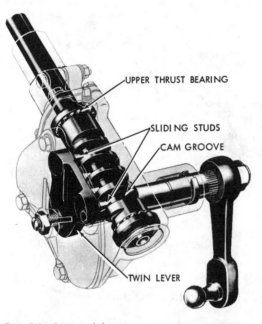

UPPER THRUST BEARING

SLIDING STUDS

CAM GROOVE

TWIN LEVER

Fig. 5-6. Cam and lever type steering gear. (*Ross Gear and Tool Co.*)

The cam groove is tapered, being narrower at the bottom. The cam which is integral with the steering shaft is mounted in the housing on thrust type ball bearings. An adjustment in the form of shims located between the housing end plate and the housing or a threaded bearing adjuster nut is used to establish and maintain the correct bearing preload.

A lever is affixed to the cross shaft. This lever lies at the side of the cam and has a tapered stud projecting from it. The stud fits into the cam groove so that when the cam turns the stud moves along the cam, thereby swinging the lever and turning the cross shaft. The cross shaft is mounted within removable bushings to reduce friction and wear. An adjusting screw in the housing cover can be used to move the lever closer to the cam. As the stud is tapered, moving the lever closer to the cam reduces back lash. Figure 5-6, shows a lever with two studs, both of which ride the cam. The unit is known as a twin lever type steering gear.

Most cam and lever steering gears are of the twin lever type. The two studs may be an integral part of the lever or they may be mounted on tapered roller bearings. Those that are an integral part of the lever have a sliding contact on the cam and are known as *sliding studs.* Studs mounted in the lever on tapered roller bearings have a rolling contact and are known as *rolling studs.* Sliding or rolling studs may be used on either single or twin lever type steering gears.

Rack and Pinion Type Steering Gear. One make of American passenger vehicle presently uses a rack and pinion type of steering gear assembly on some models. The steering shaft, to which the steering wheel is attached, is connected to the steering gear assembly input shaft by means of a flexible cable. The flexible cable (shaft) is enclosed in a synthetic

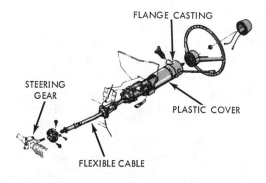

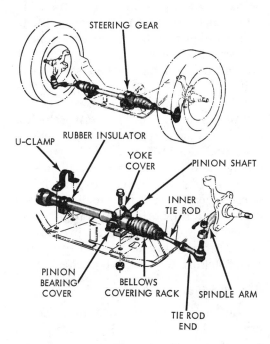

Fig. 5-7. Steering column installation (top) and rack and pinion steering gear installation (bottom). (*Ford Customer Service Div., Ford Motor Co.*)

rubber cover. A pinion gear is machined as an integral part of the steering gear input shaft and is in constant mesh with a rack, Fig. 5-7. *Note:* A rack is a flat bar with teeth on one face for meshing with the teeth of a pinion. As the steering wheel is turned, the input shaft and pinion revolve, causing the rack to move laterally. A tie rod is attached to each end of the rack by means of ball and socket joints. Movement of the steering wheel is thus transmitted to the front wheels for steering purposes and the tie rods can move up and down with the movement of the front suspension. The rack is sealed at each end with a synthetic rubber bellows to prevent dirt from entering the moving mechanism and causing wear. The rods attached to the rack cannot be serviced. The tie rod end attached to the steering arms have adjustable sleeves so as to permit changing the toe in setting. The tie rod ends can be replaced if they become worn.

Power Steering

Throughout the past few years several things have occurred that tend to make steering an automobile more difficult. The weight of the vehicle has been increased, more weight has been moved forward, wheels have become smaller, tires are wider and carry lower air pressure, and cars are capable of higher speeds. These factors have increased the effort required to turn the wheels while the vehicle is in motion. The greatest amount of effort, however, is required in parking. Parking requires that the wheels be turned while the vehicle is not moving or barely moving.

Due to the angle of the steering knuckle, the front wheels have a tendency to remain in a straight-ahead position. When the wheels are straight ahead, the front of the car is closest to the surface of the road. This means that when the wheels are turned from the straight-ahead position the front end of the car must be lifted slightly. While the weight of the front end helps the driver to maintain a straight-ahead course, it increases the effort required to turn the wheels from the straight-ahead position. This is most noticeable as you turn the wheels when parking.

To help offset these steering difficulties, car manufacturers, by means of gears and levers, have provided more and more mechanical advantage to the driver through the steering mechanism. A practical limit, however, exists as to the steering ratio. The greater the mechanical advantage, the more the steering wheel must be turned to move the front wheels a given number of degrees. The obvious answer to this problem is to provide mechanical assistance rather than mechanical advantage. This has been accomplished by the power steering systems now available as optional equipment. Over 80% of the American passenger vehicles being manufactured today are equipped with power steering.

An important safety factor of the power steering system is that it reduces the tendency of the front wheels to make unwanted turns. With manual steering, if one front wheel should suddenly hit a bump, or a front tire blows out, there is often a tendency for the steering wheel to be violently jerked out of the driver's hand. In power steering systems this is reduced to a moderate tendency of the steering wheel to turn which is easy for the driver to control. Therefore, the basic reasons for using power steering are: ease of steering, especially in parking; contribution to safety in heavy traffic conditions, and reduction of driver fatigue.

The fundamental principle behind power steering is simple. A hydraulic booster arrangement goes into operation when the steering wheel is turned with the engine running, taking over a great deal of the steering effort.

Before discussing the individual types of power steering systems, there are a few units and characteristics which are common to all power steering systems. First of all, a sense of steering *feel* must be retained. For this reason, all power steering systems have been designed so that some

manual effort on the part of the driver is necessary before the power mechanism takes over. This generally amounts to from one to four pounds of pull at the steering wheel rim before power assistance is provided. Without this resistance the driver would have a feeling of uncertainty.

All power steering systems require the engine to be running in order to supply steering assistance. Therefore, if the car is being towed or pushed with the transmission in neutral, power is not available to assist in steering. Should the power steering system fail or not be brought into operation, the vehicle can be steered manually.

There are two types of power steering assemblies in use on modern vehicles: (1) the linkage type, where the power operating unit is a part of the steering linkage, and (2) the integral type, where the power operating unit is part of the steering gear. The principle of operation is the same for both. A hydraulic pump is used to supply fluid under pressure to the steering system to multiply the driver's effort at the steering wheel.

Hydraulic System

An engine driven hydraulic pump supplies the necessary oil pressure to the system as needed. The pump is belt driven and delivers approximately 700 to 1450 psi pressure.

Always check the manufacturer's recommendations for the type of fluid to use. Some manufacturers recommend Type "A" automatic transmission fluid. Some automobile manufacturers make a special power steering fluid which they recommend, however, if this is not available, the Type "A" automatic transmission fluid can be used. Chrysler recommends not using transmission fluid; use only a special power steering fluid. A reservoir attached to the pump is a means of storing the hydraulic fluid. A pressure relief valve is incorporated within the pump to prevent the fluid pressure from exceeding a predetermined maximum pressure. Without this feature, should a front wheel become jammed against a curb so the wheel couldn't be turned, the pressure could build up to a point where the steering linkage or hydraulic system might be damaged.

Flexible hoses carry the fluid from the pump to the power cylinder control valve. The control valve used in all power steering systems is of the spool type and constructed in such a manner that a small amount of steering wheel movement aligns different passageways within the system. In a straight-ahead position, fluid under pressure is equally directed to both sides of the piston. In either a

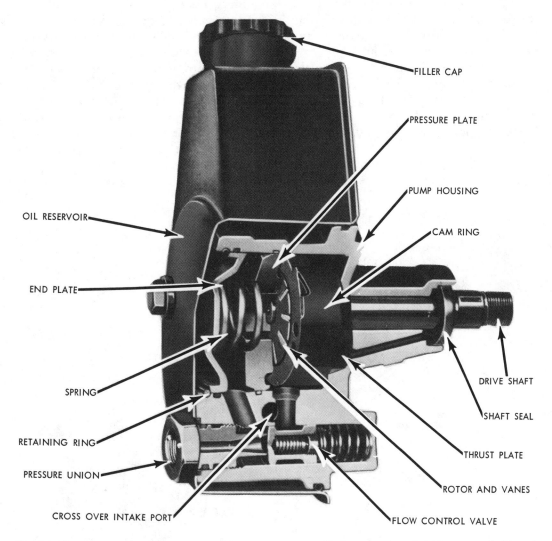

Fig. 5-8. Vane type power steering pump. The vanes are assembled in the slotted driving rotor (hub) and slide outward to contact the inner face of the pump body. The inner face is oval shaped so as to provide two pumping chambers within the pump. (*Ford Customer Service Div., Ford Motor Co.*)

right- or left-hand turn, the flow of fluid from the pump is shut off on one side of the piston, allowing the pressure to build up on the other side of the piston. After the turn has been completed, the control valve opens a return passageway which allows the fluid to return to the reservoir. The fluid then continues to circulate within the system.

Power Steering Pumps

The pump may be of the vane type, the rotor type, or a variation of the vane type. Figure 5-8 illustrates a typical vane type of power steering pump.

Variations of the same type pump are the roller and slipper types. Both pumps are similar in construction to the vane type pump except that rollers or sliding blocks (slippers) are used in place of vanes.

Figure 5-9 shows a disassembled roller type of power steering pump. Instead of

sliding vanes contacting the cam ring, rollers are used to form the seal between the cam ring and rotor.

Figure 5-10 shows the slipper arrangement in a rotor of the slipper type of power steering pump.

All power steering pumps, regardless of design, are of the constant displacement type. In the vane type pump, the vanes are located either in the hub or the rotor. In operation, these vanes slide in a manner (either inward or outward, depending upon design) to contact the inner surface of the pump housing. As the rotor revolves, the vanes slide inward and then outward to increase and then decrease the space between the inner surface of the housing and the rotor. Fluid is then forced from the inlet side of the pump to the pressure check valve at the outlet side of the pump. Oil enters the pump when the vanes, rollers, or slippers are at the low side of the eccentric inside

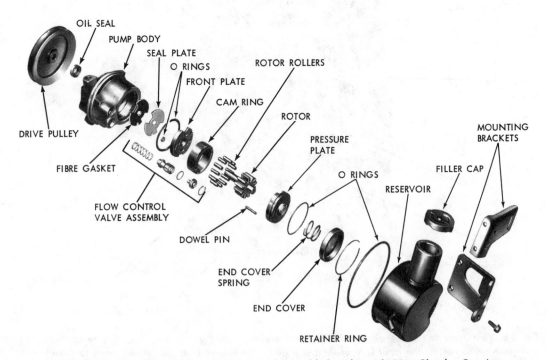

Fig. 5-9: Roller type power steering pump (disassembled). (*Plymouth Div., Chrysler Corp.*)

SLIPPER

ROTOR

Fig. 5-10. Slippers installed in a rotor of the slipper type of power steering pump. (*Ford Customer Service Div., Ford Motor Co.*)

diameter of the housing and exits after being forced to the high side of the eccentric. Orifices (openings) at the valve permit fluid to flow into the system until a maximum or predetermined pressure is reached. At maximum pressure, excess fluid flows back into the reservoir.

An exploded view of the rotor type pump is shown in Fig. 5-11. The inner (drive) rotor is located off center within the pump housing. As the inner rotor is turned, the outer rotor turns with it. As both rotors revolve, the space between the drive rotor and the driven rotor first increases and then decreases in size. During increase, fluid flows from the reservoir and into the space between the rotors through the inlet port. During decrease this fluid is forced out of the pump through an outlet port, into the lines and back to the reservoir. The same valve arrangement is used as in the vane type

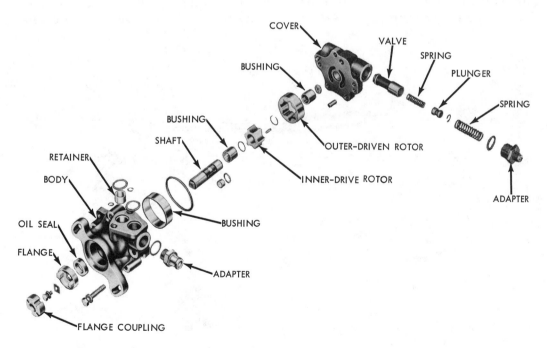

COVER
VALVE
SPRING
PLUNGER
BUSHING
SPRING
BUSHING
SHAFT
OUTER-DRIVEN ROTOR
RETAINER
INNER-DRIVE ROTOR
BODY
ADAPTER
OIL SEAL
BUSHING
FLANGE
ADAPTER
FLANGE COUPLING

Fig. 5-11. Exploded view of the rotor type power steering pump, showing the inner or drive rotor and the outer or driven rotor. The inner rotor rotates on the pump shaft, driving the outer rotor, thereby forcing hydraulic fluid into and out of the pump housing. This action provides the power steering assistance as the driver turns the steering wheel. (*Plymouth Div., Chrysler Corp.*)

pump. When maximum pressure is reached, excess fluid is bled back into the reservoir in such amounts as to maintain a working pressure.

Linkage Type Power Steering

The linkage type of power steering differs from the other hydraulic power steering systems in that a conventional type of steering gear is used.

The hydraulic power steering mechanism consists of an engine driven pump with check valve and reservoir, a double acting hydraulic power cylinder which assists linkage movement, and a control valve to direct the flow of fluid. The hydraulic pump, reservoir, and check valve are similar to those used with the integral type of power steering system, Fig. 5-12.

In some of the older installations, the control valve was incorporated within the power cylinder, thereby forming a single unit with an internal valve for directing fluid to the power cylinder passages. In today's installations, the control valve which is shown in Fig. 5-13 is a separate assembly. The control valve assembly is connected to the hydraulic pump by means of two flexible hoses. Oil, under pressure, is delivered from the hydraulic pump to the control valve assembly, shown in Fig. 5-12, and from the control valve assembly to the power cylinder assembly by means of flexible hoses.

The power cylinder contains a piston which is attached to a cylinder rod, the end of the rod being anchored to a frame bracket. The opposite end of the cylinder is attached by a ball joint to the relay rod. When oil pressure is applied to one side of the piston, the cylinder (not the piston) is actuated. The movement of the power cylinder is transferred to the steering linkage through the relay rod, thereby reducing the effort required to steer the vehicle.

The pitman arm actuates a spool valve within the control valve assembly.

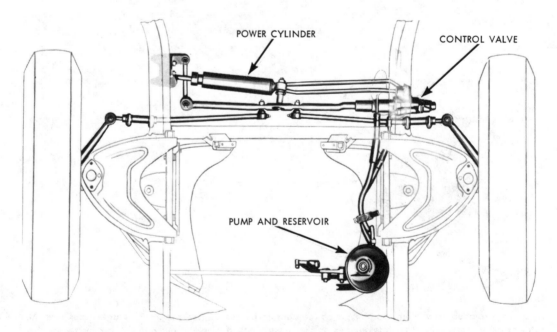

Fig. 5-12. Linkage type of power steering in which the power cylinder and control valve are an integral part of the steering linkage and not part of the steering gear. (Ford Div., Ford Motor Co.)

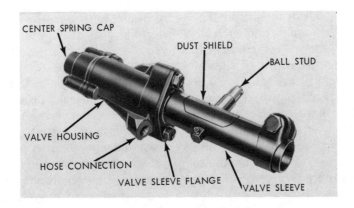

Fig. 5-13. Control valve assembly as used in the linkage type of power steering system. When the vehicle makes a turn, the control valve assembly directs fluid from the hydraulic pump to the power cylinder, thereby providing the power steering assistance needed. (Ford Div., Ford Motor Co.)

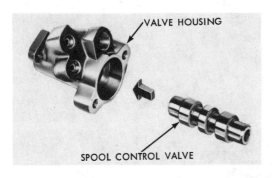

Fig. 5-14. Spool control valve which controls the flow of fluid within the linkage type of power steering system. The spool valve is contained within the control valve assembly. (Ford Div., Ford Motor Co.)

Figure 5-14 illustrates the spool valve used in this type of installation.

Initial movement of the steering wheel overcomes the spring pressure that holds the spool valve in a neutral position, thereby actuating the spool valve. This action shuts off the flow of fluid under pressure to one side of the power cylinder piston, directing fluid pressure to the other side. The spool valve is so constructed that the movement which closes off the fluid from the pump also lines up a passage which permits fluid on that side of the piston to flow back to the reservoir.

Integral Type Power Steering

An integral type of power steering system is constructed in such a manner that the power assist operating mechanism is part of the steering gear assembly.

Several different types of integral power steering units have been used by the various automobile manufacturers over a period of years. However, all integral types of power steering systems presently being used operate in the same manner and have the same basic components. The commonly used integral power steering systems are the Saginaw, Ford and Chrysler. Construction details will vary to some degree with the different makes and models.

The recirculating ball type steering gear is used by all manufacturers, although the worm and roller type has been used on some installations in the past. Fundamentally, the pump, reservoir, and check valve all function in the same manner. The system operates at pressures of from 700 to 1450 psi and in most cases uses a Type "A" transmission fluid. A double acting piston is used to assist in movement of the cross shaft which, in turn, moves the pitman arm. A spool valve is used to direct the flow of fluid to the proper side of the piston. The spool valve, at the same time, permits fluid to return to the reservoir by allowing excess fluid to bleed out of the opposite end of the piston cylinder. The steering wheel pressure required to move the spool value varies with different makes and models of automobiles. The method of moving the spool valve may also vary with the different makes of power steering installations.

Saginaw Integral Power Steering Using a Rotary Valve. Manual steering effort at the steering wheel is transmitted to the steering gear assembly through a flexible coupling. The flexible coupling absorbs shock and vibration and overcomes slight misalignment conditions.

This steering motion is transmitted by the coupling to the stub shaft in the steering gear assembly. A rotary control valve assembly, in turn, receives the steering effort from the stub shaft. The rotary valve controls the flow of oil to the proper side of the rack-piston nut according to the direction of the turn of the steering wheel and cuts off flow when power assistance is not called for.

The major components of the rotary valve type power steering assembly are: a hydraulic control valve body assembly, a piston, one side of which is in the form of sector gear rack teeth, a worm shaft and a cross shaft mounting a sector gear. The pump creates hydraulic pressure to aid in movement of the steering gear components, therefore producing a steering assist action, Fig. 5-15.

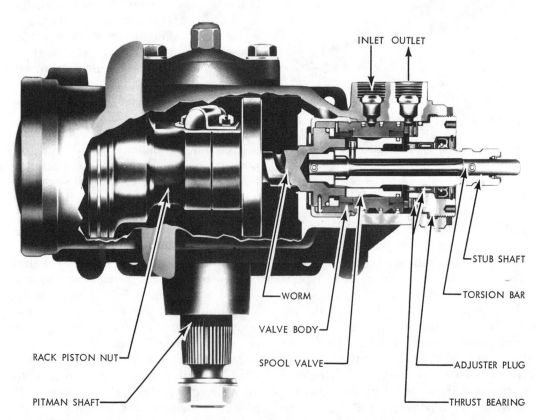

Fig. 5-15. Saginaw integral power steering using a rotary valve. (*Chevrolet Div., General Motors Corp.*)

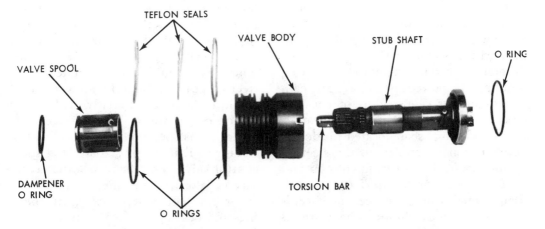

Fig. 5-16. Rotary valve disassembled. (Ford Customer Service Div., Ford Motor Co.)

The mechanical element uses a recirculating ball system, in which steel balls act as a rolling thread between the worm and the piston. The piston rack assembly meshes with the sector gear which is mounted on the cross shaft (pitman shaft). The hydraulic control valve is contained within the front section of the steering gear housing.

A variable steering ratio is built into the steering gear assembly on a number of late model passenger vehicles. This is brought about by using a longer middle tooth on the sector shaft and shorter teeth on either side.

In the mid-position of the gear, such as for straight ahead highway driving, the steering ratio is higher, approximately (16 to 1) for greater steering stability. For greater ease in maneuvering when making sharp turns for parking, the steering ratio is lower (approximately 13 to 1).

The rotary control valve is, basically, two assemblies fastened together by a torsion bar. The first subassembly which is connected to the upper end of the torsion bar and then to the coupling, shaft and steering wheel includes the stub shaft and spool valve. The second sub-

assembly, connected to the lower end of the torsion bar and eventually to the front wheels through the steering linkage, consists of the worm, valve body, and valve body cap. Figure 5-16 shows a disassembled rotary valve.

When the steering wheel is turned, resistance between the front wheels and the roadbed causes the torsion bar to deflect. Deflection of the torsion bar rotates the spool valve, changing the relationship between the grooves in the spool valve and the grooves in the valve body. This action directs the flow of fluid to the proper end of the piston chamber and releases the fluid in the opposite chamber. Fluid, under pressure, is equally directed to both sides of the piston when the steering wheel is motionless.

A cross shaft adjusting screw is located in the housing side cover. This adjustment is provided to remove cross shaft end play and establish a pre-load between the worm and sector gear.

An adjusting plug is located in the upper end of the gear housing to establish and adjust the preload on the valve body thrust bearings.

Chrysler Integral Type Power Steering. The Chrysler integral power steering gear assembly uses a different control valve arrangement than that used in the Saginaw power steering assembly. A cross shaft with a sector gear is supported by the housing at right angles to the steering column. The power piston has gear teeth milled into its side, and is in constant mesh with the cross shaft sector gear. A worm on a short shaft located inside the power piston is coupled to the steering column shaft. The steering column and shaft extends upward into the driver's compartment where the steering wheel is mounted in the column. The worm is meshed to the piston by means of a recirculating ball contact. Figure 5-17 illustrates the Chrysler integral type power steering.

The control valve assembly is mounted above the steering gear and directs the flow of fluid to either end of the power piston. The upper end of a control valve pivot lever is fitted into the spool control valve which is located in the valve body. The valve assembly is incorporated in the steering gear housing. The lower end of the lever fits into a radially drilled hole in the center thrust bearing race. The center thrust bearing race tips the valve lever which in turn, actuates the spool control valve. The thrust bearing center race is held firmly against a shoulder on the worm shaft between two thrust bearings and bearing races. An adjusting nut is incorporated on the worm shaft to permit adjustment. The center thrust bearing race is, in effect, clamped axially to the worm shaft and must move with the worm shaft whenever the steering wheel is turned.

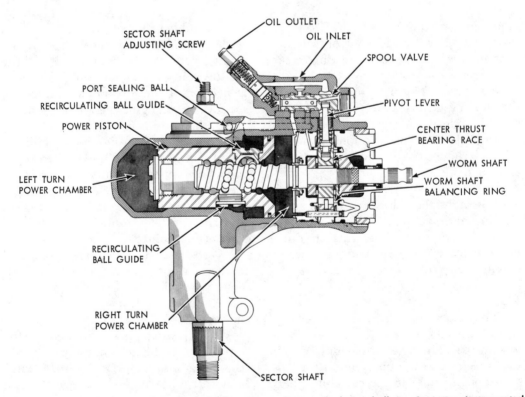

Fig. 5-17. The Chrysler integral power steering system uses a recirculating ball steering gear incorporated within a hydraulic power piston. (*Plymouth Div., Chrysler Corp.*)

The spool valve is in neutral when in a straight-ahead position and fluid is delivered under equal pressure to both piston chambers. When the steering wheel is turned, the worm and shaft rotate inside the piston. Due to the resistance of the steering linkage and front wheels, the power piston does not move immediately. Instead, the worm and shaft are withdrawn from the piston a few thousandths of an inch. The center thrust bearing race moves in the same distance as the worm shaft. The center race thus tips the pivot lever which, in turn, moves the spool valve. Fluid is now directed under pressure to one of the piston chambers while a passageway at the opposite piston chamber is opened, permitting fluid in that chamber to return to the reservoir. Hydraulic pressure now assists in moving the piston which, in turn, causes the cross shaft to rotate.

An adjusting screw located in the cross shaft housing permits adjustment of cross shaft end play.

Proper operation of the control valve is set by the up-and-down location of the valve body in relation to the gear housing.

Ford Integral Type Power Steering. The Ford power steering assembly is, basically, the same as the Saginaw type which is controlled by the twisting action of a torsion bar. Although the control valve housing is separate and mounted on the end of the gear housing, all lines between the control valve and rack piston are internal, Fig. 5-18.

The principal difference between the Saginaw and the Ford unit is that the Ford unit has a selective shim arrangement in the valve housing to adjust steering effort and balance the effort between right and left turns. Changing shim size changes steering effort.

Other Types of Power Steering Systems. Other types of power steering units have been used on various makes of automobiles. However, in every case, the basic operating principles and general

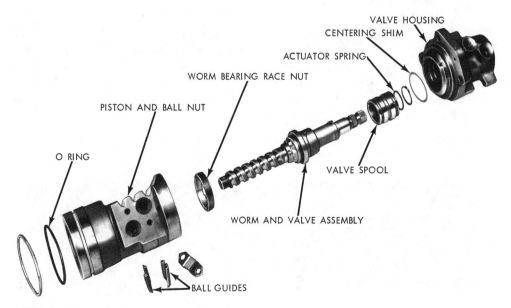

Fig. 5-18. Ford integral type power steering ball nut and valve housing disassembled. (*Ford Customer Service Div., Ford Motor Co.*)

construction will be the same. Variations, if any, generally occur in the relative position of the various components.

Steering Linkage

The rods, arms, and levers by which the steering knuckles are connected to the steering gear pitman arm are known collectively as the steering linkage. Various designs of steering linkages have been used in automative vehicles, but they all perform the same function.

All steering linkages used today are of the same basic design. A pitman arm is attached to the steering gear assembly cross shaft (pitman arm shaft). One end of a relay rod is attached to the pitman arm, the other end is supported by means of an idler arm attached to a frame member. Two tie rods, of equal length, are fastened by ball joints to the relay rod with the outer ends attached to the steering knuckle arms. Figure 5-19 illustrates a typical steering linkage arrangement.

Pitman Arm

The steering gear assembly has a pitman arm attached to the cross shaft that extends out of the steering gear housing, Fig. 5-19. The pitman arm swings from one side to the other, or forward and backward on some older designs, as the steering wheel is turned.

Relay Rods

The relay rod is used to transmit motion from the pitman arm to the tie rods. One end of the relay rod is attached to the pitman arm by a ball joint while the other end is supported by an idler arm attached by means of a bracket to a frame member. One end of each tie rod is attached to the relay rod by means of ball and socket joints, Fig. 5-19. The pitman arm moves the relay rod back and forth at right angles to the vehicle frame.

Steering Knuckles

The steering knuckle consists of a spindle for mounting the wheel, a means of attaching the unit to the control arms, and an arm for attaching the linkage to the knuckle in any desired position in its swing or travel. The knuckle, spindle, and steering knuckle arm are forged in one piece.

Steering Knuckle Arm

The steering knuckle arm is a lever for swiveling the knuckle. One end of the arm is secured to the knuckle. The free end of the arm is made with a hole for attaching the tie rod, which connects the

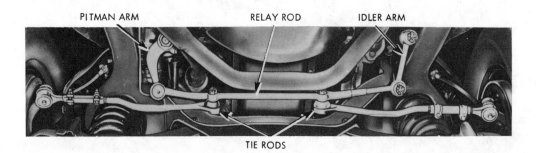

Fig. 5-19. A typical steering linkage arrangement. (Ford Div., Ford Motor Co.)

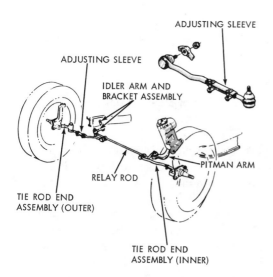

Fig. 5-20. Linkage system using a relay rod. (*Ford Customer Service Div., Ford Motor Co.*)

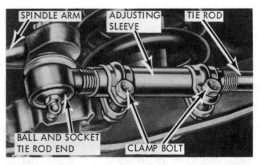

Fig. 5-21. The tie rod end is screwed into the sleeve and locked with the clamp bolts. This type of installation is known as a ball and socket tie rod end. (*Ford Div., Ford Motor Co.*)

right and left steering knuckle arms, as shown in Fig. 5-20.

Tie Rods

The tie rod is a hollow tube used to connect the steering knuckle arms together. Two tie rods are used on all independent front suspension systems. On present day vehicles, a relay rod is located between the two equal length tie rods and connects the pitman arm to the tie rods.

The tie rod is attached to the steering knuckle arm by means of a ball and socket joint which is known as the tie rod end. The tie rod and tie rod end have matching threads, enabling the tie rod to screw into the tie rod end while the opposite tie rod end always has a left-hand thread. The threads are cut in this manner so that the tie rod assembly can be lengthened or shortened by turning the tie rod, either inward or outward on the two tie rod ends. The end of each tie rod is fitted with clamp bolts to prevent either or both tie rods from turning, once the desired length is established. Most

installations employ a tie rod which is threaded only on one end. Therefore, a threaded sleeve is installed between the tie rod end and the tie rod as shown in Fig. 5-21. The sleeve has right-hand threads on one end and left-hand threads on the other. The sleeve is adjusted in the same manner as the tie rod; that is, the sleeve is turned either inward or outward to shorten or lengthen the tie rod. Clamps are used to keep the sleeve from turning when the vehicle is in use.

The threaded portion of the ball end joint forms the socket for holding the ball. The ball is a spherical end on a short bolt which is tapered and made expressly for attachment to the steering knuckle arm. The joint is fitted with a seal to keep dirt and moisture out of the socket. Ball end joints cannot be disassembled.

Another type of ball and socket joint assembly was used over the past years. The socket was part of the end of the tie rod or drag link. A ball was attached to the pitman arm and/or steering knuckle arm. The socket could be separated from the ball, therefore, the assembly was adjustable. Concave washers and one or more springs were located in the socket to maintain a slight tension on the ball. A threaded end plug in the socket enables adjustment of spring tension on the ball thereby compensating for wear and preventing free play.

The independent front suspension system uses a separate tie rod for each steering knuckle. Separate tie rods are used, because the distance between steering knuckle arms varies as the wheels move up and down independently of each other. If a constant distance is maintained by using a single tie rod, the wheels would swivel or turn, at least to a small degree, at every road irregularity.

Several linkage methods have been used to keep the wheels in a straight-ahead position in spite of spring deflections. All present linkage systems have tie rods of the same length as the lower suspension control arms and are parallel to them, Fig. 5-20. By this means, the tie rods swing in the same arc as the control arm and consequently maintain the same distance from the center of the vehicle throughout the spring action. On turns, however, the tie rods do not remain parallel to the control arms, because the arc of action on the pitman arm causes the inner ends of the tie rods to rise and fall. To maintain steering stability, the tie rods are connected to a relay rod which is connected on one end to the pitman arm and on the other end to an idler arm which is the same length as the pitman arm.

Other Types of Steering Linkage

A type of steering linkage which was formerly used employed a center pitman arm and long and short tie rods, Fig. 5-22. In this system, the steering gear was so constructed that the pitman arm swings crosswise under the vehicle frame. A short tie rod connects the pitman arm directly to one steering knuckle arm, while a long tie rod reaches directly to the other. In order to compensate for the difference in the lengths of the tie rods (which affects the amount the wheels are turned), they are attached at different points on the pitman arm. When the pitman arm swings in making a turn, the short arm rises in a sharper arc and consequently does not move as far in a cross wise direction. This difference in travel at the pitman arm causes the two wheels to swivel a corresponding degree.

A second type of unequal tie rod design was one in which the short tie rod was attached to the long rod at a point

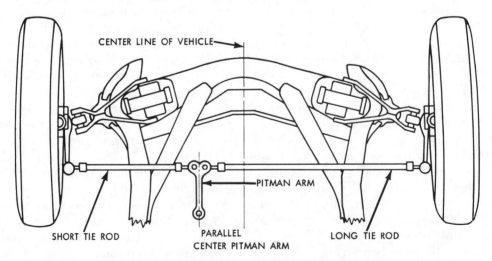

Fig. 5-22. Steering linkage using a center pitman arm.

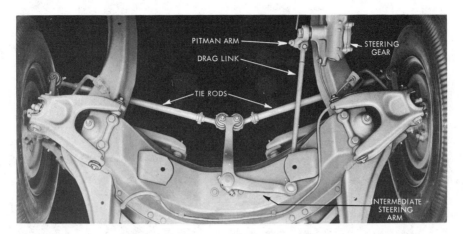

Fig. 5-23. Steering linkage using a drag link.

near the center of the vehicle, the long tie rod being attached directly to the pitman arm. This construction gives the effect of two equal arms.

Another type of linkage system, also no longer being used, had equal length tie rods, the tie rods being attached to an intermediate steering arm at the center of the vehicle. The steering knuckle arms are actuated by the tie rods, which in turn are actuated through a short drag link by the pitman arm, Fig. 5-23.

Numerous other designs of steering linkages have been used, but the operating principles, basic components, and servicing procedures are the same for all types of linkages.

Any free play that may develop in the steering linkage which cannot be removed by adjustment, necessitates the replacement of parts, generally: the tie rod, the relay rod, or the tie rod ends. Proper front wheel toe-in must be maintained by correct adjustment of the tie rods. Adjustment of the tie rods also affects the midposition of the steering wheel.

Steering Columns

The steering column is the mast jacket or shroud which encloses the steering gear shaft and shift tube as well as containing the anti-theft lock system and the turn signal switch. All steering columns on older vehicles were made in one piece. Today's passenger vehicles all use a collapsible type of column.

Collapsible Steering Column

As a safety feature, vehicles now being manufactured have an energy absorbing (collapsible) steering column. This applies to the tilt steering wheel, the telescoping steering column as well as the regular steering column. At a pre-determined force, such as that brought about by various front impact conditions (collision), the column (mast jacket), shift tube and steering shaft are designed to collapse (push forward and downward), approximately six inches at a controlled rate.

Some steering columns are constructed to collapse in an accordion fashion, at a prescribed force, Fig. 5-24. This may be accomplished by constructing a section of the column with diamond shaped perforations having accordion pleats. Other columns may have a ball bearing energy absorbing device. Ball bearings are imbedded in plastic and pressed between

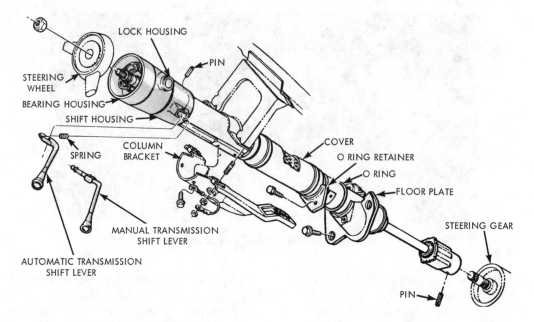

Fig. 5-24. Collapsible type steering column. (*Plymouth Div., Chrysler Corp.*)

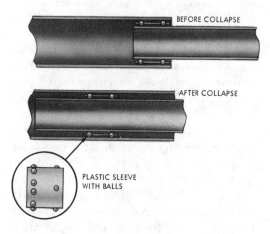

Fig. 5-25. Energy-absorbing steering column. (*Chevrolet Div., General Motors Corp.*)

the upper and lower steering column jackets. Upon impact, the columns (jackets) slide together, Fig. 5-25.

The steering shaft and shift tube are made in two pieces, one sliding over the other so that they will slide further together upon impact. Some are held in place by plastic pins which shear upon impact.

On some installations "break-away" column mounting brackets are used which shear upon impact, permitting the entire assembly to move forward. The bracket, in some cases, will allow the column to slide forward but will block its rearward movement.

Tilt and Telescoping Steering Column

Many auto manufacturers make available a tilt type steering wheel, as well as a telescoping type steering column, as optional equipment. Both features are generally combined.

This type of equipment permits the steering wheel to be tilted to best fit the individual driver or tilted for ease of entering or leaving the vehicle. The telescoping column permits the driver to adjust the height of the steering wheel for more comfortable driving. By lowering the steering wheel it is easier to enter or leave the vehicle from the driver's seat.

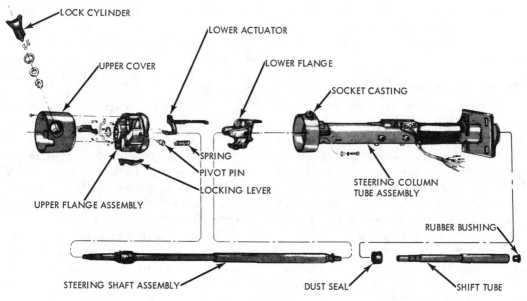

Fig. 5-26. Tilt column disassembled. (*Ford Customer Service Div., Ford Motor Co.*)

By lifting a small control lever located below the steering wheel, it is possible to tilt the steering wheel to fit the needs of the individual driver. Some assemblies have five driving positions at which the wheel may be set: straight, two up or two down. A two-piece steering shaft permits this flexibility. Figure 5-26 shows the tilt steering column assembly disassembled. As illustrated each shaft has a yoke on one end. The universal joint yokes are attached to one another by a centering sphere.

The steering column in Fig. 5-27 can be telescoped to better fit the driver. Both the steering shaft and shift tube are

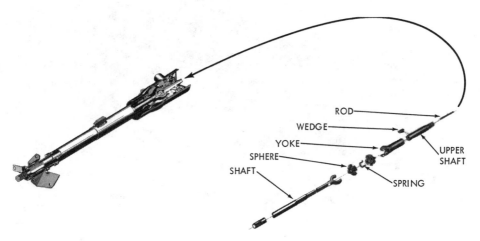

Fig. 5-27. Tilt and telescoping steering column. The driver can adjust the steering wheel to the most comfortable position. (*Oldsmobile Div., General Motors Corp.*)

made in two pieces. One shaft slides inside the other for the telescoping effect. The shift tube is constructed in the same manner.

Steering Column Ignition Lock

Regardless of the type of steering column used, tilt, telescoping or regular, late model passenger vehicles will all have an ignition lock system located in the steering column. The steering column incorporates an ignition lock, starting motor switch, ignition switch and an anti-theft system. The ignition key cannot be removed unless the transmission is in "Park" on a vehicle with an automatic transmission or reverse on a manual transmission. The lock bezel must also be turned to the "lock" position.

When the switch is in "lock" position, the steering wheel and shift lever are automatically locked by a rod and lock plate mechanism inside the column assembly, Fig. 5-28. A mechanical linkage between the floor shift transmission control and steering column provides the necessary

anti-theft features for all floor mounted controls.

When the lock bezel is turned, a rod is engaged with the lockplate preventing the steering shaft from being turned and the shift shaft from being moved out of "Park" on the automatic transmission or out of reverse on the manual shift transmission.

As part of the anti-theft system, an electrical circuit is incorporated which sounds a warning buzzer when the ignition key is all the way in the lock and the door on the driver's side is open.

The horn button or shroud, steering wheel and turn signal switch must be removed in order to service the anti-theft system.

Servicing the Steering Gear and Linkage

The safe operation of a vehicle depends a great deal upon the mechanical

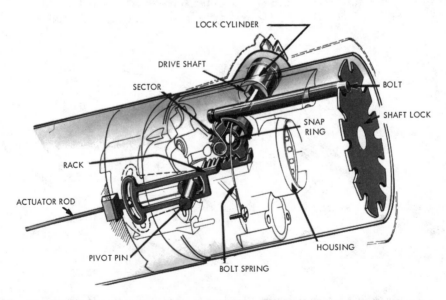

Fig. 5-28. Anti-theft ignition lock system. (*Oldsmobile Div., General Motors Corp.*)

condition of the steering gear and its connections through the various types of linkage to the front wheels.

All steering gears are adjustable either within themselves or externally. Therefore, when the front wheels are in the straight-ahead position, there should be no lost motion or lash between the gears. If excessive lash does exist within the steering system, the innumerable slight bumps in the road that normally are absorbed by the steering connections will be transformed into hammer-like blows that are felt in the steering wheel. Such a condition is described as road shock.

To check the amount of lost motion in the steering system, turn the steering wheel until the front wheels are in the straight-ahead position. Then lightly grasp the steering wheel between thumb and forefinger at the rim and move the steering wheel back and forth to determine the amount of play. Manufacturer's specifications vary with respect to steering gear no lash adjustment. However, if any steering wheel play is found at the rim, the steering gear requires adjustment.

Binding of the various steering components is known as hard steering and is usually the result of improper (too tight) no lash adjustment, tight or worn bearings, or distortion of the steering column. Such conditions will affect the control and stability of the vehicle, resulting in wander and hard steering when the vehicle is in motion as well as when stationary.

After considerable use, a steering gear may become worn to the extent where adjustment is no longer able to restore satisfactory operating limits. Then, it becomes necessary to replace some of the working parts. Damage from undue stress or collision may also make repairs necessary.

Adjustment of Manual Steering Gears

As previously discussed, there have been several different types of steering gear assemblies used over the years. However, for the past several years the recirculating ball type of steering gear has been used almost exclusively for both manual and power steering systems.

Regardless of the type of steering gear assembly, the purpose of adjusting is to remove the lash or adjust the tightness in the steering gear.

In all systems the worm shaft is mounted on bearings in the housing, and the bearings can be pre-loaded (set with a slight drag) by an adjusting screw or shims. The roller, sector, lever or ball nut must engage the worm shaft with a minimum of friction and is called high point. This is generally adjusted by an adjusting screw located in the steering gear housing, Fig. 5-29.

As the recirculating ball type of steering gear is the common type of assembly in general use, the adjustment procedure will be directed toward this type of steering gear system, all others will be adjusted in much the same manner. Figure 5-30 shows a disassembled recirculating ball nut steering gear.

There are two basic adjustments that must be made on a manual steering gear. These are the worm shaft bearing pre-load adjustment and the pitman or cross shaft over-center pre-load (high point). It may also be necessary to adjust the pitman shaft end play on some installations. Since these adjustments made on the steering gear are for taking up normal wear, they consist of tightening only and should, therefore, result in a definite drag or pre-load but should *not* cause binding. It is advisable to disconnect the steering linkage from the lower end of the pitman arm when checking or making steering gear adjustments.

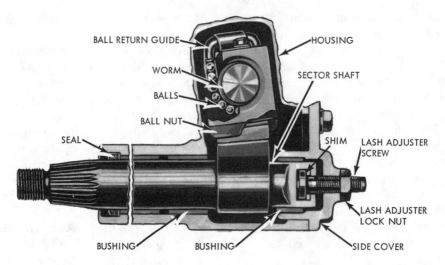

Fig. 5-29. Cross shaft construction in relation to the steering gear. Cross shaft lash is taken up by means of an adjusting screw located in a T slot within the cross shaft. The adjusting screw extends through the cross shaft housing cover and is held in position by means of a lock nut. (*Buick Div., General Motors Corp.*)

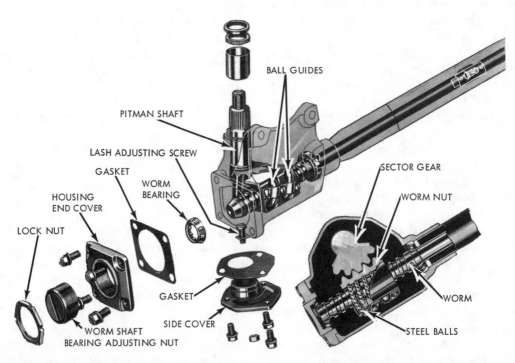

Fig. 5-30. Recirculating ball type of steering gear showing the arrangement of the various components in relation to the steering wheel shaft. The sector gear, which is mounted on the end of the cross shaft, meshes with the sector teeth cut on the worm nut. (*Buick Div., General Motors Corp.*)

Worm Bearing Pre-load Adjustment. In general, the worm shaft bearing adjustment (amount of bearing pre-load) is determined by the amount of effort it takes to turn the worm shaft when mounted between its bearings. The effort required to turn the worm shaft is measured on the rim of the steering wheel by a spring scale somewhat similar in design and operation to that of a fish scale. If a spring scale is not available, a torque wrench may be used instead. Attach the torque wrench to the nut that mounts the steering wheel to the worm shaft.

An average worm shaft bearing pre-load reading using the spring scale should be approximately one-half pound or eight ounces depending on the type of scale used. An average torque wrench reading would be six inch ounces.

Two basic methods have been used to adjust the worm shaft bearing pre-load. One method, used on older model vehicles, is the use of shims between the housing and a plate that is bolted to the lower or upper end of the housing. To increase the worm shaft bearing pre-load, remove one or more shims from between the housing and the plate until the correct worm shaft bearing pre-load is achieved. If too much pre-load is obtained, for example the spring scale reads one pound at the rim of the steering wheel, a very thin shim would be replaced between the housing and the plate and the bolts re-tightened.

The method of adjustment used on most vehicles today employs a large adjuster nut that screws into the steering gear housing. (See Fig. 5-30.) This nut may be located at either the upper or lower end of the housing. A steering gear that employs this type of adjustment is regulated by first unscrewing the jam nut that locks the adjusting nut in position, and then turning the adjusting nut into the housing to increase the bearing load or out of the housing to decrease bearing load. When the spring scale reads approximately one-half pound (or whatever the manufacturer's specifications call for) pull on the rim of the steering wheel, the adjusting nut should be locked in position by the jam nut.

Pitman or Cross Shaft End Play. On some model steering gears, the pitman or cross shaft end play adjustment is an internal adjustment maintained by selective washers between the head of the adjusting screw and a T-slot milled in the end of the cross shaft. Figure 5-29 illustrates this type of adjustment. This can be accomplished only when the steering gear is removed from the vehicle or the steering gear is being serviced.

The clearance between the head of the adjusting screw and the bottom of the T-slot should not exceed .002 inch. Upon disassembly, the adjustment should be checked by installing a feeler gage between the bottom of the T-slot and the head of the bolt. If the clearance is greater than .002 inch, the end play of the cross shaft will be excessive. To correct this excessive end play, place selective shim washers beneath the head of the screw until the correct clearance is obtained.

Pitman or Cross Shaft Over-Center Pre-Load. To check and adjust the cross shaft over-center pre-load, turn the steering wheel from one stop all the way to the other, carefully counting the total number of turns. Turn the wheel back exactly half-way to center position. Loosen the lock nut on the lash adjusting screw and turn the adjusting screw to remove all lash between the pitman shaft teeth and the ball nut.

Check the torque at the steering wheel, taking the highest reading as the wheel is turned through the center position. Check the manufacturer's specifications and, if necessary, readjust the lash adjusting screw to obtain the proper torque. Tighten the lock nut.

On older model vehicles or vehicles using a different type of steering gear assembly, the cross shaft end play will be adjusted in basically the same manner.

The re-circulating ball steering gear must have the correct lubricant in order to give adequate service. Hence, a special steering gear grease is available for this type of installation. A steering gear that cannot be adjusted properly should be disassembled and the worn or otherwise defective parts replaced.

Power Steering Adjustments

The types of adjustment made on a power steering installation depends upon whether it is a linkage system or an integral system.

Linkage Type Power Steering Adjustments. The linkage type of power steering system consists of hydraulically controlled linkage used in conjunction with a conventional manual steering gear.

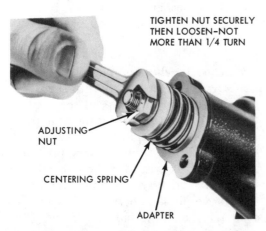

TIGHTEN NUT SECURELY THEN LOOSEN—NOT MORE THAN 1/4 TURN

ADJUSTING NUT

CENTERING SPRING

ADAPTER

Fig. 5-31. Adjusting the control valve on the linkage type of power steering system. (Ford Div., Ford Motor Co.)

Such steering gears are adjusted in the same manner as any other manually operated steering gear. The hydraulic part of the steering system has one adjustment. To make this adjustment, just remove the small cover at the end of the control valve which screws into the end of the relay rod. Under this cover is either a small self-locking nut or cotter keyed nut as shown in Fig. 5-31. This nut must be tightened firmly and then backed off a quarter of a turn or, if using a torque wrench, until the torque reading is 25 foot pounds. Later model vehicles using this type power steering employ a different method of adjusting the nut. Support the car on a hoist and disconnect the hydraulic ram from the frame of the vehicle. Start the engine, then turn the control valve nut in one direction until the cylinder or piston rod moves. Then turn the nut in the opposite direction until the cylinder or piston rod again moves. Notice the total turns made by the nut and turn the nut halfway between position where cylinder or push rod moved. If this adjustment is not made properly, the vehicle will pull or steer itself to one side of the road. Should the control valve leak hydraulic fluid, the valve may be removed and the hydraulic seals replaced. The seal in the hydraulic cylinder is also replaceable and should the cylinder leak fluid around the piston rod the seal should be replaced. The piston and piston rings within the cylinder cannot be serviced and, therefore, if either fail, the unit must be replaced.

Integral Type Power Steering Adjustments. There are two basic adjustments to the integral type power steering system: the thrust bearing pre-load adjustment and the high point adjustment.

The integral type of power steering worm bearing pre-load and the over-center (high point) adjustment is performed in the same manner as for the manual recirculating ball type steering gear.

Some installations will require adjustment of the control valve assembly. The Chrysler integral power steering gear has the control valve mounted on the top of the steering gear. If the control valve has been removed, it must be properly centered when reinstalled. Install the spool valve in the valve body so the valve lever hole is aligned with the lever opening in the valve body. The valve must be free in the valve body without sticking or binding.

Install the assembly on the gear housing, making sure the valve lever enters the hole in the valve spool and the key section on the bottom of the valve body fits with the keyway in the housing. Install the two screws, attaching the valve body to the housing. Tighten the screws partly, (7 ft. lb.).

With the steering wheel in the straight ahead position, start and stop the engine several times, tapping the valve body up or down, as required, until there is no movement of the steering wheel when the engine is started and stopped. The control valve is now properly centered. Tighten the valve body to housing screws to the correct torque.

In the case of the Ford integral power steering gear, the control valve is mounted inside the gear housing. A selective shim in the valve housing provides a means of adjusting the steering effort. If steering effort is heavy to the left, the shim thickness can be increased to correct the problem. If the steering effort is light to the left, decrease the shim thickness to correct the problem.

If all excess play is not removed from the steering gear after a few turns of the adjusting screw, the thrust bearings or the worm and ball nut are excessively worn, therefore necessitating the removal of the steering gear for overhaul.

A pressure gage and valve attachment should be used when checking all power steering gear systems. The pressure gage and valve are mounted between the hydraulic pump and the high pressure hose leading to the steering gear. If the power steering unit fails to give hydraulic assistance, the trouble may be due to either a faulty pump or a faulty steering gear. By using the gage, the faulty unit may be detected and repaired, thereby eliminating the possibility of testing both units. Turn the front wheels to their maximum position either left or right. The hydraulic fluid pressure within the system should be approximately 1,000 pounds. If the gage reads 500 pounds, the system is failing. Close the valve mounted between the gage and the steering gear. If the pump does not produce maximum pressure, it is faulty.

Steering Linkage Service

The steering linkage, which connects the steering gear to the front wheels, must be maintained with a minimum of looseness at the connections for ease of steering and safe steering control. The various joints in the linkage must be properly lubricated since tightness or binding at the connections prevents self-correction by the other factors of alignment. To check the tie-rod and drag link ends for wear, grasp the front of the front wheels as shown in Fig. 5-32, first pushing them away from each other and then pulling them toward each other. At the same time, observe the tie rod and drag link ends for looseness. Either adjust or replace loose tie rod and drag link ends, and straighten or replace bent tie rods or drag linkage.

Adjustable Ball and Socket Joint. Figure 5-33 illustrates an adjustable type ball end joint. Adjustment plugs are provided at the ends of the relay or tie rod to compensate for wear between the tie rod

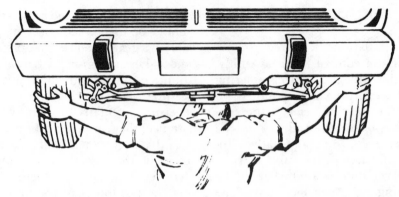

Fig. 5-32. Checking tie rod and drag link ends for excessive free play. Grasp the front of the front wheels and push them away from each other and then bring toward each other, observing the tie rods and drag link ends for looseness. (Ford Div., Ford Motor Co.)

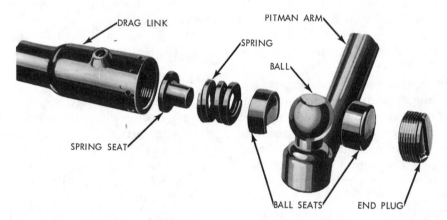

Fig. 5-33. Construction of a typical adjustable tie rod ball end joint and drag link. The drag link is similar in construction to the tie rod and is the link which connects the steering gear pitman to one of the steering knuckles. Adjustment is made by means of a threaded end plug. (Chevrolet Div., General Motors Corp.)

ball stud and the pitman arm ball stud, idler arm ball stud, and respective sockets or seats.

To adjust these various components, screw the adjustment plug into the end of the relay rod until it can go no further. Then back the plug approximately one-half to one turn and lock with a new cotter key. Be careful not to over-tighten as this will cause the vehicle to wander.

Replacing Tie Rod Ends. To replace the tie rod ends, it is necessary to press or drive the tapered shank of the stud out of the hole in which it is mounted. The tool shown in Fig. 5-34 is typical of the many excellent pullers that are available for this purpose.

After the tie rod end stud has been removed, remove the end from the sleeve by first loosening the clamp and then

Fig. 5-34. Ball stud press. This tool is used to remove the tapered stud of the tie rod end from the steering arm in which it is mounted. (K. R. Wilson Co.)

unscrewing the end from the sleeve rod. Count the number of turns necessary to unscrew the end. When installing the new tie rod end, screw it in exactly the same number of turns so that the assembly will have approximately the original length. To keep the toe-in adjustment nearly the same, lubricate the new ball end joint.

Insert the ball stud into the steering knuckle arm and draw up tight by means of the nut. Always recheck the toe-in and adjust as required after installing new tie rod ends. Tighten the clamp bolts.

Rebush Idler Arm. The idler arm bushing which connects the idler arm to the idler arm bracket often becomes worn, allowing the relay rod to become loose. A quarter of an inch up and down movement is permissible, although more than a quarter of an inch of travel will cause the right front wheel to shimmy. When the bushing becomes worn, a new idler arm bushing must be installed.

TRADE COMPETENCY TEST

1. What are the functions of a steering gear assembly?
2. What is the pitman arm attached to and what is its function?
3. What is the cross shaft mounted on within the housing?
4. What type of adjustment is used on all manual steering gear assemblies to remove excessive cross shaft end play?
5. What are some of the factors which have brought about the need for power steering?
6. What are the characteristics that are common to all types of power steering?
7. What are the types of power steering now in use?
8. What kind of fluid is used in a power steering system?
9. What type of control valve is used in a power steering system and how does it operate?
10. Why are two tie rods used to connect the steering knuckle arms together on an independent front suspension system?
11. What is the most common reason for adjusting the steering gear and linkage?
12. Why is it important that the tie rods be adjusted to a certain length?
13. How is an energy absorbing steering gear assembly constructed?
14. How does a steering column ignition lock system operate?
15. How does the steering gear assembly using a tilt type steering wheel differ from the conventional type of steering assembly?

CHAPTER 6

WHEELS AND TIRES

Wheels

Wheels used on today's passenger vehicles are of the drop-center, demountable, steel disc type. The center of the rim is lower than the tire bead seat, to permit the forcing of part of the tire bead into the drop-center section, thereby, allowing for removal of the tire. Rim flanges keep the sidewall of the tire from expanding in an outward direction when the tire is inflated. A typical wheel and rim assembly is shown in Fig. 6-1. Note the position of the rim flanges. Some rims have a raised section between the rim flange and the rim drop center (well). Inflation forces the bead over the raised section of the flange. Tire-wheel separation under extreme cornering conditions is prevented by air pressure and the raised section. In the case of tire failure, the raised section helps to hold the tire in position on the rim until the vehicle is brought to a stop.

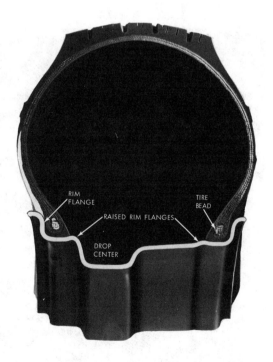

Fig. 6-1. Cutaway of a tire and rim assembly. (Plymouth Div., Chrysler Corp.)

Wheels must be sufficiently rigid and flexible to carry the weight of the vehicle, transfer driving and braking torque to the tires and withstand side thrusts under different load and speed conditions. The wheel is attached to a machined surface of the hub or axle shaft with bolts or stud nuts. The matching surface of the wheel and hub or axle must be kept clean. Stones, lumps of mud, or grease wedged between the wheel and matching surface to which the wheel is attached can unbalance a wheel and tire assembly. The bolts or stud nuts must be kept tight to prevent movement between the wheel and the hub. Loose wheel bolts or stud nuts can result in an elongation of the stud holes. Figure 6-2 is a wheel bolted to a front hub.

The rim must be kept clean and free from nicks and roughness in order to provide an airtight seal between the rim and tire bead. If a wheel or wheel rim which is bent cannot be straightened, it must be replaced.

The typical wheel has a wheel cover to enclose the tire mounting studs.

Tires

Tires perform several functions. The tire forms a cushion between the wheel and road surface. When the wheel passes over bumps in the surface of the road, the tire flexes, thereby, reducing the shock transmitted to the passengers. Tires also provide a friction contact between the wheel and road surface. A high friction contact creates good traction for transmitting power on acceleration and braking, as well as reducing the tendency of the vehicle to skid on turns.

Tires used on today's passenger ve-

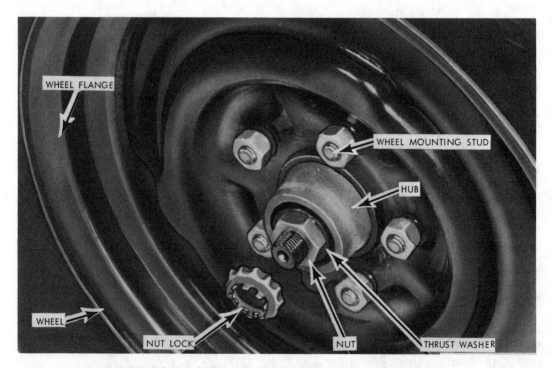

Fig. 6-2. Wheel bolted to a front hub. (*Plymouth Div., Chrysler Corp.*)

hicles are of the low pressure, air cushion type. Over a period of years, wheel diameters have been reduced and wheel rims made wider. This has permitted tire manufacturers to develop a tire with a wide cross sectional diameter. This type of tire requires a large volume of air which will carry the vehicle weight at a low air pressure, thereby providing greater cushioning effects.

Types

Tires are classified according to either the tube type or the tubeless type. The tube type consists of an outer tire with a replaceable inner tube. The tubeless type, introduced in 1955, does away with the inner tube.

The chief advantage of the tubeless type of tire is less weight, improved balance, and cooler running characteristics.

Construction

The structural parts of a tire are shown in Fig. 6-3. The outermost portion of a tire is known as the *tread*. It is the

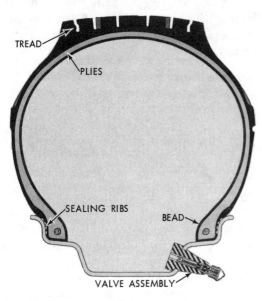

Fig. 6-3. A cross-sectional view showing tire construction. (*Pontiac Div., General Motors Corp.*)

wearing surface consisting of a layer of synthetic rubber. It has grooves cut lengthwise to give road traction. The so-called *snow tires* have deep grooves of a variety of designs to give even better road traction in snowy weather conditions.

Grooves serve an important purpose in tires. As tires flex, excess rubber piles up and must compress into the grooves, or else lumps form and cause a cupping condition on the tread.

The plies, which make up the foundation of the tire, are made of different materials and may be arranged in different configurations.

Tire Plies

Different materials are used in the plies of tires that are in general use today. Cotton cord was employed exclusively for many years by the various tire manufacturers.

Rayon was one of the original manmade fibers to be used and is still very popular. This type of material provides a comfortable ride.

Nylon is strong, durable and resistant to heat but will "flat spot" when the vehicle is not moved for a period of time. The "flat spot" will work itself out when the vehicle is driven.

Polyester is, presently, a popular cord material. It combines the better features of rayon and nylon. While it is as strong as nylon, it will not "flat spot."

Fiberglass is known for its strength. It is flexible but does not stretch. It makes a good belt material. Steel is now being used as belt material also.

In addition to the material which is used in the makeup of the plies, another important feature is the manner in which the plies are used in the construction of the tire.

Bias-Ply (Cross Bias). The bias-ply or conventional tire may have from two to six plies (layers or cord) at angles of 30°

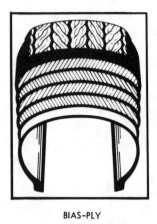 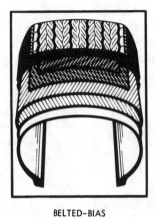 

BIAS-PLY   BELTED-BIAS   RADIAL

Fig. 6-4. Types of tire construction. (*The Firestone Tire & Rubber* Co.)

to 40° to the bead. Each alternate ply is angled opposite to the one beneath it, giving a crisscross pattern. This type of tire is inexpensive to manufacture, has good sidewall strength, makes for a smooth ride and provides for adequate handling on the road.

Radial-Ply. The radial tire is now being used as standard equipment on some vehicles. This tire was first introduced in France in 1948 by Michelin. In radial tires, the main body plies, from one to three, usually two, run from bead to bead at 90 degrees. This arrangement permits the tire to deform when cornering, while the belts that encircle the outside of the main body plies, just under the tread layer, prevent the tire from slipping. The radial belt may be made of fiberglass, rayon, nylon or steel wire, usually two or four plies to a belt. The cords in the belt are usually angled approximately 16 degrees, rather than straight around the tire. The radial ply tire has good sidewall flexibility, thus creating a minimum of friction and heat. The tire provides for good tread life, good traction and is resistant to impact.

Belted Bias-Ply. The belted bias ply tire, basically, is a combination of the conventional tire and the radial tire. The two main plies of polyester, nylon or rayon are angled at about 30 to 40 degrees. On top of these are belts of two or four plies of fiberglass or steel. These belts are usually angled at about 25 to 30 degrees. The belted bias-ply is less expensive than the radial tire, operates cooler than a conventional tire and has a somewhat longer tread life than the conventional tire. Figure 6-4 shows the three different types of bias ply in use today.

Tire Markings

Changes have been made in tire marking which indicate the quality of tires. Tires presently being manufactured have standard information marked on the tire which gives dimensions and load information.

As of May 1971, all American-made tires are required to carry a letter code which indicates the manufacturer's plant, tire size, type of construction and when the tire was manufactured.

The following information is also found on present day tires: the name of the manufacturer, type of tire (tubeless, radial), load carrying capacity, tire size

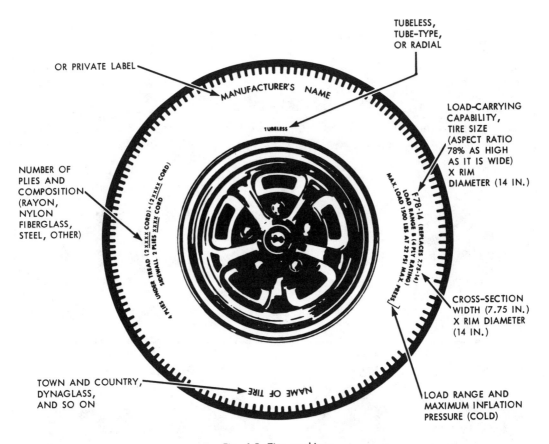

Fig. 6-5. Tire markings.

(ratio: width to height in percent), rim diameter, load range and maximum cold inflation, cross-section (width and rim diameter) brand name of tire and the number of plies and composition. Figure 6-5 shows the type of information which is found on today's tires.

Tire Sizes

Instead of a size designation, such as 7.75-14, today's tires have a letter and two numbers, such as F 78-14. The letter is the load carrying capacity. The first number is the aspect ratio; this is the ratio of the tire's height to its width. The last number is the wheel size. A comparison of the numbering system presently in use is as follows:

Tire Size	Replaces
C78-14	6.95-14
E78-14	7.35-14
F78-14	7.75-14
G78-14	8.25-14
H78-15	8.55-15
L78-15	9.15-15

A load range designated by a letter is also marked on the sidewall. The load range represents the inflation limits as follows:

Load Range	Maximum Pressure
A	28psi
B	32psi
C	36psi
D	40psi

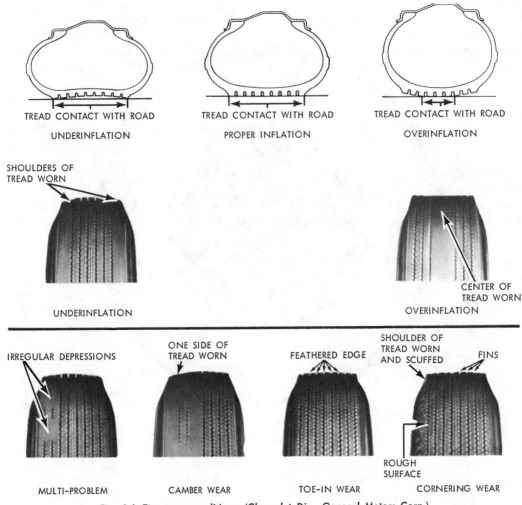

TREAD CONTACT WITH ROAD   TREAD CONTACT WITH ROAD   TREAD CONTACT WITH ROAD

UNDERINFLATION   PROPER INFLATION   OVERINFLATION

SHOULDERS OF
TREAD WORN

CENTER OF
TREAD WORN

UNDERINFLATION   OVERINFLATION

IRREGULAR DEPRESSIONS   ONE SIDE OF TREAD WORN   FEATHERED EDGE   SHOULDER OF TREAD WORN AND SCUFFED   FINS

ROUGH SURFACE

MULTI-PROBLEM   CAMBER WEAR   TOE-IN WEAR   CORNERING WEAR

Fig. 6-6. Tire wear conditions. (Chevrolet Div., General Motors Corp.)

Tire Wear

Tires normally last as much as 40,000 miles or more before replacement or repair is necessary. But often tire life is greatly reduced because of poor driving habits, improper inflation, and misalignment. Several different examples of abnormal tire wear are pictured in Fig. 6-6. The speed of driving is a major factor in tire wear. A "jack rabbit" fashion of driving wears out the tires rapidly because of quick accelerations and sudden stops. High speed around turns also subjects the

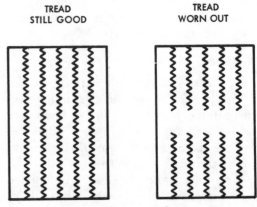

TREAD STILL GOOD   TREAD WORN OUT

Fig. 6-7. Tire wear indicators.

tires to undue side thrusts. At speeds above 70 mph the tread wear is considerably more rapid than at lower speeds.

Some tires incorporate built-in tread wear indicators, Fig. 6-7, to assist in determining when the tire has worn to the point where it should be replaced. The indicators are molded into the bottom of the tread grooves and will appear as approximately one-half inch wide bands when the tire tread depth wears to within $\frac{1}{16}$ inch of the bottom of the tread. When the bands appear in two or more adjacent grooves, the tire should be replaced.

Tire Rotation

It is recommended that all tires except radial be rotated (interchanged) approximately every 6,000 miles, as shown in Fig. 6-8. Radial tires should be rotated forward or rearward on the same side of the car; in other words, radials should always rotate in one direction to achieve maximum tread life. The purpose is to obtain the most uniform tread wear and minimize the possibility of tire noise. This is also a good time to inspect the tires for nails, bruises, or cuts.

Removal and Mounting

Removal. Although tire-changing machines are used by a majority of service men, the basic principles of tire removal can best be learned by the use of hand tools.

To remove a tire, the location of the valve should be first marked with chalk on the casing. Any puncture should also be marked for easy location upon disassembly.

Release the air by screwing out the valve stem core, and break loose the bead

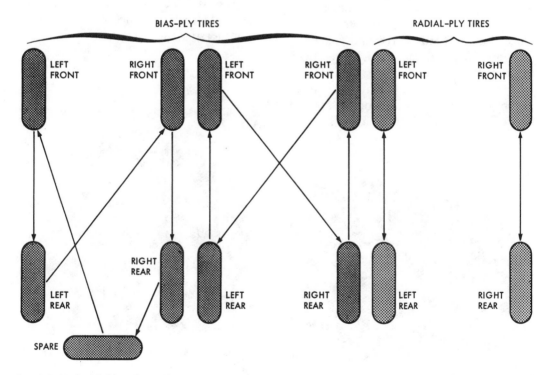

Fig. 6-8. Methods of switching tires with a spare (left) and without a spare (center) to equalize tire wear. Radial tires (right) should be rotated front to back on the same side only.

Fig. 6-9. Separating the tire bead from the rim. (Plymouth Div., Chrysler Corp.)

from the rim by using a special bead loosening tool on both sides, Fig. 6-9. Push the bead down into the drop center of the rim opposite the valve and, starting at the valve, using two tire irons, pry the top bead up over the rim flange. Use clean, polished tire irons to prevent bead damage (very important on tubeless tires). Once the top bead is free and removed, the opposite bead can then be removed up over the same rim flange.

Mounting. Tire mounting requires proper care to obtain the correct air seal between the rim and bead. The rim should be checked for dents and rust which may cause poor sealing. Steel wool may be used to remove rust, and any rim dents should be removed with a hammer. Check the valve stem in the rim for a tight seal, and coat the beads with a special rubber lubricant to aid in mounting. Work the bottom bead over the top rim flange, Fig. 6-10. Using tire irons, start the top bead over the rim and gradually work the bead over the rim, taking care not to damage the bead. A tire mounting band is used to spread the beads out against the rim flange before the tire is inflated, see Fig. 6-11. Give the tire a few quick bursts of air to seat the bead properly in the rim. Inflate the tire to 40 psi. Check to see if the bead positioning ring (ring molded in the tire sidewall near the rim) is evenly visible. If the ring is not even, deflate the tire completely and reinflate until the bead is in place. Deflate the tire to the correct pressure. The mounted tire can be checked for air leaks by immersing the rim and tire in water.

Fig. 6-11. The tire beads are expanded against the rim so that the tire will hold air. The bead expander is removed after the tire is partially inflated. (Plymouth Div., Chrysler Corp.)

Fig. 6-10. Mounting a tire. (Plymouth Div., Chrysler Corp.)

Tire Repairs

When a tire loses all or most of its air, particularly when driving, the recommended procedure is to remove the tire from the wheel for complete inspection. Punctured tires should be removed from the wheel and permanently repaired from the inside.

Externally applied plug type repairs should be considered temporary and the tire should be permanently repaired as soon as possible.

Never attempt to repair a puncture in a tire which has a ply separation, chafed fabric injuries, damaged bead wires, flex breaks, loose cords or has evidence of having been run flat, tread separation, cracks which extend into the fabric or tires worn below $\frac{1}{16}''$ depth in major grooves.

Preparation of Puncture. Throughly dry the area around the puncture. Pour vulcanizing fluid on the probe tool and the outside of the puncture. Carefully follow the puncture hole with the probe to clean out the puncture. If the hole is too small for the probe tool, a plug is not required.

Scrape the inner tire surface around the puncture with a sharp tool then buff with a hand buffer or wire brush. Buff an area slightly larger than the patch you intend to use. Take care not to damage the inside of the tire, Fig. 6-12. Lubricate the puncture inside and outside with vulcanizing fluid. Lubricate the plug insertion tool and insert it into the injury, moving it in and out to completely lubricate the inside of the injury.

Place a straight plug either of the head type or headless type in the eye of the insertion tool so one end extends less than $\frac{1}{4}''$ from the tool eye. Lubricate the tool and plug with vulcanizing fluid.

Insert the plug into the puncture from inside the tire. Hold and stretch

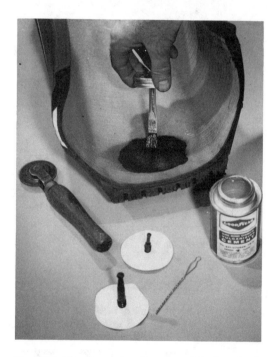

Fig. 6-12. The tire casing is prepared (top) and vulcanizing cement applied to the punctured area (bottom). (Goodyear Tire & Rubber Co.)

the long end of the plug as it is forced into the hole until one end extends through the hole, Fig. 6-13. Remove the tool and cut off the plug $\frac{1}{16}''$ above

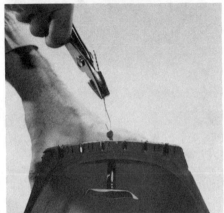

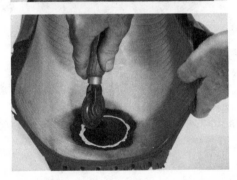

Fig. 6-13. Cement is applied to the puncture hole (top). A plug of the proper size is inserted from the inside and pulled through the hole (center). The base of the plug is stitched to remove trapped air (bottom). (Goodyear Tire & Rubber Co.)

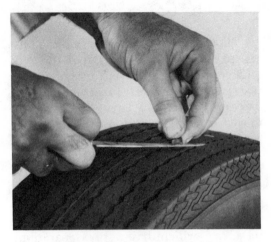

Fig. 6-14. Finally the plug is trimmed. (Goodyear Tire & Rubber Co.)

day, recommend a patch even if the plug is of the head type. The patch is used to cover and seal the head.

Cold Patch. Pour a small amount of vulcanizing fluid over and around the injury, spread evenly with your finger and allow to dry for approximately five minutes. Always follow the manufacturer's directions for the patch being used. Remove the backing from the patch, center the patch on the plug and firmly press into place. Use a stitching tool to work the air out from under the patch and to form a good seal at the edges.

Hot Patch. The hot patch method utilizes heat to vulcanize the patch to the tire and plug repair. The steps to follow are essentially the same as for the cold patch.

The patch is centered on the spot to be repaired. The clamp is placed over the patch and tightened. Heat is applied. When cool, the clamp is removed. Remount the tire.

Tires with worn treads may be retreaded or recapped if the casing is still in good condition. If a single tire is to be replaced due to wear, usually it is best to replace all four tires. Otherwise, when

the surface. Do not stretch the plug while cutting, Fig. 6-14.

Headless plugs must be backed up with either a cold self-vulcanizing patch or a hot patch. Many manufacturers, to-

mounted with a worn tire, the new tire will wear out rapidly.

Tire Inflation

Tires should be regularly checked for proper inflation when they are cool. As the car is driven, the air pressure will increase, due to the frictional heat developed. An increase of 2-6 psi is normal; therefore, the pressure should not be readjusted while the tires are hot. The manufacturer recommends specific pressures for proper inflation. Air may be let out from, or added to, the tire, by way of the valve to maintain this pressure. A tire pressure differential, front to rear is recommended by some manufacturers to insure optimum directional stability. Tire pressures should be checked at least once a month and should be checked and adjusted before any long trips.

As shown in Fig. 6-6, improper inflation cuts down on tire life. Under-inflation causes undue flexing, weakening the plies and making the tire more prone to bruising and tread wear. Due to unequal distribution of the car weight on the tires, the chances of premature failures are increased.

Over-inflation, on the other hand, subjects the tire to undue tension and tread wear and results in a rough ride. At any rate, improper inflation creates an additional burden on the driver because of the added difficulty in steering.

When checking pressure, it is a good policy to examine the tread for undue wear so that an early correction can be made. This also gives you a chance to detect the presence of any foreign matter that may have become imbedded in the tire. These precautions aid in removing the source of tire trouble.

When replacing tires or wheels, it is mandatory that only the standard or optional tire sizes and types recommended by the manufacturer be used. Rim width and offsets must be those recommended by the manufacturer for the particular tire size. Tire and wheels other than those recommended can adversely affect the safety and durability of the vehicle.

All tires and wheels should be of the same size, type and load carrying capacity. Never mix belted, radial and/or conventional type tires.

Tires, larger or smaller than originally installed, may affect the accuracy of the speedometer and require a change of speedometer drive gears.

Space Saver Spare Tire

Some manufacturers make available a space saver spare tire for the purpose of providing more room in the luggage compartment. The tire is installed on the wheel in a deflated condition and barely extends beyond the periphery of the wheel; thereby, leaving more room in the trunk compartment.

The tire is not designed for extended milage but rather as an emergency tire to enable the driver to proceed to the nearest service station at a normal speed. The tire cannot be used as a permanent substitute for a conventional tire.

The tire is inflated with a tire inflator can which is included with the assembly. Do not use any other method of inflating the tire.

Operation of Wheel and Tire Assembly

The rotation of the wheel and tire as an assembly can be affected by several factors, some of which are created by the alignment of the front end, while others are created by the assembly itself. A wheel assembly that is out of balance or alignment may affect the riding qualities of the vehicle, cause hard steering, or be responsible for rapid tire wear. Several symptoms which appear to be caused by wheel and tire troubles are also common to suspension and steering troubles. Therefore, an understanding of the construction and maintenance of the wheel and tire assembly will assist in determining where malfunctions of the steering system are located.

The wheel and tire assembly includes the wheel, a hub, a brake drum or disc, a grease cap, a wheel cover, and the tire. The front hub is attached to the brake drum or disc, the wheel in turn being bolted to the brake drum or disc. The bearing cone and roller assemblies are mounted on the steering knuckle spindle and rotate within the bearing cups. The bearing cups are pressed into the hub. A grease retainer is installed at the inner end of the hub to prevent lubricant from leaking into the brake. Figure 6-15 illustrates a typical front wheel assembly. The correct bearing pre-load is established by means of an adjusting nut which is mounted on the wheel spindle. To take up the bearing pre-load, tighten

the adjusting nut and to back off, loosen the nut.

When a vehicle is in motion, the entire wheel and tire assembly becomes a rapidly rolling mass. If a passenger vehicle that uses a F78-14 tire is driven at a speed of 60 miles per hour, the wheel will roll approximately 800 revolutions per minute (the exact number of revolutions is difficult to calculate, as the weight of the vehicle compresses the tire). The wheel and tire assembly represents a considerable weight, and when rolling on the road surface at this speed, sets up considerable centrifugal force. Any condition that disturbs this rolling mass creates vibrations which are not only dangerous but destructive to structural parts of the vehicle.

An understanding of the effect of centrifugal forces which are produced when a wheel and tire assembly is in motion is important. A slight amount of weight added to one side of the wheel or tire and not counterbalanced by an equal amount of weight on the other side will result in

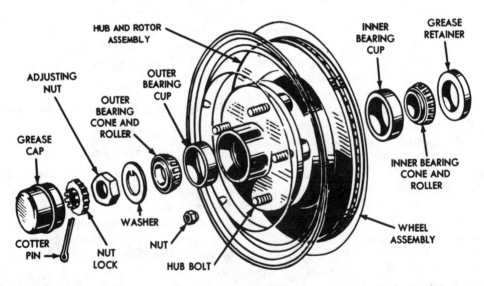

Fig. 6-15. Front wheel assembly: this type of construction is typical of automotive wheels. (*Ford Customer Service Div., Ford Motor Co.*)

a tendency for the heavy spot to travel in a straight line, rather than in an arc. This is due to the ever increasing speed of the heavy spot as it moves toward the top of the wheel and tire assembly. The result is a tendency for the wheel and tire assembly to move up and down or back and forth, causing a bouncing or jerking, commonly referred to as *wheel tramp*. Uneven tire wear also results.

Static and Dynamic Balance

Whenever an unbalanced condition exists in the wheel and tire assembly, steps must be taken to correct the condition. Two types of wheel balancing, referred to as *static balance* and *dynamic balance* must be taken into consideration when checking and correcting an unbalanced condition.

Static Balance

When the weight of a wheel and tire assembly is equally distributed around a spindle, the assembly will not rotate by itself (if the wheel is off the ground and free to rotate), regardless of the position in which it is placed. Such a wheel assembly is said to be in static balance (not moving). A wheel and tire assembly that is out of balance will rotate by itself until the heavy side is at the bottom. As an example, a tire rolls over a muddy spot on the road and in doing so the tire picks up a small portion of the mud. The piece of mud that the tire has picked up will cause one end of the tire to become heavier than the other end, throwing that end out of balance with the other end of the wheel. If the wheel is free to rotate by itself, the end of the tire with the mud will cause the wheel to rotate until the heavy end is at the bottom. See Fig. 6-16.

Balancing a wheel statically is accomplished by adding an equal amount of

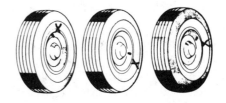

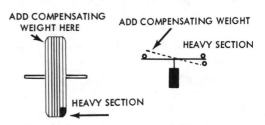

ADD COMPENSATING WEIGHT HERE

ADD COMPENSATING WEIGHT

HEAVY SECTION

HEAVY SECTION

Fig. 6-16. *Top*, static balance: balancing a wheel at rest. A wheel is said to be in static balance when it has the weight equally distributed around the circumference in such a manner that there is no tendency for the wheel to rotate by itself. *Bottom*, static balance correction. A wheel that does have an unbalanced condition due to a heavy spot will tend to rotate by itself until the heavy portion of the assembly is down. Add compensating weight at top. (*Bear Manufacturing Co.*)

weight on the opposite end of the wheel from the axis as the point to be balanced. This principle is shown in Fig. 6-16.

When tires are manufactured, great care is taken to keep the weight equally distributed around the tire to prevent an out-of-balance condition. Manufacturers of other parts such as the wheel, hub, and brake drum or disc also exercise care to retain balance in these parts. However, when component parts of the wheel and tire assemblies are removed and re-installed, or when tire repairs are made, a shifting of weight can occur, causing the assembly to become out of balance. For this reason the complete assembly may require balancing to offset an out-of-balance condition.

When a wheel is out-of-balance, the amount of unbalance is stated in *inch ounces.* A simple explanation of the term inch ounce is as follows:

If a one-ounce weight, placed one inch from the axis of the wheel, would turn the wheel until the one-ounce weight is at the bottom, regardless of where on this one-inch circle the weight would be placed, the wheel would then be balanced to one inch ounce or less.

If a 10 ounce weight were placed one inch from the center of the wheel, or if a one-ounce weight were placed 10 inches from the center of the wheel, the balance test would be stated as *10 inch–ounces. Formula: Weight in ounces multiplied by the radius in inches equals inch-ounces.*

Dynamic Balance

So far we have considered weights that may be added to the outer flange of a wheel so as to balance it statically. It is possible for a wheel to be perfectly balanced statically (not in motion) and at the same time be unbalanced dynamically (inmotion).

A rotating wheel will run true without any tendency to wobble or shake, if it is in dynamic balance. Dynamic balance takes into consideration the distribution of the weight to be added to the wheel.

When the amount of weight required to maintain dynamic balance in a wheel and tire assembly is known, it is usually necessary to attach one half the amount of weight needed to the outside of the wheel rim flange and at 180° the other half of the weight to the inside of the wheel rim flange. This principle is illustrated in Fig. 6-17. By dividing the weight as required, an out-of-balance condition in the wheel assembly while it is rotating can be corrected and the wheel assembly will be in both static and dynamic balance.

A wheel balancer is needed to cor-

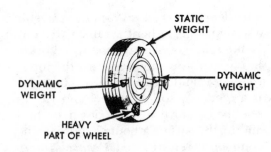

Fig. 6-17. Dynamic balance. To eliminate this "couple" action compensating weights (dynamic) are placed at 180° opposite each other. Dynamic balance is obtained while static balance remains unaffected. (*Bear Manufacturing* Co.)

rectly balance the wheel and tire assembly. Various types of wheel balancing equipment are on the market, some of which check the balance of the wheel and tire only, while others check the balance of the wheel, tire, brake drum, or disc and hub as an assembly. Some equipment balances the wheel and tire assembly while on the vehicle spindle, while other equipment necessitates the removal of the assembly from the spindle.

Two other factors react in the same manner as unbalance in relation to satisfactory steering control. These are: lateral run-out (wheel wobble) and radial run-out.

The condition in which the top and bottom of a wheel alternately moves in toward and out from the center of the vehicle as the wheel rotates on the spindle is known as *lateral run-out.* A wheel and tire assembly having lateral run-out could be perfectly balanced statically but be out of dynamic balance. This condition is illustrated in Fig. 6-18. Lateral run-out may be caused by a bent wheel or an improperly mounted tire. Generally the maximum allowable run-out is ⅛ of an inch.

Excessive radial run-out of the wheel, generally in the form of a bounce, has a very pronounced effect on the steering of

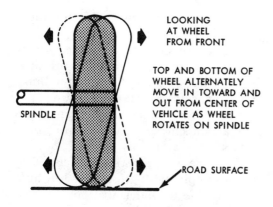

LOOKING AT WHEEL FROM FRONT

TOP AND BOTTOM OF WHEEL ALTERNATELY MOVE IN TOWARD AND OUT FROM CENTER OF VEHICLE AS WHEEL ROTATES ON SPINDLE

SPINDLE

ROAD SURFACE

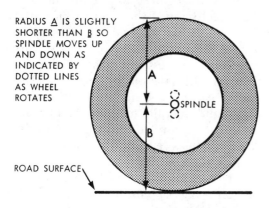

RADIUS A IS SLIGHTLY SHORTER THAN B SO SPINDLE MOVES UP AND DOWN AS INDICATED BY DOTTED LINES AS WHEEL ROTATES

A

SPINDLE

B

ROAD SURFACE

Fig. 6-18. Lateral run-out of wheel (top) and radial run-out of wheel (bottom).

the vehicle. Radial run-out, in addition to destroying the balance of the wheel (both static and dynamic), causes the spindle to rise and fall in the amount of the run-out on each revolution of the wheel. This condition is shown in Fig. 6-18. Radial run-out occurs when the radius of the tire, when it contacts the road, is not equal around the entire tire circumference.

Corrections and Adjustments

Tire Movement on the Road

Tire wear, aside from cutting as oc-

curs on crushed stone, shell, or cinder roads, is always the result of one of the following conditions:

1) Anything that has a tendency to restrain the wheel from rolling or any tendency of the wheel to spin.

2) Any condition that causes the tire to leave the road at a different point than where contact was first established.

3) Any condition that in effect causes the tire or a portion of the tire to have a smaller rolling diameter than its actual diameter.

The rolling radius of the wheel and the area of tire contact with the road are controlled by the amount of air in the tire and the load that the vehicle imposes upon it. Automobile and tire manufacturers publish specifications for correct tire pressures for the various sizes of tires in use. Tire pressures should be maintained as recommended.

If the tire pressure is lower than recommended or required by the particular tire or load, the increased contact area between the tire and road will change the self correcting influences of the other factors of steering control. In addition, abnormal tire wear will result.

Too high a tire pressure will cause the tire to wear in the center of the tread; however, the total wear may be less than would be true with the recommended pressure. Overinflation increases the tire rolling radius as well as creating a hard ride.

The grooves incorporated in all tread designs provide space for the excess rubber that piles up as the wheel revolves. This condition is brought about because the rolling radius of the tire is smaller than the actual tire radius. If a tire is worn smooth, underinflated or overloaded, the grooves in the tread are no longer effective and the excess rubber piles up ahead of the point of contact, as

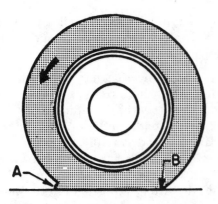

Fig. 6-19. Excess rubber will pile up ahead of the contact area (A) if the grooves of the tire are no longer effective in providing space for the excess rubber which results from tire rotation. Since the rolling radius of the wheel is smaller than the actual radius of the tire, space in the tire groove must take up the excess rubber as the tire rotates.

shown at A in Fig. 6-19. When the limit of distortion is reached, the excess rubber is compressed and finally passes under the wheel in a lump. Slippage occurs at B (in Fig. 6-19) as the distorted rubber is released from the restraint of the road and the tread resumes its original position. This results in *cupping* of the tire, which wears away tread rubber. However, more serious than the wasted rubber is the fact that once the cupping has developed, the tread obtains a series of depressions on its surface. These depressions transmit a jerking effect through the steering mechanism, causing wear of the steering gear, and the steering linkage and jerking of the steering wheel.

Improper Tire Wear

Normal tire tread wear varies in relation to the type and condition of road surface, the amount of traffic, temperature, and the driving habits of the driver. Abnormal tire wear will occur under certain circumstances. Therefore, the type of tire wear found is often an indication of a particular condition in the suspen-

sion or steering system, or of improper operation or abuse. Abnormal wear in varying degrees can be accounted for by such conditions as incorrect tire pressure, faulty wheel alignment, improper brake operation, and vehicle overloading.

Tire wear can be divided into two general classifications which are: fore-and-aft wear, and cross wear.

The tire wear illustrated in Fig. 6-20 is an example of lengthwise or fore-and-aft wear due to underinflation. The excessive rubber forced to pile up ahead of the wheel scraped the road surface as it returned to its original shape, causing uneven wear around the tread as already mentioned. Excessive flexing of the tire side wall will take place due to underinflation, causing the side wall to crack or break, and the plies to separate. The tire is also more prone to bruising if underinflated when it encounters road irregularities, thereby shortening tire life.

Wear around the tread is also due to the following: 1) Fore-and-aft wear is accelerated by anything that increases the tendency to either spin or resist rotation, as, for example, dragging brakes, excessive use of brakes, tight wheel bearings or spinning of the wheels during rapid acceleration. 2) Due to excessive camber the tire will have several diameters.

When the wheels have the correct amount of toe-in, little or no cross wear occurs on the tires. Therefore, if you look for indications of cross wear, it will become an easy matter to identify vehicles which need attention (provided, of course, that they are operated mostly on pavement).

Pass the palm of your hand across the tread of the tire, first in one direction and then in the other. The presence of crown wear will be indicated by one or the other edge of the tread being either sharp or featheredged, as shown in Fig. 6-21. The sharp edge can be felt as the

Fig. 6-20. Cupping of tread on the shoulder of the tire. In the above illustration the fore-and-aft wear of the tread was caused by underinflation. (*Ford Div., Ford Motor Co.*)

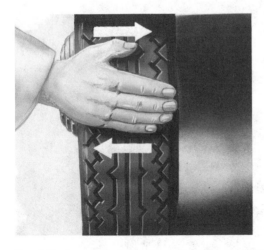

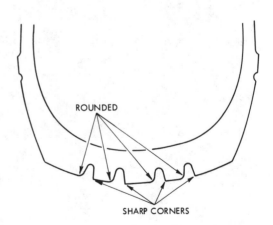

Fig. 6-21. A method of detecting tire cross wear (left) by pressing the palm of the hand first toward and then away from the vehicle center. The presence of cross wear will be indicated by one or the other edge having sharp corners as compared to the rounded corners of the tire tread (right). (*Ford Div., Ford Motor Co.*)

palm is passed over the tread. If the sharp edge is felt as the hand is moved toward the center of the vehicle, the tire does not have enough toe-in. If the sharp edge is felt as the hand is moved away from the center of the vehicle, the tire has too much toe-in.

Servicing the Wheel Assembly

The wheel assembly includes the hub, the brake drum, the wheel, the tire, the grease cap, and any decorative rings that are mounted on the assembly. Since the wheel assembly includes everything that revolves on the spindle any factor that has an influence on the revolving wheel also influences steering control and tire wear.

Tire Inflation

Check the air pressure in the tires with a tire gage and inflate to the recommended pressure. If the front tires are cupped or show signs of uneven wear, they should be changed to a different location in accordance with tire switching recommendation.

Front Wheel Bearing Adjustment

Raise the front wheels off the ground. It would be a good idea to check the front wheel bearings for packing since the wheel is off the ground and if the bearing grease is dirty, repack the bearing with clean grease. Rotate one front wheel slowly and note any tendency of that wheel to bind. Grasp the front wheel at the front and back, alternately

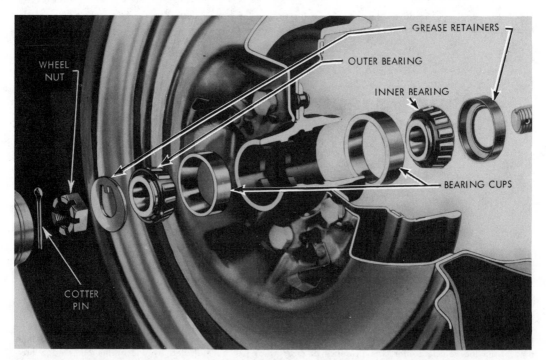

Fig. 6-22. Exploded view of the various wheel spindle mounting parts showing both tapered front wheel bearings which are known as the inner and the outer bearings. (*Dodge Div., Chrysler Corp.*)

push it in toward and away from the center of the vehicle. Repeat this procedure for the opposite wheel. If any free play (or binding) is noticed, adjust the wheel bearings.

To adjust the front wheel bearings, remove the grease cap and the cotter pin and run the adjusting nut up as tight as it will go. A cut-away view showing the relation of the front wheel bearings is shown in Fig. 6-22. Rotate the wheel to insure that the bearings are not cocked or misaligned. Then back off the nut completely and tighten the nut with your fingers. Install a new cotter pin. Replace the grease cup and lower the wheel to the ground.

Check Wheel Wobble

Raise the front wheels off the ground. Spin one wheel by hand and observe the amount of wheel wobble. If the wheel wobble is more than $\frac{1}{8}$ of an inch the wheel should be straightened or replaced.

Check Wheel Run-out

Spin the front wheel by hand and observe the radial run-out at the top of the wheel. If the run-out is in excess of $\frac{1}{16}$ of an inch make sure that the tire is seated properly on the wheel rim. If the tire is installed properly but still has excessive run-out, it may be advisable to install the wheel on the rear axle.

Wheel Balancing

A wheel that is statically unbalanced will rotate upon a near frictionless axle until it comes to rest at the same place from which rotation started. A simple method to statically balance the front wheels of a vehicle equipped with drum brakes is to loosen the wheel bearing adjusting nut and back off the brake shoes from the brake drum. This lets the wheel's heavy spot settle to the bottom. A weight made of lead which can be attached to the wheel rim by means of a steel clip, is then attached to the rim to balance or equalize the heavy spot.

Wheel weights normally range in size from one quarter ounce to four ounces, in quarter ounce increments. From four to six ounces, these weights are usually available in $\frac{1}{2}$ ounce increments. When a tire and wheel assembly requires two or more ounces to balance it statically, the amount of weight needed is divided into two equal parts. For example, a wheel needing two and one-half ounces to balance it statically would have a $1\frac{1}{4}$ ounce weight on both sides of the wheel. These weights would be placed directly opposite the heavy spot of the tire and directly opposite each other on both sides of the wheel. By correcting the static unbalanced condition in this manner, the wheel will not be thrown out of dynamic balance.

A number of balancing machines of the teeter totter design or bubble balancer, as shown in Fig. 6-23, are used instead of the above method since too much time must be taken to loosen the wheel bearing and back off the brake shoes.

Another type of static balancer, as shown in Fig. 6-24, is one which may be used without removing the wheel from the vehicle. This type of balancer used a wheel spinner to rotate the wheel at the approximate speed where static unbalance is felt when the car is driven. The balancing head which attaches to the wheel of the vehicle determines the amount of weight needed to smooth out the vibrations of the wheel as it is rotated. One advantage of this type of balancer over the balancer shown in Fig. 6-23 is that the balancer statically balances not only the tire and wheel, but also the hub and the brake drum. Many of our modern day passenger vehicles which are supported on coil springs have

Fig. 6-23. Static type of wheel balancer. This machine balances the wheel and tire assembly statically. The bubble of the level will be in the center of the level when the wheel and tire have been balanced, that is, when the correct weights are added to the assembly in the correct spot, opposite the heavy spot of the wheel and tire. Usually this type of balance procedure requires that the correct weight be halved, one portion of the weight added to either side of the wheel. (*John Bean Corp.*)

problems of wheel balance which did not exist some years ago. The hub and drum in some cases must be balanced or a vibration will be felt.

Generally the wheel and tire assembly should be removed from vehicles equipped with disc brakes in order to perform balancing operations. This is necessary due to the drag of the spring-loaded brake shoes on the disc. However, on vehicles equipped with single piston disc brakes the front wheels and tires may be balanced on the vehicle by removing sufficient brake fluid from the master cylinder to bring the level to at least one-half inch below the lowest edge of the front reservoir of each filler opening. Using a screw driver or suitable pry bar apply pressure against the back of the caliper to push the piston into its bore, thus permitting the wheel to spin freely. Refill the master cylinder after the balancing operation is completed.

The *on the car balancer may* also be

Fig. 6-24. On-the-car type of wheel balancer being used to statically balance the front wheel of a vehicle. The vehicle is supported by a floor jack placed at the center of the front suspension cross member. The balancing head which is attached to the wheel determines the amount of weight needed to statically balance the wheel and tire assembly. Spin test each wheel separately for unbalance which may cause wheel tramp and/or vibration. By spinning the wheel assembly slowly a bent wheel or out-of-round tire may be detected. (*Bear, The Wheel Service Division, Applied Power, Inc.*)

used to statically balance the rear wheels. When balancing the rear wheels with this type of balancer, the rear end of the vehicle must be supported by a floor jack. Place the jack against the body or frame and in front of the wheel to be balanced. One wheel rests on the ground and the other wheel is free to rotate. After the balancer is attached to the rear wheel, start the engine and place the vehicle in drive position. Caution: one person should remain in the vehicle at all times when the engine is running to maintain constant speed of the rear wheel. As a statically unbalanced rear wheel is revolved, the rear axle will vibrate. The

Fig. 6-25. Strobe light on-the-car wheel balancer. This type of balancer tells you how much weight is needed and at what point to install the correct weight to achieve balance of the wheel, tire, hub, and brake drum assembly. (*Stewart Warner Corp.*)

balancer is then operated to smooth out the rear wheel vibration. Be careful not to exceed 35 miles per hour on the speedometer as this is the speed of 70 miles per hour at the rear wheel due to gearing in the differential.

When balancing the rear wheels of a vehicle which is equipped with a limited slip or positraction rear axle, support the frame or body of the vehicle so both rear wheels are off the floor and remove the tire and wheel from the rear axle of the wheel that is not being balanced.

A strobe light (an instrument which uses a light for measuring motion) type of on-the-car balancer uses a pickup (jack) which rests against the suspension of the vehicle, as shown in Fig. 6-25. When the pickup is placed under the suspension, the machine balances the wheel assembly statically. When the pickup is placed against the brake back-

Fig. 6-26. Off-the-car type static and dynamic wheel balancer. The hub and drum of the wheel assembly are mounted on the balancer shaft. Static balance is accomplished by letting the heavy spot of the tire turn the wheel to the proper position to attach the wheel weights. A light beam will show how much weight must be added and to what spot to the rim when the wheel is spun in order to balance the wheel dynamically. (*Bear, The Wheel Service Division, Applied Power, Inc.*)

Fig. 6-27. Combination static and dynamic wheel balancer. This machine determines the amount of weight and location to correct both static and dynamic balancing at one time. (FMC Corp.)

ing plate in a horizontal position, the machine will dynamically balance the wheel, hub, and brake drum assembly.

Stationary or off the car wheel balancing equipment are capable of balancing a wheel both statically and dynamically. Two types of these machines which will either balance the tire and wheel assembly or balance the hub, brake drum, and wheel assembly as a unit are shown in Figs. 6-26 and 6-27. From the point of view of safety, balancing the wheel, the hub, and the brake drum assembly not only takes the vibration out of the front suspension, but also enables the wheel balancing operator to inspect the wheel bearings and condition of the brake system of each wheel.

TRADE COMPETENCY TEST

1. What are several factors which affect the rotation of the wheel and tire assembly?
2. Describe the action of a wheel and tire assembly as it rotates.
3. What is static balance and how is it corrected if an unbalanced condition exists?
4. What is dynamic balance and what is the effect of operating a tire that is dynamically unbalanced?
5. What could cause wheel wobble?
6. Why are all new tires made with grooves in the tread?
7. What are the causes of improper tire wear?
8. How do you check for abnormal tire wear?
9. What are the advantages of switching tires around on a vehicle?
10. How do you adjust front wheel bearings?
11. What is the advantage of balancing the wheel assembly while it is on the vehicle?
12. What precaution should be taken where an on-the-car type of balancer is used to balance the rear wheels?
13. How often do most car manufacturers recommend switching tires?
14. What are the different ways in which the plies are used in the construction of a tire?
15. What are the different materials used in the plies of a tire?

CHAPTER 7

WHEEL ALIGNMENT FACTORS

The satisfactory operation of a vehicle is possible only when it can be so controlled that it will maintain a true course on the highway. Any looseness in the steering wheel, shake, wobble, or tendency of the vehicle to pull, either constantly or intermittently to either side, is intolerable and quickly tires the driver. The driver must have absolute steering control at all times. Any sense of insecurity takes away the pleasure of driving and driving then becomes work.

A vehicle propelled over the highway represents a heavy mass traveling at high speed creating tremendous forces that tend to resist any change in the direction of vehicle travel. Even at high speed, the driver must be able to change the direction of the vehicle at will. When the direction of the vehicle has been changed, it must be possible for the driver to resume a straight ahead course with ease.

The need for almost effortless control of the vehicle has resulted in the development of stable suspension systems and easily controlled steering gears. As speeds and loads increased, the early concepts of what was required had to be changed repeatedly. Often as new problems of control arose and were mastered, either the problem or the cure imposed added problems of tire wear. Thus the first successful attempts to improve stability and ease of steering control also resulted in rapid tire wear, and many designs had to be either discarded or changed. As a result, stability, control of the vehicle, and tire life are now considered as one common problem, usually thought of and referred to as *wheel alignment. Stability: The word* stability *as used in connection with wheel alignment means the ability of a vehicle to maintain a true course on the highway without the need for continual steering effort on the part of the driver.*

Any condition which affects the movement or the rolling of the wheel and tire assembly is a factor contributing to unstable steering.

The ball joints which allow the front wheels of a vehicle to turn and the spindles, which carry the front wheels on bearings, are positioned at various angles to attain ease of steering, stability, and maximum tire life.

The mechanism used to connect the steering gear and linkage to the front wheels must provide a minimum of friction to allow the driver to hold the front wheels in any desired position while operating the vehicle. The steering connections must be able to flex with the movement of the front suspension and front wheels without restraining the stabilizing influences of the other factors of wheel alignment. Any condition which affects the adjustment or operation of the steering gear and its connections is a factor of wheel alignment.

Any condition that alters the positioning or operation of the springs, shock absorbers, frame, and other parts which are used to support the weight of the vehicle are factors that affect wheel alignment.

Springs, shock absorbers, the vehicle frame, and other parts that support the weight of the vehicle control the positioning of the wheels in relation to the vehicle as a complete assembly. Misalignment of the wheels may be the result of misalignment of structural parts which support the wheels.

In all types of suspensions, automotive manufacturers strive to accomplish two major objectives in suspension design. These objectives are 1) stability with ease of steering control and 2) maximum tire life.

While some factors of wheel alignment create stronger influences than others, no single factor (or angle) in itself imparts stability to the vehicle. A single misalignment factor, however, can destroy stability. In other cases, rapid tire wear or the lack of stability can be the result of a combination of things.

Likewise, two misalignment factors, each of which alone would create instability, may cancel out each other, with the result that the vehicle has stability when in motion. In such a case, the correction of only one factor might remove the counteracting force with the result that the vehicle would lose its stability.

Therefore, while each factor of wheel alignment may be considered as an individual subject, the combined result of all factors produce the desired objectives—proper contact between the tire and the road for stability, ease of steering control and maximum tire life.

The influences and factors that combine to create stability, ease of steering control and maximum tire life are brought about by the angular relationship between the front wheels, the front wheel linkage, and the vehicle frame members. The angle of the steering knuckle (away from the vertical), the toe-in or toe-out of the front wheels, and the tilt of the front wheels from the vertical are all involved in front-end geometry. Each angle imparts an influence upon the front wheels causing the wheels to either toe-in or toe-out. By offsetting one influence with an opposing influence, it is possible to create steering stability as the vehicle travels in a straight ahead direction. The various factors that enter into front-end geometry and influence steering are classified as 1) caster, 2) steering axis inclination or angle, 3) camber, 4) point of intersection, 5) toe-in, and 6) toe-out on turns, Fig. 7-1. When all of these factors and influences are in the correct relationship to one another the wheels will tend to remain in a straight ahead position when in that direction, and minimum effort will be required to steer the vehicle. Also the front wheels will straighten themselves out after the vehicle has made a turn.

In all factors of wheel alignment, a true appreciation of the influences created by each individual factor or angle is possible only if its contribution is considered alone so as not to confuse its influences with those of other factors. For this

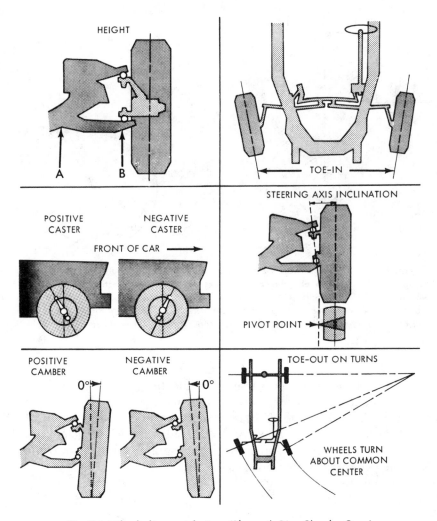

Fig. 7-1. Wheel alignment factors. (*Plymouth Div., Chrysler Corp.*)

reason the tendencies created by each of the various angles are treated as though they are the only factors to be considered.

Caster

Directional stability is obtained in varying degrees on the different makes of passenger vehicles by using the caster principle for attaching the steering knuckle. An understanding of the caster principle can be obtained by examining

an ordinary furniture caster, as shown in Fig. 7-2.

When a piece of furniture mounted on casters is pushed, the caster wheel lines itself up with the direction of travel because it is being pulled by its spindle pin. The caster wheel trails behind its spindle pin. This action of the furniture caster causes the piece of furniture to roll easily and in a straight line. It should be noted that a vertical line projected through the center of the wheel contacts the floor behind the center line of the

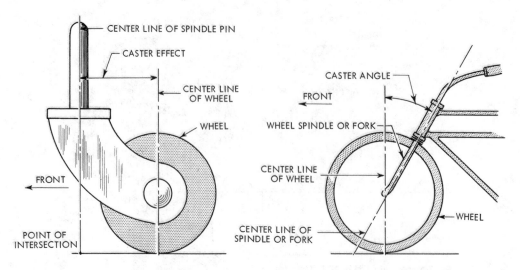

Fig. 7-2. *Left,* caster effect of a furniture caster. When the piece of furniture is moved, the caster wheel will line itself up with the direction of travel because it is pulled in that direction by its spindle pin; that is, the wheel will trail behind the spindle pin, causing the furniture to move in a straight line. The same principle applies to the automotive wheel, giving the vehicle directional stability. *Right,* caster effect in a bicycle. The fork of the bicycle serves as a spindle which causes the wheel to move in a straight line.

spindle pin. The distance between these two center lines is known as *caster effect.*

Another example of the same effect is employed in bicycles. The front wheel of a bicycle is mounted in a fork in such a manner that the projected center line of the wheel is also behind the projected center line of the fork, as shown in Fig. 7-2. This causes the wheel to trail behind the center line of the fork in the same manner as a furniture caster. When the speed of the bicycle is increased, it has more directional stability. The front wheel has a tendency to stay in the straight ahead position as long as the rider keeps the bicycle vertical and does not turn the handle bars. In an automobile, caster is the term applied to a similar trailing effect imparted to the front wheels. This effect is established by the projected center line through the ball joints intersecting the road surface at a point ahead of a vertical line projected through the center of the wheel. It

should be noted that the positioning of the steering knuckle on late model passenger cars is controlled by ball joints. On older model vehicles the tilt of the steering knuckle was controlled by king-

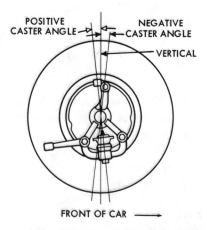

Fig. 7-3. Caster effect on automobile front wheels. A backward tilt of the steering knuckle produces a positive caster effect while forward tilt of the steering knuckle produces a negative caster effect. (Cadillac Div., General Motors Corp.)

pins. The same principles apply in both cases. As shown in Fig. 7-3, this effect is obtained by tipping the top of the steering knuckle rearward from the straight up-and-down position.

On most vehicles the steering knuckle is tipped backward to obtain a caster effect while on other vehicles the steering knuckle is placed ahead of the center line of the wheel. When the steering knuckle is placed ahead of the center line of the wheel the steering knuckle may be exactly vertical; however, the caster effect is the same as that obtained with the furniture caster. With this design, the top of the steering knuckle might actually be tipped forward slightly without losing the caster effect. This is also illustrated in Fig. 7-3.

Regardless of design, caster effect is always obtained if the center line through the steering knuckle intersects the road at a point ahead of a vertical line through the center of the wheel.

Tipping the top of the steering knuckle forward results in negative caster, whereas tipping the top of the steering knuckle rearward results in positive caster. Some vehicles are designed with positive caster, while others are designed with negative caster.

When the steering knuckle is tipped rearward to create a positive caster effect, the vehicle lowers slightly when the front wheel is turned toward the center of the car (straight ahead position). This is easily demonstrated by means of two pencils as shown in Figs. 7-4 and 7-5. In both illustrations, imagine that the vertical pencil and the ruler are both standing on

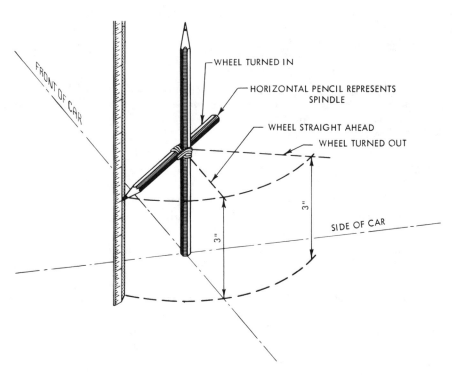

Fig. 7-4. Example of a vertical steering knuckle. The vertical pencil is tilted neither forward nor backward and, therefore, can be compared to a steering knuckle having no caster.

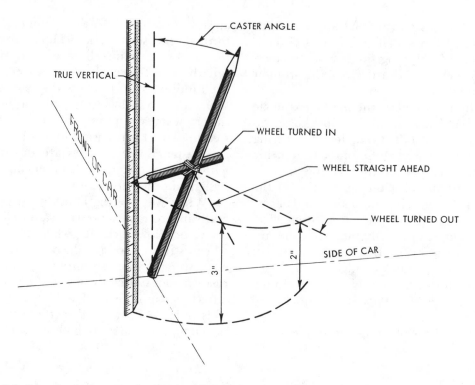

Fig. 7-5. Example of a steering knuckle having positive caster. Since the vertical pencil is tilted backward, it can be compared to a steering knuckle having positive caster, the caster angle being the difference between the top of the tilted pencil and a true vertical as seen from the front of the vehicle.

the same flat surface which we will refer to as a table. In Fig. 7-4, the vertical pencil can be compared to a steering knuckle having no caster. As the vertical pencil is turned, the horizontal pencil (representing the wheel spindle) maintains the same distance from the table. In a vehicle, if the steering knuckle were exactly vertical, the front of the vehicle would neither raise nor fall when the front wheels were turned.

In Fig. 7-5, the vertical pencil representing the steering knuckle has been tipped to simulate the caster angle of the steering knuckle in a vehicle. As the horizontal pencil (representing the spindle) is turned forward (representing front wheel turned in) the distance from the pencil to the table increases. When the horizontal pencil is turned rearward

(representing front wheel turned out), the distance from the pencil to the table decreases.

In a vehicle, the same results are obtained except that the distance from the end of the spindle to the road remains the same, since this is established by the size of the wheel. Therefore, instead of the spindle rising and falling, the steering knuckle and the front end of the vehicle rise as the front wheel is turned inward and falls as the front wheel is turned outward.

With positive caster, the front of the vehicle is nearer to the surface of the road when the wheel is turned inward (straight ahead position). Therefore the weight of the vehicle working through the caster angle of the steering knuckle creates a tendency for the front wheel to toe-in. This, then is the influence of positive caster. With negative caster (top of the steering knuckle tipped forward) the opposite tendency is created. Negative caster creates a tendency for the wheel to toe-out.

If the positive caster angle is the same on both sides, a tendency is created for the front of both wheels to turn in toward each other. However, the distance between the wheels is rigidly maintained by the suspension system and the tie rod. Therefore the tendency of one wheel to turn inward is balanced or offset by the same tendency of the other wheel.

If caster on left and right wheels were uneven, however, the tendency of the side having the most caster would be stronger than the tendency at the other wheel, with the result that the wheel having the most caster would turn inward, causing the wheel having less caster to

turn outward. With such a condition, a tendency would be created for the vehicle to pull constantly to one side (away from the side having the most positive caster) .

Caster angle can change in a vehicle due to bent, distorted, or worn parts involved in the establishment of the caster angle. Any change in caster due to damage resulting from an accident may affect the camber angle, toe-in or toe-out of front wheels, or the steering axis inclination.

A caster adjustment is incorporated into the front suspension system to permit making caster corrections. Before making adjustments all worn or damaged parts should be repaired or replaced.

The most common method of caster adjustment is by the use of adjusting shims. Figure 7-6 illustrates the shim arrangement used for setting caster. Add-

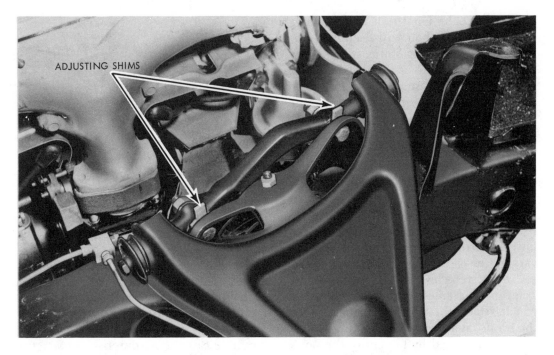

Fig. 7-6. Caster adjusting shims. Shims, mounted between the frame and the pivot pin on mounting bolts, provide a means of reducing or increasing caster. To make an adjustment, either remove or add shims as needed. (*Chevrolet Div., General Motors Corp.*)

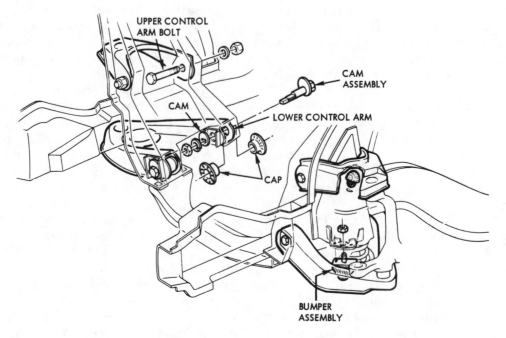

Fig. 7-7. Cam bolt and cam used to adjust caster. (*Chevrolet Div., General Motors Corp.*)

ing shims at the front bolt or removing shims at the rear bolt will decrease positive caster. Removing shims at the front bolt or adding shims at the rear bolt will increase positive caster. The removal or addition of shims at one bolt or the other tilts the steering knuckle either backward or forward thereby changing the caster angle.

On some vehicles, the caster angle is established by a cam bolt and cam which is used to attach the lower control arm to the frame member, Fig. 7-7. Turning the rear lower control arm cam will move the lower control arm fore or aft thereby varying the caster.

Other vehicles will have elongated holes in the frame member, for the bolts which attach the upper control arm to the frame, as a means of adjusting caster. Caster is adjusted by loosening the bolts that attach the inner shaft of the upper control arm to the frame and installing a special tool which is used to move the

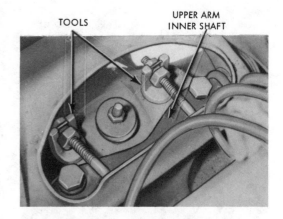

Fig. 7-8. Caster and camber adjusting tool. (*Ford Customer Service Div., Ford Motor Corp.*)

shaft in or out, Fig. 7-8. Positive caster is increased by tightening the front tool hook nut or loosening the rear hook nut. Negative caster is accomplished by tightening the rear hook nut or loosening the front hook nut.

On one installation, the caster is con-

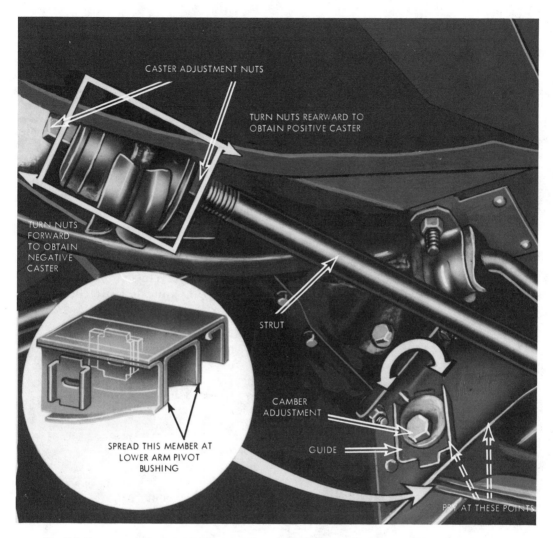

Fig. 7-9. Front suspension strut used to control caster. (Ford Customer Service Div., Ford Motor Corp.)

trolled by the front suspension strut, Fig. 7-9. To obtain positive caster, loosen the strut rear nut and tighten the strut front nut against the bushing. To increase negative caster, loosen the strut front nut and tighten the strut rear nut against the bushing.

In the past most vehicles were designed with relatively high caster for the directional stability obtained through the trailing action that caster imparted. This tendency, however, can be created by several other means, chief of which are sidewise inclination of the steering knuckle and increased tread width of the tires.

Steering Axis Inclination

The sidewise tilt of the steering knuckle is referred to as the *steering axis inclination angle.*

Steering axis inclination of the steer-

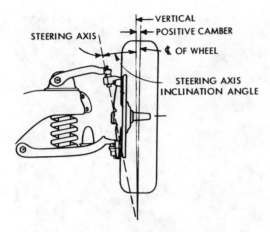

Fig. 7-10. Steering axis inclination. Steering axis inclination is the difference between the vertical center line of the ball joints and the vertical center line of the wheel, as viewed from the front of the vehicle. (Cadillac Div., General Motors Corp.)

ing knuckle establishes the point of intersection of a center line projected through the center of the ball joints and a center line projected through the center of the tire. These two center lines intersect at approximately the center of the area of the tire in contact with the road, as shown in Fig. 7-10. This provides a pivot point on which the wheel can be turned easily, especially when the vehicle is not in motion, as is the case when parking. Steering axis inclination of the steering knuckle also aids directional stability.

Steering axis inclination is created between the center line of the steering axis and a true vertical line is viewed from the front of the vehicle. The upper end of the steering knuckle is attached to the

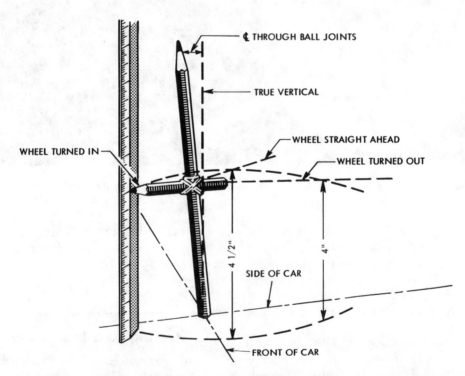

Fig. 7-11. Example of steering axis inclination. Note that the horizontal pencil representing the wheel spindle is farther away from the table when the pencil is at right angles to the true vertical. In the automotive vehicle, the wheel spindle is farther away from the road surface when the vehicle is in a straight ahead position.

upper control arm so that it is closer to the center of the vehicle than the bottom of the steering knuckle; thus it tilts the steering knuckle inward.

If the steering knuckle was not tilted in this manner, the wheels would roll in an arc around the point where the center line projected through the ball joints contacts the road surface. By tipping the steering knuckle sidewise, as shown in Fig. 7-11, the projected center line is made to contact the road approximately in the center of the contact area of the tire. This results in the wheel pivoting around the point of intersection without acually rolling.

Disregarding that the steering axis may be tipped backward to create a caster effect, the two pencils shown in Fig. 7-12 demonstrate that steering axis inclination angle causes the end of the horizontal pencil to be farther away from the table when it is at right angles to the direction of travel, that is, when the wheels are in a straight ahead position. This demonstrates what happens to the steering knuckle due to steering axis inclination.

In actual practice, the diameter of the wheel establishes the distance from the end of the spindle to the road, and instead of the end of the spindle rising and falling as the wheel is turned, the steering knuckle and the front end of the vehicle rises and falls. This means that the vehicle is closer to the road when the wheels are in a straight ahead position, due to the steering axis inclination of the steering knuckle. As a result, the weight of the vehicle actually must be lifted in order to turn the wheels to any other than the straight ahead position.

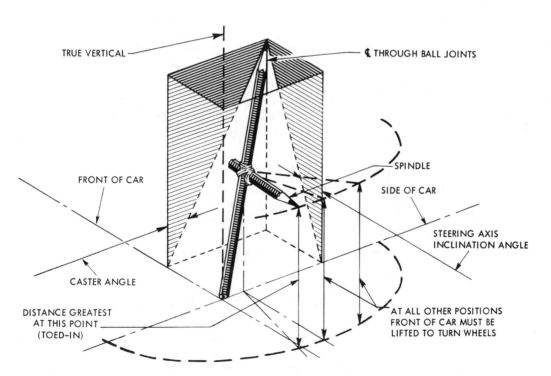

Fig. 7-12. Example of combined caster and steering axis inclination. The two pencils illustrate the result of both caster and steering axis inclination.

Steering axis inclination, therefore, has a stabilizing influence which tends to keep the front wheels in a straight ahead position. In many vehicles, the tendency of the wheels to maintain a straight ahead course created by the steering axis inclination and the width of the tire contact permits a reduction in caster angle. In fact, in some vehicles the tendencies are so pronounced that the front end is designed with no caster, or with negative caster, so as to reduce or counteract these tendencies and reduce steering effort while still retaining the desired amount of directional stability.

Figure 7-12 illustrates the net result of a combination of both caster and steering knuckle angle.

There is no adjustment provided for steering axis inclination. If other alignment angles are correct and the steering axis inclination is incorrect, the knuckle or attaching parts are bent and must be straightened or replaced.

Camber Angle

Camber is the tilting of the wheel from the vertical. The front wheels of most passenger vehicles are tipped outward at the top, a condition known as positive camber. The camber angle is shown in Fig. 7-13. If the wheels are tipped inward at the top, the condition would be known as negative camber. Some cars are designed with positive camber while others are designed with negative camber.

Camber is established by tipping the outer end of the spindle downward. The combination of camber angle and steering knuckle sidewise inclination is sometimes referred to as the combined angle.

Camber in effect makes a cone of the front wheels. With positive camber, unless restrained, the wheel will roll outward in a circle around the apex (point) of the cone. If the degree of this tendency

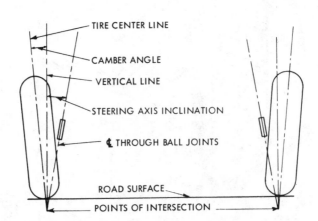

Fig. 7-13. Camber angle and steering axis inclination. The top of the front wheels of an automobile are tipped either inward toward the vehicle center or outward away from the vehicle center providing a condition which is known as camber. The difference between the tire center line and a true vertical is known as the camber angle. Where the tire center line, the vertical center line, and the steering axis center line meet is the point of intersection.

to roll outward is the same at both front wheels (since the tie rods prevent their turning in opposite directions), the tendency of each will cancel out or counteract the same tendency in an opposite wheel and the vehicle will travel straight ahead.

When a cone effect is present the wheel and tire assembly will have several diameters. Since the actual diameter at both sides of the tire is the same and since all of the tread makes the same number of revolutions, the outermost portion of the tread (smallest rolling radius) must move faster than the actual vehicle speed. Therefore, the excess tread must slip over the road, resulting in tire wear.

The tendency toward the use of tires with larger cross sections and larger areas of contact has caused manufacturers to design vehicles with less camber and with greater steering knuckle sidewise inclination to maintain steering stability. Since camber causes tire wear, it is desirable to have no camber so as to reduce tire wear.

Usually, maximum tire life and mileage are obtained when the average *running* camber angle is zero, since all portions of the tread have the same rolling radius. This does not necessarily mean that the camber angle should be zero when the vehicle is unloaded. It does mean, however, that with an average load and average operating conditions the tire wear will be less if the camber is approximately zero.

Referring back to the two pencils in Fig. 7-5, it will be noted that in addition to the fact that the end of the horizontal pencil (representing the spindle) rises and falls due to the caster angle, the angle of this pencil in relation to the horizontal also changes.

Due to the caster angle, this is likewise true of the spindle on which the front wheels turn. As a result, when the wheel is turned toward the center of the vehicle, the camber angle is reduced. As the wheel is turned away from the center of the vehicle, the camber angle is increased. Both of these changes are accounted for by the caster angle of the steering knuckle, and the degree of camber change is in proportion to the caster angle. The more the caster, the more the camber change. This provides a means of measuring the caster angle through the change in camber during a turn of an exact number of degrees.

A camber adjustment is provided to permit compensation for changes which

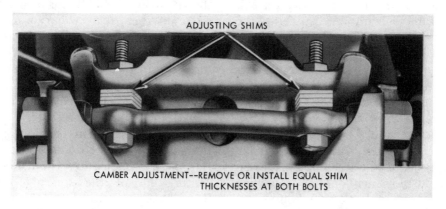

Fig. 7-14. Camber adjusting shims. Shims are mounted on the bolts which mount the pivot pin to the vehicle's frame. (Ford Div., Ford Motor Co.)

may take place due to wear or distortion. The most common method is the type using adjusting shims. The camber adjustment is usually combined with the caster adjustment. Figure 7-14 shows the shim arrangement used for making camber adjustments. Adding an equal number of shims at both bolts increases the camber angle while removing an equal number of shims at both bolts decreases the camber angle (positive camber). Removing an equal number of shims at both bolts tips the top of the steering knuckle toward the center of the vehicle whereas adding an equal number of shims at both bolts tilts the top of the tire away from the center of the vehicle.

On vehicles where cam bolts and cams are used to establish caster, the same cam arrangement also permits establishing camber, Fig. 7-7. Turning the front lower control arm cam after loosening the pivot bolt will move the lower control arm in or out thereby varying the camber setting.

When elongated bolt holes in the frame member are used for the bolts which attach the upper control arm to the frame, Fig. 7-8, to permit changing the caster setting, the same tool and procedure are used for camber adjustment. Moving both front and rear bolts an equal amount in the same direction will change camber without disturbing the caster setting.

The installation, which uses a front suspension strut to establish caster, uses an eccentric cam located at the lower arm attachment to the side rail, Fig. 7-9. To change camber setting, loosen the adjusting bolt nut at the rear of the body bracket. Spread the bracket at the camber adjustment bolt area enough to permit lateral movement of the arm when the bolt is turned. Rotate the bolt as necessary to increase or decrease camber.

The combined angles of caster, steering knuckle sidewise inclination, and camber are interrelated. A change in either caster angle or steering knuckle angle or both will also cause a change in the camber angle as well. It is necessary, therefore, to recheck the camber angle if either of these factors are changed.

Point of Intersection

The point of intersection, as shown in Fig. 7-13, is controlled by camber, steering axis inclination of the steering knuckle, the rolling radius of the wheel, and the distance from the wheel to the pivot points of the steering knuckle. These conditions impart a tendency to the wheel to either toe-in or toe-out, depending on whether the point of intersection is above or below the surface of the road.

If the point of intersection for each front wheel is above the road surface, the front wheels will have a tendency to toe-in. If the point of intersection for each front wheel is below the surface of the road, the wheels will have a tendency to toe-out. This tendency can be demonstrated by pushing a sheet of paper over the surface of a table with a pencil, as shown in Fig. 7-15. If the pencil is centered on the paper, you can move the paper forward without its turning. If, on the other hand, the pencil is not centered on the paper, you cannot move the paper forward without its turning toward the side of the paper that has the largest contact with the table.

If the point of intersection is below the surface of the road, the largest portion of tire contact area is outside of the center line of the steering knuckle. Therefore, a tendency for the wheel to turn out (toe-out) is created. If the point of intersection is above the surface of the

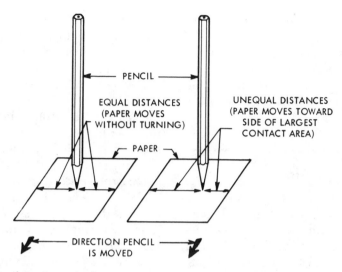

PENCIL

EQUAL DISTANCES
(PAPER MOVES
WITHOUT TURNING)

UNEQUAL DISTANCES
(PAPER MOVES TOWARD
SIDE OF LARGEST
CONTACT AREA)

PAPER

DIRECTION PENCIL
IS MOVED

Fig. 7-15. Tendency of the front wheels to turn in (toe-in) or turn out (toe-out) changes with the point of intersection, as shown by the two pencils in the above illustration. With the pencil placed on the center of the paper, the paper can be moved forward without the paper turning. However, if the pencil is placed away from the center of the paper, the paper, when moved forward, will turn in the direction of largest contact area.

road, the largest portion of tire contact area is inside the projected center line through the ball joints of the steering knuckle. Therefore, a tendency for the wheel to turn in (toe-in) is created.

If the point of intersection is neither above nor below the road surface under normal loading, each slight change of rolling radius would change the location of the point of intersection. At one moment the point of intersection might be slightly below the road surface, and a tendency for the front wheels to turn out would be created. At the next moment the point of intersection might be above the road surface, and a tendency for the front wheels to turn in would be created. Under such conditions a tendency for hunting, wandering or darting could result.

In all factors of wheel alignment, it is usually more desirable to create positive tendencies which can be counter-balanced by other positive tendencies in the opposite directions than to have indefi-

nite tendencies. For this reason, most vehicles are designed with the point of intersection below the surface of the road, thus creating a positive tendency for the wheels to turn out.

If the point of intersection is higher on one front wheel than the other, the tendency of the wheels to either toe-in or toe-out will not be equal on both wheels, and the vehicle will pull toward the side having the lower point of intersection (lower combined camber plus steering knuckle sidewise inclination angle).

Changes in the point of intersection are usually the result of a bent steering knuckle, worn ball joints, or loose wheel bearings. However, if front wheels or tires are used which are larger than originally intended, the point of intersection will then become raised. Wheels having a greater "dish" will also raise the point of intersection, if installed. If wheels of less "dish" are used, the point of intersection will be lowered. Note: *The dish of the wheel is a term used to indicate the dis-*

tance from the center line of the tire to the mounting surface of the wheel.

Considered separately, the point of intersection is not a factor in tire wear. However, camber, which is one of the factors that establish the point of intersection, *is* a factor of tire wear.

Toe-in

The various rods and levers that make up the steering linkage and steering connections either restrain the influences of the other factors of alignment or transmit them. They likewise transmit to the front wheels the turning force from the steering gear. The prevailing tendencies of the front wheels to turn out are restrained by the tie rods. The tie rods hold the front wheels parallel in the straight ahead position and maintain the correct relationship between the front wheels on turns. To keep the front wheels parallel in a straight ahead position while the vehicle is moving, it is generally necessary to adjust the tie rods so that the front wheels have toe-in when the vehicle is stationary.

The term toe-in refers to a condition that exists when the front of the wheels are closer together than the rear of the wheels, as shown in Fig. 7-16. If the front wheels are exactly parallel, the condition is referred to as zero toe-in. If the front of the front wheels are farther apart than the back of the front wheels, the condition is referred to as toe-out. Toe-in of the front wheels is maintained by means of adjustable tie rods which are connected to the steering knuckle arms.

Toe-in (even the correct amount) is an evil that always results in tire wear. The ideal condition is for the back portion of the tire to begin its forward and upward movement at the exact point where it contacts the road. Since there are more factors which create a tendency for the front wheels to toe-out (camber and point of intersection below the road) than there are factors which create a tendency for the front wheels to toe-in (caster), the resultant tendency is for the wheels to turn outward. The tie rods, which are used to establish toe-in, restrain this influence. However, some lash always exists in the steering connections which permits the wheels to turn out slightly in spite of the tie rods. To compensate for this slight movement, the tie

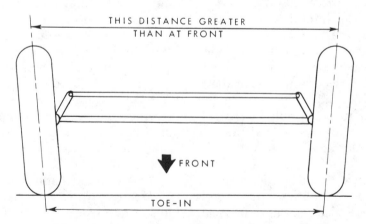

Fig. 7-16. Toe-in of the front wheels. Toe-in is a condition that exists when the wheels are closer together at the front than they are at the rear.

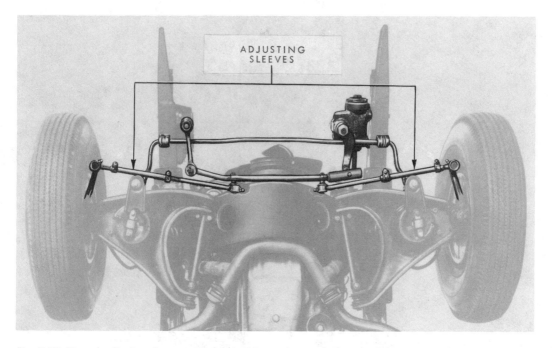

Fig. 7-17. Tie rod adjusting sleeves make it possible to change the length of the tie rod. After the tie rod has been adjusted to the correct length, tighten the clamp bolts on the sleeve to prevent the sleeve from loosening. (*Chevrolet Div., General Motors Corp.*)

rods are adjusted so that when the vehicle is stationary and the influence to toe-out is not in effect, a slight toe-in is established. When the vehicle is in motion, the strong tendency for the wheels to turn out will take up this lash, and hence the wheels will have no toe-in.

A change in one or all of the various factors of alignment will result in a change in the toe-in of the front wheels. Thus, toe-in and/or the resultant tire wear become the best means of spotting trouble.

In addition to tire wear, when the adjustment of toe-in is not correct, a condition sometimes results in which first one wheel aligns itself, throwing all the error to the opposite wheel, then the opposite wheel aligns itself, throwing the first wheel out of alignment. This cycle may be repeated several times for each revolution of the wheel, resulting in a shimmy of the wheel and, of course, excessive tire wear.

The front wheels can be adjusted to correct a condition of excessive toe-in or toe-out. Toe-in is adjusted by changing the length of the tie rods. The tie rods are usually built with an adjusting sleeve between the fitting and the tie rod, as shown in Fig. 7-17. One end of the fitting has a right-hand thread, while the other end of the fitting has a left-hand thread. This arrangement makes it possible to change the length of the tie rod by turning the sleeve.

Toe-out on Turns

Toe-out on turns refers to the difference in angles between the two front wheels during turns.

When a vehicle is traveling straight

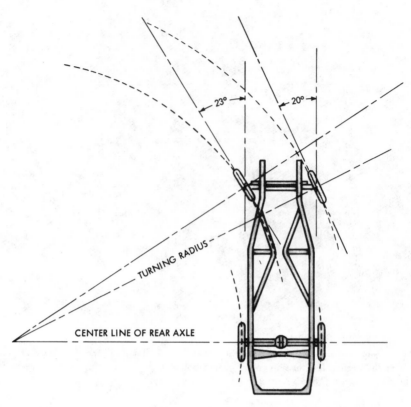

Fig. 7-18. During a turn the front wheels are toed-out, and as a result the distance between the front of the front wheels is greater than the distance between the back of the front wheels.

ahead, both front wheels must be parallel in a straight ahead position if the vehicle is to maintain steering stability. During a turn, however, this is not true. Figure 7-18 illustrates the positions assumed by the front wheels during a turn. The inner wheel is rotating on a smaller radius than the outer wheel when the vehicle is rounding a curve, therefore the spindle of the inside wheel must be turned at a sharper angle to reduce side slippage. As shown in Fig. 7-18 the outside wheel is turned at a 20° angle from straight ahead position while the inside wheel is turned at a 23° angle from the straight ahead position. When this situation exists the wheels are no longer parallel or toed-in, but are actually toed-out, resulting in a greater distance between the front of the

front wheels than the rear of the front wheels. This is known as toe-out on turns and is always referred to by its full name to avoid confusion with toe-out as referred to when the wheels are in the straight ahead position.

Some late model cars having link type rear suspensions with coil springs turn about a center that is midway between the front and rear suspension as shown in Fig. 7-19. The toe-out on turns specification is reduced because the rear wheels also steer in a cornering.

Toe-out on turns is accomplished by having the center line which extends through the ends of the steering knuckle arms closer together than the center line which extends down through the steering knuckle ball joints. The design of the

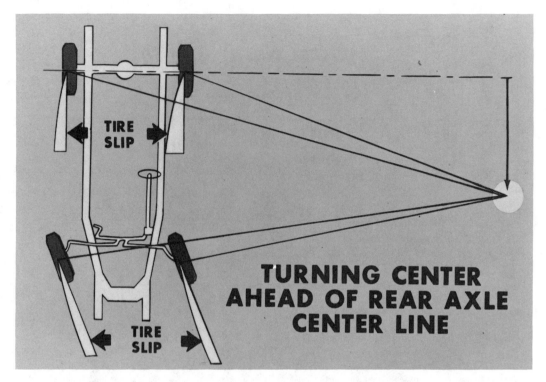

Fig. 7-19. Turning center is ahead of the rear axle center line on some vehicles to reduce the toe-out on turns required which also reduces tire slip and wear.

steering knuckle arms controls the toe-out on turns. If the steering knuckle arms are bent, there is little to be gained by attempting corrections other than by replacing the bent steering knuckle arm.

Wheel alignment factors may be arranged in two groups: The first group consisting of camber, toe-in, toe-out, and toe-out on turns are related in that each deals with the wheel's position in reference to the road. The second group consisting of caster and steering axis inclination are related in that they both deal with the steering axis.

Direct measuring methods are used to check camber and toe-in or toe-out. Direct measuring means that the measurement is taken directly from some part of the wheel assembly. Indirect measuring methods are those that measure the an-

gles through the change of some other angles or parts.

There are a number of different gages and machines manufactured to determine the wheel alignment angles. Some of the basic gages and machines will be briefly discussed here. A complete operating manual is available for a specific type of machine from its manufacturer.

Camber Angle Adjustment

Camber is the tilting of the wheel from the vertical. All instruments measure camber by the actual tilt of the wheel from the vertical line.

Camber reading gages may be mounted against the tire, on the rim of the wheel, on the hub, or on the spindle.

Before these gages that mount to the wheel or the tire are used (Figs. 7-20 and

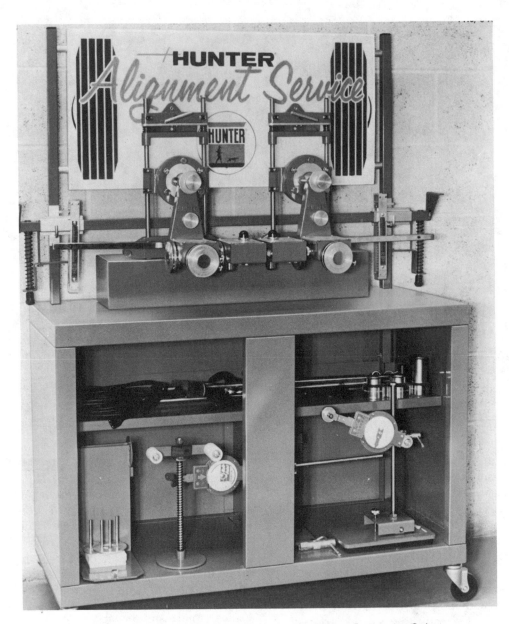

Fig. 7-20. Portable wheel alignment equipment. (*Hunter Engineering* Co.)

7-21), a provision must be made to compensate for the lateral run-out of the wheel. Lateral run-out is a sidewise movement of the wheel as it rotates. This can easily be determined by holding a piece of chalk against the tire or wheel, depending on where the gage will come in contact with the wheel. A chalk mark on the wheel or tire will indicate where the wheel and tire assembly is bent. Before attaching the type of gage shown in Fig. 7-21 to measure camber, rotate the wheel until the chalk mark is facing the front of the car. Fig. 7-22B shows position

Fig. 7-21. Portable wheel alignment gage mounted to the rim of the wheel. The gage is adjusted until the bubble is centered in the spirit level. Camber reading will be shown on the 60-degree scale of the gage. A reading which is outside of zero would indicate negative camber. Readings toward the wheel from zero would be positive camber readings. (Ammco Tools Inc.)

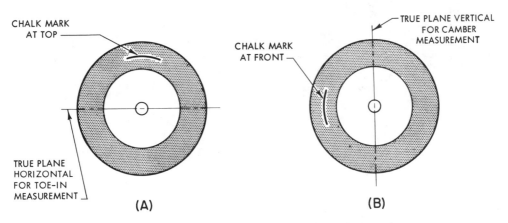

Fig. 7-22. Chalk marks for measuring (A) toe-in and (B) camber.

Fig. 7-23. Portable caster, camber and steering inclination gage. (*Snap-On Tools Corp.*)

of wheel for measuring camber. Fig. 7-22A shows position for measuring toe-in.

The portable caster, camber and steering inclination gage shown in Fig. 7-23 is of the magnetic type. After removing the grease cap the gage is attached directly to the outer edge of the hub. Strong magnets hold the gage in place. The gage is centered on the spindle by a pointer located in the center of the gage and placed in the centering hole of the wheel spindle.

Turn tables are required so as to be able to turn the front wheels the specified amount when checking caster and steering inclination.

The Lite-A-Line alignment rack shown in Fig. 7-24 uses a precise lens system with a light beam that projects the alignment angles on a large panel located in front of the rack.

The Visualiner, as shown in Fig. 7-25, uses a mirror assembly which is mounted to the rim of the wheel. Run-out must be compensated for in order to obtain accurate readings on both machines.

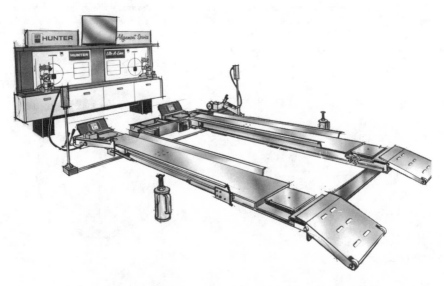

Fig. 7-24. Lite-a-line alignment rack. (*Hunter Engineering Co.*)

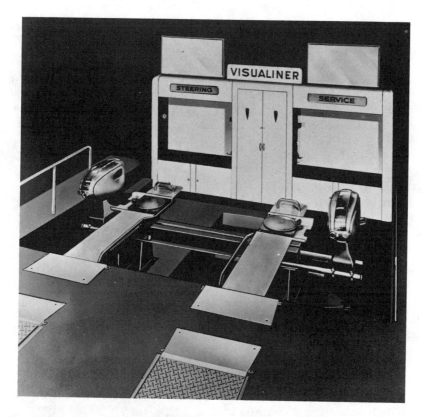

Fig. 7-25. Visualiner with a short rack installed in a pit. Tools can be added to this type of rack to enable a wheel alignment operator to correct damage to a vehicle as a result of a collision as well as all normal wheel alignment of vehicles regardless of their tread width. (*John Bean Corp.*)

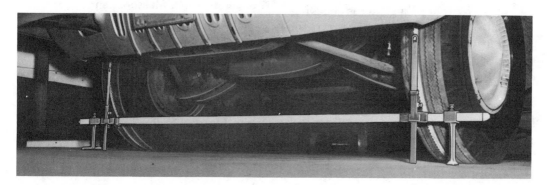

Fig. 7-26. Trammel used to check toe-in from scribed line. (*Bear Manufacturing* Co.) (*Bear, The Wheel Service Division, Applied Power, Inc.*)

Toe-in or Toe-out

Toe-in or toe-out is measured by determining the distance between the two front wheels at the front of each wheel as compared to the distance between the front wheels at the rear of each wheel. If the distance at the front of the front wheels is greater than the distance at the rear of the front wheels, the wheels are toed out. If the distance at the front of the front wheels is less than the distance at the rear of the front wheels, the wheels are toed in. The simplest way to check toe-in is to use a tape measure and measure the distance between the front of the front wheels and compare it to the distance between the rear of the front wheels. However, this method could give an incorrect reading since a bent wheel would give an erroneous width dimension.

Figure 7-26 illustrates a trammel which determines the amount of toe-in or toe-out by using a line previously scribed around the tire. The two lines (one on each tire) are accurate measuring points not affected by wheel run-out. Figure 7-27 illustrates a scribing tool for making the line. This method may also be used to measure toe-in of the rear wheels which in most cases should be 0.

Figure 7-28 shows a gage for checking the toe of the front wheels. This type of gage is part of a regular wheel aligning rack.

Figure 7-29 shows a type of wheel alignment gage for checking the toe of the front wheels by the use of a light beam. The toe readings are magnified several times and reflected by mirrors to the panel. The toe reading may be noted as the adjustment is made, thereby, eliminating the numerous rechecks that otherwise may be necessary.

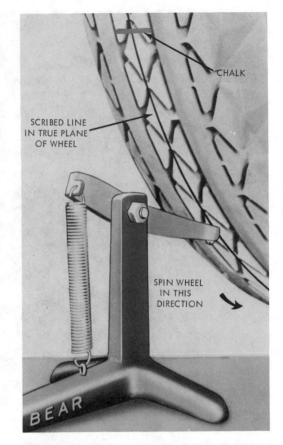

Fig. 7-27. Tire scriber in position to mark the tire. The wheel is rotated against a sharp point of the scriber leaving a mark completely around the tire. (*Bear Manufacturing Co.*)

Toe-out on Turns Measurement

To measure toe-out on turns, a degree plate or a graduated turntable is used. Figure 7-30 shows a turntable.

To measure toe-out on turns, turn the wheels to the right until the left wheel is at 20 degrees in a right hand turn. The right wheel will now show the amount of toe-out. Next, turn the wheels to the left until the right wheel is at 20 degrees in a left hand turn. The left wheel will now show the amount of toe-out. The two readings should agree with

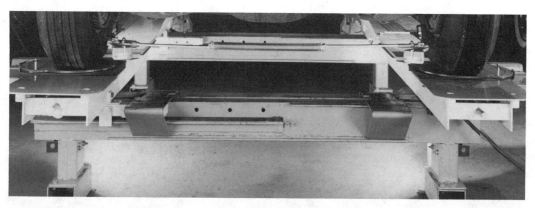

Fig. 7-28. A gage that fits between the wheels for checking toe-in and toe-out. (Bear, The Wheel Service Division, Applied Power, Inc.)

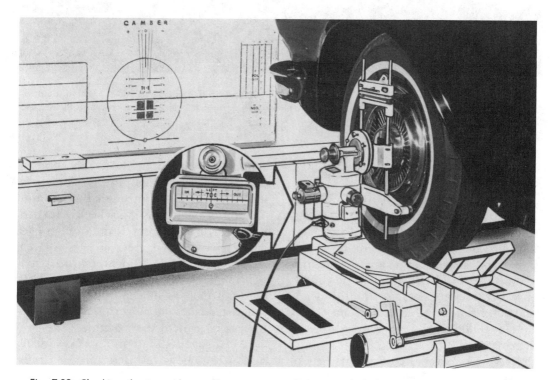

Fig. 7-29. Checking the toe with an alignment gage which uses a light beam. (Hunter Engineering Co.)

or be within 1 degree of each other. If the two readings are not within 1 degree of each other, one or both steering arms are bent. Vehicle manufacturer's manuals usually will give the recommended toe-out on turns for their vehicles.

Fig. 7-30. A pointer attached to the graduated turntable shows the amount of table turns in degrees. Straight-ahead position is zero. Turning the wheels either left or right is calibrated on the scale 30 degrees each way.

Caster Adjustment

Caster is the rearward tilt of the top of the steering axis. Since positive caster is the rearward tilt of the top of the steering axis, the upper ball joint on a ball joint type suspension would be slightly behind the lower ball joint. When reference is made to caster, it usually means that condition by which the front wheels are controlled by the rearward tilt of the steering axis.

Negative caster occurs when the upper ball joint is in front of the lower ball joint. Sometimes negative caster is called reverse caster.

If a vehicle has positive caster, the right wheel is turned to the right and the camber of the wheel is taken, then the wheel is turned inward or to the left, a change in camber of the wheel will be noticed. Caster gages are designed to measure the caster through the amount of camber change as the wheel is turned in an arc of 40 degrees. If the camber of a wheel changes 3 degrees as it is rotated from 20 degrees to 20 degrees, the caster will be approximately 2 degrees. This does not have to be computed each time the caster is taken since this is built into the caster scale of the machine.

Most gages operate in the above manner. A few, however, determine a caster reading by turning the wheel inward at the front 20 degrees and setting the gage on 0 on the caster scale, then turning the wheel until the wheel is turned 20 degrees inward at the rear and the scale will now give the caster reading. Either method will give you the same numerical

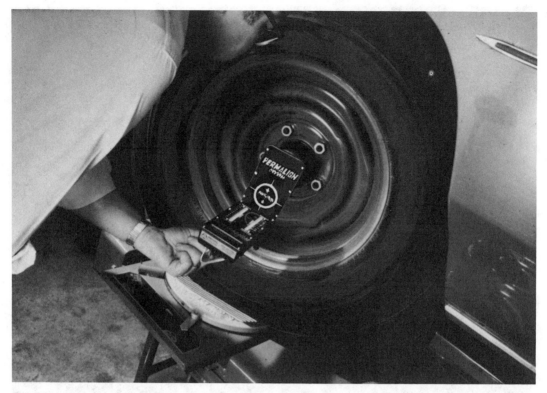

Fig. 7-31. Note that the wheel is turned 20 degrees inward at the rear. At this point the caster scale is adjusted to read zero. The wheel is then turned about its steering axis until the gage reads 20 degrees with the wheel turned in at the front. The caster scale will now indicate the caster reading. (*Bishman Manufacturing*)

value of the caster angle, but if a gage is designed to read caster by turning the rear of the wheel in first and then it is done in a reverse manner, the caster will change signs. Or in other words, if the steering axis of the wheel has positive caster, and the gage is used in the reverse manner of which it is designed, the gage will read that the wheel has a negative caster. Figures 7-31 and 7-32 illustrate how a typical hub-mounted camber and caster gage measures caster. A turntable with a degree plate as shown in Fig. 7-30 is required to measure caster.

Steering Axis Inclination Measurement

When the steering axis is tilted inward toward the center of the vehicle from a vertical line, the included angle is called S.A.I. or *steering axis inclination*. This angle is not adjustable. Steering axis inclination is a built-in feature of the steering knuckle. As the camber of the wheel is changed, so is the steering axis inclination changed. As camber is increased in the positive direction, the steering axis inclination is decreased. Therefore, the reverse is true in that as the camber is moved in the negative direction, the steering axis inclination is increased.

Steering axis inclination is measured in the same manner as caster is measured, that is, by turning the wheel about its steering axis until the rear of the wheel is in 20 degrees. The steering axis gage,

Fig. 7-32. A combination alignment machine using an electronic device for measuring camber and caster and a light beam to determine toe-in. (*Bishman Manufacturing*)

which is usually built into most wheel alignment equipment, is set on 0 on the steering axis scale. The gage must be mounted to the spindle; however, it may be mounted to the hub or to the wheel if the brakes are applied. As the wheel is rotated about its steering axis, the steering axis inclination causes the spindle to turn or roll about its center. When the wheel reaches 20 degrees in at the front, the steering axis gage will give the steering axis inclination of that wheel.

If the steering axis inclination reading does not agree with the specifications, the spindle or another part of the steer-

ing knuckle may be bent. Steering axis inclination, S.A.I., is given as so many degrees at a certain camber angle. For example, a typical steering axis inclination angle may be stated as 4 degrees steering axis inclination or kingpin inclination at ½ degree positive camber. A steering axis inclination will be 4 degrees only when the camber angle is ½ of a degree positive. If the camber of the wheel is 0 degrees, the steering axis inclination angle should be 4½ degrees. If the camber is 1 degree positive then the steering axis inclination should be 3½ degrees.

If the steering axis inclination in the above example was taken and found to be 3 degrees when the camber was 0, then the steering knuckle is damaged. A steering knuckle cannot be repaired and therefore should be replaced.

TRADE COMPETENCY TEST

1. What are the objectives which automotive manufacturers strive to attain in suspension design?
2. What should be the results of a properly aligned front-end?
3. What is the principle of caster and what is its effect on steering?
4. Why can correct wheel alignment factors be obtained with negative caster?
5. What is the effect of uneven caster?
6. What are the methods of caster adjustment and how is caster changed?
7. What is the purpose of steering axis inclination?
8. What influence does camber have on a rolling wheel?
9. What will cause the camber angle to change?
10. Where should the point of intersection be located in relation to the road and why?
11. Why are front wheels toed-in and what controls toe-in?
12. Why is toe-out on turns necessary?
13. How is toe-out on turns accomplished?
14. What alignment factor do we check in order to measure the caster?
15. What are the various factors that enter into front-end geometry and influence steering?

CHAPTER **8**

CUSTOMIZED VEHICLE ALIGNMENT

Various steering control and tire wear problems arise due to misalignment, wear, unbalance, improper tire pressures, and defects in the suspension system and the related steering linkages. Misalignment cannot be corrected unless the cause can be found. Each abnormal steering condition or excessive tire-wear pattern should be checked since it should provide a valuable indication as to the cause of the trouble. Frequently more than one condition is at the root of the trouble. It is best to make a complete front-end check whenever steering difficulties and/or excessive tire wear become apparent.

This chapter outlines the procedure for checking the vehicle and provides the information needed to carry out an alignment once the nature of the problem has been analyzed.

Pre-Alignment Visual Inspection

Before the actual adjusting of the vehicle alignment takes place, the vehicle must be visually inspected. Bear in mind that the way the vehicle handles on the road may be a valuable aid in making the proper diagnosis and in repairing the vehicle. Steps to follow are explained below.

Curb Height

First, inspect the vehicle to see how it sits in relation to the road surface. Curb height, which is usually specified by the manufacturer, is the distance between a stated point on the car (usually the lower edge of the bumpers) and the road sur-

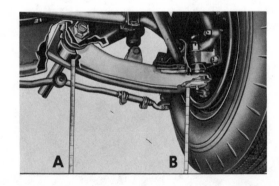

Fig. 8-1. The lower arm of the front suspension system measures lower at the wheel (B) than at the center of the vehicle (A). This condition indicates that the curb height is satisfactory. (*John Bean Corp.*)

152

face when the vehicle is fully loaded with fuel, oil, and coolant—standing free and without driver, passengers, or load.

When looking at an independent suspension, if the lower control arm is higher at the center of the vehicle than at the outer end, or if it is horizontal, the curb height is usually satisfactory. See Fig. 8-1.

Tire Condition

To insure the best alignment service a vehicle must be equipped with good front tires. A worn front tire, even though the vehicle is properly aligned, may cause erratic steering. Look at the tires for the following wear:

Camber Wear. This condition is caused by the design of the front suspension and by worn or bent suspension parts. Excessive negative camber causes wear on the inside tread of the tire. Improper positive camber causes wear on the outside tread. See Fig. 8-2.

Under-Inflation Wear. Observe the tire inflation and note if tire wear is caused by improper inflation. See Fig. 8-3, *top.*

Over-Inflation. Excessive inflation

Fig. 8-2. Camber wear on tires results in unevenness at the edges. Positive camber wear appears on the outside tread. Negative camber wear appears on the inside tread. (*John Bean Corp.*)

Fig. 8-3. *Top,* under-inflation wear appears on both edges of the tire, because the center treads have recessed under the weight of the vehicle. *Bottom,* over-inflation wear is the opposite of this condition. (*John Bean Corp.*)

pressure will wear the tire in the middle of the tread. See Fig. 8-3, *bottom*.

Toe Wear. Observe the toe wear of the tires which may be caused by maladjustment or by worn or bent steering linkage. Place your palm on the tire tread and move your hand, first, toward and then away from the center of the vehicle. Toe-out wear may be ascertained by feeling sharp edges on the tread design when pushing the hand inward toward the center of the vehicle. Toe-in wear is noted if the edges are sharp when the hand is pulled away from the center of the vehicle. See Fig. 8-4.

Scalloping Wear. This may be the result of several causes. The wheels may be out of balance; severe brake application may have worn an initial flat spot; either excessive positive or negative caster may have caused a shimmy which has become exaggerated; steering system parts may

Fig. 8-5. Scalloping or heel-and-toe may be caused by a number of road conditions, certain driving habits, and faulty adjustments in the automotive suspension system. It is an uneven and eccentric condition. (*John Bean Corp.*)

be worn; or inoperative shock absorbers may have caused uneven and eccentric tire wear. See Fig. 8-5.

Cornering Wear. This condition is caused by excessive speed in turning or by extreme negative caster. See Fig. 8-6. The wear pattern looks like camber wear on both edges of the tire or like under-inflation wear.

Steering System Inspection

Check the steering system for excessive looseness by turning the wheels straight ahead and then moving the steering wheel back and forth. *No* play should exist between the steering wheel and the road wheels. A vehicle must have a tight steering system if any realignment correction is to be effective. For this reason adjustment of the steering gear and linkage must be part of the alignment job.

Fig. 8-4. Toe-in and toe-out wear occur as a result of worn or bent steering linkage. Test for it by feeling for sharp edges when pulling the hand across the tire. If the inner edges are sharp, the condition is toe-in wear. If the outer edges are sharp, the condition is toe-out wear. (*John Bean Corp.*)

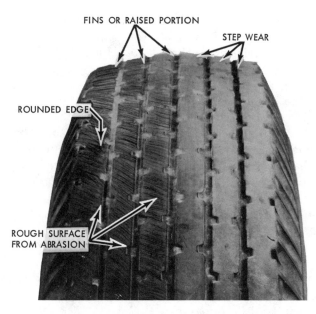

FINS OR RAISED PORTION

STEP WEAR

ROUNDED EDGE

ROUGH SURFACE
FROM ABRASION

Fig. 8-6. A typical example of cornering wear brought about either by excessive turning at high speeds or by extreme negative caster. (*John Bean Corp.*)

Vehicle Track

This term applies to the rear wheels following directly behind or in the tracks of the front wheels. A vehicle which is out of track may not handle properly on the road even though the front wheels are in correct alignment. There are two ways of visually detecting this condition. The first is to follow directly behind the

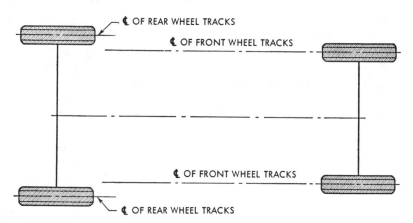

℄ OF REAR WHEEL TRACKS

℄ OF FRONT WHEEL TRACKS

℄ OF FRONT WHEEL TRACKS

℄ OF REAR WHEEL TRACKS

Fig. 8-7. Vehicle in track may be observed by watching the marks made by the front and rear wheels after the automobile has been driven more than twenty feet. Tracks should be parallel, but they need not overlap. (*John Bean Corp.*)

car as another person drives it on a straight road, observing the offset condition of the rear wheels in relation to the front wheels. Do not be misled by a vehicle on which the rear tread width (distance between wheels) is more or less than the tread width of the front wheels. The other method is to observe the imprint of the tire tracks on a garage floor after the vehicle has been driven in a straight line for a dozen feet. If the rear wheel imprints evenly overlap or are parallel to the front wheel imprints the vehicle is in track. See Fig. 8-7.

General Vehicle Appearance

A final and important check pertains to the general appearance of the vehicle. An obviously new paint job or apparent repair work on the body may be indications that a collision could have damaged the suspension system. Unless you check it this damage will go undetected and unrepaired.

Pre-Alignment Road Test

After visual inspections have been made and the operator is still not satisfied as to the nature of the car's trouble, the car should be road tested. A definite route *typical* of roads regularly used by the vehicle should be chosen for the test. During the road test the operator should watch for the following conditions:

Pulling

A vehicle will pull or drift to one side because of faulty brakes, a tire with low pressure, or improper alignment.

Excessive Noise and Vibration

Pitted or loosely adjusted wheel bearings will cause excessive noise and vibration. A *clunking* sound as the brakes are applied may be due to worn ball joints, worn upper or lower outer pivot pins, or worn bushings. Unbalanced wheels and loose steering parts will also cause a vibration.

Hard Steering

A vehicle may be hard to steer because of inadequate lubrication, an improperly adjusted steering system, excessive positive caster, or under-inflated tires.

After completing the road test the operator should have an idea of the cause of the vehicle's erratic handling.

Vehicle Repair

All parts that are worn or bent should be replaced before alignment of the vehicle is undertaken. An alignment rack—which is an expensive piece of equipment—is to be used for the correction of a vehicle's alignment and *not for the replacement of parts*. Parts which are bent or worn can be replaced in any stall in the shop.

Wheel Alignment Equipment

There are many different makes and models of wheel aligning equipment in general use. Some are of the portable type while other types are incorporated into a rack. A number of present alignment racks are an integral part of a hydraulic lift arrangement which permits the vehicle to be raised for front-end correction and repairs. When not being used for front-end service the rack can serve as a regular hydraulic lift for other types of repair work.

A shop that does a volume of front-end alignment work should definitely have an up-to-date alignment rack. While portable equipment can do the job it is decidedly more convenient and faster to use an alignment rack.

Every manufacturer of alignment equipment has detailed instructions on how to properly and efficiently use their equipment. Always follow these directions carefully and completely.

So as to make the alignment procedure more meaningful a step by step operation of the John Bean Visualiner follows. While the information is specifically directed to the one brand of commonly used alignment equipment the basic procedure will apply to a number of alignment racks using light beams.

Before starting any alignment job, the equipment must be checked for calibration. In general, all alignment machines must be level. They are usually calibrated to zero degree camber and zero inch toe. All manufacturers provide calibration instructions with their equipment, and it is advisable to check these instructions before beginning calibration. See Fig. 8-8.

The caster measuring feature of pres-

ent equipment cannot be calibrated by the operator. If there is any reason to doubt its accuracy, the manufacturer must be informed so that he can adjust it.

Vehicle Alignment

The vehicle is ready to be aligned after the steps outlined above have been completed. The procedure described in this section applies to aligning a vehicle on a John Bean Visualiner.

Putting the Car on the Rack

First, adjust the alignment rack to the wheel tread width of the vehicle to be aligned. Next, drive the vehicle on the rack up to the turntables and block one rear wheel. Caution: Do not let the engine run while the vehicle is on the rack. Then, inflate all four tires to the manufacturer's specifications.

Adjusting Vehicle Curb Height

Adjust the vehicle to the manufacturer's specified curb height. (Refer to Fig. 8-1.) If the vehicle is lower in the rear

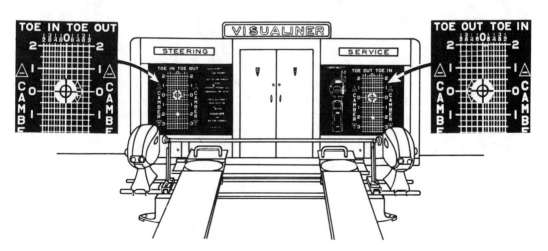

Fig. 8-8. All alignment equipment should be regularly tested for accuracy. Equipment must be absolutely level and ordinarily set at zero degrees camber and toe. (*John Bean Corp.*)

Fig. 8-9. Adjusting bars by means of a Torsion-air gage installed to aid in getting the correct curb height. Compare with Fig. 8-1. (*John Bean Corp.*)

than in the front, the condition may be due to broken or fatigued rear springs, lowering-blocks on the vehicle, or an excessive load in the trunk. If, however, the load of the vehicle is the one it normally carries (for example, a heavily loaded salesman's car), proceed with alignment with the load in the car. Requirements are different. Weak rear springs may be boosted by overload springs and spacers may be used to strengthen coil springs.

If the vehicle leans to the left or to the right, the reason may be a sagged spring on the weak side. Usually the only occupant of a vehicle is the driver; accordingly, it is not abnormal for a vehicle to lean slightly to the left.

To correct fatigued front springs replace the sagged springs with new ones. Always replace front springs in pairs

since failure to do so may cause the vehicle not to be level. Another method of correcting faulty curb height is to insert spacers or blocks between the coils of the spring. Still a third means is to use spacers underneath the spring—that is, between the bottom of the spring and the lower control arm. Torsion bar readjustment is accomplished by means of special adjustment screws, which are part of the bars themselves. Specifications for this operation are supplied by the manufacturer. See Fig. 8-9.

Adjusting and Checking Wheel Bearings for Loose Parts

Pull the vehicle on the turntables and reblock the rear wheels. Lift the left front wheel under the lower control arm until the wheel just clears the turntable.

Check for loose parts by shaking the wheel in a direction horizontal to the ground. This test will reveal loose ball joints and steering system parts. By shaking the wheels vertically, you will be able to check loose kingpins, worn ball joints, and loose wheel bearings. A movement of more than one-quarter inch of the wheel either inward or outward—at the bottom of the wheel—must be considered excessive. Such a condition may necessitate replacement of the kingpins or ball joints.

To adjust the wheel bearings, first tighten the spindle nut firmly and then back off one-sixth of a turn. If a cotter pin hole is not lined up with a slot in the nut, move the nut slightly to align the hole with a slot. When the nut is correctly adjusted, you will not be able to move it with the fingers if the installation is of the ball-bearing type. Roller bearing installations require that the nut be movable by the fingers. Finally, install the cotter pin and be sure to bend it properly so that it will not interfere with the static collector in the grease cap. Note: From this point on it is essential that you understand the contents of Chapter 7 as background for the technical instructions which follow.

Clamp Mirror to Wheel

Place two mounting feet (brackets to hold mirror to wheel) against the lip of

Fig. 8-10. In checking the mirror assembly located next to the projection head, rotate the mirror about its axis and note if the cross hair spot stays at the same place on the screen. If the spot moves, the mirror assembly should be sent to a factory service center for readjustment. (*John Bean Corp.*)

Fig. 8-11. Mounting mirror on the wheel. *(John Bean Corp.)*

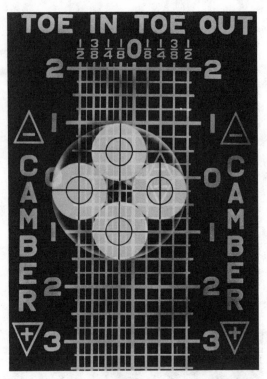

Fig. 8-12. Vertical travel is the distance from the negative one-half degree to the positive one degree. One-half of the total movement is three-quarters of one degree. A vehicle wheel that has a total run-out of three-quarters of one degree vertically or three-eighths of one inch horizontally would have to be straightened or replaced. *(John Bean Corp.)*

the wheel rim. Slide the mirror on its bar assembly until the shaft of the mirror is in line with the center of the wheel's spindle. Place a third mounting foot against the wheel rim and rotate the clamp to lock the mirror assembly on the wheel. Rotate the mirror assembly to check for the accuracy of the wheel mirror assembly. The cross-hairs should remain in the same spot on the screen. See Figs. 8-10 and 8-11.

Rotate Left Wheel to Compensate for Lateral Run-Out

Lift the vehicle with a jack and observe the pattern that the cross-hair spot makes on the screen. Observe the total vertical travel of the cross hair. See Fig. 8-12. Lower the wheel to the turntable when the cross-hair spot is in the lowest position on the screen. Divide the total amount of vertical travel by two and mark the spot corresponding to this calculation on the wall chart below the zero degree line. (A good way to mark

the spot is to use a small bar magnet and assume its center is the line you want.) Now turn the knob on the rear of the projection head to bring the zero degree camber mark in line with the center of the magnet you have placed on the chart. The cross-hair spot will now show the camber of the left wheel. Record this reading. See Fig. 8-13.

Camber Reading of the Right Wheel

Lift the vehicle with a jack and repeat the procedure described above for the right wheel. Record the camber reading. See Fig. 8-14.

Fig. 8-13. Camber reading of the left wheel shows the cross hair at one-half degree below the zero mark. This means the reading is one-half degree positive. (*John Bean Corp.*)

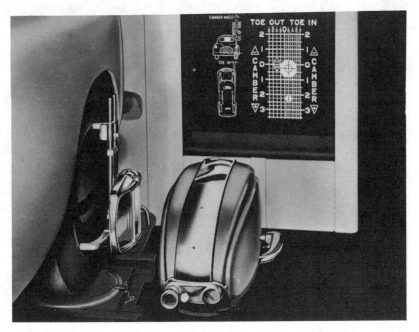

Fig. 8-14. Camber reading of the right wheel shows the cross hair at one-quarter degree below the zero mark. This means the reading is one-quarter degree positive. (*John Bean Corp.*)

Check Toe of Both Wheels

Manipulate the left front wheel until it is recorded at zero degree toe. The cross-hair spot on the right wheel screen will now indicate the total front wheel toe-in. This reading has no relationship to the final toe reading since readjustment of camber or caster will change the toe of the front wheels. The real purpose of checking toe at this stage is to aid in making an accurate check of the toe-out on turns. This is the difference in angles between the two front wheels and the car frame when a turn is made. The inner wheel turns out more.

Check Caster of Right Wheel

Turn the knob on the rear of the projection head until the caster chart is shown on the screen. To determine the caster of the right wheel, move the rear of the wheel inward toward the body of the car (which means the car would be turning to the right) until the cross-hair spot on the caster chart on the screen shows the wheel is turned twenty degrees. See Fig. 8-15. Now turn the knob on the rear of the projection head until the zero degree line on the caster chart falls on the horizontal line of the cross-hair spot.

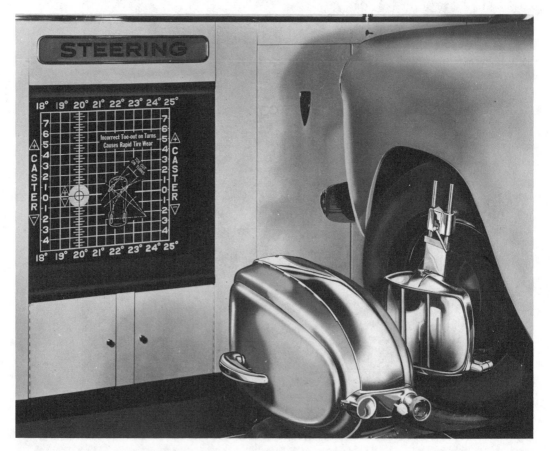

Fig. 8-15. To set the caster chart turn the rear of the wheel in 20 degrees and move the 0 degree mark on the caster chart over the cross hair spot. (*John Bean Corp.*)

Fig. 8-16. When the wheel is turned in 20 degrees at the front, the cross hair spot shows the caster of the wheel. Caster reading indicated in the photograph above is one and one-half degrees positive. (*John Bean Corp.*)

Now turn the wheel inward at the front an arc of twenty degrees (vehicle turning to the left). The location of the cross-hair spot on the caster chart now indicates the caster angle of the right wheel. See Fig. 8-16.

Check the Toe-out on Turns of the Left Wheel

Move to the left wheel and turn the knob on the projection head until the caster chart is on the screen. Since the right wheel has been left at a twenty-degree angle, the caster chart on the left side of the machine will indicate the number of degrees of toe-out on turns of the left wheel. If the toe reading when the wheels were straight ahead was toe-out, then the toe-out on turns will be too high.

Check Caster of Left Wheel

Follow the steps in the section on checking caster of right wheel, above. Make sure the wheel is turned twenty degrees into a left turn. See Figs. 8-15 and 8-16.

Check the Toe-out on Turns of the Right Wheel

After recording the left wheel caster, note that the left wheel is in twenty de-

Fig. 8-17. The steering axis inclination gage is installed on the nut. The movement of the bubble as the wheel is steered through an arc of 40 degrees is the steering axis inclination. The space between each full line on the bubble represents one degree. (*John Bean Corp.*)

grees into a left turn. This means that by looking at the right wheel caster the right wheel toe-out on turns may be recorded.

Steering Axis Inclination

All readings have now been taken except steering axis inclination. Normally such inclination is not measured unless the steering knuckle is suspected of misalignment. Fig. 8-17 illustrates the steering axis inclination gage in use.

Caster and Camber Specifications

Read from the specification chart the camber and caster angles and toe-in adjustment for the year and model of the vehicle. A specification of one-half degree for either camber or caster means *plus* (positive) one-half degree. A tolerance of plus or minus one-half degree applies to all camber and caster specifications on the chart when a single angle is shown. For example, one-half degree is given as a caster angle; therefore one-half degree positive caster with the tolerance may be adjusted on the vehicle from one-half plus one-half or one, to one-half minus one-half, or zero. Record the camber, caster, and toe-in specifications.

The specifications as given on the chart are for both front wheels. If the vehicle were driven on a flat level road and with a uniform passenger load, the same caster and camber angles for each wheel would be satisfactory. Since, however, most roads are crowned to promote drainage, and most vehicles carry only a single person, setting the camber and caster of each wheel the same amount may not always result in a satisfactory alignment job.

The Customized Alignment Job

There are some useful guides for doing a proper alignment job. A few of them are included.

A vehicle will pull to the wheel having the most positive camber. Details are explained in Chapter 7. The left wheel, accordingly, should have the more positive camber setting to compensate for the road crown which tends to pull the vehicle to the right. For example, if the camber specification is zero degree or zero plus one-half or minus one-half or minus one-half to plus one-half, the left wheel could be set at plus one-half degree camber and the right wheel at zero degree camber. This is the maximum difference allowed between front wheels. An average crowned road would be compensated for by a one-quarter degree difference between the camber of the two front wheels. An example would be: left wheel plus one-half degree, right wheel plus one-quarter degree.

Practical camber specifications are from zero to plus one-half of a degree. Setting camber at less than zero may cause inside tire wear, while adjusting camber at more than plus one-half on the left wheel may cause outside tire wear.

A vehicle will pull toward the wheel having the least positive or the most negative caster. Therefore, the left wheel should be adjusted to have less positive or more negative caster than the right wheel. This arrangement will compensate for the crown in the road. If the caster specification is minus one-half degree, leeway—with the permissible varia-

tion of one-half degree—would be from zero to minus one degree. The left wheel could then be set at minus one-half degree and the right wheel at zero degree. To compensate for the crown of the road, one-half degree caster is the maximum permissible difference allowed between front wheels.

Either camber or caster may be used to compensate for the right pull of the vehicle on the crowned road. On severe crowns both camber and caster adjustments may be used.

If a heavy person rides in a small car by himself, adjust the camber equally on both front wheels. The driver's weight will cause the vehicle to lean to the left, making the left wheel camber become positive and the right wheel camber become negative, automatically compensating for the crown in the road.

Caster is usually varied in its range of specification to give better handling of the vehicle. The mechanic should adjust caster toward the negative extreme of the specifications (that is, zero plus or minus one-half degree would be adjusted to minus one-half degree) if the vehicle is to carry heavy loads or if the driver wants a vehicle that is easy to steer. On the other hand, he should adjust caster toward the positive side (plus one-half degree) if the vehicle is to travel mountain roads or if the driver wishes more stability on flat, level roads.

Determine Corrections

Determine the camber and caster angles from the specifications and alter them to suit the needs of the vehicle. Record these angles next to the angles you wrote down when you checked the vehicle. With the two readings side-by-side determine which way you must move the wheel or the steering axis to readjust camber and caster on the left front wheel. For example, if the actual

Fig. 8-18. Eccentric pin.

three-quarters of a degree. If the caster reading had been plus one-half degree and should be zero degree, the top of the kingpin or upper ball joint should be moved one-half degree toward the front of the car.

Camber Adjustments

Eccentric pins have been used on early independent front suspension in connection with kingpins. To operate the eccentric a screwed-in grease fitting must be removed from the upper pin bushing and a lock bolt holding the pin loosened. Insert an Allen wrench into the pin through the grease fitting hole. Turning the pin one-half turn changes camber approximately one degree. A full turn will not change camber because the pin is an eccentric. See Fig. 8-18.

Eccentric bushings are located on the upper control arm outer pin inside the steering knuckle support. They are kept from turning by a bolt which is fitted

camber reading had been minus one-quarter degree and the new specification calls for plus one-half degree, you should move the top of the wheel outward

Fig. 8-19. Eccentric bushing.

through the steering knuckle support. Camber change per turn of the bushing is approximately the same as with the eccentric pin. One-half turn of the bushing will change the camber angle a maximum of one degree. See Fig. 8-19.

An eccentric bushing is located between the steering knuckle and the upper ball joint stud on Cadillac cars to adjust camber. See Fig. 8-20. The caster is adjusted by changing the length of the lower control arm strut rod. See Fig. 8-21.

Eccentric washers are used to connect either the upper pivot shaft to the upper control arm or the lower pivot shaft to the lower control arm. In either instance both washers (one at each side of the control arm) must be rotated the same amount and in the same direction or the caster angle will be changed. See Fig. 8-22.

Shims are usually used between the upper pivot shaft and the vehicle frame to change camber. They can also be placed between the upper pivot shaft bracket and the frame side rail. Adding shims will result in positive camber in some installations; in others it will result in negative camber. See Fig. 8-23.

Caster Adjustments

Caster is usually the first element checked because more adjustment is possible for caster than for camber. There are several ways to accomplish the necessary adjustments.

As explained above in the section on camber adjustments, eccentric pins and bushings are used in installations with

Fig. 8-20. Upper ball joint eccentric.

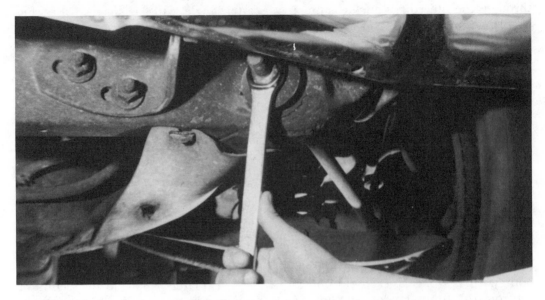

Fig. 8-21. Strut rod caster adjustment.

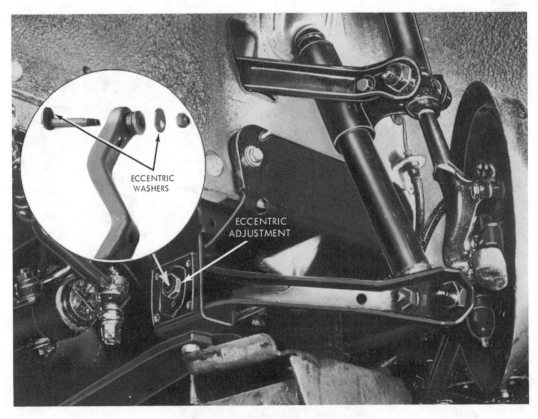

ECCENTRIC
WASHERS

ECCENTRIC
ADJUSTMENT

Fig. 8-22. Eccentric washers on cams.

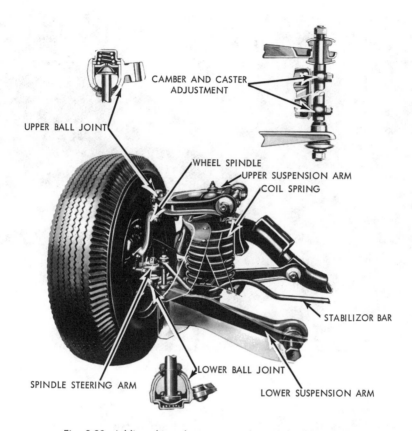

CAMBER AND CASTER ADJUSTMENT

UPPER BALL JOINT

WHEEL SPINDLE

UPPER SUSPENSION ARM

COIL SPRING

STABILIZOR BAR

SPINDLE STEERING ARM

LOWER BALL JOINT

LOWER SUSPENSION ARM

Fig. 8-23. Adding shims decreases camber. (*John Bean Corp.*)

kingpins. Camber adjustment is accomplished by manipulation of these eccentrics. As the pin or bushing is turned to achieve a camber change, however, the steering knuckle support is moved either forward or backward. This movement causes a change in caster. A forward placement of the steering knuckle support results in a negative caster. A backward movement produces positive caster. Usually, two turns of the bushing or pin will result in a total caster change of about two degrees. See Figs. 8-18 and 8-19.

Shims are used to change caster only if they are changed equally at both front and rear shaft mounting bolts. If only one shim is removed from the front mounting bolt, the camber goes in the positive direction and the caster goes in the positive direction. See Fig. 8-23.

Lower control arm strut rod nuts can be used to shorten or lengthen the distance between the lower control arm and the frame. When the distance is shortened on a strut rod mounted in front of the wheels, the caster becomes more positive. Increasing the distance will move the caster in a negative direction. See Fig. 8-21.

Many late model cars now adjust camber and caster by sliding the upper control arm shaft on the frame. The bolts that clamp the shaft to the frame are mounted in slotted holes. Special tools that hook over the shaft and into a hole in the frame are available to aid in adjustment. See Fig. 8-24.

Fig. 8-24. Slotted hole adjustment.

The tools are locked into place before the shaft bolts are loosened. Sliding the front bolt outward (away from the engine) will cause camber and caster to become more positive.

Most alignment equipment manufacturers have charts available that aid the front end mechanic in determining how he should perform the various adjustments to achieve the camber and caster specifications he desires. The Bishman Company provides a computer-like device which uses cards that correspond to the vehicle's make and model. Fig. 8-24 shows how the camber and caster adjustments are made to car factory specifications.

Steering Wheel Alignment and High Point Centering

If the steering wheel is not properly centered and/or the steering gear is off the high point with the front wheels in a straight ahead position, check and adjust in the following manner. Set the front wheels in an exact straight ahead position by driving the vehicle a short distance on a smooth surface to determine the steering wheel position at which the vehicle follows a straight path. Some vehicles will have a flat on the worm shaft. This should be at the top side when the wheels are straight ahead.

To adjust, loosen the adjusting sleeve clamps on both left and right hand tie rods. Turn both sleeves an equal number of turns in the same direction to bring the gear and wheel back on the high point (centered). Turning the sleeves an unequal amount will change the toe-in setting of the wheels. When correctly lined up, retighten the adjusting sleeve clamps.

After caster and camber have been

adjusted, the steering gear and linkage should be adjusted.

Make sure that the steering wheel is centered before the toe-in is adjusted. When the vehicle is traveling in a straight-ahead direction, certain factors are true with regard to the relation between the vehicle and the road. These factors are:

1) The rear wheels have approximately zero inches toe unless the rear axle housing is bent.

2) The steering wheel is in its position of high point; that is, in the correct, straight ahead driving position.

3) The front wheels are at zero inches toe.

These three factors are correlated by a process known as sighting the wheels. The process is the same regardless of the kind of rack used. It consists of the following steps:

1) Measure toe of the vehicle with either a toe bar or an alignment machine.

2) Center the steering wheel. Determine whether the steering wheel is in its correct position on the shaft. For full data refer again to Chapter 5.

3) Sight along the side of each front wheel, noting the amount of each rear wheel seen. From this observation determine which front wheel toes out or toes in more than the other.

4) Adjust the toe-in on the front wheel needing the most correction. Do this by turning sleeves on the tie rod. Be certain in this operation that you use the sleeve nearest the wheel you wish to adjust.

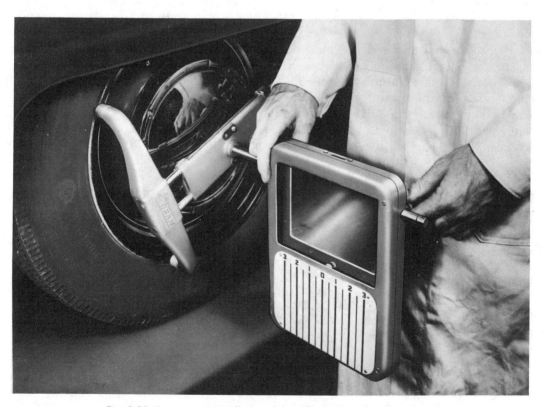

Fig. 8-25. Rear mirror installed on left rear wheel. (John Bean Corp.)

5) Resight the wheels. If the same amount of the rear wheel is not visible with the toe-in set, then adjust both sleeves equally until the wheels sight the same, keeping the steering wheel in the same straight ahead position.

Centering the Steering System on the Visualiner

One rear wheel is set on zero degrees toe—or in a straight ahead position—as shown on the screen. To achieve this position, clamp a mirror to a rear wheel (usually the left rear wheel) in a manner similar to that used with regard to the front wheel. See Fig. 8-25.

A light beam is projected from the rear of the alignment head to the mirror mounted on the rear wheel. The mirror then projects an image in the shape of a cross on the screen. By turning the knob on the rear of the projection head, a rear wheel toe chart can be made to appear on the screen. See Fig. 8-26.

Before an accurate reading may be taken, the lateral run-out of the rear wheel must be taken into account. To compensate for this factor, jack up the rear axle and rotate the left rear wheel. The cross on the screen will move on the left rear wheel chart if the wheel or axle

shaft is bent. Rotate the wheel to split the total run-out. This maneuver will place the cross hair on one-eighth of one inch toe-out. Lower the wheel and remove the jack. Move the vehicle sideward on the alignment rack until the left rear wheel toe reads zero inches. See Fig. 8-26. The left rear wheel is now in the straight ahead position.

Adjust the left front wheel toe-in at zero inches. Then turn the tie rod adjusting sleeve on the right front wheel until it reads the toe-in specified by the vehicle manufacturer. Make certain the steering wheel is in the straight ahead position.

Recheck All the Nuts and Bolts You Have Loosened

Remove the mirror assembly and push the vehicle off the turntable. Back the vehicle off the rack and road test it.

Know how to interpret your diagnosis and remedy the faults you find. Learn how to start with a known fault and, by a study of the conditions revealed in the course of an inspection, learn the specific remedies for specific faults. Make corrections without requiring costly and extensive rebuilding of the entire suspension system to create a "like new" situation.

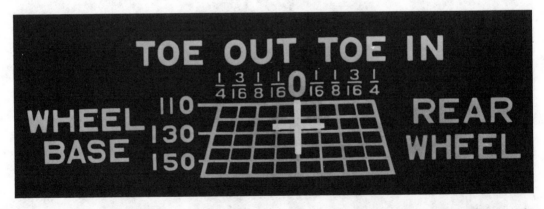

Fig. 8-26. The cross on the rear wheel toe chart shows the rear wheel is on zero or straight ahead. (John Bean Corp.)

TRADE COMPETENCY TEST

1. What is the purpose of making a pre-alignment visual inspection before attempting correction?

2. What misalignment conditions may be indicated by tire wear?

3. Why should a vehicle be road tested before checking for misalignment?

4. If worn suspension and steering parts are not repaired before an alignment job is done what may be the results?

5. How often should you check the wheel alignment equipment?

6. Why should springs be replaced in pairs?

7. How do you adjust front wheel bearings?

8. Why should the left front wheel have more positive camber, in some cases, than the right wheel?

9. What different types of adjustments may be used to control camber setting?

10. Why is caster usually adjusted first during the alignment procedure?

APPENDIX
REVIEW OF MATH—
INCLUDING METRIC

Only basic information and items which have general use in the trade can be covered, including:

> Operations with Fractions and Decimals
> Changing Fractions to Decimals and Decimals to Fractions
> Metric-to-English and English-to-Metric Conversions

It is assumed that all readers understand the fundamental processes of adding, subtracting, multiplying and dividing whole numbers and are familiar with common units of measurement such as feet, yards, pounds, gallons, etc.

For a more detailed study of mathematical problems and formulas, mathematics books should be consulted.

Operations With Fractions

Addition

To add fractions with the same *denominator* (lower part), such as $\frac{1}{8}$ + $\frac{2}{8}$, add the *numerators* (upper parts) and place this sum over the *common denominator* (bottom number). Thus, $\frac{1}{8} + \frac{2}{8} = \frac{3}{8}$. When the sum

174

of numerators is larger than the common denominator, such as $9/8$, divide this new numerator (top) by the denominator (bottom), giving a *mixed number* (whole number with fractional remainder). Thus, $9/8 = 1\frac{1}{8}$.

To add fractions with different denominators, multiply both numerator and denominator of each fraction by a number that will make the denominators equal. Any multiplier may be used without changing the quantity of the fraction. For example, $\frac{1}{4} = \frac{2}{8} = \frac{4}{16} = \frac{8}{32}$, etc. Similarly, $\frac{1}{4} = \frac{3}{12} = \frac{9}{36}$, etc.

After all fractions to be added have been changed so as to have a common denominator, add the new numerators (top numbers) and place this sum over the common denominator (the bottom number). If the new fraction is larger than 1, it can be changed to a mixed number, as already explained. For example, if $\frac{1}{2}$, $\frac{3}{8}$ and $\frac{2}{3}$ were to be added, the common denominator (the bottom number) would be 24. Thus $\frac{1}{2}$ would become $\frac{12}{24}$, $\frac{3}{8}$ would become $\frac{9}{24}$ and $\frac{2}{3}$ would become $\frac{16}{24}$. To add: $\frac{12}{24} + \frac{9}{24} + \frac{16}{24} = \frac{37}{24} = 1$ and $\frac{13}{24}$. (Note that $\frac{37}{24}$ breaks down into $\frac{24}{24} + \frac{13}{24}$, thus, since $\frac{24}{24} = 1$, we get 1 and $\frac{13}{24}$, or $1\frac{13}{24}$.)

In some cases the various fractions to be added can be changed to have a common denominator by dividing instead of multiplying both numerators and denominators by the same number. Again, the quantities would not be changed. For example, $\frac{8}{32} = \frac{4}{16} = \frac{2}{8} = \frac{1}{4}$.

Although both numerator and denominator of *each individual fraction* must be multiplied or divided by the same number, it is not necessary that the same multiplier or divisor be used for *all fractions* to be added. Thus, to add $\frac{1}{5} + \frac{2}{3}$, the first fraction could be multiplied by $\frac{3}{3}$ giving $\frac{1}{5} = \frac{3}{15}$. The second fraction could be multiplied by $\frac{5}{5}$, giving $\frac{2}{3} = \frac{10}{15}$. The addition would then be $\frac{3}{15} + \frac{10}{15} = \frac{13}{15}$.

Subtraction

Change the fractions to have a common denominator as in the case of addition. Subtract the smaller of the new numerators from the larger and place this subtracted number over the common denominator. It is assumed that no negative fractions will be used, such as $-\frac{3}{8}$ or "minus three-eighths".

Multiplication

To multiply fractions there is no need to change them first so as to have a common denominator. Simply multiply all the numerators to obtain a new numerator and multiply all denominators to obtain a new denominator. Thus, $\frac{2}{3} \times \frac{1}{8} \times \frac{3}{5} = \frac{6}{120}$. (For the numerator: $2 \times 1 \times 3 = 6$; for the denominator: $3 \times 8 \times 5 = 120$.) This can be simplified to $\frac{1}{20}$ by dividing both numerator and denominator by 6.

Another method to simplify calculations is called *cancellation*. In multiplying a series of fractions with no intervening subtractions or additions, it often happens that the same digit appears in a numerator and a denominator. In such cases both numerator and denominator can be cancelled. Thus, in the above case, the digit 3 appears as the denominator in $\frac{2}{3}$ and as the numerator in $\frac{3}{5}$. These 3's cancel each other and disappear in the multiplication. Thus, $\frac{2}{3} \times \frac{1}{8} \times \frac{3}{5} = \frac{2}{40}$. This is readily simplified by dividing both numerator and denominator by 2, giving $\frac{1}{20}$ as the answer, exactly as before.

Division

Division of fractions is very simple but is best understood by example. Consider the problem $\frac{1}{2} \div \frac{2}{3} = ?$ Here the *dividend* (number to be divided) is $\frac{1}{2}$ and the *divisor* (number that divides it) is $\frac{2}{3}$. To do this operation, re-write the dividend without change, change the division sign $\div$ to a multiplication sign $\times$, invert numerator and denominator of the divisor $\frac{2}{3}$ to read $\frac{3}{2}$, and proceed to multiply as the sign directs. Thus $\frac{1}{2} \div \frac{2}{3} = \frac{1}{2} \times \frac{3}{2} = \frac{3}{4}$.

It comes as a surprise to some people unused to calculations with fractions that generally the quantities decrease when they are multiplied and increase when they are divided. In common speech, when a person speaks of "half an apple" he is multiplying $\frac{1}{2} \times 1$ apple, and thus decreasing the quantity.

Operations With Decimals

Decimal numbers, unlike ordinary fractions, have only numerators. Denominators are implied by the place of the last digit to the right of the decimal point. Thus, $0.1 = \frac{1}{10}$, $0.01 = \frac{1}{100}$, $0.001 = \frac{1}{1000}$, etc.

Any number of zeros may follow the significant digits in the decimal number without increasing the quantity. Thus, $0.68 = 0.680 = 0.680000000000$. Zeros to the left of the significant digits and immediately following the decimal point are another matter; the quantity decreases by a factor of 10 for each zero preceding these digits. Thus, $0.75 = \frac{75}{100}$, $0.075 = \frac{75}{1000}$, and $0.0075 = \frac{75}{10000}$.

(Note: It is generally considered good practice to place a zero before the decimal point where no whole number is included with the decimal remainder.)

Operations with decimals differ in no way from those used with whole numbers except in placement of the important decimal point. Because United States money is based on the decimal system, these operations are already familiar to nearly everyone.

Addition

Line up decimal numbers to be added so that the decimal points are directly under each other. Add as with whole numbers and place the decimal point in the sum in exactly the same location as in the numbers added. This is a case where neatness counts.

For example, add 3.236, 0.75, and 107.205. Arrange as:

$$3.236$$
0.750—Adding zero
107.205   to right

Adding gives 111.191

This is read as "one hundred eleven and one hundred ninety-one thousandths."

Subtraction

As with addition, arrange the decimal numbers with the decimal points directly underneath each other. Subtract as with whole numbers, and place the decimal point directly under those of the listed numbers.

For example, subtract 0.9 from 2.356. Arrange as:

                2.356
Subtracting   −0.900—Add 2 zeros
    gives   1.456   to right

Multiplication

Multiplication of decimal numbers differs from that of whole numbers only in placement of the decimal point in the product. Multiply the numbers. Then place the decimal point as many places to the left of the significant digits as the sum of such places in the numbers multiplied.

For example, multiply 0.9 × 0.3 × 0.5. The digits in the product will be 135. Since there are three places to the right of the decimal point in the numbers multiplied, the answer is pointed off as 0.135. Here the zero to the left of the decimal point has no meaning other than to assure that there is no whole number. The answer is read as "one hundred thirty-five thousandths."

Division

Division of decimal numbers differs from that of whole numbers only in placement of the decimal point in the *quotient* (the number resulting from the division). Consider the problem 7.835 ÷ 0.5 = ? Here 7.835 is the dividend and has three places of decimals to the right of the decimal point. The divisor, 0.5, has one place to the right of the decimal point. In this particular case the dividend has *two more places* of decimals than the divisor. This difference will determine the placement of the decimal point in the quotient. Dividing gives the digits 1567, the quotient, which is pointed off *two places* as 15.67, read as "fifteen and sixty-seven hundredths".

Changing Fractions to Decimals

A common fraction, such as ⅛, is an instruction to perform an operation. It says "divide 1 by 8". Doing this operation, as shown, converts it to a decimal number.

Set down and divide:

```
      0.125
  8 ) 1.000
      8
      ─────
      20
      16
      ─────
      40
      40
```

The quotient, 0.125 (read as "one hundred twenty-five thousandths), is

the conversion. Similarly, ⅜ is an instruction to divide 3 by 8:

```
      0.375
  8 ) 3.000
      2 4
      ─────
      60
      56
      ─────
      40
      40
```

TABLE 1 DECIMAL EQUIVALENTS OF COMMON FRACTIONS OF AN INCH

Common Fractions	Decimal Equivalents	Common Fractions	Decimal Equivalents	Common Fractions	Decimal Equivalents	Common Fractions	Decimal Equivalents
1/64	.015625	17/64	.265625	33/64	.515625	49/64	.765625
1/32	.03125	9/32	.28125	17/32	.53125	25/32	.78125
3/64	.046875	19/64	.296875	35/64	.546875	51/64	.796875
1/16	.0625	5/16	.3125	9/16	.5625	13/16	.8125
5/64	.078125	21/64	.328125	37/64	.578125	53/64	·828125
3/32	.09375	11/32	.34375	19/32	.59375	27/32	.84375
7/64	.109375	23/64	.359375	39/64	.609375	55/64	.859375
1/8	.125	3/8	.375	5/8	.625	7/8	.875
9/64	.140625	25/64	.390625	41/64	.640625	57/64	.890625
5/32	.15625	13/32	.40625	21/32	.65625	29/32	.90625
11/64	.171875	27/64	.421875	43/64	.671875	59/64	.921875
3/16	.1875	7/16	.4375	11/16	.6875	15/16	.9375
13/64	.203125	29/64	.453125	45/64	.703125	61/64	.953125
7/32	.21875	15/32	.46875	23/32	.71875	31/32	.96875
15/64	.234375	31/64	.484375	47/64	.734375	63/64	.984375
1/4	.25	1/2	.50	3/4	.75		

Thus, ⅜ = 0.375 (three hundred seventy-five thousandths).

Conversions of this type are required so frequently that tables such as the one shown in Table 1 have been compiled for quick reference.

Not all conversions are as neat as

the ones illustrated. For instance, $1/12 = 0.083333333333333333$ . . . (approx.) As many significant figures are retained in the conversion as practicality requires. For most applications 0.083 would be acceptable.

Changing Decimals to Fractions

Translate the decimal number to fractional form, then reduce this

fraction to its simplest form by dividing both numerator and denominator by the same number. For example, $0.84 = {}^{84}\!/_{100}$. This can be reduced to ${}^{42}\!/_{50}$ (dividing by 2), and again to ${}^{21}\!/_{25}$. No number can evenly divide both 21 and 25, so ${}^{21}\!/_{25}$ is the simplest form and the fractional conversion.

Metric-to-English and English-to-Metric Conversions

Rapid expansion of trade and industry on an international basis in the past two decades has increased the need for understanding of both the *metric* or CGS (Centimeter-Gram-Second) system used by nearly all countries of the world and the *English* or FPS (Foot-Pound-Second) system used by the United States and some other English-speaking countries.

If the co-existence of two systems seems inconvenient, as it is, remember that in respect to worldwide agreement we are the exception. In view of the increasing need for a universal system to measure lengths, areas, volumes, weights, temperatures, etc., it now seems likely that the CGS system will ultimately replace the FPS system despite immense costs and problems that will be involved in making the changeover.

Table 2 lists factors for converting units from metric to English, while Table 3 lists factors for converting from English to metric units.

To convert a quantity from *metric* to *English* units:

1. Multiply by the factor shown in Table 2.
2. Use the resulting quantity "rounded off" to the number of decimal digits needed for practical application.
3. Wherever practical in semi-precision measurements, convert the decimal part of the number to the nearest common fraction.

To convert a quantity from *English* to *metric* units:

1. If the English measurement is expressed in fractional form, change this to an equivalent decimal form.
2. Multiply this quantity by the factor shown in Table 3.
3. Round off the result to the precision required.

Relatively small measurements, such as 17.3 cm, are generally expressed in equivalent millimeter form. In this example the measurement would be read as 173 mm.

TABLE 2 CONVERSION OF METRIC TO ENGLISH UNITS

LENGTHS:		WEIGHTS:	
1 MILLIMETER (mm)	= 0.03937 IN. OR = 0.003281 FT	1 GRAM (g)	= 0.03527 OZ. (AVDP)
1 CENTIMETER (cm)	= 0.3937 IN.	1 KILOGRAM (kg)	= 2.205 LBS
1 METER (m)	= 3.281 FT OR 1.0937 YDS	1 METRIC TON	= 2205 LBS
1 KILOMETER (km)	= 0.6214 MILES	**LIQUID MEASUREMENTS:**	
AREAS:		1 CU CENTIMETER (cc)	= 0.06102 CU IN.
1 SQ MILLIMETER	= 0.00155 SQ IN.	1 LITER (= 1000 cc)	= 1.057 QUARTS OR 2.113 PINTS OR 61.02 CU INS.
1 SQ CENTIMETER	= 0.155 SQ IN.		
1 SQ METER	= 10.76 SQ FT OR 1.196 SQ YDS	**POWER MEASUREMENTS:**	
		1 KILOWATT (kw)	= 1.341 HORSEPOWER
VOLUMES:		**TEMPERATURE MEASUREMENTS:**	
1 CU CENTIMETER	= 0.06102 CU IN.	TO CONVERT DEGREES CELSIUS TO DEGREES FAHRENHEIT, USE THE FOLLOWING FORMULA: DEG F = (DEG C X 9/5) + 32	
1 CU METER	= 35.31 CU FT OR 1.308 CU YDS		

SOME IMPORTANT FEATURES OF THE CGS SYSTEM ARE:
1 CC OF PURE WATER = 1 GRAM. PURE WATER FREEZES AT 0 DEGREES C AND BOILS AT 100 DEGREES C.

TABLE 3 CONVERSION OF ENGLISH TO METRIC UNITS

LENGTHS:		WEIGHTS:	
1 INCH	= 2.540 CENTIMETERS OR 25.40 MILLIMETERS	1 OUNCE (AVDP)	= 28.35 GRAMS
1 FOOT	= 30.48 CENTIMETERS OR 304.8 MILLIMETERS	1 POUND	= 453.6 GRAMS OR 0.4536 KILOGRAM
1 YARD	= 91.44 CENTIMETERS OR 0.9144 METERS	1 (SHORT) TON	= 907.2 KILOGRAMS
1 MILE	= 1.609 KILOMETERS	**LIQUID MEASUREMENTS**	
AREAS:		1 (FLUID) OUNCE	= 0.02957 LITER OR 28.35 GRAMS
1 SQ IN.	= 6.452 SQ CENTIMETERS OR 645.2 SQ MILLIMETERS	1 PINT	= 473.2 CU CENTIMETERS
		1 QUART	= 0.9463 LITER
1 SQ FT	= 929.0 SQ CENTIMETERS OR 0.0929 SQ METER	1 (U.S.) GALLON	= 3785 CU CENTIMETERS OR 3.785 LITERS
1 SQ YD	= 0.8361 SQ METER	**POWER MEASUREMENTS**	
VOLUMES:		1 HORSEPOWER	= 0.7457 KILOWATT
1 CU IN.	= 16.39 CU CENTIMETERS	**TEMPERATURE MEASUREMENTS**	
1 CU FT	= 0.02832 CU METER	TO CONVERT DEGREES FAHRENHEIT TO DEGREES CELSIUS, USE THE FOLLOWING FORMULA: DEG C = 5/9 (DEG F-32)	
1 CU YD	= 0.7646 CU METER		

INDEX

Numerals in **bold type** refer to illustrations.

Part Two
Disc
and
Drum
Brake
Service

CONTENTS

CHAPTER 1

BRAKE ASSEMBLIES

Purpose of Brakes

The purpose of the brake system on an automobile is to stop the vehicle, or to slow down its rate of travel, as required at any time during operation. Whenever an automobile is in motion the safety of the operator, passengers, pedestrians, other vehicles, and public property depends upon the proper functioning of the brakes with which the vehicle is equipped. The brakes must be capable of stopping the vehicle quickly and reliably at all times and under varying conditions to avoid collisions and to permit the operator to retain control of the vehicle.

In all states, regulations exist which require that vehicles be equipped with brakes which possess definite performance characteristics. In most instances, these standards are set by law. Many states or communities require periodic brake examinations, carried out by qualified authorities, to insure the highest possible standards of safety.

Automotive vehicles are equipped with two braking systems to conform to existing automotive safety regulations. The service brake system, which operates on all four wheels is applied through hydraulic pressure brought to bear when the operator applies pressure to the brake pedal. The second system is the parking brake system, which operates the service brake shoes on the rear wheels through a lever and cable arrangement. On most vehicles, the parking brake is also operated by foot pressure.

Any mass in motion represents energy. This energy must be absorbed or converted to some other form to stop the motion. In the braking system, this is accomplished by converting the energy of motion into heat.

Brakes are mechanical devices using the force of friction to overcome motion. Any two surfaces in contact with each other resist the movement between them. The brake drum or disc and the wheel that turns with it is slowed by applying pressure of a non-rotating shoe and lining assembly against it.

1

The speed of a vehicle is built up by the power of its engine or gravity, or both. As the speed increases, the momentum or kinetic energy is also increased. This energy increases with the square of the speed. For example, if the speed is doubled, the energy developed is increased fourfold.

Under certain circumstances, an automotive engine capable of developing 100 hp may accelerate the vehicle to 60 mph in 30 seconds. The brakes of the vehicle, however, must be capable of stopping it in about ⅕ of this time—6 seconds. The comparative horsepower then required to stop is 500 hp.

The kinetic energy developed, due to the weight and speed of the vehicle, is converted into heat energy by the friction of the brake shoe and drum. This heat is dissipated into the surrounding air.

Factors Controlling the Stop

The speed of the vehicle and the type and condition of the road are usually considered the chief factors which control the vehicle's stop. Actually, a number of factors are involved.

Since stopping involves the absorption of energy, the greater the speed and the greater the vehicle load, the more energy that must be absorbed to stop the vehicle.

The maximum work the brakes can do is to hold the wheels from turning. However, the quickest stop is made not with the wheels sliding, but with the wheels just ready to slide. The coefficient of friction between the road surface and the tire is highest just before the wheels start to slide. The coefficient of friction between the tire and the road varies for different types and conditions of road surfaces.

Coefficient of Friction. Friction is the resistance to motion which takes place when one body is moved upon another and can be defined generally as the force acting between two bodies at their surface contact so as to resist their sliding upon each other. The ratio of the force required to slide a body at constant velocity along a horizontal plane surface, to the weight of the body is called the coefficient of friction. The greater the coefficient of friction, the more frictional force developed.

The condition of the tire tread is an important factor in controlling the stop. A new tread with adequate grooves between the rolling ribs provides a greater coefficient of friction than a smooth tire. With good tires and a good road surface, the effort to stop the wheel from turning increases. If the vehicle is traveling up a hill at the time of the stop, the force of gravity will assist in making the stop.

If a vehicle which is under load is traveling downhill at the time of the stop, the force of gravity will tend to keep the vehicle moving, therefore increasing the braking effort required.

All wheels, which carry any part of the load, should be equipped with brakes in order to provide the maximum braking effort. Any part of the load being carried by a wheel not equipped with brakes will increase the time required for the stop. For this reason, automotive vehicles are equipped with brakes at each wheel (four-wheel brakes).

The ability of the brakes to prevent the wheels from turning is controlled by the coefficient of friction between the brake lining and the brake drum (or brake disc, depending on the type of brake). Different grades of brake lining will have different coefficients of friction. Grease-soaked or glazed linings may have a tendency either to slip over the brake friction surface rather than hold to it, or to cause the brake to grab.

Another factor controlling the stop is the multiplication of the applied force by means of leverage. The increase over the applied physical force, when the driver pushes the brake pedal, depends on the mechanical ratio built into the (lever) brake pedal.

When the brake shoes are forced into contact with the rotating brake drum, there is a natural tendency for the shoe to follow the drum in the direction of rotation and thus to wedge the shoe more tightly against the drum. Drum brake design utilized today is such that the tendency to wedge the brake shoe more tightly against the revolving drum is used to increase the applied pressure. This factor is referred to as self-energization which increases the applied pressure to the brake shoe and thus reduces the physical effort required to apply the brakes.

The weight on both the front suspension and the rear axle is approximately equal on most vehicles when carrying average loads properly distributed. However, when the brakes are applied, there is a transfer of weight from the rear wheels to the front wheels, caused by the tendency of the vehicle to continue in its forward motion. The greater the deceleration (braking action), the greater the transference of weight from the rear to the front wheels. During the stop, the weight on the rear wheels is lessened, while the weight on the front wheels is increased by exactly the same amount. For this reason, brakes are designed so that more braking is accomplished on the front wheels than on the rear wheels.

The engine is used as a braking device, particularly when coasting or descending long grades. The braking effect of the engine is less when the transmission is in direct drive than when it is in the lower gears.

Stopping Distance

An important factor in braking is the stopping distance. This is the distance between the point the driver actually applies the brakes, and the point when the vehicle rolls to a full stop. The stopping distances shown in Table I are based on favorable road conditions and on average driver reaction time. Stopping distances will vary from those shown, depending on the type and condition of the road surface, the mechanical condition of the vehicle, and the variation of individual drivers' reaction time.

Some variations exist between individual drivers, as not all react in the

TABLE I STOPPING DISTANCES

VEHICLE SPEED M.P.H.	DISTANCE TRAVELED DURING DRIVER'S REACTION TIME	DISTANCE TRAVELED AFTER APPLICATION OF BRAKES	TOTAL STOPPING DISTANCE
20	22 FT.	22 FT.	44 FT.
30	33 FT.	50 FT.	83 FT.
40	44 FT.	88 FT.	132 FT.
50	55 FT.	138 FT.	193 FT.
60	66 FT.	200 FT.	266 FT.

same period of time when applying the brakes. The distances shown on Table I are based on average driver reaction time: that is, between the instant the driver decides to use the brakes, and the instant he actually moves his foot to the brake pedal.

Brakes are designed to stop a vehicle within the indicated distances while it is carrying its rated load on average road surfaces.

Poor road conditions or an overloaded vehicle will also increase the stopping distance. Worn linings, worn drums or discs, glazed linings, or grease-soaked linings also increase stopping distances by lowering the coefficient of friction.

NOTE: *The ideal lining is not necessarily the one with the highest coefficient of friction. Linings are selected according to the design of the brake and the particular vehicle on which they are to be used.*

Poor brake shoe-to-drum fit after a relining job prevents the full application of braking effort due to lack of full contact between the shoe and the rotating friction surface. Improper adjustment or wear, also prevents the full application of braking force.

Two types of brakes are being installed on present passenger vehicles. Until recently, the front and rear brakes were of the internal expanding type that contact the inside diameter of a drum upon application.

Most manufacturers are now installing a disc brake system on the front wheels with the conventional drum brake used on the rear wheels. A few vehicles will have disc brakes on both front and rear wheels. It is quite apparent that the disc brake is becoming more popular and will eventually replace the drum type brake system. For the sake of clarity, the two types of brakes will be discussed separately.

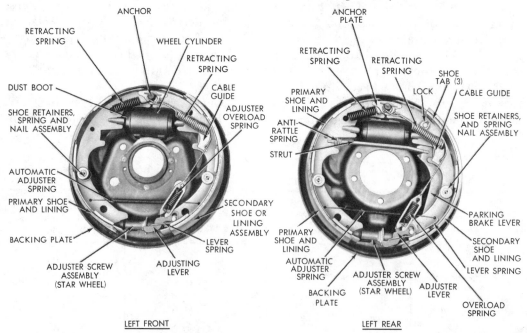

Fig. 1-1. Typical front and rear self-adjusting drum brake assemblies with components identified. (*Plymouth Div., Chrysler Corp.*)

Construction of Drum Brakes

Passenger vehicle drum brakes are of the hydraulic type whereby hydraulic pressure operates pistons inside wheel cylinders to force the brake lining into contact with the brake drum, when the brakes are applied.

Certain parts are common to all passenger vehicle drum brake assemblies. Included among these are a backing plate, brake shoe anchors, brake shoes, retracting springs, brake linings, brake drum, wheel cylinder and adjusting mechanisms. Figure 1-1 illustrates typical front and rear drum brake assemblies (shown at left and right respectively) with the drums removed.

Backing Plate

The backing plate, usually of ribbed pressed-steel construction, is rigidly bolted to the rear wheel axle housing for the rear brakes and to the steering knuckle assembly for the front brakes. See Fig. 1-1. This plate acts as a support for the anchor pins, wheel cylinder, retracting springs, adjusting mechanism and brake shoes. The brake backing plate carries the entire braking load for each wheel. It also forms a dust shield for the operating parts of each wheel brake.

Anchors

Anchor bolts (pins) provide a means of mounting the brake shoes to the backing plate and provide a pivot for the brake shoe. On most vehicles a single anchor bolt is used for both shoes, while on some older models one anchor bolt is used for each shoe. Some anchors are adjustable to permit adjustment of the anchored end of the shoe toward or away from the drum, to secure proper clearance between brake shoe and drum. All modern brake designs, however, feature a fixed anchor.

Brake Shoes

Brake shoes are of a *T*-section steel construction and are curved to fit the drum. A frictional material (brake lining) is either riveted or cemented (bonded) to the brake shoe.

One end of the brake shoe is attached to or held against the anchor bolt or pin. At the opposite end, the shoes are held in position by an adjuster screw. See Fig. 1-1. Pressure is applied by the wheel cylinder to force the shoes outward toward the drum. The shoes and lining are free to move outward to the drum. Springs or spring clips of various designs hold the shoes in proper position on the backing plate.

The terms used to distinguish between the two brake shoes vary with the design of the brake. If the brake is a non-servo brake (shoes not connected) the shoes will be referred to as the forward and reverse shoes, or as the leading and trailing shoes. If the brake is a servo-type brake, the shoes are referred to as the primary and secondary shoes. The primary brake shoe is the first shoe in the direction of forward rotation from the point of actuation (wheel cylinder). In a brake assembly using two wheel cylinders, both shoes are forward shoes.

Retracting Springs

Retracting springs are used to return the brake shoes to their released position. This is necessary to prevent any possible drag. In hydraulic brakes, the retracting springs also return the hydraulic fluid to the master cylinder. The location and number of retracting springs vary with the design of the brake. See Fig. 1-1.

Brake Lining

A molded type of brake lining (friction material) is used on automotive vehicles. The basic material of all brake lining is asbestos, used because of its high heat-resistant quality. Since the amount of work done by the secondary brake shoe is usually greater than the amount of work done by the primary shoe, the use of lining with a different coefficient of friction on each shoe is not uncommon.

Brake lining is usually purchased in sets attached to brake shoes by a bonding or riveting process. The edge of the lining of each shoe will be marked *primary* or *secondary*. Some linings are marked *forward* (primary) or *reverse* (secondary). Letter markings *A* through *G* indicate the manufacture of the material and the friction characteristics of the lining. The *G* code indicates that the material can withstand higher temperature before loss of friction than *A* coded lining.

Lining should be replaced before it is worn down to within $\frac{1}{64}''$ of the rivet heads or, in the case of bonded lining, before the lining is worn down to within $\frac{1}{32}''$ of the shoe.

Wheel Cylinders

Hydraulically operated wheel cylinders are used to force the brake shoe assembly into contact with the drum. Common practice is to use one wheel cylinder with two opposed pistons at each wheel. Each piston moves one brake shoe. If two separate wheel cylinders are used at one wheel, each wheel cylinder contains only one piston and operates one shoe.

Varying the size of the wheel cylinder will vary the amount of force exerted on the different brake shoes.

Brake Drums

Brake drums are usually made of cast iron fused to a pressed steel disc. This type of construction usually has cooling ribs cast around the drum providing the assembly with a better dissipation of heat. The drum, when mounted, is accurately centered on the hub and wheel. The friction surface of the drum is machined to present a smooth surface to the brake lining. The inner edge of the drum generally has an annular groove located between two flanges to assist in keeping dirt and moisture from entering the brake mechanism. A coil spring (dampener spring) is sometimes used around the outside of the drum to reduce brake noises.

Another type of brake drum construction is that made of cast aluminum alloy with a cast iron liner, as shown in Fig. 1-2. This type of installation has

Fig. 1-2. Brake drum made of cast aluminum alloy with a cast iron liner used for the friction surface. (Pontiac Div., General Motors Corp.)

ribs and fins to help dissipate heat to the air.

Drum Brake Design Variations

Self-Energizing Action

When the brakes are applied and the shoes are moved into contact with the rotating drum, the shoes have a tendency to follow, or rotate with, the drum. The shoe may be connected directly to the anchor or may float on its anchor (as in Fig. 1-3) so that a slight movement occurs before the shoe firmly seats on its anchor.

After the initial movement, the anchor prevents further movement of the shoe. Since the forward, or *leading,* shoe cannot move in the direction of drum rotation, it tends to pivot about its anchor. This has the effect of wedging the shoe into the drum. This wedging action greatly increases the stopping pressure applied by the shoe to the drum, and is referred to as *self-energizing action.* Because the *trailing* shoe pivots *away* from the drum, only the leading shoe possesses this self-energizing characteristic. If the drum rotation reverses, then the trailing shoe will become the shoe with self-energizing action.

Various degrees of self-energization

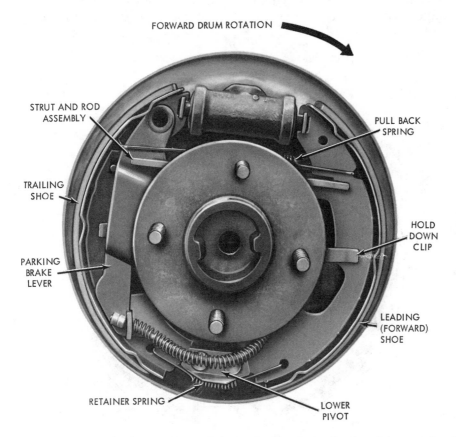

Fig. 1-3. Energizing action. The drum tends to pull the leading shoe in the direction of drum rotation. The shoe, pivoting on its anchor, wedges tightly against the drum. Only the leading shoe has self-energizing action, since the trailing shoe pivots away from the drum. (*Chevrolet Div., General Motors Corp.*)

have been used, depending upon the design of the brake.

Self-Energizing Brakes (Non-Servo)

Drum brakes have been classified by the extent to which their designs utilize self-energizing action.

The Lockheed two-forward-shoe brake design, shown in Fig. 1-4, featured two separate wheel cylinders and two anchors. The wheel cylinders and anchors were positioned so that *both* shoes were self-energizing in the forward direction. However, this design did not provide for self-energizing action in reverse braking.

The eccentric adjuster was used for minor adjustments to reduce wheel cylinder piston travel due to lining wear. The anchors were adjustable so that the shoes could be centered in the drum after a reline.

The Chrysler Corporation's center plane brake design, shown in Fig. 1-5, also employed two wheel cylinders and anchors. The shoes were inserted between the brake shoe support plate, and butted against an anchor block. The shoes were called floating shoes because they could move with respect to the anchor block when the brakes were applied. A major adjustment (centering the shoes to the drum after a reline) was not required on this brake design. A minor adjustment was made by rotating the adjusting cams in a forward drum direction to compensate for lining wear.

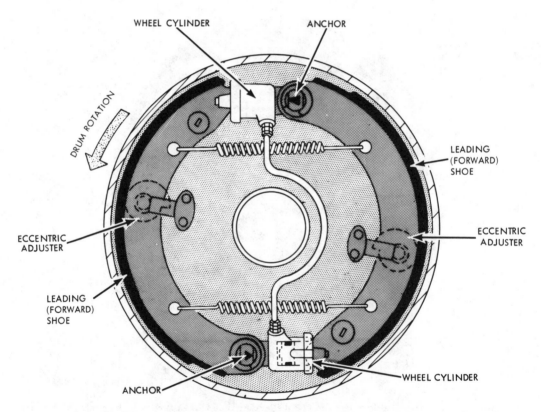

Fig. 1-4. In this design, two single-piston wheel cylinders and two anchors are positioned so that both shoes are self-energizing in the forward direction. (*Barrett Brake Co.*)

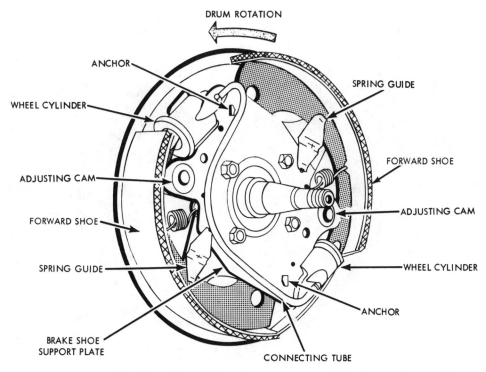

Fig. 1-5. In this design, both shoes are equally self-energizing. In addition, the floating shoes are free to center themselves in the drum when the brakes are applied. (*Barrett Brake Co.*)

Servo Brakes

Servo brakes are the most efficient drum brake design in terms of stopping pressure developed. The duo-servo brake has long since been adopted by all car manufacturers; brake servicemen will seldom be called on to service any other type of drum brake.

The servo brake employs a single anchor pin and a single, two piston, wheel cylinder. The shoes are free to float and are coupled together by an adjusting screw at the bottom, as shown in Fig. 1-6. When the brakes are applied, the friction between the linings and the rotating drum moves the primary shoe downward against the adjusting screw mechanism. The adjusting screw acts as a link transmitting the movement of the primary shoe to the lower end of the secondary shoe. The upper end of the secondary shoe is forced against the anchor. Self-energizing force develops in the primary shoe and is transmitted through the adjusting screw, where it contributes to a much greater self-energizing force in the secondary shoe. The secondary shoe develops approximately twice as much frictional force as the primary shoe because of this servo action—i.e., the primary shoe "serves" the secondary shoe to develop twice as much stopping pressure against the drum.

Fig. 1-6 illustrates the duo-servo brake, which has a two-piston wheel cylinder and functions equally well in both the forward and reverse directions.

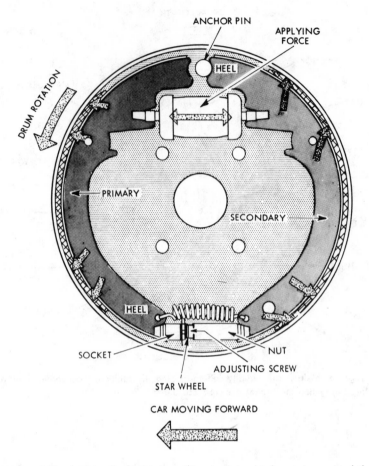

Fig. 1-6. Servo action. Self-energizing force developed by the primary shoe is transmitted through the adjusting screw to develop a still greater self-energizing force in the secondary shoe.

Self-Adjusting Duo-Servo Brakes

The latest design change involving the duo-servo brake is the self-adjusting mechanism. This mechanism is designed to continuously maintain the proper lining-to-drum clearance, which eliminates the periodic minor brake adjustment. This mechanism was first used in 1958.

Bendix Self-Adjusting Brakes. The self-adjusting mechanism is made up of a cable, cable guide, adjusting lever, adjusting screw assembly and adjuster springs, Fig. 1-7.

The brake will adjust itself whenever the vehicle is braked in reverse if the linings on the shoes have become worn to the point where the lining-to-drum clearance is too great. As the brakes are applied, the secondary shoe contacts, and tends to move in the direction of, the rotating drum. The secondary shoe moves *away from* the anchor pin since the car is moving in reverse.

The lever of the self-adjusting mechanism is attached to, and tends to move with, the secondary shoe (Fig. 1-7). However, the cable hooked to the lever is attached at its opposite end to the fixed anchor pin. Thus, the effect of the cable

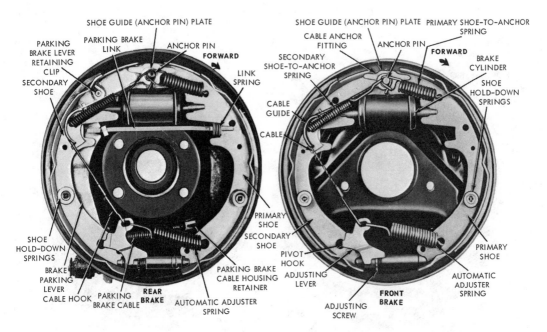

Fig. 1-7. Bendix-type, self-adjusting, duo-servo brake. (*Ford Customer Service Div., Ford Motor Co.*)

is to pivot the lever upward as the secondary shoe shifts away from the anchor pin. If the secondary shoe moves far enough away from the anchor pin (depending on the amount of lining worn from the shoes) the flange on the arm of the lever will catch in a new notch on the star wheel. When the brakes are released and the lever moves downward to its at-rest position, the star wheel spring rotates the star wheel by one notch, expanding the adjusting link.

This brake self-adjustment will provide trouble-free operation of the brakes. Rapidly backing the vehicle and applying the brakes while the drums are hot may result in the brake over-adjusting itself. This results in little or no drum-to-lining clearance. When the drum cools and contracts, the reduced clearance causes rapid brake lining wear as well as erratic brake operation.

Delco-Moraine Self-Adjusting Brakes. A great many automobiles use the Delco-Moraine self-adjusting brake shown in Fig. 1-8 which is very similar to the Bendix self-adjusting brake.

The self-adjusting mechanism consists of an adjuster lever, an actuating link, an adjusting screw assembly, an adjuster lever return spring, an override pivot and an override spring.

The self-adjusting mechanism operates only when the vehicle is moving backward and the brakes are applied. There must be sufficient clearance so the secondary shoe is able to move a predetermined distance toward the brake drum before adjusting will occur.

When the car is moving backward and the brakes are applied, friction between the primary shoe and the drum forces the primary shoe against the anchor pin. As the secondary shoe moves away from the anchor pin, the upper end of the adjusting lever is prevented from moving by the actuating link. This causes the adjuster lever to pivot on the sec-

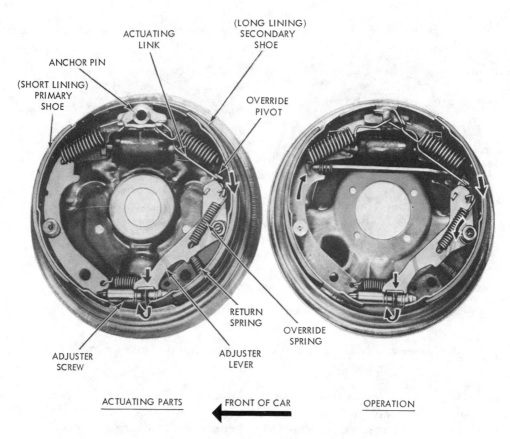

Fig. 1-8. Delco-Moraine, self-adjusting brake. (*Oldsmobile Div., General Motors Corp.*)

ondary shoe forcing the adjuster lever against the adjusting screw sprocket. If the linings are worn enough to permit the secondary shoe to move the predetermined distance, the adjuster lever will turn the adjusting screw one tooth, depending on the amount of lining wear. If the secondary shoe does not move the necessary distance, the movement of the adjuster lever will not be great enough to turn the adjusting screw. When the brakes are released, the adjusting lever return spring will move the adjuster lever into the adjusting position on the sprocket.

An override feature is built into the brake mechanism which allows the sec-

ondary shoe to be applied in reverse in the event the adjusting screw becomes "frozen" preventing the self-adjuster from operating.

When the vehicle is moving forward and the brakes are applied, the upper end of the secondary shoe is forced against the anchor pin due to the self-energizing action of the brakes and, therefore, the self-adjuster will not function.

Construction of Disc Brakes

The disc brake is a friction device similar to the drum brake which slows down and stops a moving vehicle. The rotating friction surface of a drum brake is a cylinder. Inside the cylinder are two brake shoes which are forced outward against the inner wall of the cylinder by

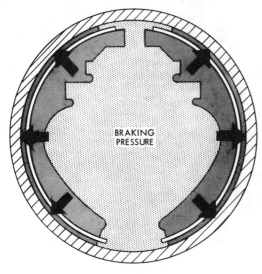

Fig. 1-9. Braking forces in a drum brake system *(Management and Marketing Institute)*

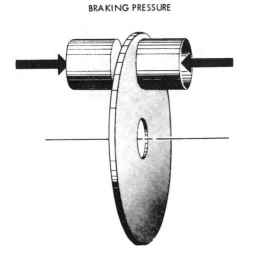

Fig. 1-10. Braking forces in a disc brake system. *(Management and Marketing Institute)*

hydraulically activated pistons and self-energizing forces, Fig. 1-9.

The rotating friction surface of a disc brake is a flat, circular plate. The brake shoes are positioned on both sides of the plate and push against the plate or disc when activated, as illustrated in Fig. 1-10.

All disc brake shoes are operated by hydraulic fluid pushing against one or more pistons, which in turn force the disc brake shoes against the sides of the disc. The components which make up the disc brake assembly are discussed below. The following section will discuss the more common variations in disc brake design.

Caliper

As stated above, the braking pressure applied to the disc (Fig. 1-10) is brought about by pistons which force the disc brake shoes against the disc. The pistons move inside cylinders which are machined inside a heavy malleable casting called a *caliper*.

A caliper may have one, two, or four pistons. A typical four-piston caliper is shown mounted on the brake disc in Fig. 1-11. Two and four-piston calipers are made up of two halves: an inner caliper housing and an outer caliper housing. The inner and outer housings are joined with special high-strength bolts and bridge the brake disc. The mating faces of the inner and outer housings of a four-piston caliper are shown in Fig. 1-12. The four pistons are clearly visible, together with the dust boots which keep the cylinders free of road dust and other contaminants.

The two-piston and four-piston caliper housings are connected hydraulically by either an external brake fluid transfer tube or by internally drilled passageways. An *O*-ring seal, Fig. 1-12, is used at the mating surfaces of the caliper halves to assure leak-proof connections between

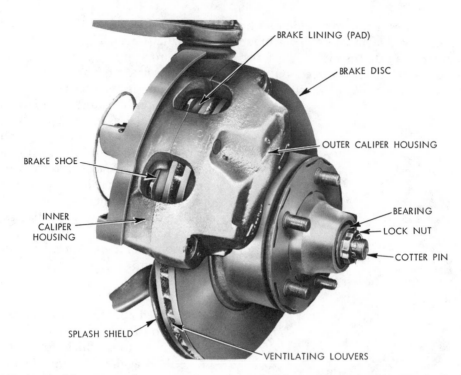

Fig. 1-11. A typical four-piston caliper mounted on a front wheel brake disc. (*Dodge Div., Chrysler Corp.*)

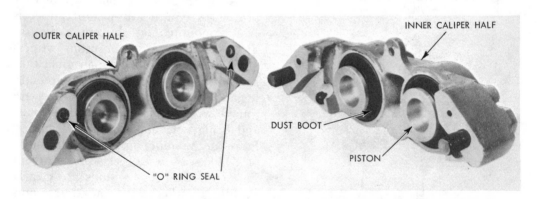

Fig. 1-12. A four-piston caliper is shown split into its inner and outer halves. The halves are turned to show the pistons in the caliper bores, the dust boots which keep the bores free of dirt, and the hydraulic passageways which connect the caliper halves. (*Oldsmobile Div., General Motors Corp.*)

the internal passageways of the caliper halves.

Caliper Mounting Bracket

The caliper is mounted either to a bracket bolted to the steering knuckle, as shown in Fig. 1-13, or by bolts directly to the steering knuckle, as shown in Fig. 1-14. In some designs, shims are used between the caliper and the mounting

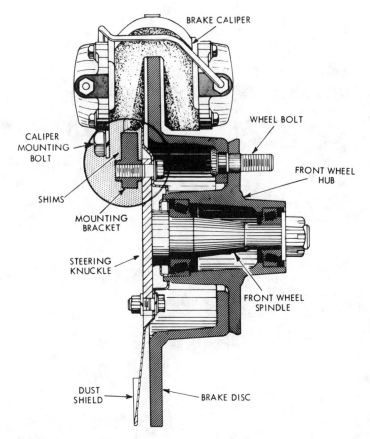

Fig. 1-13. Brake caliper mounting method. In this design the caliper is bolted to a mounting bracket, which in turn is bolted to the steering knuckle flange. The disc is attached to the hub by the wheel bolts.

bracket to center the caliper to the brake disc. See Fig. 1-13.

Brake Disc (Rotor)

The brake disc is usually made of cast iron. The disc is cast so that it is either solid (Fig. 1-13) or has ventilating slots (Fig. 1-11). The ventilating slots allow air to flow between the two friction surfaces of the disc for more efficient cooling.

The disc is fastened to the hub by wheel mounting stud hub bolts, as shown in Fig. 1-14, or by special bolts that are used only to hold the disc to the hub, as shown in Fig. 1-15.

Most hubs and discs are now cast together in one piece identified as a rotor.

Splash Shield

The inner surface of the brake disc is protected from road dirt and water by the splash shield, as shown in Fig. 1-15. The outer surface of the disc is protected by the wheel.

Disc Brake Pads or Shoes

Early disc brake designs used on cars imported from Europe had small two-piston calipers, which employed square-shaped friction pads. When the four-piston caliper became popular on American automobiles the friction device became more rectangular than square, and its name was changed from "friction pad" to

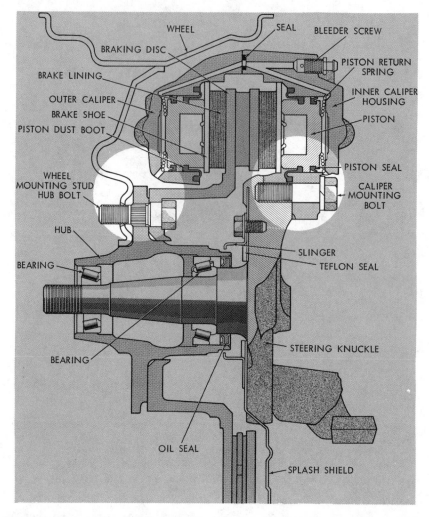

Fig. 1-14. In this disc brake design (Bendix Series E), the caliper is bolted directly to the steering knuckle with caliper mounting bolts. The brake disc is attached to the front wheel hub by the wheel mounting stud hub bolts. (*Plymouth Div., Chrysler Corp.*)

"disc brake shoe". A typical four-piston caliper disc brake shoe is illustrated in Fig. 1-16.

The "telltale tabs" bent into the metal back of the shoe rub against the outer circumference of the brake disc when the brake lining becomes worn to a thickness of $\frac{1}{32}$ of an inch or less. The rubbing of the metal backing of the brake shoe against the disc causes a noise which warns the driver that the brake shoes are worn and require replacement.

Disc Brake Shoe Retaining Devices

Since the disc brake shoe floats within the caliper, it must be held into the caliper by an external retainer or by internal depressions (pockets) machined into the caliper.

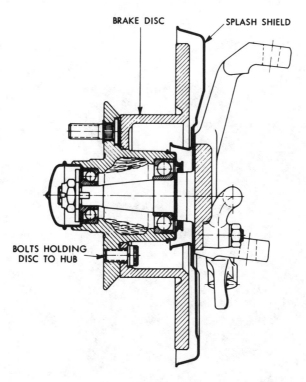

Fig. 1-15. In this disc brake design, the disc is attached to the hub by separate bolts. That is, the wheel studs are not used to hold the disc to the hub. (*Opel Div., General Motors Corp.*)

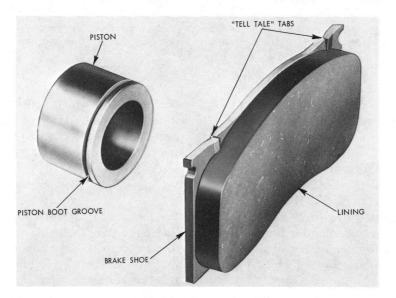

Fig. 1-16. A typical disc brake shoe is shown together with one of the pistons which force the shoe into contact with the disc. The piston is hollow for much of its length to facilitate its removal from the cylinder bore and to reduce heat transfer from the shoe to the hydraulic fluid. The piston is also grooved to provide a seat for the dust boot. (*Plymouth Div., Chrysler Corp.*)

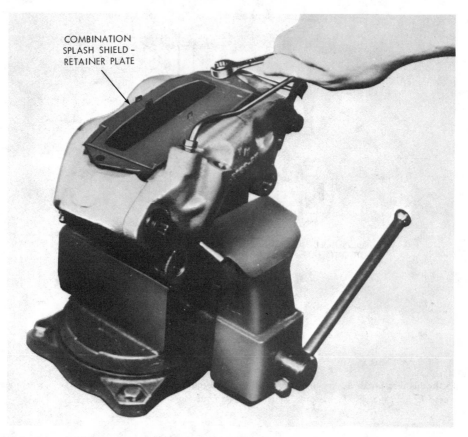

COMBINATION
SPLASH SHIELD –
RETAINER PLATE

Fig. 1-17. In this early design of a Kelsey-Hayes disc brake caliper, the shoes are held in the caliper by a re tainer plate. To remove the shoes, the caliper must be removed from the disc. (*Ford Motor Co.*)

The external retainer may be in the form of a *clip* held in place by a bolt. A retainer *plate,* which also serves as a road splash shield, is shown in Fig. 1-17. The plate contains two leaf springs that bear against the shoes to reduce brake shoe vibration and noise. Still another external retention method is the use of a retainer *pin,* as shown in Fig. 1-18. The pin fits through matching holes in the inner and outer housings and through a hole in the metal backing of each brake shoe.

The *internally-retained* disc brake shoe fits into a contoured pocket machined on the inside of the caliper as shown in Fig. 1-19. The contoured pocket provides a positive method of shoe retention which precludes slipping or misalignment. However, the caliper must be removed from the spindle and inverted to remove the shoes.

Disc Brake Wheels

Most cars with disc brakes require a different wheel than that used when the car has drum brakes. The cut-away view of a disc brake wheel, Fig. 1-20, shows that the center section of the wheel is welded at the extreme outer edge of the wheel rim. This must be done to provide clearance between the wheel and the caliper.

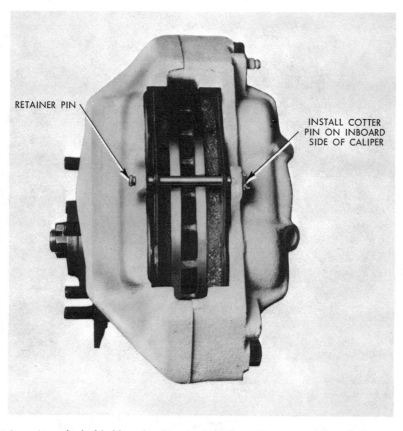

RETAINER PIN

INSTALL COTTER
PIN ON INBOARD
SIDE OF CALIPER

Fig. 1-18. Retainer pin method of holding the shoes in the caliper. The pin goes through the outer caliper half, outboard brake shoe, inboard shoe, and inboard caliper half. In this design, the shoe can be removed without removing the caliper. (Oldsmobile Div., General Motors Corp.)

Disc Brake Design Variations

Disc brake designs can be classified according to (1) the number of pistons in the caliper, (2) whether the caliper is fixed to the spindle or slides on its mounting bracket, and (3) whether the brake disc is solid or has cast-in ventilating fins.

One of the first American cars to use disc brakes was the 1950 Crosley. The design used had single-piston calipers which were fixed to both the front spindle and to the rear axle. An adjustment was provided to compensate for wear between the inner shoes and the brake disc. The Studebaker Company, from 1962 until they stopped manufacturing automobiles, offered a two-piston, fixed-caliper disc brake which had previously been used successfully on European cars.

Most disc brakes used on modern American cars through 1967 are of the four-piston, fixed-caliper design. Internally, all calipers have either lip-type piston seals (with piston return springs which hold the shoes against the disc at all times) or square seals which ride on the outer surface of the piston. The seal also provides a running clearance between the disc and the shoe.

The trend in disc brake designing in

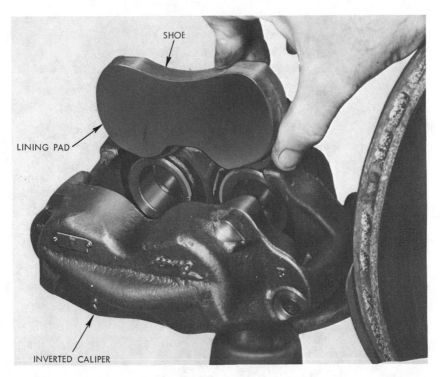

Fig. 1-19. In this Bendix design, the shoe is held in the caliper by the contour of the caliper. To remove the shoe the caliper must be removed from the disc. The shoe is then lifted out of the pocket. (*Plymouth Div., Chrysler Corp.*)

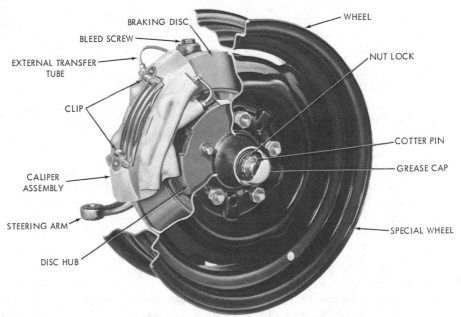

Fig. 1-20. Note how the wheel is shaped to clear the caliper assembly. In this disc brake design, the shoes are held in the caliper with retainer clips. (*Plymouth Div., Chrysler Corp.*)

the last few years has been to use a caliper that slides or floats on its mounting bracket so that an adjustment device is not required. Also, a ventilated disc is usually used in preference to a solid disc for better cooling.

Single-Piston, Sliding-Caliper Disc Brakes

From 1968 to 1972 all Ford passenger cars (except Lincoln) which are equipped with power brakes have a front spindle-mounted, single-piston, sliding-caliper disc brake. A self-adjusting, duo-servo drum brake is used for the rear brakes.

A single piston pushes the inner disc brake shoe against the inboard face of the brake disc. Then the caliper housing slides in its mounting bracket to bring the outer shoe into contact with the outer face of the disc. A single-piston, sliding-caliper disc brake assembly is illustrated in Fig. 1-21. The exploded

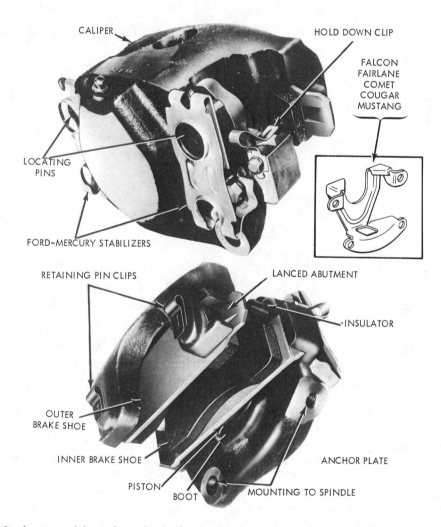

Fig. 1-21. Single-piston, sliding-caliper disc brake. In this design the single inboard piston forces the inner shoe against the disc while the sliding caliper moves inward, bringing the outer shoe against the disc. (*Ford Div., Ford Motor Co.*)

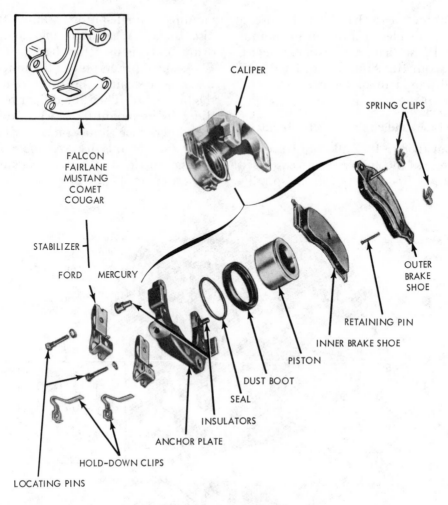

CALIPER

SPRING CLIPS

FALCON
FAIRLANE
MUSTANG
COMET
COUGAR

STABILIZER

FORD   MERCURY

OUTER
BRAKE
SHOE

RETAINING PIN

INNER BRAKE SHOE

PISTON

DUST BOOT

SEAL

INSULATORS

ANCHOR PLATE

HOLD-DOWN CLIPS

LOCATING PINS

Fig. 1-22. Exploded view of the single-piston, sliding-caliper assembly. (Ford Div., Ford Motor Co.)

view shown in Fig. 1-22 identifies the components of the single-piston caliper.

On General Motors cars, which employ a single-piston sliding caliper, a wide, shallow groove has been machined on each side of the disc. The groove causes a corresponding ridge to be formed on the brake shoes. A C-clamp must be used to pull the shoe out of the groove in the disc face, since a ridge forms on the face of the shoe. Also, before the sliding caliper can be removed from the spindle, a C-clamp should be used to retract the brake shoes. The C-

clamp forces the single piston into its cylinder bore so that the caliper can be lifted off the brake disc. See Fig. 1-23.

When new disc brake shoes are assembled into the caliper, new locating pin insulators should be used. See Fig. 1-22. The pins should be inserted into the new insulators when they are dry or a fast evaporating fluid such as denatured alcohol can be used.

The single-piston caliper disc brake tends to wear the disc brake shoes unevenly as shown in Fig. 1-24. When the caliper forces the shoes against the rotor,

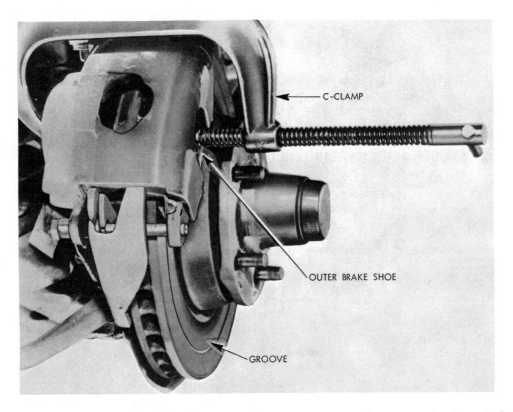

Fig. 1-23. A C-clamp is shown being used on a sliding-caliper brake assembly to retract the pistons in their bores prior to removal of the brake shoes. (*Cadillac Div., General Motors Corp.*)

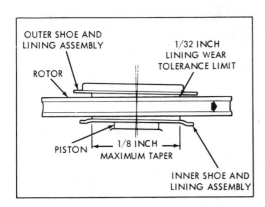

Fig. 1-24. Tapered shoe wear on both inner and outer shoe. (*Ford Div., Ford Motor Co.*)

the caliper tends to move with the rotation of the rotor, which in turn twists the caliper out of square with the rotor. This action causes the shoes to wear unevenly or with a taper. The caliper can twist because the adaptor or bracket that supports the caliper is not located directly over the shoes but to one side.

Fig. 1-25 shows a late model caliper that is supported by abutments directly over the center of the rotor. This design minimizes the tapering of the shoes compared to the early caliper design.

The positioner shown in Figs. 1-25 and 1-26 is used in the Kelsey-Hayes design to limit the clearance between the disc brake shoes and the rotor when the brakes are released. The "O" rings of the Delco-Moraine disc brake design shown in Fig. 1-27 serve this function for General Motor vehicles.

Another basic difference between

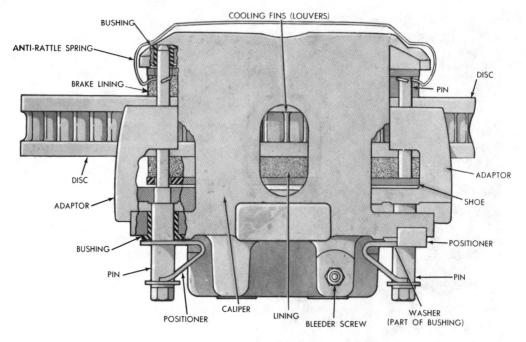

Fig. 1-25. Kelsey-Hayes disc brake. (*Chrysler Div., Chrysler Corp.*)

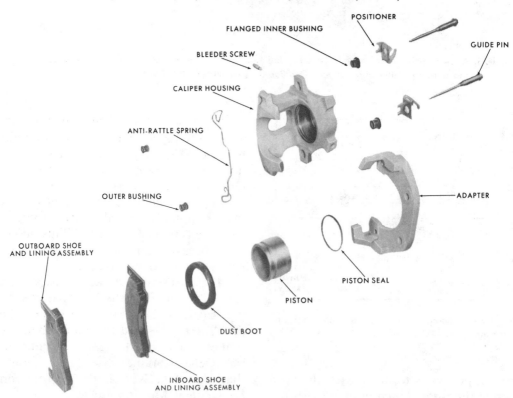

Fig. 1-26. Exploded view of the Kelsey-Hayes sliding-caliper disc brake. (*Chrysler Div., Chrysler Corp.*)

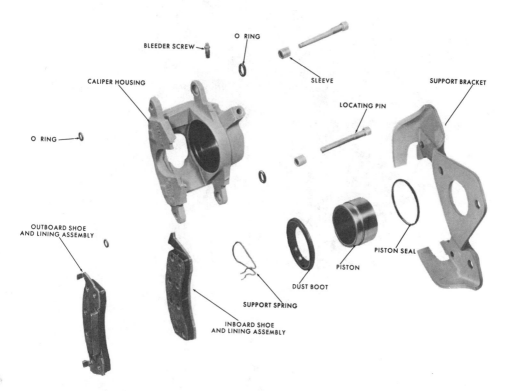

Fig. 1-27. Exploded view of the Delco-Moraine sliding-caliper disc brake. (*Pontiac Div., General Motors Corp.*)

Delco-Moraine and Kelsey-Hayes is the method used to retain the disc brake shoes in the caliper. The Kelsey-Hayes design shown in Fig. 1-26 uses the guide pins and an anti-rattle spring. The Delco-Moraine design in Fig. 1-27 uses pins and a spring to retain the inboard shoe, but the outboard shoe is locked to the caliper by bending the tabs on the brake shoe.

The Ford disc brake caliper shown in Fig. 1-22 and the Kelsey-Hayes shown in Fig. 1-28 both retain the dust boot in the caliper by trapping it between the piston and the caliper bore. The Delco-Moraine design retains its dust boot, (Fig. 1-29), by pressing it into a recess in the caliper. Chapter 4 of this

book will give details on how these dust boots are installed.

Two-Piston, Fixed-Caliper Disc Brakes

An exploded view of a typical two-piston, fixed caliper is shown in Fig. 1-30. In this design, a piston is located on each side of the disc. The caliper is fixed, and all lateral movement (forcing the shoes against the disc) is provided by the two pistons moving within their cylinders.

The brake disc is held to the hub by four bolts in this design. Most American-made front rotors are now cast in one piece. The disc brake shoes, or pads, are removed from the caliper by driving out the two brake shoe retaining (or mounting) pins as shown in Fig.

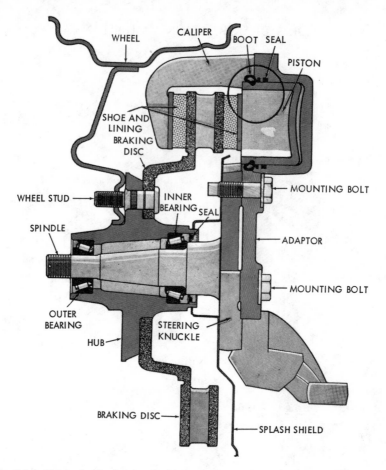

Fig. 1-28. In the Kelsey-Hayes disc brake design the boot is trapped between the piston and the groove in the wall of the caliper bore. (*Chrysler Div., Chrysler Corp.*)

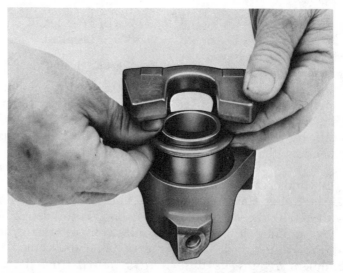

Fig. 1-29. The dust boot is being placed over the piston before it is pressed into the recess in the caliper. (*Chevrolet Div., General Motors Corp.*)

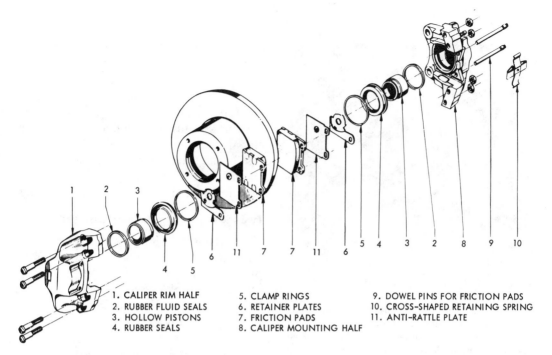

1. CALIPER RIM HALF
2. RUBBER FLUID SEALS
3. HOLLOW PISTONS
4. RUBBER SEALS

5. CLAMP RINGS
6. RETAINER PLATES
7. FRICTION PADS
8. CALIPER MOUNTING HALF

9. DOWEL PINS FOR FRICTION PADS
10. CROSS-SHAPED RETAINING SPRING
11. ANTI-RATTLE PLATE

Fig. 1-30. Exploded view of a two-piston, fixed-caliper design. (*Opel Div., General Motors Corp.*)

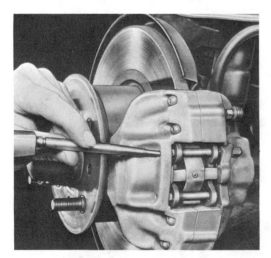

Fig. 1-31. Driving out the disc brake shoe retaining pins of the two-piston, fixed caliper. (*Opel Div., General Motors Corp.*)

Fig. 1-32. Once the shoe retaining pins are removed, the shoe can be lifted from the caliper. (*Opel Div., General Motors Corp.*)

1-31, permitting the brake shoes to be pulled out either by hand (Fig. 1-32) or with the help of two pairs of pliers gripping the flanges on the metal backing of the shoe.

The two caliper pistons must be forced into the bottom of their bores in order to provide space for the new (thicker) disc brake shoes. A screw driver with a soft handle can be used to bottom

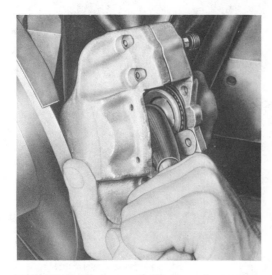

Fig. 1-33. To facilitate installing new shoes in the caliper, the pistons should be bottomed to provide clearance for the new (thicker) shoes. Where caliper design permits, the pistons can be bottomed using the handle of a screwdriver. (*Opel Div., General Motors Corp.*)

out the piston in the caliper, as illustrated in Fig. 1-33. Opening the bleeder valve to reduce the resistance of the fluid helps in this operation.

The Chevrolet Vega sliding caliper disc brake shown in Fig. 1-34 is a different approach to disc brake design. The disc brake shoes butt directly against the anchor instead of the caliper which results in more uniform wear of the shoes.

Two-Piston, Sliding-Caliper Disc Brake

Starting in 1968 Ford Motor Company made disc brakes optional on its pick-up trucks. In this two-piston, sliding-caliper brake design, both pistons are located on the inboard side of the disc, as shown in Fig. 1-35.

In this design, an *anchor plate* provides the support for the entire caliper assembly; it bolts to the front wheel spindle and does not move laterally. The *caliper* is attached to the anchor plate by

Fig. 1-34. Chevrolet Vega disc brake. (*Chevrolet Div., General Motors Corp.*)

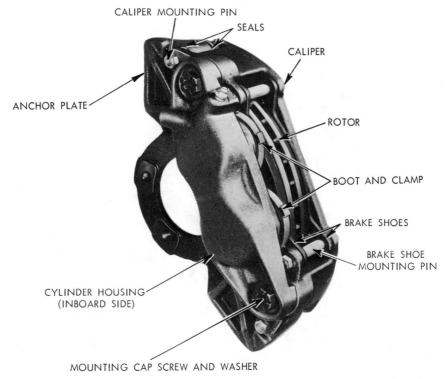

CALIPER MOUNTING PIN

SEALS

CALIPER

ANCHOR PLATE

ROTOR

BOOT AND CLAMP

BRAKE SHOES

BRAKE SHOE
MOUNTING PIN

CYLINDER HOUSING
(INBOARD SIDE)

MOUNTING CAP SCREW AND WASHER

Fig. 1-35. Two-piston, sliding-caliper, disc brake assembly. In this design the inner shoe is forced against the inboard face of the disc by the two inboard pistons. The cylinder housing is bolted to the caliper, which slides on caliper mounting pins. The outer shoe is brought against the outboard face of the disc by the sliding caliper. (Ford Div., Ford Motor Co.)

means of two caliper mounting pins and is free to slide on these pins. See Fig. 1-36. The cylinder housing (which contains the two pistons) bolts to the caliper; the cylinder housing and the caliper slide as a unit on the caliper mounting pins.

The brake shoes are retained in the caliper by brake shoe mounting pins, as shown in Figs. 1-35 and 1-36. When the brake is applied, the two pistons advance within the cylinders to force the inner shoe against the disc. When the shoe contacts the disc the forward movement of the pistons stops. However, since the cylinder housing is not fixed, the applied brake pedal force pushes against the cylinder housing, moving the cylinder housing away from the pistons (i.e., the housing moves relative to the temporar-

ily fixed pistons). The caliper is bolted to the cylinder housing, so that the movement of the housing brings the outer shoe into contact with the outboard face of the disc. A friction ring attached to each piston limits the inward travel when the brake is released.

Four-Piston, Fixed-Caliper Disc Brakes

In the four-piston, fixed-caliper disc brake design, the caliper is made up of two, almost identical caliper halves. The caliper halves are fixed; the shoes are moved (by opposing pairs of pistons) against the faces of the disc entirely by the action of the pistons moving within their cylinders. The four-piston, fixed calipers can be further classified accord-

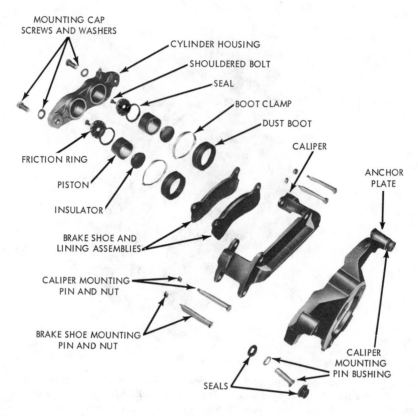

Fig. 1-36. Exploded view of the two-piston, sliding caliper. (*Ford Div., Ford Motor Co.*)

ing to the method employed to retain the brake shoes. Some designs retain the shoes in the caliper with external clips, plates, or pins; other designs use internal-retention pockets.

The Caliper Pocket Method of Shoe Retention. The Bendix Series E disc brake, as used by American Motors, Buick, and Chrysler Corporation's medium-sized cars, is of the internal retention type. This design retains the brake shoes in contoured pockets machined inside the caliper. The ledges on which the brake shoes rest are shown in Figs. 1-14 and 1-19.

The Budd disc brake, used on Chrysler Corporation's larger automobiles,

also retains the disc brake shoes within the caliper by means of pockets machined into the caliper. For both models of the internal retention design (Bendix Series E and Budd) the caliper mounting bolts must be removed so that the caliper assembly can be lifted away from the disc to remove the brake shoes. Fig. 1-19 shows how the shoe is withdrawn from the caliper. Once the caliper is removed, the shoe can be easily removed from the caliper by sliding it forward along the pocket and out through the brake disc opening. Fig. 1-19 also illustrates how the pocket holds the shoes in position.

The Retaining Pin Method of Shoe Retention. The retaining pin method

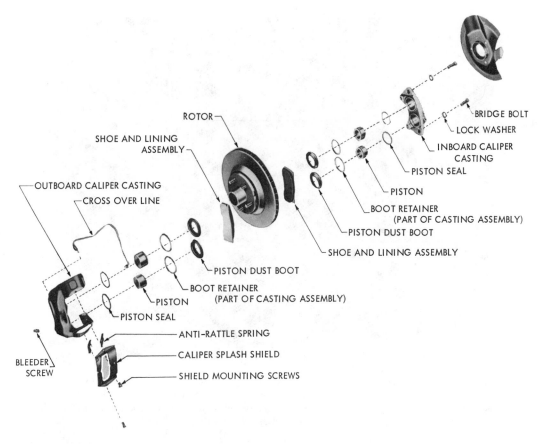

Fig. 1-37. Exploded view of the Kelsey-Hayes, four-piston, fixed caliper design. This design features square piston seals which seat in grooves in the cylinder walls. The dust boots are held to the pistons by retaining rings. The shoes are retained in the caliper by a combination splash shield-retainer plate which bolts to the outboard caliper casting. *(Ford Div., Ford Motor Co.)*

for holding disc brake shoes in the caliper is used in the Delco-Moraine four-piston, fixed-caliper disc brake. Fig. 1-18 shows a similar retaining pin in position.

After the retaining pin has been withdrawn, the disc brake shoe can be removed from the caliper by pulling on the top end of the shoe. A pair of pliers may be needed to remove the shoes from the caliper.

Retainer Plate (Splash Shield) Method of Shoe Retention. The caliper splash shield was used on early models of the Kelsey-Hayes disc brake to hold the shoes into the caliper. Fig. 1-37 shows the position of the two shield mounting screws holding the caliper splash shield to the outboard caliper housing. Both large and small designs of the Kelsey-Hayes four-piston, fixed-caliper disc brake have been used on all Ford vehicles from 1965 through 1967 and on the 1968-69 Lincoln. Chrysler Corporation's smaller cars used the smaller version of the Kelsey-Hayes brake. The Eldorado and the Toronado used the large version of the Kelsey-Hayes disc brake through 1968.

Fig. 1-38. To remove the shoes from the Kelsey-Hayes, four-piston, fixed caliper, remove the splash shield-retainer plate and the anti-rattle springs. For the shoes to clear the rust ridge built up on the outer edge of the disc, it may be necessary to bottom the pistons in their bores with a water pump pliers (insert). The shoes can then be removed using two pairs of pliers as shown. (*Plymouth Div., Chrysler Corp.*)

After the splash shield is removed from the caliper, the brake shoes and lining assembly can be removed from the caliper. The insert at the upper right in Fig. 1-38 illustrates how the pistons are forced into the cylinders with a pair of pliers to gain the clearance necessary to remove the brake shoes.

TRADE COMPETENCY TEST

1. What are the factors that control the stopping of a vehicle?
2. What should the total brake stopping distance be for a car traveling at 20 miles per hour?
3. What is the most common brake lining material?
4. How does a wheel cylinder operate?
5. What is the purpose of the dampener spring around the outside of the brake drum?
6. What two forces apply the brake shoe to the drum?
7. How does the self-energizing brake differ from the duo-servo brake?
8. Does the secondary shoe exert more stopping pressure than the primary shoe? Why?

9. How do you operate the drum brake self-adjusting mechanism?

10. What drum brake design is most efficient in terms of stopping pressure developed?

11. The brake shoes in a drum brake push outward against the inside of the drum. How do disc brake shoes work?

12. The brake shoe actuating pistons travel inside wheel cylinders on drum brakes. The pistons travel within what part on disc brakes?

13. How is the caliper held in position on the brake disc?

14. What two methods are used to connect the cylinders in disc brake cylinders?

15. How can brake discs be constructed so that they run cooler?

16. A disc brake shoe should be replaced when the lining has worn to what thickness?

17. Is it necessary to remove the caliper when replacing brake shoes?

18. What are the basic methods used to retain disc brake shoes in the caliper?

19. Do cars with disc brakes use the same wheels as cars equipped with drum brakes?

20. Calipers are designed with varying numbers of pistons. How many different types of calipers are there?

21. Do most disc brakes require adjustment?

22. What are the two methods used to hold the brake disc to the hub?

23. Are all two-piston calipers of the fixed-caliper design?

24. What are the two functions of the caliper splash shield?

CHAPTER 2

BRAKE APPLICATION SYSTEMS

Brake Actuating Mechanisms

Several methods of applying the brake shoe assembly to the drum have been used in the past. The brake shoes on all present day passenger vehicles are actuated by hydraulic pressure. The parking brake is applied by mechanical means through the use of cables and levers.

Mechanical Brakes

Older passenger vehicles used a system of levers, rods and/or cables to create a mechanical advantage for expanding the brake shoes when the driver depressed the brake pedal. See Fig. 2-1. The rods and cables were adjustable to permit removal of slack or free play, keeping the levers at the correct angle. A cam, toggle, or wedge located between the ends of the brake shoes, was used to expand the shoe assembly. Various types of adjustments located within the brake assembly were used to adjust the lining to brake drum clearance.

Electric Brakes

The use of electric brakes is con-fined primarily to house trailers. The use of electricity to operate the drum-type brakes of a detachable unit permits a simplified hook-up between the two units. An electric cable from the brake controller (rheostat) in the vehicle to a detachable plug connector at the trailer hitch provides a convenient coupling for separating the control circuit from the trailer brake circuit.

The brake shoes are actuated by an electromagnet which is attached to the brake backing plate. As the control lever of the controller (rheostat) is moved toward the apply position, current flows through the electromagnet energizing the magnet. The magnetic field developed causes the magnet to be shifted which in turn moves the brake shoe actuating mechanism. The actuating mechanism may be in the form of a lever operated cam or a cam which is shifted by the revolving of the armature. As more current is supplied to the magnet, more force is developed on the actuating mechanism.

One type of electric brake is illustrated in Fig. 2-2. An armature (in this case a metal ring which revolves to complete a circuit) (1) revolves with the

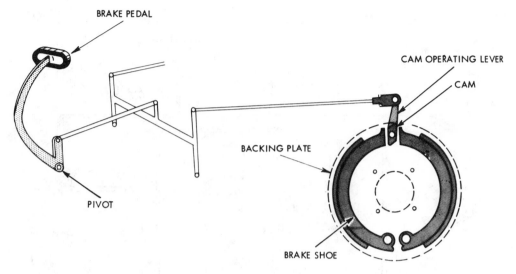

Fig. 2-1. Components of a mechanical brake system.

Fig. 2-2. Electric brake assembly.

drum. As current is supplied to the electromagnet (2), the magnet attempts to cling to the armature which causes the magnet to shift, forcing the cam (3) against the end of the brake shoes. This action applies the brake. When the control is moved to the off position, current ceases to flow and the electromagnet becomes demagnetized. Retracting springs then return the brake shoes to their released position.

Air Brakes

Air brakes are used on most heavy trucks and buses. In an air brake system, compressed air, controlled by the operator by means of a foot treadle or hand valve or both, is employed to actuate the brake mechanism. Air pressure in a closed system is transmitted equally in all directions, the same as fluid pressure in a hydraulic brake system. Air from the compressor is transmitted to the wheel brake assemblies where it is used to actuate mechanical or hydraulic mechanisms that apply the brake lining to the brake drum.

The air brake system consists of a

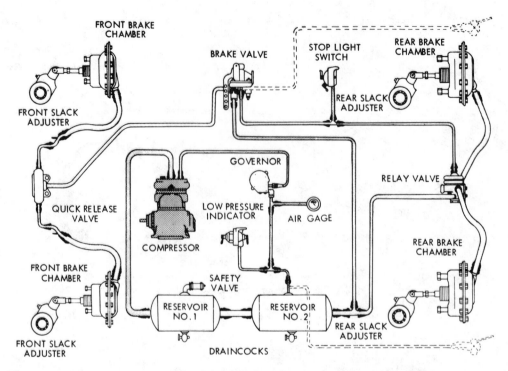

Fig. 2-3. Air brake system.

compressor, a governor, a reservoir, brake control valves, a brake chamber containing a diaphragm, a quick-release valve, and a relay valve. Figure 2-3 illustrates a typical air brake system.

The engine driven compressor, which supplies air under pressure to the reservoir, may be of the rotary type or the reciprocating-piston type and will be either air-cooled or water cooled.

A governor regulates the pressure in the reservoir and prevents the building up of excessive pressure in the system. The reservoir is usually in the form of a welded steel tank designed to withstand pressure greatly in excess of the pressure required to operate the system. A safety valve is incorporated within the system (usually located at the tank) to relieve air pressure when it reaches a predetermined high.

The brake control valve, which may be operated by foot or by hand or both, is placed in the air line between the reservoir and the lines leading to the individual wheel brakes. When the brake control valve is in the applied position, air under high pressure from the reservoir is admitted to the diaphragm in the brake chamber at each wheel. In the off position, the air pressure from the reservoir is cut off and the lines are opened to the atmosphere. The valve is so designed as to permit controlled application of the brakes.

The brake chambers are equipped with a movable diaphragm connected by a rod to the brake shoe operating mechanism at the wheels. The admission of air pressure to the front side of the diaphragm moves the diaphragm and linkage which actuates the brake shoes.

A quick release valve is used in the front brake lines to speed up the release of air from the brake chambers directly to the atmosphere.

A relay valve is used to speed up the application and release of air at the rear brakes. A small amount of air from the brake control valve opens the relay valve directly to the reservoir, bypassing the control valve, permitting a more direct flow of air to the rear brake chambers for faster action.

One type of air brake uses spring pressure to apply the rear brakes when no air pressure is available in the brake system. When air pressure reaches normal operating pressure, the spring is compressed and the rear brakes are released. Two air pressure application circuits are employed, one for the rear brakes and the other the front brakes. A third circuit services the spring cavity of the spring brake actuator through a parking valve and modulating spring brake control. The spring action mechanism serves as an emergency brake when there is no air pressure available.

For several years light trucks used an air-over-hydraulic brake system. In this system, when the brakes are applied, hydraulic pressure from the master cylinder actuates an air valve which directs air pressure from the brake compressor system to the air chamber. Air pressure on the air chamber piston is transmitted through a piston rod to the master cylinder piston. This type of system has been discontinued in favor of a vacuum booster with a basic hydraulic brake system.

Two other methods of power braking have been developed recently. One system is a hydro-boost power brake whereby hydraulic pressure for power braking is supplied by the power steering pump. A control valve meters hydraulic fluid from the power steering pump through the master cylinder for a power boost upon brake application.

A full power hydraulic brake system uses two pumps, either engine driven or electrically driven to provide high pressure for brake application. The pressurized fluid is delivered to accumulators from which it is metered to the wheel cylinders when the brakes are applied.

Hydraulic Application

In a hydraulic brake system, movement of the brake shoe assembly against the drum is accomplished by the movement of a column of liquid.

Before describing the hydraulic braking system it is necessary to take into account two important elementary principles of hydraulics:

(1) No liquid can be appreciably compressed. To all intent and purposes a column of liquid confined in a tube represents a solid linkage, when pressure is applied to the liquid. The pressure is transmitted just as though the liquid was a solid rod.

(2) The pressure in every part of a hydraulic system is the same. When pressure is applied to a column of liquid, confined within the system, that same pressure exerted by the piston in the liquid is transmitted equally in all directions.

Four cylinders of various diameters are shown in Fig. 2-4. The cylinders are connected by means of suitable tubing and the entire system is filled with liquid (hydraulic brake fluid). The piston in cylinder A, called the *master* cylinder, is linked directly to the brake pedal. The other cylinders in this system are called the *wheel cylinders.*

If a force of 100 lbs. is exerted on the brake pedal, the resultant force on the master cylinder piston will be 700 lbs. This increase in pressure is due to a mechanical advantage ratio of 7 to 1, since the length of the lever between the pedal and the pivot point of the brake pedal is 7 times as long as the length of the lever be-

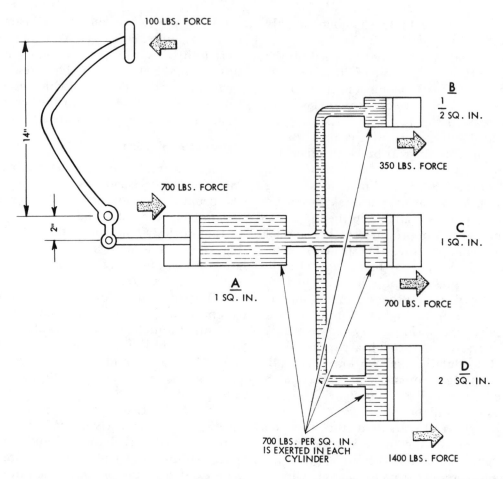

Fig. 2-4. Hydraulic brake principle: a force applied to a confined fluid is transmitted equally by that fluid in every direction. Since the applied force per square inch of fluid surface is everywhere equal, the total force delivered to any part of the enclosed circuit can be varied by changing the cross-sectional area of that part of the circuit.

low the pivot point. Therefore, the piston moves along the cylinder A with a force of 700 lbs. If the area of the piston is 1 sq in. the pressure throughout the system will be $700 \div 1$ or 700 lbs per sq in. (psi).

Since the pressure is equal in all directions, wherever the lines lead, the pressure will be 700 lbs per sq in. In case of cylinder B having ½ sq in. area, the force will be $700 \times$ ½ or 350 lbs. Cylinder C, having the same area as cylinder A,

will exert the same force of 700 lbs. The force in cylinder D, however, which has an area of 2 sq in. will be 700×2 or 1,400 lbs. By varying the size of the cylinder it is possible to distribute the available pressure throughout the system as desired.

The components of a simple drum brake hydraulic system are shown in Fig. 2-5. In this system the brake shoe assembly is moved in contact with the drum by pistons, in the wheel cylinder

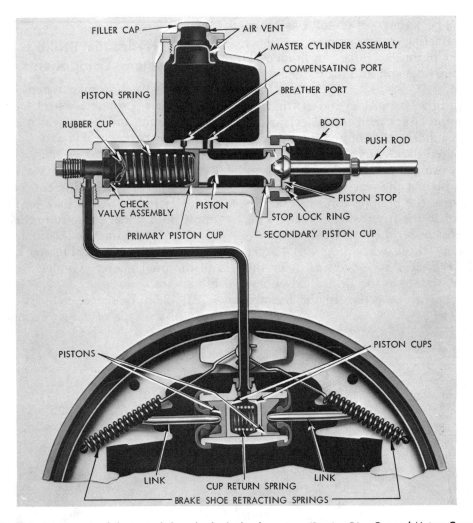

Fig. 2-5. Components of the typical drum brake hydraulic system. (*Pontiac Div., General Motors Corp.*)

connected directly to the shoes by links. When the brake pedal is depressed, the master cylinder piston is moved within the master cylinder, putting the hydraulic brake fluid under pressure. This hydraulic pressure is transmitted through the connecting tubing to the wheel cylinders, forcing the wheel cylinder pistons outward.

The pressure on the wheel cylinder pistons forces the brake shoes outward, overcoming the tension of the retracting springs and bringing the lining into contact with the drum. When the driver removes his foot from the brake pedal, the strong action of the retracting (return) springs pull the brake shoe assemblies back to their normal released position so that they are clear of the drums. The return action of the foot pedal also permits the master cylinder piston to return to its original position, thus leaving space in the master cylinder for the return of the fluid which has been pushed into the lines. The strong action of the brake shoe retracting springs enables the wheel cylinder pistons to force the fluid back along the lines and into the master cylinder.

By using stepped cylinders (having one piston larger than the other) at the wheel cylinders, the applied force can be distributed differently to the two shoes. Also by using larger cylinders at the front wheels than at the rear wheels, a greater portion of the braking force can be distributed to the front wheel brakes. This compensates for the transfer of weight to the front wheels when stopping. Larger wheel cylinders have been used for the primary shoe so as to gain full advantage of the energizing action in the forward direction.

Hydraulic Brake System Components

The hydraulic brake system consists of a master cylinder, wheel cylinders and the lines and hoses which connect the various parts. See Fig. 2-6.

Master Cylinders

There are three different types of master cylinders which may be used to supply fluid under pressure to the wheel cylinders. These include the single piston master cylinder, the dual master cylinder and the dual master cylinder used with disc brakes.

All older passenger vehicles used a single piston type of master cylinder. As

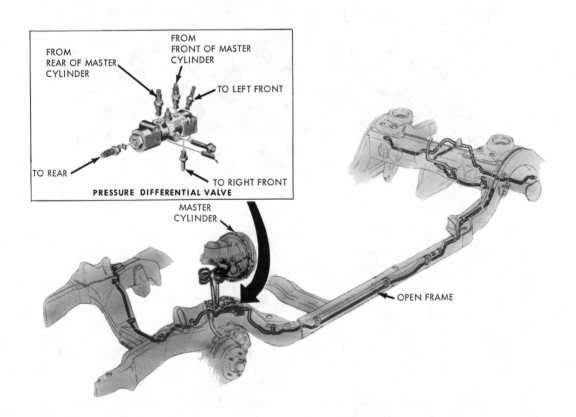

Fig. 2-6. Hydraulic brake system. (*Courtesy Oldsmobile Div., General Motors Corp.*)

this type will still require service for several years, it is well to have an understanding of the construction and operation of this particular type of unit.

All passenger vehicles presently being manufactured must have a dual master cylinder as an added safety feature. Essentially, this gives the effect of having a separate master cylinder for the front wheels and one for the rear wheel brakes.

Because of the particular retracting feature of the disc brake, residual pressure cannot be utilized in the hydraulic system for disc brakes. This brings about a different type of valve arrangement.

For clarity, each type of master cylinder will be discussed separately.

Single Piston Master Cylinder

Figure 2-7 illustrates a typical hydraulic brake single piston master cylinder. It consists of two main chambers: the cylinder in which the piston operates, and a fluid reservoir. The reservoir stores fluid which permits additional fluid to enter into or return from the lines to maintain a constant volume when the fluid is affected by expansion (heat) or contraction (cold). In addition, any seepage of fluid, due to wear at sealed points, is compensated for by the reservoir.

The master cylinder piston is shaped like a spool and when in the released position as shown in Fig. 2-7, the space around its center is kept full of fluid which enters through the inlet or bypass port. A rubber cup which acts as a seal is provided at each end of the piston.

The rubber cup at the return spring end of the piston is called the primary cup and is designed to form a seal as the piston is moved forward toward the fluid outlet. A two-way fluid check valve is located at the cylinder outlet. The rubber cup mounted on the piston at the brake pedal rod end serves to prevent leakage of fluid at this point. This cup is called the secondary cup.

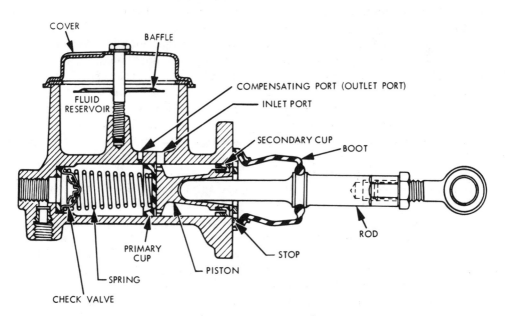

Fig. 2-7. A master cylinder is shown with the master cylinder piston in the released or at-rest position. (*Plymouth Div., Chrysler Corp.*)

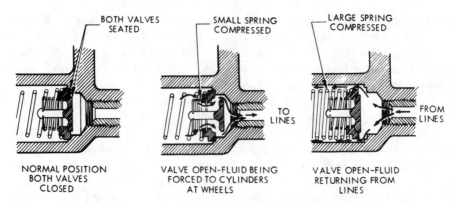

Fig. 2-8. A fluid check valve. The purpose of a fluid check valve, which is actually two separate valves in a single assembly, is to keep the hydraulic system under sufficient pressure to prevent air from entering the system.

The pedal rod is connected to the brake pedal. A rubber boot over the back end of the master cylinder and around the pedal rod prevents dirt from coming in contact with the cylinder wall. When pressure is applied to the brake pedal, the pedal rod forces the master cylinder piston forward against the return spring. As the piston moves, it pushes the fluid through the small compensating (outlet) port into the reservoir. When the piston cup has moved sufficiently to cover the compensating port, the only remaining outlet through which the fluid can flow is the fluid check valve which leads into the hydraulic lines. The pressure exerted by the fluid forces the fluid check valve open against the tension of a small spring or diaphragm and fluid is forced into the lines. The pressure thus transmitted is exerted on the wheel cylinder pistons which forces the brake shoe assembly into contact with the drum.

Figure 2-8 illustrates the action of the fluid check valve. Actually two valves incorporated within one unit are involved. The fluid pressure exerted during brake application overcomes the tension of the small valve spring and moves the small valve off its seat, Fig. 2-8, *center*. The fluid passes around the valve and into the lines.

When the brakes are released, the brake pedal is returned to its normal position by the brake pedal retracting spring. The master cylinder piston is returned to the released position by its return spring. This same spring holds the control valve momentarily closed, preventing the return of fluid from the lines to the master cylinder. As the piston moves away from the fluid check valve, the primary cup collapses, allowing the fluid from around the center of the piston to flow through holes in the head of the piston and into the cylinder. See Fig. 2-9. The action of the powerful retracting springs on the brake shoes forces the fluid back through the lines and into the master cylinder. The master cylinder return spring, however, presses against the large valve and in order to enter the cylinder bore, the fluid from the lines must overcome the tension of the piston return spring and lift the large valve from its seat, Fig. 2-8, *right*.

When the brake shoe retracting springs have returned the brake shoe assemblies against their stops, movement of the fluid in the lines also stops. However,

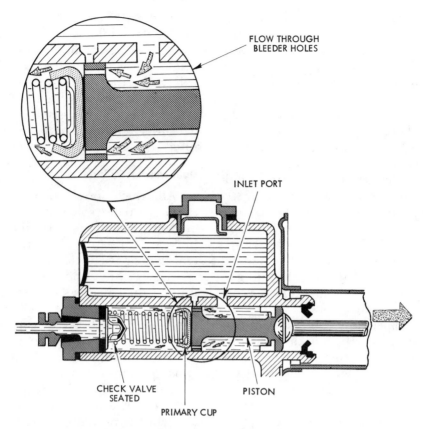

FLOW THROUGH
BLEEDER HOLES

INLET PORT

CHECK VALVE
SEATED

PISTON

PRIMARY CUP

Fig. 2-9. The master cylinder piston cup is shown collapsing at its edges as the brake pedal is released. The insert shows fluid running from the master cylinder inlet port, through special ports in the head of the piston, and around the partly collapsed primary cup to keep the master cylinder filled with fluid. (*Buick Div., General Motors Corp.*)

the large valve has closed before the pressure in the system reaches zero, thereby maintaining residual pressure.

The master cylinder piston is returned very quickly to its released position, and since the fluid is slow in returning, a vacuum is created in the section of the cylinder vacated by the piston. When this vacuum is created within the cylinder, the rubber cup on the front end of the piston collapses. Therefore, atmospheric pressure on the fluid in the reservoir forces fluid to flow from the space around the piston through bleeder holes in the piston head, around the partly

collapsed rubber cup, and into the front of the cylinder, Fig. 2-9. The space around the center portion of the piston is maintained full of fluid through the inlet port from the reservoir.

When the piston has been returned to its stop, the fluid in the lines is still being forced back into the master cylinder. The master cylinder, however, is already filled and the excess fluid being returned by the tension of the brake shoe retracting springs is forced into the reservoir through the compensating port.

The tension exerted by the piston return spring closes the fluid check valve and maintains a residual pressure of about seven psi in the system. This pressure exerted on the lip of the wheel cylinder cups seals the system and prevents air from entering when the brakes are released.

If the clearance between the brake lining and drum is excessive so that a full stroke of the pedal will not bring about an effective pressure at the shoes, a quick release of the pedal will permit additional fluid to enter the cylinder. A second quick stroke of the pedal will force additional fluid into the lines. Sufficient fluid can usually be pumped into the system by this means until effective braking force is obtained. Adjusting the lining to drum clearance will usually correct a condition of this kind.

The compensating port, in addition to permitting the return of the fluid, prevents a build-up of pressure due to the expansion of the fluid. Every time the brakes are applied, heat is generated at the drums. Some of this heat is transferred to the fluid, causing it to expand. The extra volume of fluid represented by the expansion flows into the reservoir through the compensating port when the piston is against its stop. Without this compensating port, *or if this port is blocked,* the extra volume would overcome the tension of the brake shoe retracting springs and cause the brake shoes to move toward the drums. After several applications of the brakes, the brake shoes would be dragging, creating more heat and still further expansion, causing the brakes to seize.

An incorrectly adjusted brake pedal rod that prevents the master cylinder piston from completely returning to its stop, can cause the primary cup to block the compensating port. Likewise, harmful fluids can cause the rubber cup to swell, effectively blocking the compensating port. Even with satisfactory fluids, it is possible for the cup to expand after many thousands of miles so as to block the port.

Any leakage of fluid past the primary piston cup when the brakes are applied will cause the master cylinder to lose pressure. When this occurs, the master cylinder must be disassembled, the cylinder surface cleaned and new rubber parts installed.

Dual Master Cylinder

All vehicles presently being manufactured are required to have dual master cylinders, sometimes referred to as a split brake system, as a safety feature. The system is designed with separate hydraulic systems for the front and rear brakes using a dual master cylinder. Should a wheel cylinder or brake line fail at either the front or rear brake system the vehicle can still be brought to a controlled stop.

The tandem dual master cylinder has two separate reservoirs covered by a common cover (Fig. 2-10). A rubber diaphragm between the cover and the master cylinder prevents moisture-laden air from contaminating the brake fluid.

The rear piston (the primary piston, nearest the rear of the car) applies either the front or rear brakes, depending upon the specific design; in addition it activates the front floating piston which in turn provides hydraulic pressure to the remaining brakes. When functioning properly, a hydraulic link connects the two pistons when the brakes are applied. (When the brake linkage moves the primary piston past the compensating port, the fluid trapped under pressure between the two pistons forces the front piston forward.) If, however, the rear system should fail because of loss of fluid its piston will bottom against the front piston. The rear piston would then push the front piston forward mechanically providing hydraulic pressure to the system operating from the secondary portion of

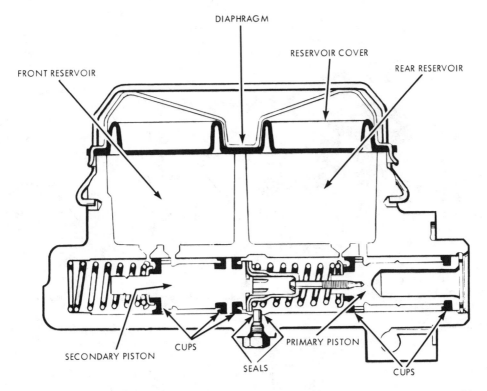

Fig. 2-10. Dual master cylinder. The dual master cylinder has separate (but connected) piston assemblies and separate fluid reservoirs. (Chevrolet Div., General Motors Corp.)

the master cylinder. When the front system loses fluid its piston will bottom against the end of the master cylinder. The brake system connected to the rear portion of the master cylinder will continue to function.

Dual Master Cylinder
Used With Disc Brakes

The master cylinder, employed in a disc brake system, is very similar to the dual master cylinder just discussed. However, the master cylinder used with the drum brakes uses a check valve to maintain a static pressure within the hydraulic system to keep air from entering the system. This is known as residual pressure. If that section of the hydraulic system, which serves the disc brake cylinders, generally the front brakes, is pressurized,

even slightly, the brake lining would drag excessively on the brake disc. Because of this, the master cylinder used for a disc brake system, must not have a check valve assembly in the hydraulic circuit to the disc brake actuating unit. In most cases this is the front brakes only, however, some vehicles use disc brakes on all four wheels. This system would not require check valves.

When drum brakes are used only at the rear brakes, a check valve (residual check valve) will usually be inserted in the master cylinder outlet which goes to the rear brakes, Fig. 2-11. Late model G.M. products do not use residual check valves in any of their master cylinders, neither drum nor disc systems.

Brake Valves. Certain valves are used in the hydraulic system which has a dual

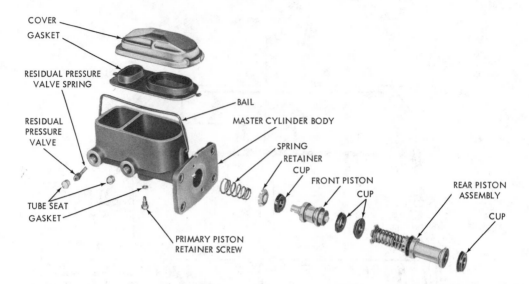

Fig. 2-11. Dual master cylinder with check valve at the outlet to the rear drum brakes. (*Chrysler Div., Chrysler Corp.*)

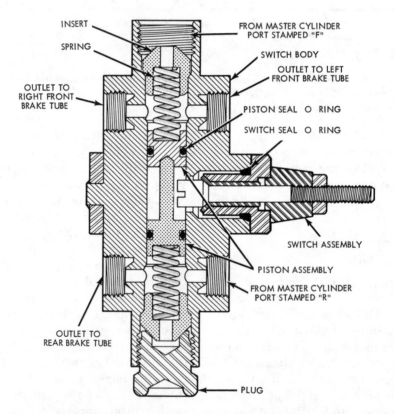

Fig. 2-12. Section view of a typical hydraulic safety switch. When a drop in line pressure on one side of the switch occurs, the switch piston is forced to the low side, contacting the terminal which extends into the cylinder bore and activating the brake warning light. (*Chrysler Div., Chrysler Corp.*)

master cylinder to act as a safety warning device, to proportion pressure between the front and rear actuating cylinders and to balance hydraulic pressure between the front and rear brakes. Various arrangements may be used, depending upon the design of the system. The various valves may be independent or in combination with one another.

Hydraulic Safety Switch. A hydraulic safety switch (brake pressure differential warning switch) is located between the brake line to the front brakes and the brake line to the rear brakes. All dual master cylinder hydraulic systems on American cars built since 1967 are required by law to have a safety switch, regardless of the type of brake system.

Figure 2-12 is a sectional view of a typical safety valve. The piston is normally centered in the switch assembly. The switch will be connected to a brake warning light on the instrument panel of the vehicle. If a hydraulic leak should occur in either the front or rear systems, brake fluid could escape from the defective half of the system. When the brakes are applied, there would be more pressure developed on the sealed side of the safety switch's piston assembly than on the leaking side. The piston within the safety switch would move to the low pressure side, contacting (and grounding) the electrical terminal protruding into the cylinder. This causes the brake warning light to glow, indicating to the driver that a brake failure has occurred within the system.

Proportioning Valve. A proportioning valve is located between the master cylinder and the rear brakes, so as to reduce the tendency of the rear drum brakes to lock upon severe brake application. The duo-servo type rear drum brake used in conjunction with front disc brakes will lock the rear brakes with less line pressure than is required to

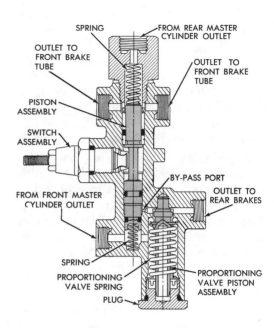

Fig. 2-13. Proportioning valve and warning switch (sectional). *(Plymouth Div., Chrysler Corp.)*

lock the front disc brakes. When a predetermined pressure is reached, the proportioning valve functions to limit the amount of increase in pressure to the rear wheel cylinders. This prevents the rear brakes from locking before full effective braking effort is produced by the front disc brakes.

In the event of a front hydraulic system failure, the proportioning valve has a "bypass" feature to direct full pressure to the rear brakes to insure a safe stop using only the rear brakes. Figure 2-13 is a sectional view of a proportioning valve and brake warning switch. This is a common arrangement. On some high-performance cars with conventional drum brake systems, a proportioning valve may be used to balance the operation of the front and rear drum brakes. The purpose of the proportioning valve in this case is to compensate for the tendency of the rear wheels to lock up because of the disproportionate weight of the front of the vehicle.

Metering Valve. The metering valve is located in the hydraulic system between the master cylinder and the front disc brake caliper assembly. The purpose of the metering valve is to balance the operation of the front disc brakes with the rear drum brakes at low hydraulic pressure. The valve operates to "hold-off" hydraulic flow to the front disc brakes until a predetermined pressure is reached. This "hold-off" action allows the rear drum brakes to build up sufficient pressure to overcome the opposing force of the brake shoe retracting springs in order to actuate the rear drum brakes. The metering valve, sometimes referred to as a balancing valve, controls the fluid flow to the front disc brakes, and will not open until the line pressure has overcome the tension of the rear brake shoe return springs; or, the metering valve will not activate the front brakes before the rear brakes are applied. Thus, front and rear brakes will work simultaneously.

Combination Valve. The combination valve, which was introduced on 1971 model cars equipped with front disc

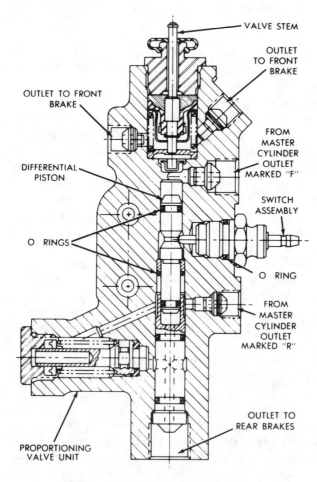

Fig. 2-14. Combination valve. (*Chrysler Corp.*)

Fig. 2-15. Metering valve tool. A special tool must be used on most combination valves to hold the valve open. This allows low pressure brake fluid to pass through the valve when bleeding the system with a pressure bleeder. (*Chrysler Corp.*)

brakes, included the metering valve hydraulic safety switch and the proportioning valve all in one housing as shown in Fig. 2-14. A tool is required as shown in Fig. 2-15 to bleed a system which uses a combination valve. Figure 2-16 is a sectional view of a combination brake warning, proportioning valve and metering valve assembly. The valve must be replaced as a unit should it fail to function properly.

Drum Brake Wheel Cylinders

Each drum brake backing plate is equipped with one or two wheel cylinders connected to the master cylinder by means of hydraulic lines. A wheel cylinder having two opposed pistons is shown in Fig. 2-17. Each brake shoe either fits into a slot at the outer end of the piston, or is connected to the piston by a short connecting link. As the brake pedal is depressed, the master cylinder forces fluid along the brake lines and into the wheel cylinders, the fluid entering between the two pistons. Pressure is exerted between the two pistons, forcing the shoes and lining outward against the drum. Leakage of fluid is prevented by the rubber cups between the pistons and the fluid. A spring between the two piston cups keeps them firmly seated against the piston at all times. Each wheel cylinder is provided with a bleeder valve to permit the removal of any air in the hydraulic system. A rubber boot fits over each end of the cylinder to prevent dirt and foreign matter from entering the cylinder.

When it is desirable to have a greater

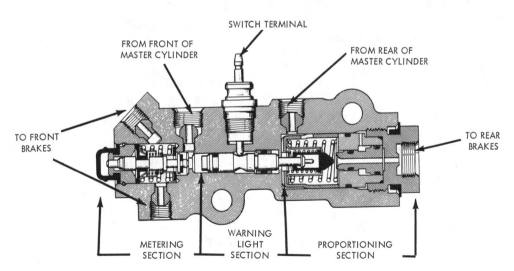

Fig. 2-16. Combination brake warning, proportioning valve and metering valve assembly (sectional). (*Oldsmobile Div., General Motors Corp.*)

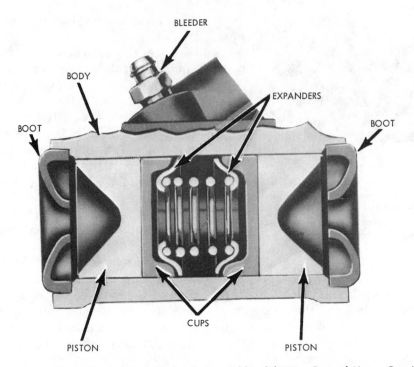

Fig. 2-17. A typical two-piston wheel cylinder. (Oldsmobile Div., General Motors Corp.)

pressure applied to one shoe, than to the other shoe, one end of the cylinder may be made larger and fitted with a larger piston. This is known as a step type of wheel cylinder.

Another drum brake design used on some import vehicles has two, separate, single-piston, wheel cylinders mounted 180° apart on the backing plate. One end of each wheel cylinder is closed, and tubing connects the two wheel cylinders hydraulically. The function of the wheel cylinders is the same as that of the single, two-piston, wheel cylinder. However, the effect of locating the wheel cylinders and anchor pins 180° apart is that both brake shoes act as forward, or leading shoes and apply equal force to the drum.

Should fluid leak past the rubber piston cups and into the boots, the wheel cylinder must be disassembled, the cylinder wall cleaned and new rubber parts,

after being lubricated with brake fluid, installed.

Disc Brake Calipers

The caliper assembly of the disc brake is the equivalent of the drum brake wheel cylinder and brake shoe assembly. Most disc brake calipers are castings made of malleable cast iron, although some imported car disc brake calipers are made of aluminum. The caliper houses both the brake shoes and the pistons which force the shoes into contact with the disc. A caliper must, therefore, be made of metal tough enough to resist deformation due to the reaction force of the piston pushing against the brake disc. A weak caliper would distort when the brakes are applied, causing a spongy feeling in the operation of the brake pedal.

Caliper Pistons. Depending on the design, disc brake calipers may have one, two, or four pistons. The pistons are located in cylinders machined in the caliper casting. The piston is hollowed for much of its length in order to reduce piston weight and to provide a convenient method for piston removal. Depending on the caliper design, grooves may be machined in the outside of the piston to provide a seat for either the dust boot, the piston seal, or both.

Dust Boots and Piston Seals. Dust boots are used to protect the caliper bores (cylinders) from rust and contamination. Depending on the design of the caliper, one side of the boot is seated in a groove machined in the piston and the other side is seated in either a groove in the cylinder wall or on a boot retainer ring pressed onto the cylinder boss. Figure 2-18 illus-

trates the method most commonly used, where the boot is seated in a groove in the piston and in the cylinder wall.

Rubber piston seals, roughly analogous to automobile piston rings, prevent leakage between the piston and the cylinder wall. Caliper piston seals are designed in two ways: square seal and lip seal.

The square seal type, shown in Fig. 2-18, is of rectangular cross-section and seats in a groove machined in the wall of the cylinder. The inner seal surface is the outer diameter of the piston. The square seal also functions as a device to maintain a certain amount of clearance between the disc brake shoe and the brake disc. Figure 2-19, *left,* shows the seal distorted when brake pressure is applied. When the brake pressure is released, Fig. 2-19, *right,* the seal assumes its undistorted shape and retracts the piston. This action

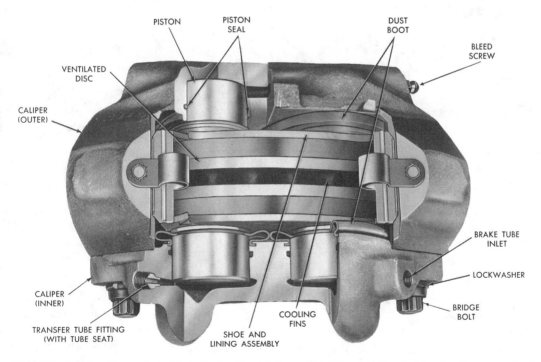

Fig. 2-18. A Kelsey-Hayes, four-piston, fixed-caliper design, which illustrates the way the dust boots are fitted on the piston and the use of square piston seals which seat in grooves in the cylinder bores. (*Plymouth Div., Chrysler Corp.*)

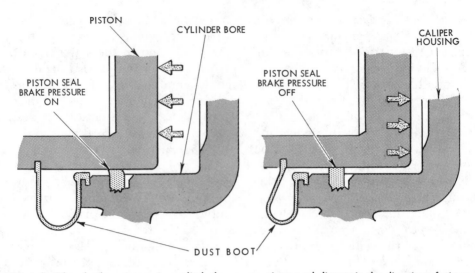

Fig. 2-19. *Left:* When brake pressure is applied, the square piston seal distorts in the direction of piston movement. *Right:* When the brake pressure is relaxed the seal rights itself and retracts the piston. (*Plymouth Div., Chrysler Corp.*)

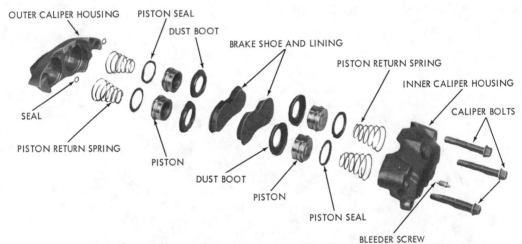

Fig. 2-20. A four-piston, fixed-caliper design with a lip-type piston seal. In this design the pistons do not retract from the brake shoe when the brake pressure is relaxed. Instead, piston return springs hold the shoes lightly against the disc. (*Plymouth Div., Chrysler Corp.*)

provides the running clearance between the shoe and the disc.

The lip-type seal, with a skirt-like or tapered cross-section, is usually used in conjunction with a piston return spring. An exploded view of a four-piston caliper employing lip seals and piston return springs is shown in Fig. 2-20. The piston return spring holds the piston against the back of the brake shoe. Thus, in this caliper design, the shoe is lightly held against the brake disc when the brake is in the "at rest" position. This causes a slight amount of brake drag, although the

PISTON BOOT

PISTON SEAL

PISTON

Fig. 2-21. A close-up of the piston, piston boot, and lip-type seal used in the design shown in the preceding illustration. (*Plymouth Div., Chrysler Corp.*)

brake pedal is released. Figure 2-21 is a close-up of a lip-type piston seal mounted on the piston. Note that the lip-type seal is anchored in a groove in the piston instead of being anchored in a groove in the cylinder wall, as in the square seal design.

Brake Lines

Steel tubing which resists corrosion while withstanding high pressure is used between the master cylinder and frame connections, and between the rear flexible hose and rear wheel cylinders. Flexible hoses connect the tubing to the front wheel cylinders.

If it is necessary to replace brake tubing, always use metal tubing which is designed to resist corrosion and withstand the high pressures encountered within the hydraulic system. The tubing must be double flared at the connections so as to produce a strong leak-proof joint. Low pressure copper tubing must not be used.

Brake Fluid

The liquid used for a hydraulic brake system is called brake fluid. Brake fluid is one of the most important parts of the brake system. Any fluid leak within the system will cause loss of pressure and ineffective braking action.

All brake fluid must meet SAE specifications as well as Federal motor vehicle safety standards. The fluid must have a high boiling point to withstand high temperatures and avoid vapor lock but not become so thin that leakage will occur. In cold weather the fluid must not separate or become too thick so as to prevent proper performance. In addition, the brake fluid must lubricate the rubber parts of the system as well as reduce rust and corrosion.

Many automobile manufacturers recommend a DOT 3 type fluid, other fluid manufacturers designate their fluid as heavy-duty, super heavy-duty and extra heavy-duty. Regardless of what the name may imply, always make certain that the fluid is of the correct type for the system being serviced.

Brake fluid ages in service and should be replaced periodically. Brake fluid also has a very strong attraction (affinity) to water. Uncovered fluid can easily become contaminated by the humidity in the air. It is good practice to flush the brake system of old fluid and renew with new fluid at least every two years.

System to Prevent Wheel Lockup

An electronic brake control mechanism labeled "Sure-Brake," "Track Master" or "True Track Brakes" may be obtained as optional equipment for some makes of passenger vehicles. The system is designed to keep the wheels rolling by preventing wheel lockup during brake applications at speeds over five m.p.h. but still maintain maximum stopping effort. It is much the same effect as "pumping" the brake pedal. This prevents lateral movement, provides decreased stopping distances under certain conditions and prevents flat spots on tires during severe brake application.

The system consists of a mechanically driven speed sensor at each wheel or at the transmission, a logic controller (computer) and three pressure modulators, one for each of the front wheels and one for the rear wheels. The speed sensors are sensitive to rapid deceleration, which takes place when the brakes are applied as in an impending wheel lockup. When this happens, an electrical signal is sent to the controller, which in turn activates the modulator to shut off hydraulic pressure until the possibility of lockup has passed.

The speed sensors are mechanically driven electromagnetic devices which generate electricity that causes the modulator to function. The modulator consists of a vacuum chamber, bypass tube, air valve, endplate, bypass valve and pressure modulator switch. There is also a hydraulic cylinder which is part of the endplate assembly that is actuated by the vacuum chamber assembly and controls the hydraulic pressure to the brakes. Fig-

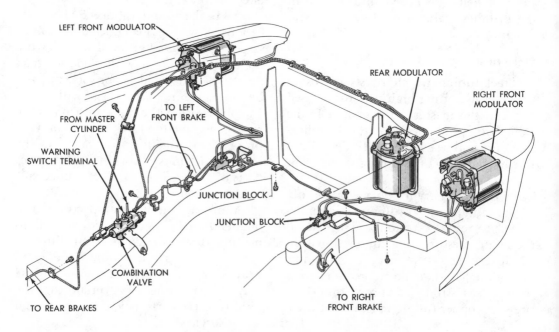

Fig. 2-22. Hydraulic components of a "Sure Brake" system. (*Plymouth Div., Chrysler Corp.*)

ure 2-22 illustrates the hydraulic components of a "Sure Brake" system.

Parking Brakes

Parking brakes are located in the rear wheel brake assembly. Some older model vehicles had a parking brake mechanism located on the back of the propeller shaft. The brakes are actuated by cables and levers. Most brakes are applied by a foot-operated lever in the driver's compartment. When a console is located between the individual front seats, a hand operated lever may be used to apply the parking brakes.

Figure 2-23 pictures the cable-and-linkage arrangement used on parking brakes at the rear wheels. The control system consists of a hand or foot-operated brake lever, cables enclosed in a conduit (channel), with brake shoe levers and struts to apply the rear brakes.

The brake lever cable connects to a sheave (equalizer), located at the center of the brake cable, with an adjusting nut to take up cable slack. Each end of the brake cable is attached to the free lower end of a brake shoe lever which pivots on each secondary brake shoe. A strut is mounted between each brake shoe lever and the front brake shoe, Fig. 2-24. When the brake lever is pulled, the brake cables apply an equal pull to each brake shoe lever and strut, forcing the brake shoes and lining into contact with the drum.

Strut action against the primary shoe causes a servo-action which provides a good parking brake effect in the forward action. However, the secondary shoe is not forced into the drum with sufficient pressure to give servo-action if the service brake is applied first and then the parking brake. The parking brake is effective in reverse for holding the vehicle. The parking brakes are adjusted by taking up cable slack.

Beginning with the 1971 model Chevrolet Vega, the self-energized rear brake shown in Fig. 1-3 was adjusted each time the parking brake was used. The strut be-

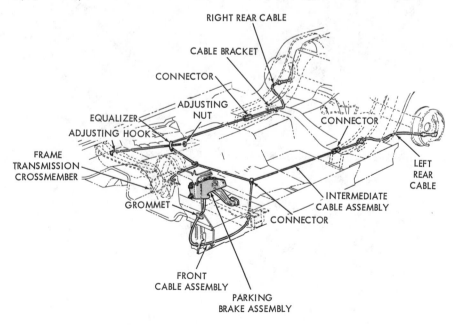

Fig. 2-23. Parking brake control system. (*Plymouth Div., Chrysler Corp.*)

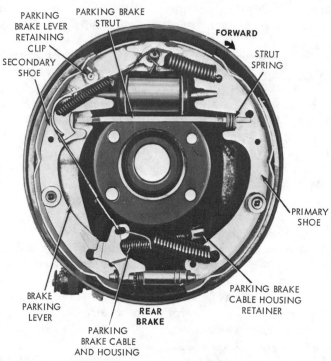

Fig. 2-24. Parking brake link and lever arrangement. (*Ford Customer Service Div., Ford Motor Co.*)

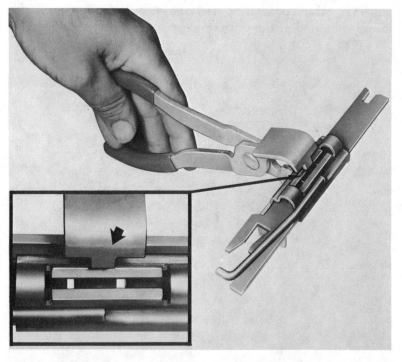

Fig. 2-25. Vega parking brake strut adjustment tool. (*Chevrolet Div., General Motors Corp.*)

tween the shoes becomes longer as the lining wears. A special tool is shown in Fig. 2-25 that is used to pre-set the strut when the brake shoes are installed.

Parking Brake Used With Rear Wheel Disc Brakes

When disc brakes are used on both front and rear wheels, provisions must be made for a separate parking brake system.

A small drum brake assembly, which is the same as a regular rear drum brake assembly, only smaller, is built into the hub of the disc brake rotor, Fig. 2-26.

Vacuum Control Release Parking Brake

Some passenger vehicles are equipped with a vacuum control release arrangement in the parking brake system.

A vacuum power unit is mounted on the parking brake control assembly, Fig. 2-27. A vacuum actuated piston within the power unit is connected by a rod to one end of the parking brake release lever. The vacuum assembly is actuated to release the parking brake when the engine is running and the transmission is in a forward or reverse range. The brake

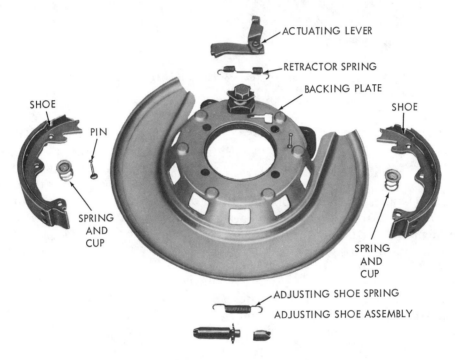

Fig. 2-26. Parking brake used with rear wheel disc brakes. (*Chevrolet Div., General Motors Corp.*)

The cable and linkage arrangement is the same as for the parking brake used with the regular rear drum brake assembly.

The shoe-to-drum clearance can be adjusted through an access hole in the drum after removing the wheel.

can be released manually in the event of a vacuum loss.

The vacuum power unit receives vacuum from the intake manifold. The vacuum release control valve is generally located on the backup light switch or firewall.

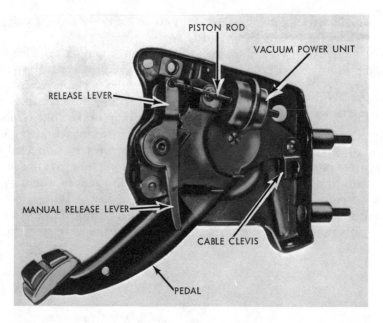

Fig. 2-27. Vacuum parking brake control assembly. (*Ford Customer Div., Ford Motor Co.*)

Power Brakes

For quick stops and severe braking, considerable pressure must be exerted on the brake pedal. The higher the speed of the vehicle and the greater its load, the more effort that is required to stop the vehicle.

In a hydraulic brake system there are limitations as to the size of the master and wheel cylinders which can be practically employed. Furthermore, the physical strength of the driver limits the amount of force which can be applied. These factors restrict the brake shoe to brake drum pressures obtainable.

To increase or boost the braking force, automobile manufacturers have made available vacuum assisted brake systems which are called *power brakes*. Different makes and designs of power brakes are on the market, but basically they all

operate in the same manner. When the brake pedal is depressed, a valve arrangement is actuated, and engine vacuum from the intake manifold is then applied to one side of a diaphragm, while atmospheric pressure is applied to the other side. Since the pressure is greater on the one side of the diaphragm, it is then forced to the vacuum side. This movement assists (in varying degrees depending on the particular system) in supplying hydraulic pressure through the brake fluid to the different wheel cylinders.

Vacuum

When the pressure existing within a container is less than the atmospheric pressure (14.7 psi) surrounding the container—a vacuum condition then exists within the container. The measurement of vacuum is the difference between the pressure *within* the container and the pressure of the atmosphere *outside* the container. Vacuum is commonly measured in inches of mercury, with the reading representing the number of inches the atmospheric pressure will lift a column of mercury in its endeavor to flow into the container. Inches of mercury is merely a means of expressing the difference between the pressure within the container and the pressure outside the container.

If a container was completely emptied of air, the resultant pressure differential would be 14.7 pounds per square inch, which would be approximately 30 inches of mercury. If, for example, an engine develops 15 inches of vacuum (comparable here to 15 inches of mercury), this 15 inches of vacuum would represent a pressure of 7.35 psi—one half of the value of atmospheric pressure since 30 inches of mercury equals 14.7 psi. If this vacuum was applied to a diaphragm having an area of 50 square inches, a force of 367.5 pounds would be exerted on the diaphragm ($50 \times 7.35 = 367.5$).

Vacuum in itself has no power, being a negative value. Any work done as a result of a vacuum or a partial vacuum is actually done by the pressure or weight of the atmosphere as it fills up the space where the lower pressure existed.

In the case of a power brake cylinder, the amount of work the unit will do is dependent upon how much engine vacuum, obtained from the intake manifold, is present on one side of the diaphragm, and the area of the diaphragm.

The power brake cylinder may be either air or vacuum suspended. If the cylinder is air suspended, atmospheric pressure is present on both sides of the diaphragm, until the brake pedal is depressed. In the applied position atmospheric pressure is cut off on one side of the diaphragm, (brake pedal depressed) and vacuum is applied to the same side. Atmospheric pressure then forces the diaphragm, toward the vacuum side.

If the cylinder is vacuum suspended, vacuum is present on both sides of the diaphragm until the brake pedal is depressed. In the applied position (brake pedal depressed), vacuum is cut off on one side of the diaphragm and atmospheric pressure is applied to the same side. One side of the diaphragm now has more pressure applied to it than the other side of the diaphragm; therefore, atmospheric pressure forces the diaphragm toward the side which has the least pressure, the vacuum side. Most modern power brakes are of the vacuum suspended type. A piston or bellows was used in place of a diaphragm on some older model booster units. Operating principles are the same for all units.

Power Brake Operation

The power brake unit involves the master cylinder and linkage only. Other parts of the brake system are usually like those in conventional brakes. Two external lines are generally connected to the power brake assembly: a vacuum connection to the intake manifold (vacuum reservoir on some installations) and a hydraulic connection leading into the hydraulic brake system.

On many installations a vacuum reservoir is inserted between the power unit and the intake manifold. The purpose of the reservoir is to make vacuum available for a short time to the booster unit, if the vehicle must make a stop without the engine running such as when it is being pushed or towed. Also, the reservoir maintains a uniform vacuum within the system should engine vacuum drop off under certain operating conditions. A check valve must be used in conjunction with a vacuum reservoir to prevent vacuum from bleeding back to the intake manifold when manifold vacuum is less than the vacuum in the tank.

All power brakes retain some pedal

resistance permitting the driver to maintain a certain amount of pedal feel. A light pressure upon the pedal will give a light braking force while a heavy pressure upon the pedal will give a more severe braking application.

If the vacuum section of the power unit should fail, brake application can still be obtained without the use of the vacuum assist.

The vacuum-hydraulic booster unit of the integral type is used exclusively today for all passenger car power brake installations. Certain light commercial vehicles also use this type of installation. The unit is labeled an integral type because the power unit and master cylinder are a single assembly that replaces the conventional master cylinder.

The most common integral types (brand names) are the Bendix, Delco-Moraine and the Midland Ross. The Bendix and Delco-Moraine are the most extensively used on passenger vehicles. All use a single or tandem diaphragm rather than a bellows or piston and presently are of the vacuum suspended type. The power unit uses a master cylinder constructed in the same manner as the conventional dual master cylinder.

Bendix Single Diaphragm Power Brake. The Bendix system consists of a power booster unit (vacuum) located between the brake pedal linkage system and

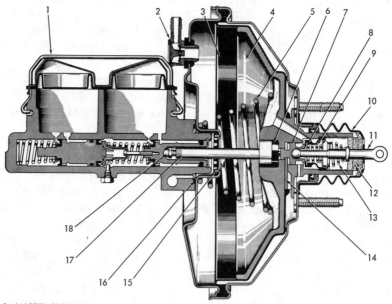

1. MASTER CYLINDER
2. VACUUM CHECK VALVE
3. DIAPHRAGM
4. DIAPHRAGM PLATE
5. DIAPHRAGM SPRING
6. REACTION DISC
7. PLUNGER
8. POPPET VALVE
9. POPPET VALVE SPRING
10. DUST BOOT
11. VALVE PUSH ROD
12. FILTER AND SILENCERS
13. VALVE RETURN SPRING
14. AIR VALVE LOCK PLATE
15. PUSH ROD SEAL
16. CYLINDER-TO-SHELL SEAL
17. HYDRAULIC PUSH ROD
18. ADJUSTING SCREW

Fig. 2-28. Bendix single diaphragm power brake. (*Chevrolet Div., General Motors Corp.*)

the master cylinder, and is bolted to the power unit, Fig. 2-28. The power unit is divided into two compartments by a flexible diaphragm. The power unit is vacuum suspended so that when the brakes are released and the engine is operating, manifold vacuum is supplied to both sides of the diaphragm.

A vacuum check valve is located in the line between the power unit and source of vacuum, (reservoir or intake manifold). The check valve prevents the loss of vacuum when manifold or reservoir vacuum falls below that in the brake system. This provides for several powered brake applications after the engine has stopped. With a complete loss of vacuum in the brake system, the brakes can be applied manually but considerable more pedal effort will be required.

The power unit is constructed in such a manner that the front and rear housings interlock to form a chamber which contains the power diaphragm assembly and valve mechanism. Located on the center portion of the diaphragm is a plate carrying the actuating and control valve mechanism. This plate is called the power piston. A diaphragm return spring is located between the housing and power piston. The control valve is of the poppet type with an atmospheric port and a vacuum port. A reaction disc made of hard rubber distributes pressure between the diaphragm plate and valve plunger in proportion to the contact area so as to provide a normal brake pedal feel. A valve push rod operates the control valve assembly and projects out of the power unit through a boot where it is attached to the brake pedal. The master cylinder, bolted to the front housing of the power unit, is actuated by the power unit through the hydraulic push rod.

When the engine is operating with the brake pedal released, engine vacuum will remove air between the power unit and the engine intake manifold. In released position, the valve operating rod and valve plunger are held in position by the valve return spring. The atmospheric port is closed and the vacuum port is open. Under these conditions both sides of the diaphragm are subjected to equal vacuum conditions. The hydraulic master cylinder will be in a released position.

As the brake pedal is depressed, the valve operating rod and plunger assembly are moved forward. This movement compresses the valve return spring and brings the poppet valve into contact with the vacuum port seat closing off the vacuum port. Further movement of the valve operating rod opens the atmospheric port admitting atmospheric pressure through the air filter to the rear half of the power unit (chamber next to the firewall). The force on the diaphragm created by this unbalanced pressure condition forces the diaphragm and hydraulic pushrod forward actuating the master cylinder piston. Movement of the master cylinder piston delivers hydraulic pressure to each individual wheel cylinder.

A reaction force is developed during the braking process by the hydraulic pressure which provides "brake feel" during the braking operation. Due to this reaction process, any degree of braking effect can be attained. When the brake pedal is held stationary, a slight movement of the diaphragm takes place which closes the atmospheric port. With both the vacuum and atmospheric ports closed, the diaphragm and piston assembly will remain stationary and the brakes will be in a "hold" position. Further movement of the brake pedal will reopen the atmospheric port for greater braking effort or release of the pedal will open vacuum to both sides of the diaphragm and power piston and braking will not be in effect.

If the power unit should fail, the

brakes may be applied manually. As the brake pedal is depressed, the valve operating rod moves forward beyond its normal travel until the master cylinder push rod is contacted. Further movement pushes the master cylinder piston into the master cylinder, causing the brakes to be applied in the conventional manner.

Delco-Moraine Single Diaphragm Power Brake. The basic construction and operation of the Delco-Moraine single diaphragm power brake, Fig. 2-29, is much the same as the Bendix single diaphragm power brake.

Bendix Tandem Diaphragm Power Brakes. The Bendix tandem diaphragm power brake contains many of the same components as the single diaphragm power unit. Using two diaphragms provides greater assistance in brake application, as atmospheric pressure and manifold vacuum is applied to a larger diaphragm area.

When the engine is operating and the brake pedal is released, vacuum from a reservoir or the engine intake manifold is admitted through the vacuum check valve to the front vacuum chamber as well as through a port in the hub of the front plate to the vacuum chamber located in front of the rear diaphragm. A sectional view of the complete unit is shown in Fig. 2-30.

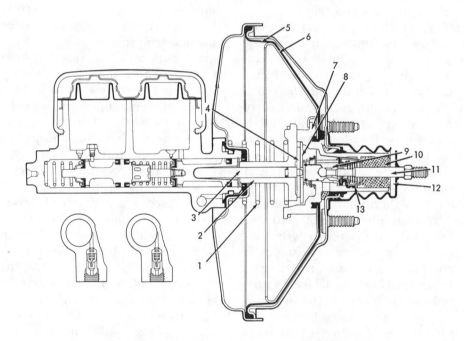

1. POWER PISTON RETURN SPRING
2. REACTION RETAINER
3. MASTER CYLINDER PISTON ROD
4. REACTION PLATE
5. DIAPHRAGM
6. SUPPORT PLATE
7. POWER PISTON

8. REACTION LEVERS
9. AIR VALVE
10. AIR FILTERS
11. PUSH ROD
12. SILENCER
13. FLOATING CONTROL VALVE
    ASSEMBLY

Fig. 2-29. Delco-Moraine single diaphragm power brake. (*Chevrolet Div., General Motors Corp.*)

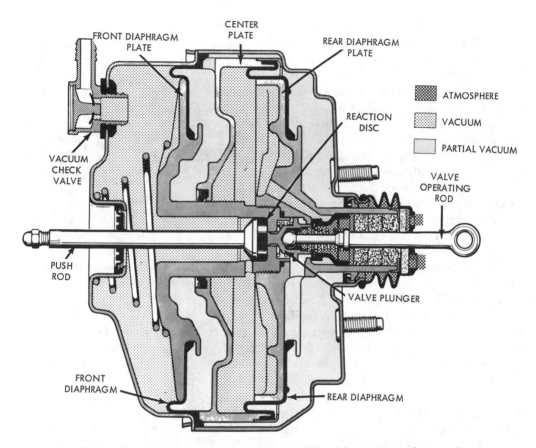

Fig. 2-30. Bendix tandem diaphragm power brake. (*Oldsmobile Div., General Motors Corp.*)

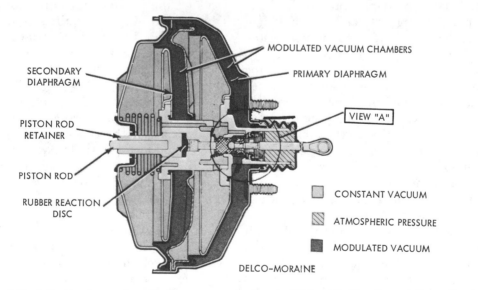

Fig. 2-31. Delco-Moraine tandem diaphragm power brake unit. (*Oldsmobile Div., General Motors Corp.*)

Delco-Moraine Tandem Diaphragm Power Brake. In addition to the single diaphragm power brake assembly, Delco-Moraine also has available a tandem diaphragm power brake unit which is used on a number of vehicles. Figure 2-31 is a sectional view of this type of dual diaphragm power brake assembly.

As illustrated, the unit has two major assemblies, a vacuum power cylinder and a hydraulic master cylinder. The power cylinder is made up of a power piston assembly and a return spring. The power piston assembly is composed of a primary power piston, a secondary piston and a steel housing divider. The primary piston contains the valve mechanism. The secondary power piston contains the reaction mechanism which balances pedal pressure against vacuum force during a fixed brake holding position. A vacuum check valve is located in the front housing at the vacuum hose connection.

Midland Ross Power Brake. The Midland Ross power brake system is available on a number of Chrysler products. The various units which are in use may be classified as single diaphragm small, tandem diaphragm small, single diaphragm large or tandem diaphragm large depending upon the weight of the vehicle in which the unit is installed.

The basic operating principles are the same as for the previously discussed power brake systems. The unit mounts on the engine side of the firewall and is externally connected to the brake system by a push rod to the brake pedal, by a vacuum hose to the intake manifold, through a check valve and hydraulic lines from the master cylinder to the wheel cylinder, Fig. 2-32.

The Midland Ross power brake unit can be identified by a clamp type band used to attach the housing and cover together. The master cylinder contains all of the regular master cylinder compo-

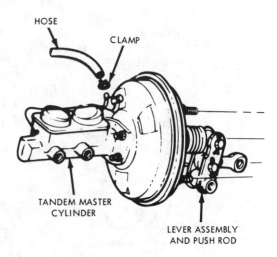

Fig. 2-32. Midland Ross power brake system. (Plymouth Div., Chrysler Corp.)

nents except for a special push rod which is part of the power unit.

The vacuum unit cannot be repaired by the usual methods, it must be exchanged for another unit should it fail to perform properly.

Power Brake Troubles

The brakes will still operate even though the booster unit fails. However, the amount of effort required to stop the vehicle will be greatly increased. The conventional brake system is left intact and the power system is added to the existing system.

If brake trouble is encountered, first check out the braking system in the same manner as for the conventional system; then proceed for possible power booster malfunctions. Air in the hydraulic lines will cause a spongy pedal feel. Oil- or grease-soaked brake lining will cause the brakes to grab. Power brakes do not require adjustment other than linkage, they either operate correctly or not at all.

To check the power booster unit for correct operation, with the engine stopped, apply the brakes several times so as to deplete the vacuum reserve in the system. Partly depress the pedal and hold lightly, start the engine. If the booster system is operating properly, the pedal will tend to fall away under foot pressure and will require less pressure to hold in applied position. If no action is felt, the booster system is not functioning.

If the power unit is not giving enough assistance, check the engine vacuum. If the engine vacuum is abnormally low (below 14 inches at idle) tune up the engine to raise the vacuum reading and try the brake assist. A steady hiss when the brake pedal is depressed indicates a vacuum leak which results in a hard pedal, that is, a lack of power assist.

Vacuum failure, which results in a hard pedal, may be due to a faulty check valve, a collapsed vacuum hose to the intake manifold or internal leaks in the power brake unit.

A tight pedal linkage will sometimes result in a hard pedal. If this connection is free and the brakes still fail to release properly, the power unit must be replaced, providing the trouble is not a restricted line or trouble in the conventional brake system.

In addition to hydraulic system problems, the brakes may fail to release as a result of a blocked passage in the power piston, a sticking air valve or a broken air valve spring.

Any malfunction occurring in the power unit will necessitate removing the unit from the vehicle. This is done by first removing the master cylinder assembly and then removing the power unit from the firewall.

The entire assembly is usually exchanged for a factory rebuilt or new unit. On-the-job overhaul of power brake units is seldom performed in auto-service shops today.

TRADE COMPETENCY TEST

1. How is an electric brake applied?
2. How does air pressure apply air brakes?
3. What two principles of hydraulics are utilized in a hydraulic brake system?
4. If you know the cross-sectional area of a piston in a hydraulic cylinder and the total force being applied to the piston, how can you calculate the pressure being applied to the hydraulic system?
5. How is the hydraulic pressure which is developed in the master cylinder delivered to the wheel cylinders?
6. What part of the brake assembly provides the force to return the fluid back to the master cylinder when the brakes are released?
7. What is a "stepped" wheel cylinder?
8. What is the purpose of the master cylinder reservoir?
9. What rubber part prevents dirt from entering the rear of the master cylinder bore?
10. What part actually comes into contact with, and pushes the fluid out to, the wheel cylinders when the brakes are applied?
11. What are the two purposes of the residual check valve?
12. What is the purpose of the rubber diaphragm under the reservoir cover of most late model car master cylinders?
13. What is the difference between a dual master cylinder used for a car with front disc brakes and a dual master cylinder used for a car with drum brakes only?
14. What are the common types of piston seals?

15. What is the purpose of the metering valve in disc brake hydraulic systems?
16. The proportioning valve is located between the master cylinder and the front or rear brakes? What is its purpose?
17. Would a proportioning valve ever be used on a vehicle having drum brakes on all four wheels?
18. What has happened in a hydraulic brake system when the warning light is illuminated on the instrument panel of the car?
19. What is the basic operating principle of a power brake?
20. What factors determine the amount of effort a power brake will apply?
21. What type of power brake is used on all vehicles today?
22. What type of parking brake is used when disc brakes are used on all four wheels?
23. Why do some vehicles use a tandem diaphragm power assist unit?

CHAPTER 3

BRAKE SERVICE

Brake service work should be of the highest standard of reliability and accuracy. Anyone doing such work should recognize and accept the responsibility which arises from the fact that the operator of the vehicle will be entrusting his safety and that of many others to the care and skill with which such brake work has been performed.

Because of the continual use of the brakes to slow down and/or stop the vehicle, automotive brakes require attention more often than most other major units on the vehicle. This chapter discusses the drum and disc brake adjustments which the mechanic will be called on to perform. A useful brake service diagnosis check list is presented at the end of this chapter which will help the mechanic to locate the brake problem by considering the road performance of the vehicle.

Common Brake Troubles

Automobile brakes are designed to give satisfactory service over long periods of time except for occasional adjustments on early model brakes to compensate for normal wear. Occasionally, some trouble occurs in the brake system which lessens the ability of the brakes to stop the vehicle within safe distances. If adjustment of the brakes does not correct such troubles, further repairs or relining of the brakes may be necessary.

All present model drum brakes use a self-adjusting mechanism, which eliminates the need for periodic minor adjustments if the mechanism functions properly. A fixed anchor pin or bolt is also used which eliminates the need for a major brake shoe adjustment. Disc brakes are self-adjusting.

Some of the common brake troubles are indicated as follows.

Brakes Lock During Operation

It is possible for the hydraulic brakes to lock in the applied position and to fail to release if the compensating port (or ports) in the master cylinder is either partially or totally blocked, which would prevent the brake fluid from returning to the reservoir after a brake application has been made. Blocking of the compensating port can result if the brake pedal linkage is not correctly adjusted, which would permit the edge of the lip of the primary cup on the master cylinder piston to completely or partially cover the port. Present brake systems use a dual master cylinder having dual fluid reservoirs. A compensating port is located in each reservoir. Blocking the port in either reservoir will effect the two brakes operated from that particular section. If the ports in both reservoirs are blocked all four wheels will be locked. Correct adjustment of the pedal linkage requires a clearance of about 0.015 to 0.020 in. between the brake pedal rod and the master cylinder piston. As a result of this clearance, the brake pedal can be moved between $\frac{1}{4}$ and $\frac{1}{2}$ in. (on some cars) before the master cylinder piston is moved (termed pedal free play). If this clearance is not maintained the lip of the primary cup may either totally or partially block the compensating port, preventing brake fluid from returning to the master cylinder reservoir. This causes the brakes to drag. The heat resulting from the friction between shoes and drums can cause the fluid to expand in the wheel cylinders, forcing the brake shoes outward against the drums and locking them in the applied position.

A swollen primary cup, due to the use of inferior brake fluid, or the presence of mineral oil in the fluid, would also block the compensating port with the same results. Dirt or other foreign matter in the fluid can also block the port, which is of very small diameter.

NOTE: If the brakes are locked, preventing movement of the vehicle, momentarily open the bleeder valve at any wheel. The pressure holding the brakes applied will force out a small amount of fluid, freeing the brakes. A car equipped with a dual master cylinder (independent front and rear brake hydraulic lines) will require that both a front and a rear brake be bled. Close the bleeder valve or valves. This does not correct the trouble, but will permit the vehicle to be moved to a location where repairs may be made.

To correct this trouble, first check brake pedal free play, if it is not within the limits required for that vehicle, adjust pedal linkage to provide correct free play. Late model vehicles do not have provision for adjustment of free play as they use a linkage of fixed dimensions, and thus require no pedal free play adjustment. If pedal adjustment will not correct the trouble, clean the master cylinder filler cap and the area around it and remove the filler cap. With a clean piece of tag wire, check through the filler port for clogging of the compensating ports either by dirt, or by a swollen primary cup. If inspection indicates dirt or a possible swollen primary cup, the master cylinder should be overhauled and hydraulic system flushed and bled.

Brakes Do Not Apply

When foot pressure is applied, the hydraulic brake pedal should travel just far enough to develop the hydraulic pressure necessary to apply the brakes. On older models if the pedal goes to the floor suddenly, it may be due to a leak in the hydraulic system (generally a faulty primary cup in the master cylinder), or the pedal linkage may be broken or disconnected.

If a fluid leak occurs in the hydraulic system having a dual master cylinder (all late model vehicles), the brakes will still apply on two wheels. A red warning light will come on in the instrument panel to warn the operator that one of the brake systems has failed. There will probably be more pedal "free play" than normally present.

Check for broken or leaking lines or

connections, especially in the flexible lines. Tighten any loose connections or replace any damaged parts. Check for leakage of the master cylinder piston cups, wheel cylinder cups and caliper piston seals. Excessive fluid in the dust boots on the master cylinder or any wheel cylinder or caliper indicates leakage past the rubber cup or seal. Correction of such leaks requires overhaul of the leaking component and replacement of all rubber parts.

If air has entered the hydraulic system, the brake pedal will have a spongy feel when depressed (since air in the system may be compressed), and may travel all the way to the firewall without developing sufficient hydraulic pressure to stop the vehicle.

Air will enter the hydraulic system if the fluid in the master cylinder is too low, if there is excessive clearance between the brake linings and the drums, if there is a faulty check valve in the master cylinder, or if the pistons of the wheel cylinders are not held firmly in place when the tension of the brake shoe retracting springs is removed while servicing the drum brakes. Bleed the hydraulic system to eliminate air that has entered the system. Adjust the brake shoes if required.

Low Pedal Reserve

During the normal operation of any brake, a little of the brake lining wears away each time the brakes are applied. On drum brakes the pedal reserve decreases as the wear increases. This wear is compensated for on drum brakes by means of a minor brake adjustment which restores the pedal reserve. Modern brakes are equipped with a self-adjusting mechanism which maintains the desired amount of pedal reserve. A low pedal with such an installation may indicate a faulty adjusting mechanism. On disc brakes there is no loss of pedal reserve;

the travel of the caliper pistons automatically compensates for lining wear. However, low spongy pedal *can* occur in disc brake systems if all the air bubbles are not bled from the hydraulic system.

Pedal Reserve: This term refers to the distance between the brake pedal and the firewall when the brakes are fully applied. Department of Transportation (DOT) used car safety rules require that 20% of total pedal travel must be available on all brake systems with a 125-lb force on the pedal. During severe application, brake drums get hot and expand, thus further reducing the pedal reserve.

Hard Brake Action

Hard brake action, or excessive brake pedal pressure required to stop a vehicle, may be caused by the normal wear of the brake linings, a heavy glaze on the lining, or grease soaked lining.

Make a minor brake adjustment to compensate for lining wear, if the brakes are not of the self-adjusting type. If this does not correct the trouble, remove the drum assembly and carefully inspect the brake assembly. Check to see if the self-adjusting mechanism is functioning properly if this type of assembly is used. Make a major adjustment if an adjustable anchor is used.

Glaze is a smooth glossy surface caused by high temperature. Glazed linings have a lower coefficient of friction and therefore reduce braking action and require more pedal effort. Remove the glaze by grinding or replace the linings.

Lack of lubrication of the pedal linkage can cause hard brake action. Check the brake lining for the wrong type of lining, or brake shoes installed in the reversed position. Replace the linings if required. Check the hydraulic lines for obstructions, kinks, dents, or dirt. Clean out lines or replace parts as required.

Check the brake fluid. If in doubt

about the fluid, drain and flush the system. Refill with fluid recommended by the manufacturer of the vehicle and bleed the brake system.

On vehicles equipped with a power brake, the unit may be inoperative and not giving any brake assistance. Check the hoses and tighten all connections in the vacuum system, clean the power brake air cleaner, and service the vacuum check valve.

Uneven Brake Action

If the brake action is uneven, that is, the car will pull to one side when the brakes are applied, check the adjustment of the drum brake shoes. Uneven brake action seldom occurs with disc brakes. If uneven braking action does occur, check the caliper for sticking pistons. If frozen or sticking pistons are found, the caliper must be rebuilt.

Check the flexible brake hoses for worn spots due to chafing and for cuts or tears of the outer surface. Look for separation of the hose from the fittings at the ends or for damage to the fittings, such as cracks, damaged threads, bends, etc. Check for soft spots in the hose, which can indicate softening of the rubber inside the hose. Check for a dented or kinked brake line.

If one wheel drags, the adjustment of the front wheel bearings should be checked and corrected to give proper wheel rotation with little or no endwise play of the wheel on the spindle. Loose wheel bearings permit the wheel to move in an endwise manner on the spindle, resulting in a misaligned contact of brake shoe and drum or disc.

Further causes of uneven brake action in drum brake systems are usually apparent from visual inspection when the drums are removed. Check for a corroded or bent shoe mechanism, a sticking wheel cylinder piston, weak or broken brake shoe retracting springs, or grease or glaze on the linings.

If grease is found on the brake lining, examine the grease seals for wear, damage, or aging (hardness of the sealing lip) which will permit grease to escape from the seal and work onto the drum and brake lining or onto the disc. Lubricant at too high a level in the differential (rear axle) can work its way past a rear wheel grease seal. On front wheels, check for an excessive amount of grease used in packing the front wheel bearings or in the cavity in the front hub. Repair or replace parts as required.

Spongy Pedal

A spongy pedal may be due to improper fit between the lining and the drum or disc, or air in the hydraulic system. Grind the brake shoe to match the drum if the system is of the drum type. If a disc brake system, check to see if the correct disc brake shoes have been installed. Finally, bleed the brake system.

Brake linings that do not fit the drum or disc make it necessary to apply sufficient pedal pressure to bend the shoes in order to obtain full contact with the drum or disc. This condition will result in a brake action that feels as though you were pushing the brake pedal against a spring instead of something solid.

Brakes Grab

When brakes grab under light pedal pressure, it may be that the lining has absorbed grease, oil or brake fluid. Linings soaked with oil or brake fluid fail to hold, and will slip, giving the effect of a grabbing brake on the opposite wheel. Loose drum brake backing plates or loose wheel bearings also are a cause of brake grab. Brake drums and discs which are rough, scored, cracked, or out of round are also causes.

Damaged brake lining must be replaced. Brake drums or discs which cannot be remachined within manufacturer's specifications must be replaced. Oil or grease seals should be replaced, if they are faulty.

Loss of Fluid

Hydraulic brake fluid can be lost if a wheel cylinder or caliper leaks, if the master cylinder leaks, or if a line or connection (cracked line, cracked or defective fittings, cross threaded, or loose, cracked flare) leaks. Loss of fluid at the master cylinder necessitates its removal for repairs. Loss of fluid at the wheel cylinder or caliper necessitates overhaul of the wheel cylinder or caliper.

Adjustment of Drum Brakes

The disc brake requires no periodic adjustment to compensate for lining wear; this section is therefore devoted exclusively to the adjustment of drum brakes.

All presently manufactured American automobiles use a self-adjusting brake mechanism which eliminates the need for minor brake adjustments. A fixed anchor pin or bolt is also used, eliminating the major adjustment feature. The following information applies to older model vehicles, large trucks and some import cars.

Drum brake adjustments are divided into two classifications: minor adjustments, which compensate for normal lining wear; and major adjustments, which involve moving both the toe and the heel of the brake shoe. Consult the vehicle manufacturer's shop manual for the specific method of making either type of adjustment.

Minor Brake Adjustment

If the condition of the lining is un-known, it is advisable to remove the right front wheel and look for the following conditions: brake drum scored, out-of-round, or bell-mouthed; brake lining soaked with oil, grease, or brake fluid, glazed lining worn to less than $\frac{1}{32}$ in. from the shoe platform; brake lining does not make full contact with the drum. If any of these conditions exist, a major brake repair is required. It may be assumed that the condition of the linings and the drums at the other three wheels is approximately the same as found at the wheel removed.

If the brake system is an earlier type (no self-adjustment), adjust all brake shoes to compensate for lining wear. An adjustment is provided at each brake that moves the brake shoes outward towards the drums, thus permitting the proper clearance to be re-established.

The procedure for making a minor brake adjustment is to reduce the lining-to-drum clearance to a point where the wheel just turns freely, without a lining drag.

Cam Adjustment. Two methods of adjusting the lining to drum clearance have been used in the past. The first method involves the use of two adjusting cams, one cam being in contact with each shoe, as shown in Fig. 3-1. With vehicle hoisted or jacked up safely, so wheels can be spun, turn the adjusting cam for the front brake shoe, Fig. 3-1 until the shoe is tight against the drum. Then carefully back off the cam until the wheel can be spun freely. Next, turn the cam for the rear brake shoe until the shoe is tight against the brake drum. Then back off carefully on the cam until the wheel spins free. Repeat this procedure for all wheels.

Star Wheel Adjustment. The other method of adjustment involves turning a star wheel adjusting screw located between the lower ends of the brake shoes.

Fig. 3-1. On this drum brake design, adjusting cams (one for each shoe) are turned to adjust the lining-to-drum clearance. *Left:* The front wheel brake assembly. *Right:* A rear brake backing plate. (*Plymouth Div., Chrysler Corp.*)

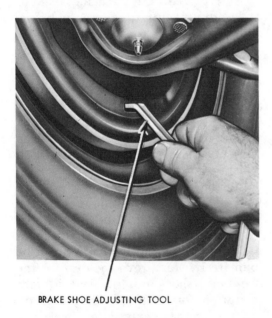

Fig. 3-2. Performing a minor brake adjustment on a brake without a self-adjustment mechanism. A brake shoe adjusting tool, inserted into a slot in the brake backing plate, is used to turn the star wheel adjusting screw which takes up the excess in the lining-to-drum clearance. (*Ford Div., Ford Motor Co.*)

This method of adjustment is shown in Fig. 3-2. Disconnect parking brake cables at the equalizer so that the parking brake is not partially applied due to shortened cables. Remove the plugs from the adjusting holes in the backing plate. Using a tool as shown in Fig. 3-2 and with the vehicle wheels off the ground, turn the star wheel until the brake shoes are hard against the drum and there is a heavy drag on the wheel. Then back off the star wheel approximately 10 to 15 notches. Spin wheel to check drag. Brake shoes should be correctly adjusted if correct procedure has been followed. If there is still a heavy drag on wheel, the brake shoe anchor pin may need adjustment as described under major adjustment. In the case of a fixed anchor design, the brake shoes must be ground. If there is no drag, replace the plugs in the adjusting slots. Then adjust the parking brake cables to give correct parking brake action.

After completing the adjustment of the shoes, check the pedal reserve. If the pedal reserve is less than half the total distance to the firewall, readjust the shoes more carefully. In the case of a car with self-adjusting brakes, apply the brakes while driving the car in reverse to establish a higher pedal.

Check for adjustment of brake pedal free play. The brake pedal is correctly adjusted when the pedal has more than ¼ in. and less than ½ in. free travel (measured at the pedal pad) before the master cylinder piston starts to move. The brake pedal lash is usually adjusted by shortening or lengthening the rod linking the brake pedal to the master cylinder piston.

Present pedal linkage is non-adjustable. Check the master cylinder reservoir and fill if necessary.

The minor adjustment described above for brake designs with a star wheel adjusting screw will apply to some older automobiles still in service.

Self-Adjusting Brake Adjustment

Modern brake designs incorporate the drum brake self-adjusting mechanism. Brakes which feature the self-adjusting mechanism may never require a minor adjustment; the brake is designed to adjust itself. However, the self-adjusting mechanism may fail, requiring a check and repair of the mechanism as well as a manual adjustment of the lining-to-drum clearance.

Some self-adjusting brakes will have an opening in the backing plate or drum to permit adjustment with the drum installed. It will be necessary to insert a long thin screwdriver or a special tool through the opening for the purpose of holding the self-adjusting mechanism away from the star wheel while making the adjustment, Fig. 3-3. Extreme care must be taken so as not to distort the adjusting arm. With the adjusting arm held

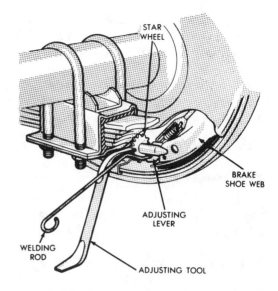

Fig. 3-3. Adjusting a self-adjusting brake. (*Plymouth Div., Chrysler Corp.*)

away from the star wheel, the drum-to-lining clearance is adjusted in the regular manner.

Many late model automobiles make no provision for this type of minor brake adjustment. No slot is machined in the brake backing plate or drum, making access to the star wheel for adjustment impossible. The recommended procedure for adjusting the lining-to-drum clearance on a brake with a self-adjusting mechanism is to remove the drum and use a special adjusting caliper tool to set the shoes to the specified size.

If the brake drums are worn considerably, it may be necessary to retract the adjusting screw before the drum can be removed. If there is an opening in the drum or backing plate, release the actuator from the star wheel with a thin screwdriver and back off the star wheel adjuster with another screwdriver.

If there is no opening in the drum or backing plate, there will be a lanced area in the web of the drum or the backing plate. A lanced area is a place which has been partially punched out. Drive out the lanced area with a punch. This will provide an opening for adjusting the star wheel. A metal hole cover is put in the opening before installing the wheel.

The following procedures, which are used to make a major brake adjustment, include adjusting the lining-to-drum clearance for a self-adjusting brake.

Major Brake Adjustment

A major brake adjustment is recommended after installation of new or relined shoes, after the drums have been turned, and in all cases where satisfactory braking is not obtained by the minor adjustment. A major adjustment also includes inspection of the hydraulic system, and bleeding of the system if necessary.

On some older cars, the brakes are provided with adjustable anchors. A major adjustment involves the resetting of these anchors along with brake shoe adjustment by means of the regular star wheel adjusting screw or cams to obtain the desired clearance. Consult the manufacturer's shop manual if there is a question as to whether or not the anchor or anchors are adjustable and for the correct specifications of the anchor settings.

When each brake shoe has a separate anchor bolt, the head of the anchor carrying the shoe is generally in the form of an eccentric. Turning the eccentric will move the shoe away from or in toward the drum.

When both brake shoe ends are in contact with one anchor pin, the anchor may be in the form of an eccentric, and shoe-to-drum clearance is adjusted by turning the anchor pin. On some installations the anchor pin is mounted in a slot. Loosening the anchor pin lock nut, expanding the star wheel adjuster, and tapping the pin upward will raise the brake shoes and reduce the lining-to-drum clearance.

Special adjusting gages or drums should be used to obtain the exact anchor setting. If a special gage is not available move the anchor until the drum locks. Then, move the anchor in the opposite direction until the drum just turns without a drag.

Adjustment of the hand brake is also generally considered as a part of a major brake adjustment.

Self-Adjusting Brake Pre-Adjustment

All present-day automobiles are equipped with a self-adjusting drum brake, Fig. 3-4. Automobiles which feature front wheel disc brakes will also employ self-adjusting drum brakes for the rear wheels. Although minor adjustments between major brake jobs are seldom, if ever, necessary, the proper lining-to-drum clearance for self-adjusting brakes must be *manually* adjusted at the conclusion of each major brake job and before the refinished drums are mounted on the car.

Adjustment of the star wheel on a self-adjusting brake is quite critical. Too often, the conventional method of adjusting the brake (through a slot in the brake backing plate) with a star wheel adjusting tool results in the brake being adjusted with too little clearance. A dragging brake results in excessive heat, causing drum expansion and an over-adjusting brake. Pushing the adjusting lever away from the star wheel with a thin screwdriver or similar tool while adjusting the brakes with a star wheel tool or screwdriver may result in a bent lever. The adjusting lever can be bent enough so that it no longer contacts the star wheel to adjust the brakes.

A special tool is available to accurately pre-adjust self-adjusting brakes with the brake drum removed. Basically, the tool is an adjustable caliper. The lower part is an inside caliper; the upper

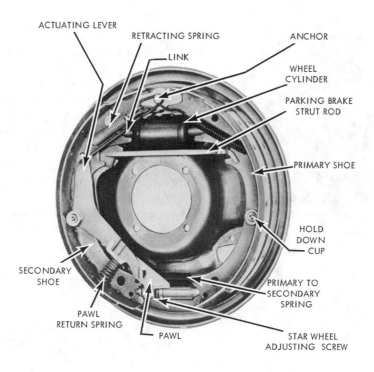

Fig. 3-4. Rear wheel brake assembly of a duo-servo brake with a self-adjusting mechanism. (Cadillac Div., General Motors Corp.)

Fig. 3-5. Adjusting the inside caliper of an adjustable caliper to the diameter of a turned drum. The outside caliper part of the tool automatically opens to the correct setting for the brake shoes. (Oldsmobile Div., General Motors Corp.)

part is an outside caliper. Expanding the inside caliper to a given setting automatically establishes the setting of the outside caliper part. The inside caliper part of the tool is first fitted to the refinished drum diameter, Fig. 3-5. The outside caliper part of the tool is simultaneously set to the corresponding brake shoe diameter. The outside part of the tool is then set across the newly-installed linings, as shown in Fig. 3-6. Since the drum is removed, the self-adjusting mechanism is fully exposed and easily accessible; the adjusting pawl or lever can be gently and safely held away from the star wheel while the star wheel is turned to expand the linings to the tool setting.

The difference between the drum setting and the shoe setting parts of the tool is fixed at 0.020 in. By using the tool, the clearance between each shoe and the drum (after setting the brake shoes) is

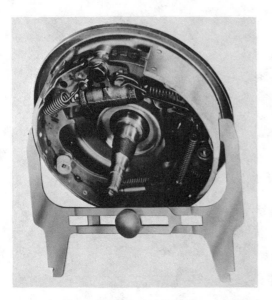

Fig. 3-6. The outside caliper of the tool is placed across the brake shoes. (*Oldsmobile Div., General Motors Corp.*)

not less than 0.010 in. After the brake job is completed, and while the car is being road tested, the final adjustment of the brakes can be accomplished by driving the vehicle in reverse and applying the brakes.

Since many late model cars do *not* have a slot in the brake backing plate for adjusting the lining-to-drum clearance with the star wheel adjusting tool, a caliper tool of the type described above is necessary to perform an adequate brake adjustment on these vehicles.

Adjust Parking Brake Cables. Adjusting the lining-to-drum clearance automatically adjusts the parking brake; however, if excess movement is necessary to apply the brakes, the cable should be shortened. The cables are adjusted by loosening the locknut on the equalizer several turns. If a clevis is used, remove the clevis pin and turn the clevis until the cables are just tight enough to remove the slack. If a nut is used on the equalizer

rod instead of a clevis, turn the nut forward until the cable slack is removed. Tighten the lock nut. Excessive tightening may pull the brake shoes off of their anchors causing the brakes to drag.

The parking brake installed on vehicles with rear wheel disc brakes consists of a small drum brake assembly inside each rotor. After removing the wheel, it is possible to adjust the lining-to-drum clearance by a star wheel adjusting mechanism through an opening in the brake rotor. The cable and linkage arrangement is the same as for the regular rear drum parking brake.

Flushing Hydraulic Brake Systems

The hydraulic brake system must be drained, flushed out, and refilled with new brake fluid of the correct type if the fluid becomes thick, dirty or contaminated with rubber or metal particles from the parts of the system. Mixing of two different brake fluids in the system may produce a chemical reaction between the fluids which can harm the rubber or metal parts, or reduce the braking efficiency. If any mineral oil, such as engine oil, has been put into the system, the rubber parts will be damaged by swelling. In any such instance, flushing is necessary to restore the braking system to normal efficiency. When flushing a brake system, use special flushing fluid recommended by the car manufacturer. Otherwise use denatured alcohol or clean brake fluid.

Remove all grease and dirt from the bleeder valve and the area around it at each wheel by wire brushing. Clean throughly around the master cylinder filler cap. No dirt should be permitted to enter the system. Remove the filler cap. Attach a bleeder hose to a bleeder valve, placing the end of the hose in a clean container to catch the fluid from the system. Flushing is performed at each wheel in turn by opening the bleeder valve 1½ turns. Pump the brake pedal with full strokes until all of the fluid emerges clear in color from each wheel cylinder. As the fluid level in the reservoir goes down, keep adding to the reservoir.

If flushing fluid or alcohol is used, after the system is clean, pump the system dry. The system should be refilled with new brake fluid and bled until all air and the remaining flushing fluid or alcohol have been removed.

Bleeding Hydraulic Brakes

When any part of the hydraulic system is disconnected for repairs or replacement of parts, air may enter the system and cause a spongy pedal action. Air can also be introduced into the sys-

tem if the brake pedal is operated when the fluid is too low in the master cylinder.

Removing air from the brake system is referred to as *bleeding*, either *manual* bleeding or *pressure* bleeding. Manual bleeding requires very little equipment, while pressure bleeding involves the use of a special brake bleeder tank. The pressure bleeder should be of the diaphragm type which prevents dirt and air from the air supply source from entering the fluid.

The bleeding procedure is essentially the same on all vehicles having hydraulic brakes. Automobile manufacturers recommend that vehicles equipped with disc brakes be bled with pressure bleeding equipment. The front and rear hydraulic systems (dual master cylinder) on today's passenger vehicles are individual systems and must be bled separately.

Most manufacturers recommend that the wheel cylinder nearest the master cylinder be bled first of the particular sys-

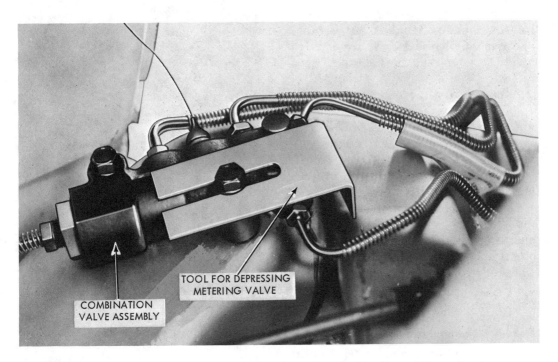

Fig. 3-7. Depressing metering valve for bleeding. (*Chevrolet Div., General Motors Corp.*)

tem (front or rear) being serviced. Other manufacturers recomend bleeding the wheel cylinder the farthest from the master cylinder. Always consult the manufacturer's manual for specific information. Regardless, the system must be bled until all air is completely removed from the entire system.

If the master cylinder is equipped with a bleeder screw or screws, bleed the master cylinder first. Loosen the bleeder screw. Push the brake pedal slowly through its full travel. Close the bleeder valve and return the pedal to the fully released position. Repeat until the fluid flows free of air bubbles. Repeat the same procedure for the remaining section of the master cylinder.

When pressure bleeding a hydraulic system, which uses a combination metering, proportioning valve and failure warning switch, the metering valve on the switch must be held open with a special tool, Fig. 3-7, while the system is being bled. Today's passenger vehicles all have dual master cylinders, but each half of the master cylinder is treated as an individual system and must be bled separately.

Remove all dirt from around the reservoir filler cap. Even one grain of sand in the brake fluid can cause serious damage to the hydraulic system. *Never* reuse brake fluid that has been bled from a brake system. Bleed the master cylinder first if equipped with bleeder valves.

If you do not have a pressure bleeder, the job is best performed by two people, one to operate the brake pedal and the other observing the discharge at each wheel. Be careful, however, as this procedure could cause damage to the dual master cylinder.

Manual Bleeding Procedure

Following is the step-by-step description of the manual bleeding procedure.

Two persons are required to do the job properly:

Step 1. Install a bleeder hose over the bleeder valve at the wheel having the shortest brake line. Insert the free end of the hose into a clean glass partially full of clean brake fluid. The end of the hose must be kept below the level of the fluid in the jar while bleeding the system. The glass jar permits you to see bubbles leaving the bleeder hose. Keep bleeder valve closed until pressure on the system is built up as explained in Step 3.

Step 2. Remove the master cylinder reservoir filler cap (previously cleaned) and fill the reservoir with clean brake fluid of the type approved by the car maker. Keep the reservoir filled during the bleeding operation to avoid the possibility of air entering the system.

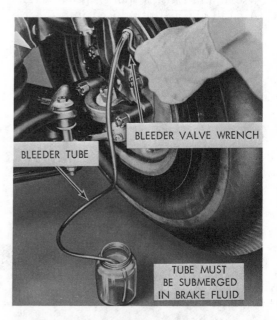

Fig. 3-8. Bleeding the drum brake wheel cylinder. Before opening the bleeder valve, one end of a tube is fitted over the valve. The other end is submerged in a jar of clean brake fluid. When the valve is opened, and bubbles no longer appear in a jar of fluid, the system is free of air at that wheel. (*Oldsmobile Div., General Motors Corp.*)

Step 3. Pump the brake pedal slowly with the bleeder closed, until pressure is built up in the brake system and the pedal no longer moves downward but has a hard, springy feel. Hold the pedal down firmly to maintain pressure in the system.

Step 4. Open the bleeder valve quickly, Fig. 3-8, watching for bubbles in the fluid leaving the bleeder hose in the jar. IMPORTANT: *Before the brake pedal goes more than halfway to the firewall, the bleeder valve must be closed to prevent loss of pressure in the system and to avoid drawing air or dirty fluid back to the system.*

Step 5. Repeat Steps 3 and 4, making sure the master cylinder reservoir is kept filled with clean brake fluid, until no air bubbles are observed in the fluid leaving the bleeder hose. Keep pressure on the system at all times. Close bleeder valve tightly while pressure is still on the system after you are sure there is no more air in the line being bled. Remove bleeder hose and wipe bleeder valve dry.

Step 6. Repeat the bleeding produre at the remaining wheel cylinders in the recommended order. NOTE: *On older vehicles having two (drum brake) wheel cylinders on the front wheels, be sure to bleed the upper wheel cylinder first, then the lower wheel cylinder last, to insure that all air is removed from that brake line.*

Step 7. After bleeding has been completed at all wheels, refill reservoir to correct level and install filler cap. Wipe clean.

Step 8. Check brake pedal action, test for proper free play of the pedal. Make brake adjustment as required, or test brakes to determine if there is any need for adjustment. Double check to make certain all bleeder valves are tightly closed.

Manually Bleeding a Hydraulic System Having a Safety Switch

The brake warning light used on today's vehicles may still be illuminated after manually bleeding the brake system even though the brake system is free of air. The safety valve piston position is normally centered in the switch as shown in Fig. 3-9, *left.* When bleeding the system, the last bleeder valve opened may

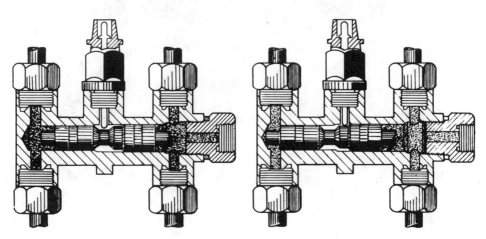

Fig. 3-9. *Left:* The normal position of the piston of a dual master cylinder safety valve. *Right:* In some cases the safety valve piston may bottom at the low pressure end of the valve as the final wheel is being bled, even though there is no longer any air in the system. The piston must therefore be re-centered to normalize the switch and shut off the brake warning light.

cause the valve piston to move to the low pressure end of the housing and stay there, closing the circuit of the warning light (Fig. 3-9, *right*).

After bleeding the hydraulic system, to re-center the piston in the safety switch and make the brake warning light go out observe the following procedure (which requires two persons):

Step 1. Turn the ignition switch to the ON or ACC position and push firmly on the brake pedal.

Step 2. Open a bleeder valve at the opposite end of the car from the last bleeder valve opened.

Step 3. As soon as the brake warning light goes out, release the brake pedal immediately, and have the other person close the bleeder valve.

If the warning light still remains lit, the piston has travelled to the other end of the valve. The procedure must be repeated, again bleeding a valve at the opposite end of the car from the last bleeder valve opened.

By pressure bleeding the hydraulic system instead of manually bleeding, the problem of an off-centered safety switch piston is avoided, since bleeding pressures of 20 to 30 psi will usually not cause

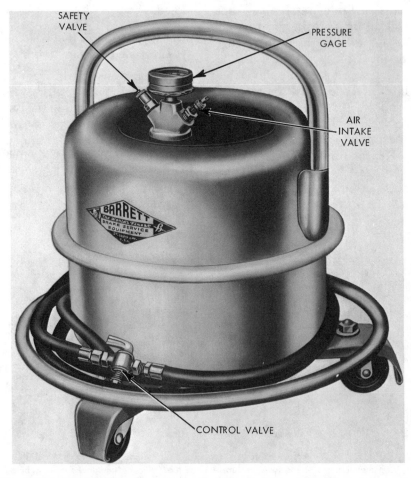

Fig. 3-10. The pressure bleeder automatically keeps master cylinder reservoir full and keeps the entire hydraulic system under steady pressure. (*Barrett Equipment* Co.)

the valve piston to stick at one end of the warning light switch housing.

Pressure Bleeding

A pressure bleeder, such as the one shown in Fig. 3-10, makes bleeding a one-man operation. The pressure bleeder not only maintains the correct level in the master cylinder reservoir, but eliminates the necessity for brake pedal manipulation. The pressure bleeder consists of a pressure tank partially filled with clean brake fluid. The pressure bleeding equipment must be of the diaphragm type that has a flexible diaphragm between the air supply and brake fluid. This prevents air, moisture, oil, dirt and other contaminants from entering the hydraulic system.

Air at 30 psi is introduced into the tank through a valve, such as used for filling a tire.

The pressure tank is connected to the master cylinder reservoir with a pressure tight connection. An adapter must be used on the dual master cylinder. The pressure bleeder is attached by means of a hose to the adapter, Fig. 3-11.

When pressure bleeding a car with front disc brakes, the pressure developed by the pressure bleeder will not be sufficient to open the metering valve which permits brake fluid flow to the disc brakes. A bleeder button, located on the metering valve must be depressed to override the valve and permit fluid to flow to the disc brake calipers at the pressure developed by the pressure bleeder, Fig. 3-7.

After the pressure bleeder line is tightly connected, the valve in the bleeder line is then opened. This places 30 psi pressure on the entire hydraulic system. If the master cylinder is equipped with bleeder valves, bleed these first and

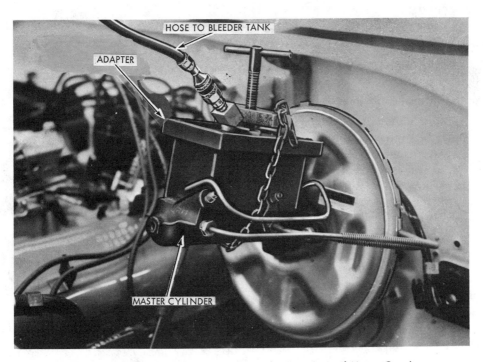

Fig. 3-11. Brake bleeder adaptor. (Chevrolet Div., General Motors Corp.)

then proceed to bleed each wheel cylinder in the same manner as when manual bleeding, using a bleeder hose and transparent jar. If a "True Track," "Sure Brake," or "Track Master" system is used, the modulator unit must be bled, in addition to the wheel cylinders. When the bleeding operation is finished, air bubbles are no longer coming out of the hose, close the bleed valve at the wheel cylinder before bleeding the next wheel cylinder.

Front disc brakes have one bleeder valve for each wheel. Rear wheel disc brakes use the bleeder valves, one inboard and one outboard, which necessitates the removal of the rear wheels to gain access to the outboard bleeder valve. Tapping the caliper with a rawhide mallet, as the fluid is flowing out, may assist in getting a good bleeding operation.

When the bleeding operation is finished, close the valve in the bleeder hose before disconnecting the hose from the master cylinder.

Brake Drum Service

Brake Drum Wear Problems

Although evidence of wear may at first glance be slight, the brake drum may under close inspection exhibit to some degree one or several of the common wear problems which will be described below. Since a smooth, regular, drum braking surface is essential to optimum braking performance, all brake drums should be machined, or "turned," whenever the brake shoes are relined or replaced.

Most automotive centers which offer complete brake service have brake drum lathes—a modified version of the machine shop lathe—on which brake drums are accurately machined to reproduce a like-

new friction surface. Some drums, however, may be too worn to be turned on a lathe. This is often true for older cars; since metal has been removed with each earlier major brake job, to turn the drums again would exceed the car manufacturer's maximum allowable oversize specification.

Drums can be reconditioned to a point if they are in good condition except for surface roughness. Most drums can be turned out to 0.060 in. oversize and oversize lining used. It is generally recommended that a drum be discarded when 0.090 in. oversize of the inside diameter as compared with the original size has been reached. The drums or discs used on late model passenger vehicles are marked with the maximum amount which can safely be removed from the inside drum diameter.

A drum micrometer is used to measure the drum diameter. A typical drum diameter micrometer is shown in Fig. 3-12.

The most common drum problems are: bell-mouthing, taper, scoring, hard spots, an out-of-round condition, and

Fig. 3-12. A drum micrometer, used to measure the diameter of the drum. (Ammco Tools, Inc.)

DRUM EXPANSION

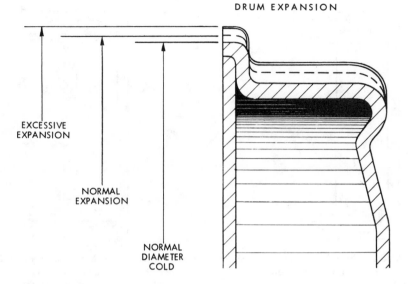

Fig. 3-13. Drum expansion due to operating pressure and temperature. *(Barrett Equipment Co.)*

eccentricity. The self-adjusting brake has made the service of drum brakes more critical. Problems which cause a self-adjusting brake to operate improperly are generally corrected by turning the drum on a lathe.

Bell-Mouthing. When the brake shoes are forced against the drum surface, the drum expands, due to the pressure and heat generated by friction, Fig. 3-13. If the elastic limit of the drum is reached and exceeded, the drum will not return to its original diameter. Since heat dissipation decreases with the distance from the hub or center section of the drum, the heat distortion will be more pronounced at the outer end of the drum. This results in a bell-mouthed drum, shown in Fig. 3-14. When bell-mouthing occurs, the linings will not uniformly contact the drum surface across their widths. Thus, a bell-mouthed drum causes low pedal reserve when the brakes are applied.

Tapered Drum. The most common wear problem is a tapered condition.

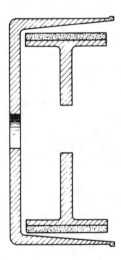

Fig. 3-14. A bell-mouthed drum results when the drum expands beyond its elastic limit. The condition is more pronounced at the outermost part of the drum friction surface.

When the drum expands as shown in Fig. 3-13, the open, outermost part of the drum expands more than the innermost part which is supported by the hub or center section of the drum. The shoe

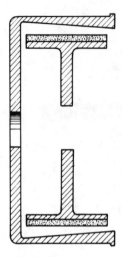

Fig. 3-15. A tapered drum is the result of severe wear along the inner part of the drum friction surface.

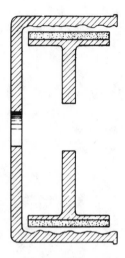

Fig. 3-16. A scored drum is caused by dirt trapped between the lining and drum or, more frequently, occurs when linings have worn so thin that the rivets which hold the lining to the shoe dig into the drum friction surface.

then presses harder against the innermost part of the drum friction surface and wears it away faster. Also, the brake dirt (old lining material) is trapped near the innermost or back part of the drum friction-surface and, acting as an abrasive, causes more wear than occurs at the outer part of the drum.

A tapered drum, shown in Fig. 3-15, is usually indicated by a low brake pedal when the brakes are applied following a minor adjustment. When the brake shoes are adjusted, the adjustment is made against the outermost, or smallest, diameter of the tapered drum. There would thus be no drag between drum and lining when the drum is replaced on the adjusted linings. But when applied against the drum the shoes go to the maximum worn diameter of the drum, which results in a low brake pedal. In some cases, brake noise will also be evidenced due to a tapered drum.

Scored Drum. Drum scoring, grooves or scratches in the drum friction surface, is caused by drum dirt trapped in the drum. More frequently, scoring occurs

when the brake shoe lining becomes worn so thin that the rivet heads contact and cut into the drum. See Fig. 3-16.

Hard Spots or Heat Checking. Hard spots are formed on the drum friction surface by excessive use of the brakes. Bluish-looking blotches in the center of the drum friction surface usually indicate hard spots. The hard spots, actually work-hardened cast iron, are formed by the extreme pressure of the brake lining being forced against the drum and the resulting excessive heat. Since the cast iron friction surface of the drum has been tempered into work-hardened cast iron in spots, the drum will present an irregular coefficient of friction to the brake shoes. This condition will show up as a hard, irregular brake pedal.

After a drum with hard spots is machined on a lathe, the hard spots may still be visible as small, raised bumps on the drum surface. If the "bumps" are present after turning, the drum will have to be ground. Heat-checks are usually an aggravated form of hard spots. See Fig. 3-17.

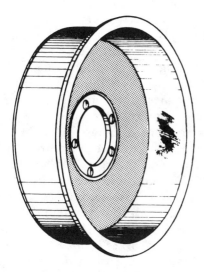

Fig. 3-17. A heat-checked drum. Drums which develop hard spots or which become heat-checked will show blue discolorations on the normally gray friction surface.

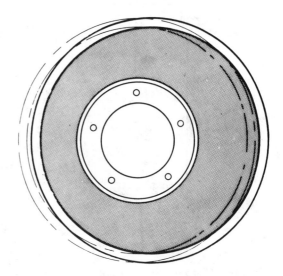

Fig. 3-19. An eccentric drum is a drum which rotates with a cam-like motion.

Out-of-Round Drum. This condition is not readily detected, and is determined by measuring the diameter of the drum with a brake drum micrometer in two or more places about its circumference as shown in Fig. 3-12. An out-of-round

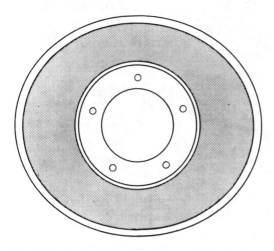

Fig. 3-18. An out-of-round drum, usually detected with a brake drum micrometer.

drum will cause a pulsating brake pedal when the brakes are applied. Turning the brake drum usually corrects this problem. See Fig. 3-18.

Eccentric Drum. An eccentric drum is a drum in which the geometric center of the friction surface is other than the center of the drum's mounting hub. See Fig. 3-19. The drum rotates with a cam-like motion. An eccentric drum is sometimes caused by improper tightening of the wheel lug nuts or excessive braking. An eccentric drum causes a pulsating brake pedal similar to an out-of-round drum.

This condition is usually discovered when the drum is mounted on the drum lathe arbor (the spindle which supports the drum). When a drum is eccentric, the tool bit will contact the drum only on a small segment of its circumference. The check for an eccentric drum is usually part of the setup of the drum on the lathe prior to machining. Figure 3-20 shows the correct lining-to-drum contact. This contact is assured when the brake drums are properly turned on a lathe.

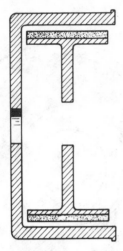

Fig. 3-20. Correct lining-to-drum contact.

Setup for Turning the Drum on a Lathe

On a brake drum lathe, the drum is mounted on a spindle, or *lathe arbor*. (The tool bar, which holds the tool bit, is usually left mounted on the lathe from job to job.) See Fig. 3-21. The drum must be perfectly centered on the arbor and rigidly secured to assure a uniform, accurate cut with an acceptable finish.

A front drum is usually mounted on the lathe arbor by means of radii adaptors or cones, which support the drum at the bearing races in its hub. See Fig. 3-22. Most rear brake drums (called "floating" drums) do not have hubs and are not supported on the rear axle by bearings. Therefore, instead of the radii adaptors and cones used to support front drums, rear floating drums are mounted on the lathe arbor by means of centering cones and aligning cups, Fig. 3-23. Older model cars have a hubbed rear drum which fits a tapered rear axle. These drums are mounted on two centering cones.

The brake drums of the different automobiles vary according to the wheel

Fig. 3-21. A front drum is shown being mounted on the arbor of a brake lathe. The tool bar is inserted in the tool holder on the lathe cross slide before the drum is mounted. The cross slide is moved as close to the housing as possible so that the cutting tool will not interfere with the drum as it is being mounted. (*Automotive Parts Rebuilders Assn.*)

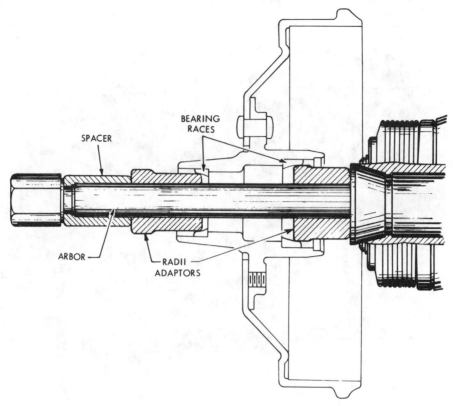

Fig. 3-22. Roller bearing and ball bearing type hub and drum assemblies are supported on the lathe arbor by radii adaptors. The radii adaptors support the hub at its bearing races.

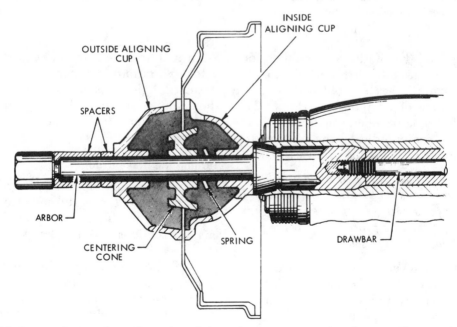

Fig. 3-23. Rear, or floating, drums do not have hubs and are not supported on bearings. They are therefore mounted on the lathe arbor by means of centering cones and aligning cups rather than with radii adaptors. (Ammco Tools Inc.)

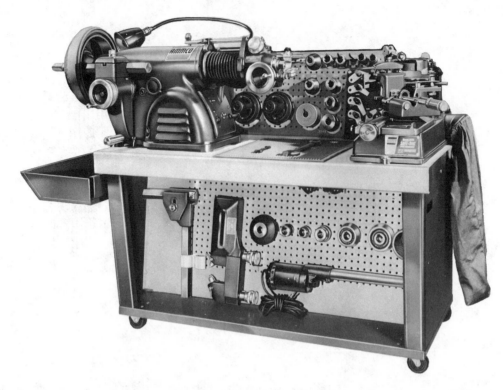

Fig. 3-24. A compact brake lathe (*left*) and a brake shoe grinder (*right*) are shown on a movable bench. The set of radii adaptors, centering cones, and aligning cones stored below enables the brake serviceman to mount and turn any brake drum. (Ammco Tools, Inc.)

size and design of the automobiles for which they are intended. For this reason, brake drum lathes are sold with a complete range of adaptors. See Fig. 3-24. The drum lathe operating instructions manual usually indicates the adaptors to be used for each specific drum setup.

Note: Always refer to the drum lathe manufacturer's operating instruction manual for detailed instructions on drum setup and turning procedures for the particular lathe being used.

Slip whatever spacers are needed onto the arbor and spin the arbor nut on by hand. Securely tighten the lathe arbor nut to firmly seat the drum on the arbor. If new bearing races have been installed in the hub, tightening the drum on the

arbor will firmly seat the races. A rubber belt (vibration dampener) is then stretched lightly around the outside of the drum, as shown in Fig. 3-21, to prevent vibration during the machining operation.

Turning the Brake Drum

The following information applies to the operation of the most commonly used brake drum machines. The manufacturer's instructions should always be followed.

Turn the lathe cross slide handwheel clockwise until the cross slide swivel block, or tool holder (which holds the tool bar), is as close to the machine housing as possible. See Fig. 3-25. Turn the cross slide handwheel counterclock-

Fig. 3-25. The controls of a typical brake lathe are identified. The cross slide handwheel moves the cutting tool toward or away from the drum friction surface. A collar on the cross slide handwheel is calibrated in thousandths of an inch, and is used to set the cutting tool for the required depth of cut. (*Ammco Tools, Inc.*)

wise one turn. Turn the drum feed handwheel (located at the rear of the machine) clockwise to bring the drum in as close to the machine as possible. Turn the drum feed handwheel counterclockwise one turn. Note: When moving the drum toward the machine with the drum feed handwheel, the cross slide swivel block, which holds the tool bar, may have to be rotated to allow the drum to clear the tool bit.

Slide the tool bar within the cross slide so that the tool bit is positioned at the innermost point on the drum's friction surface. Tighten the cross slide swivel block lock nut to hold the tool bar

in this position. Turn the drum feed handwheel counterclockwise (moving the drum outward) until the tool bit is approximately 1 inch in from the outer edge of the drum. The next step is to make sure that the drum has been properly mounted.

Turn on the lathe. With the drum rotating, turn the cross slide handwheel counterclockwise until the tool bit contacts and lightly scratches the rotating drum. Turn off the lathe. If the scratch mark on the drum wearing surface is a complete circle (tool bit contacts drum through 360° of rotation) the drum is accurately mounted, and the turning operation can proceed. If the tool bit contacts the drum surface for only a part of the drum's rotation, either the drum is non-concentric or out-of-round, or it is improperly mounted.

To check the mounting of the drum, loosen the lathe arbor nut and rotate the drum on the arbor through a half revolution. Tighten the arbor nut. Turn the drum feed handwheel so that the tool bit will contact the drum slightly to the right or left of the first scratch mark. Turn on the lathe and make a second trial scratch alongside the first. Turn off the lathe and inspect the two scratches. If the two

scratch cuts are side by side the drum is mounted correctly but is either out-of-round or non-concentric. Turning the drum will correct these defects. If the two scratches are not side by side the drum has been mounted improperly. Check the adaptors to make certain that the correct radii adaptors have been used. Make certain that the arbor nut is tight against the adjoining spacer.

When you are satisfied that the drum is correctly mounted, turn on the lathe and turn the cross slide handwheel counterclockwise until the tool bit scratches the rotating drum surface. Note the set-

Fig. 3-26. A stationary brake lathe, with provisions for turning truck drums. Lathe arbor supports must be used to assure a rigid setup and to support the weight of the drums and tires. (Kwik-Way)

ting on the micrometer collar of the cross slide handwheel. This setting is used to determine the depth of the cut to be made in the drum friction surface.

With the cutting tool clear of the drum surface, turn the drum feed handwheel clockwise until the tool bit is positioned directly in front of the deepest score or groove in the drum surface. Turn the cross slide handwheel until the tool bit strikes the bottom of the deepest score. Note the new setting on the collar of the cross slide handwheel. The change in the setting indicates the depth of the deepest score or groove in the drum, in thousandths of an inch.

Turn the cross slide handwheel clockwise to withdraw the tool bit from the groove. Turn the drum feed handwheel clockwise to position the tool bit at the maximum inner position. Turn the cross slide handwheel counterclockwise until the setting on the handwheel collar is 0.005 in. (five thousandths of an inch) greater than the setting for the deepest score. The tool is now set for the correct depth of cut.

Set the feed dial, located above the feed handwheel (Fig. 3-25), to the desired feed setting. Feed settings which range from .002 to .006 in. per revolution will produce an acceptable drum friction surface finish. Engage the power feed lever (located behind the feed dial) by moving the lever to the left (toward the drum). The drum is now being machined automatically.

If hard spots appear after turning the drum, a grinder may be employed to finish the hard spots flush with the drum surface. Some special metallic-content linings require that the brake drum be ground to a specific micro-finish after turning.

Brake drum lathes can be obtained mounted on a portable bench, as shown in Fig. 3-24, or on a separate bench with provisions to handle truck drums as shown in Fig. 3-26. After a drum has been machined on a lathe the brake lining must be ground to match the new oversize diameter of the drum.

Brake Relining

Drum and disc brakes both have a brake shoe that rubs against the drum or disc to produce friction which stops the car. The brake shoe for either type of brake is a combination of two parts: the friction material, or *lining,* and the plate, or *core,* which supports the friction material. Both components of the brake shoe are discussed in detail below.

Lining Segment

The friction material is formed into a shape called a lining segment that matches the shape of the core. Most brake lining segments are made of asbestos fibers and a bonding agent that holds the fibers together. Since the lining is that part of the shoe which contacts the drum or disc, it wears with use and must periodically be replaced. Depending on the quality of the lining material, the way in which the vehicle is used and the braking habits of the driver, a set of brake linings may last from fifteen thousand to thirty-five thousand miles before replacement is required.

In the past few years sintered iron has been made available as lining material. Sintered iron is made by fusing small particles of cast iron and carbon together. Sintered iron lining material is more resistant to fade when the brakes are overheated, however it is not extensively used.

The Core

Most brake shoe cores are constructed of stamped steel, but some imported cars use a cast aluminum core. The core of a

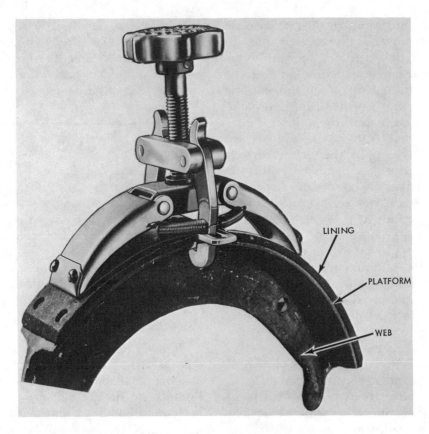

LINING

PLATFORM

WEB

Fig. 3-27. The new lining is held to the platform with a brake lining clamp while the new rivets are being installed. (*Dodge Div., Chrysler Corp.*)

disc brake shoe is a one-piece stamping. The core of a drum brake shoe is made of two parts, the platform and the web, Fig. 3-27. The platform or table supports the lining material which is either bonded or riveted to the platform. The web of the brake shoe is welded to, and acts as the backbone for, the platform. The web determines the arc of the core according to the diameter of the drum in which it will be used. The web also provides for the anchor eye of the drum brake shoe as well as holes for the various springs, actuating pins, etc. The anchor end of the brake shoe is called the heel and the actuating end is called the toe end of the brake shoe.

Drum brake shoes are available for service in two sizes: standard and oversize. A *standard* brake shoe is a lined core which has a lining thickness equal to "O.E.M."—Original Equipment Manufacture thickness. For example, if a new car has a brake lining that is $\frac{3}{16}$ (or .187) in. thick, a core with a lining of this thickness would be called a standard brake shoe. An *oversize* brake shoe is a core having a lining attached to it that has a greater thickness than the standard lining. The most common oversize brake shoe has a lining that is thirty thousandths (.030) in. thicker than the standard lining.

Brake Shoe Identification

All brake shoes are identified by number. The Friction Materials Standards Institute identifies each brake shoe according to the lining segment and the core number. For example, a box of brake shoes may have the number 2006-11 stamped on it. The first number (2006) refers to the lining segment number; the second number (11) refers to the core number. This identification code is used by most automotive parts suppliers to identify brake shoes, whereas the individual automobile dealer parts departments have their own number system.

Relining the Brake Shoe

Most automobile parts stores, or automobile dealers, carry a complete line of brake shoes with the linings already attached (either bonded or riveted) and sell them on an exchange basis. Shoes with bonded lining should be exchanged, as bonding requires special equipment.

If the lining is riveted to the shoe, the rivets may be driven out from the end opposite the head with a punch which will pass through the rivet hole. The brake relining machine shown in Fig. 3-28 is equipped with a punch to press out the rivets.

Practically all lining sold today is attached to the shoes. It is essential that the exact type of lining specified by the manufacturer for the particular vehicle be used when relining brakes. Any change in the coefficient of friction of the lining from what is intended for the specific brake may result in improper brake action.

Manufacturers of brake lining package their lining in custom sets for specific vehicles. The linings in these sets are cut, chamfered, drilled, and counterbored for the particular brake on which they are to be used. The lining will also be of the correct thickness for standard drums.

Since the disc brake shoe backing, or

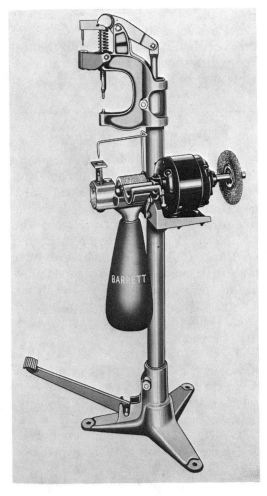

Fig. 3-28. Typical brake relining machine. (*Barrett Equipment Co.*)

core, is flat, replacement of the lining is relatively easy. The curve of the drum brake shoe, however, complicates the replacement of the drum brake shoe lining.

It is important that the lining be installed on the platform in such a manner that the lining contacts smoothly and evenly throughout the entire curve of the shoe, or more. If gaps occur between the brake lining and platform at any point between the rivets, it will be impossible to get satisfactory brake action. To insure complete contact and to prevent gaps, a brake lining clamp, such as the one shown in Fig. 3-27, or lining stretcher should be used to hold the lining tightly against the platform shoe while it is riveted.

Brake Shoe Grinding

The operation of machining the brake drum friction surface produces an oversize diameter. As-purchased, new brake shoes will not satisfactorily fit the new drum diameter. To restore the brakes to peak efficiency will require that new brake shoes be installed which have oversize or extra-thick lining corresponding to the new diameter of the drum. This is done by grinding a set of oversize shoes (lining 0.030″ larger than O.E.M. size) to match drum radius.

In disc brake servicing, brake shoe service is limited to replacement of the disc brake shoe. The brake disc, even when machined to correct problems caused by time and wear, will still present a flat surface to the lining material of the disc brake shoe. Furthermore, a worn disc brake shoe is replaced with a shoe of original (O.E.M.) size; increased caliper piston travel compensates for the slightly reduced thickness of the brake disc. Thus, disc brake shoes currently require no service beyond simple replacement. The material which follows on brake shoe grinding thus refers *only* to drum brake shoes.

In brake servicing, there are several variables which affect brake shoe fit to the drum; these variables must be clearly understood and provided for if the shoe-to-drum relationship is to be restored to like-new operating efficiency. The actual drum diameter is one variable. Lining thickness, standard or oversize, is another. Almost all cars have brakes with a non-adjustable anchor; however, the an-

chor position can still vary slightly, and this creates still another variable. The correctness of the anchor setting on older cars creates another, as do minor distortions in the brake shoes.

Effects of Improper Lining-to-Drum Fit

Figure 3-29 illustrates the ideal fit between lining and drum. A new oversize lining has been accurately ground to fit an oversize drum. In this case, top brake efficiency is combined with top life expectancy for the brake linings.

Figure 3-30 illustrates the condition that exists when a shoe with a new standard lining, which has been ground to *original* drum radius, is fitted into an oversize diameter drum. Before total lining-to-drum contact can be obtained, the brake shoe must bend to compensate for the extreme toe and heel clearances. On a light stop, only the brake shoe center contacts the drum, and on a heavy stop *extreme* shoe flexing results. Maxi-

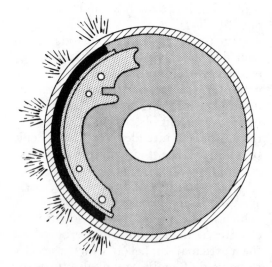

Fig. 3-29. The ideal lining-to-drum fit. To approximate this fit an oversize lining must be ground to fit the (newly-turned) oversize drum.

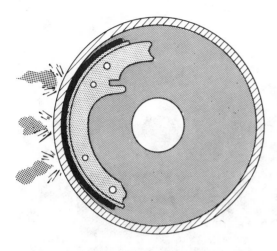

Fig. 3-30. A standard shoe fitted to an oversize drum. The result is contact (and severe wear) at the center with excessive clearance at the ends of the shoe. Hard brake application will cause the shoes to flex (spongy pedal).

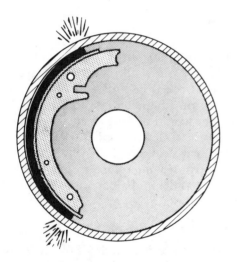

Fig. 3-31. An oversize shoe fitted to a standard or near-standard drum. Initial contact occurs at the ends of the brake shoe causing erratic brake action, uneven wear, and considerable noise.

mum brake efficiency and lining life are impossible where these conditions exist.

When a brake shoe with oversize lining is forced against a standard drum, er-ratic braking as well as noise results. Figure 3-31 illustrates this situation, where the lining contacts the drum at the toe and heel only.

"Cam Grinding" the Brake Shoe

New brake shoes should always be cam ground to assure proper shoe-to-drum fit. Sometimes this operation is referred to as "radius grinding" or "undersize grinding." Cam grinding means grinding the brake shoe to a radius *slightly smaller* than the radius of the drum.

If the brake shoe were ground to the exact arc of the drum, the shoe adjustment would have to be absolutely correct to avoid the possibility of toe or heel contact. Such "absolutely correct" adjustments are difficult to achieve. On the other hand, providing a cam ground clearance at the toe and heel of the shoe will compensate for a shoe adjustment which is slightly off. Thus, cam grinding has the intended effect of providing a slight clearance at the ends of the brake shoe in the "brakes applied" position. Note, however, that cam grinding does not create the extreme clearance at the toe and heel shown in Fig. 3-30. The clearance should only be from .005 to .008 in. at the very ends of the lining segment. This minor toe and heel clearance allows the shoe to center itself in the drum. The contact may be shifted toward the toe or the heel, but the chance of troublesome toe or heel contact is avoided.

Cam grinding also lessens the possibility of braking problems caused by distorted shoes, bent backing plates, worn shoe anchor eyes, etc. Naturally, a brake shoe that is noticeably twisted or otherwise distorted should be discarded; however, brake shoe grinding can compensate for minor shoe deformities.

Several makes of brake shoe grinders

Fig. 3-32. A bench-mounted brake shoe grinder. To set the grinder, pull the lock pin and slide the grinder table to the nearest whole number of the desired shoe diameter. The grinder is then set to within a thousandth of an inch of the desired shoe diameter with the micrometer dial located below the brake shoe grinder handle. (*Ammco Tools, Inc.*)

Fig. 3-33. Closeup view of the brake shoe grinder micrometer dial. (*Ammco Tools, Inc.*)

are available. Because of their specific use, they are similar in appearance and operation. A grinder like that shown in Fig. 3-32 will be found in every auto service shop which features major brake service. Most grinder manufacturers recommend cam grinding all shoes to a diameter 0.030 in. less than the diameter of

the drum. Thus, if the drum diameter is 11.040 in. you would set the shoe grinder to grind the shoe lining to 11.010 in. If the drum diameter is 10.015 in. the grinder would be set to grind to 9.985 in. or 0.015 in. less than 10.000 in. This is rather easily accomplished by setting the shoe grinder micrometer, Fig. 3-33, to the actual drum diameter and then backing off 0.030 in.

Brake Shoe Grinding Methods

There are two methods of brake shoe grinding. The first, the standard method, is the easier of the two. However, this method can only be used for (older) cars which feature a brake design with an adjustable anchor. Since almost all automobiles today feature a brake design with a fixed anchor, the serviceman will usually be required to grind the shoes by the second, or fixed-anchor, method.

The Standard Method. With this method, the shoe is simply placed in the shoe clamp of the brake shoe grinder and is cam ground to correctly match the arch of the drum (i.e., drum diameter less 0.030 in. Standard grinding is used in cases where the shoe is used on a brake with an adjustable anchor or when the shoe "floats."

When standard grinding, (1) set the grinder to drum diameter less 0.030 in. for cam grind; (2) place the shoe in the shoe clamp, and (3) grind the lining until it cleans up across its full arc.

When the cam ground shoes are installed on brakes with adjustable anchors, the anchors may have to be re-positioned to provide the proper shoe-to-drum fit. If, for example, the anchor is set too high, the heel of the shoe will contact the drum as shown in Fig. 3-34. If the anchor is set too low, the toe of the shoe will contact the drum as shown in Fig. 3-35. Moving the anchor up or down in its slot will re-establish the correct shoe-to-drum contact.

The Fixed-Anchor Method. Since 1955, the great majority of cars have used the duo-servo type brake with a fixed or non-adjustable anchor. Due to the stacking of tolerances at the time of manufacture, the anchor is not always exactly where it ought to be in relation to the center line of the brake assembly. Thus, even if the shoe has been cam ground to the correct arc, it would contact the drum as shown in Fig. 3-34 if the anchor is slightly high when the brakes are applied. If the anchor is slightly low, the shoe would contact the drum as shown in Fig. 3-35. Precisely because the anchor is non-adjustable, little can be done about these problems *if the shoes are ground by the standard method;* they can, and often do, lead to grabbing, pull, noise and erratic action.

Also, as has been stated, most brake shoes are re-bonded or re-riveted. Many cores have had a great many miles of use. It is not uncommon, then, to find cores with the anchor eye worn. A worn anchor eye changes the shoe geometry; as the shoe is forced into the anchor and against the rotating drum, the way in which the shoe is made to contact the drum is such that the full surface of the lining is pre-

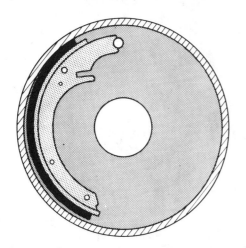

Fig. 3-34. If the anchor is high the shoe will pivot on the anchor so that only the heel contacts the drum.

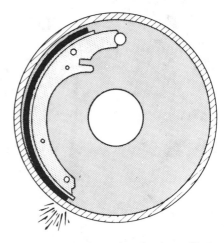

Fig. 3-35. If the anchor is low the shoe will pivot on the anchor so that only the toe contacts the drum.

vented from contacting the drum. Thus, the shoe may contact the drum improperly, even though the arc of the lining is correct and the anchor pin is in the correct position. However, no such adjustment is possible on the fixed-anchor type brake, which is now used almost universally and the type which will be encountered almost exclusively by the serviceman.

To compensate for a worn anchor eye in the shoe and the use of oversize shoes with near-standard drums (drums which needed only slight machining to restore their full effectiveness), the shoe must be ground to an anchor location on the shoe grinder that duplicates the anchor location on the car's backing plate.

Figure 3-36 shows a shoe that has been fixed-anchor ground, not only to fit the drum diameter, but also to fit the car's actual fixed-anchor position. This is done with a fixed-anchor shoe clamp. This shoe clamp allows the serviceman to

grind to the "brakes applied" position. The variables that fixed anchor grinding provides for are: (1) drum diameter, allowed for in the shoe grinder setting; (2) brake shoe arc, established through the shoe grinder setting; (3) anchor position, automatically allowed for in the settings of the fixed-anchor shoe clamp; and (4) minor shoe irregularities, also automatically compensated for in the setting of the shoe clamp. Figure 3-37 shows how a shoe with an anchor eye worn at its lower part will contact the drum.

The purpose of the fixed-anchor shoe clamp—aside from holding the shoe during grinding—is to duplicate on the grinder the exact position of the brake assembly's anchor with respect to the center of the assembly. The shoe is custom ground to the specific dimensions of the brake assembly, thus precluding a bad shoe-to-drum fit because of a slightly out-of-position anchor. On a brake with an

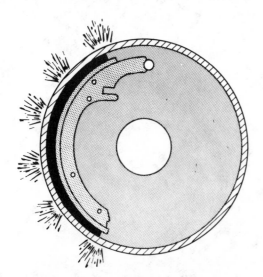

Fig. 3-36. The correct lining-to-drum fit is assured when the shoe is fixed anchor ground, since this method compensates for irregularities in the shoe-to-anchor relationship.

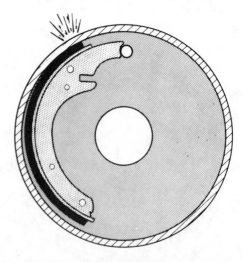

Fig. 3-37. If the brake shoe anchor eye is worn at the bottom the effect will be similar to that of a low anchor, and the shoe will contact the drum as shown if the shoe is standard ground.

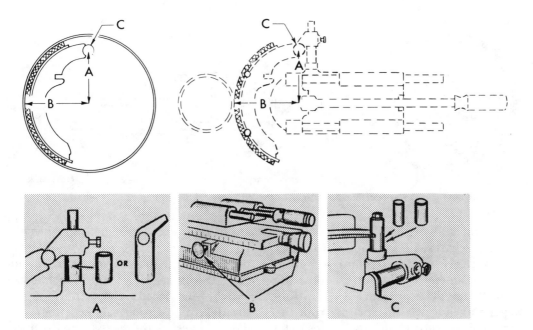

Fig. 3-38. Fixed anchor grinder settings permit the mechanic to duplicate on the grinder the size and relative position of the car's fixed anchor pin (settings C and A) in addition to providing for the proper brake shoe diameter (setting B).

adjustable anchor, this condition can easily be compensated for by raising the anchor.

The sketch shown at the upper left in Fig. 3-38 shows the drum, the shoe, and the anchor as they would be seen on the car's brake assembly. Dimension *A* is the actual distance from the center of the brake assembly to the center of the anchor. Dimension *B* is the distance from the center to the drum (or one half the turned brake drum diameter). Dimension *C* is the actual diameter of the anchor. These dimensions must be duplicated on the grinder as shown in Fig. 3-38, *upper right*.

The anchor diameter, *C,* is reproduced by slipping a sleeve of the desired outside diameter over a pin on the shoe clamp. See Fig. 3-38, *bottom right*. The distance, *A*, of the anchor from the wheel center, is reproduced by using a gage sleeve or gage plate of appropriate length

to hold the grinder's anchor at a distance *A* from the center of the grinder, Fig. 3-38, *bottom left*. Dimension *B* is set to the distance from the center of the car's brake assembly to the drum braking surface. This is accomplished by setting the slide index pin and the grinder micrometer to the turned drum diameter. (The grinder micrometer is then backed off .030 in. to provide for cam grinding.) See Fig. 3-38, *bottom center*. Remember, the shoe clamp's anchor is positioned so that it is in the same position relative to the drum braking surface, brake assembly center line, and brake shoe as the actual brake assembly anchor. The shoe is then cam ground in the "brakes applied" position.

Correctly positioning the shoe clamp anchor by means of gage sleeves or plates is relatively simple with the aid of a chart supplied by the manufacturer of the grinder. Using the chart, look up the

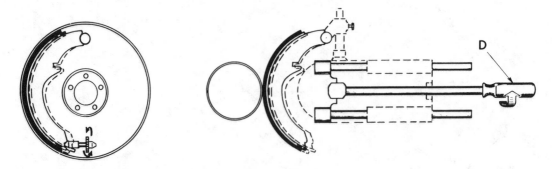

Fig. 3-39. Turning the grinder handle (D) moves the brake shoe forward into contact with the abrasive.

make and year of the car being worked on. The chart will indicate the correct anchor sleeve to use to simulate an anchor of diameter *C*. Similarly, choose the correct gage plate or sleeve for positioning the anchor at a distance *A* from the center of the shoe clamp. Next, lock the anchor in place and place the shoe in the clamp with its eye against the anchor. See Fig. 3-39.

Mark the surface of the lining with a number of evenly spaced chalk lines. Advance the shoe to the grinding position by turning the grinder handle, *D*, clockwise until the shoe contacts the abrasive. Move the handle sideways to pivot the shoe clamp and to allow grinding of the entire length of the lining segment. Proceed until the entire surface of the lining has been ground (or, until all of the chalk marks have disappeared). Note: To grind to the correct arc may require several passes across the grinder. Do not attempt to grind more than 0.010 in. in one pass.

When the shoe is assembled on the brake assembly, the lining-to-drum fit should be correct. The major brake adjustment is essentially achieved when the shoe is fixed-anchor ground. The fixed-anchor grinding operation has compensated for the minor distortions and dimensional variations.

This correction for dimensional vari-

ations is what causes some brake mechanics to wonder about the type of grind they get on the shoe. Remember—in most cases the brake shoes must be fixed-anchor ground because the anchor is not adjustable. The lining can be either standard or oversize thickness. The drum can be anywhere between standard and .060 in. oversize.

Master Cylinder and Wheel Cylinder Service

Consult the manufacturer's shop manual for exact specifications, removal, overhaul, and reassembly procedures. The master cylinder on present-day vehicles is located on the firewall in the engine compartment. When removal of the master cylinder is necessary, clean all dirt from the hydraulic line fittings at the cylinder before loosening the connection.

All vehicles now use the dual type master cylinder which means that there is a separate section for the front brakes and for the rear brakes. All are contained in a single unit.

While construction may vary slightly, according to the make of master cylinder, they are all, basically, the same as far as service is concerned. It is extremely important that the exact repair kit be used

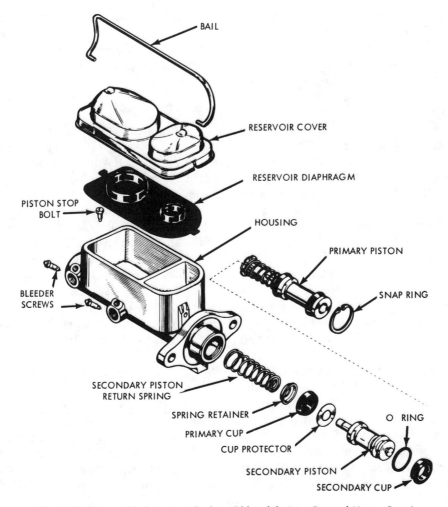

BAIL

RESERVOIR COVER

RESERVOIR DIAPHRAGM

PISTON STOP
BOLT

HOUSING

PRIMARY PISTON

BLEEDER
SCREWS

SNAP RING

SECONDARY PISTON
RETURN SPRING

SPRING RETAINER

PRIMARY CUP

CUP PROTECTOR

SECONDARY PISTON

O RING

SECONDARY CUP

Fig. 3-40. Disassembled master cylinder. (*Oldsmobile Div., General Motors Corp.*)

for the particular make and model of master cylinder being serviced.

Disassemble the master cylinder by removing the push rod boot, the snap ring, and the stop plate. A piston stop screw is located in the fluid reservoir of most dual master cylinders. This should be removed before removing the snap ring. An exploded view of a master cylinder is shown in Fig. 3-40. Use extreme care to keep all parts clean and free from oil and grease.

Inspect the cylinder bore for scoring or corrosion. Stains should not be con-fused with corrosion; corrosion is identi-fied as pits and excessive roughness. Pol-ish any stained areas with crocus cloth. Do not use any other form of abrasive. Apply the cloth with a rotary motion, not lengthwise.

If the cylinder is scored or rough, it should be polished with a hone. Do not enlarge the bore in excess of .002″. If the scores cannot be removed, the assembly should be replaced.

Delco-Moraine does not recommend honing the dual type master cylinder. If the bore is rough or scored, the cylinder should be replaced. As the cylinder bore is surface hardened and polished, honing destroys the hard surface leaving a softer and rougher bore, resulting in more rapid wear of the pistons and rubber cups.

Check the fit of the piston in the master cylinder and if not within specifications, replace both the master cylinder and the piston. Maximum allowable clearance between the piston and the master cylinder is approximately .005 in. Replacement parts for the master cylinder including oversize pistons and cups if needed, are sold in kit forms, as all the rubber parts should be replaced when overhauling a master cylinder.

Clean the master cylinder bore and other parts with clean alcohol and shake the excess fluid from the surface. Do not wipe with a cloth as lint may remain in the cylinder.

Before assembling, all parts should be coated with brake fluid. Make sure the parts are assembled in the proper sequence and the seals and cups are installed in the right direction.

It is well to bleed the master cylinder before mounting it on the firewall. This may be done by mounting the unit in a vise, filling with fluid and using a wooden dowel or plastic rod to move the pistons forward until air bubbles are no longer coming out of the master cylinder outlets.

Wheel Cylinders

The wheel cylinders are fastened to the brake backing plate by means of bolts or cap screws. If wheel cylinder replacement is necessary, loosen the flexible hose (front wheel cylinders) at the wheel cylinder. Remove the wheel cylinder, then hold the hose, and unscrew the cylinder from the hose. This saves time because the hose does not need to be disturbed where it fastens to the brake line.

Wheel cylinders usually do not have to be removed from the backing plate for disassembly or for honing. The wheel cylinder can be disassembled by removing the rubber boots after the brake shoes have been removed. A disassembled wheel cylinder is shown in Fig. 3-41. If the cylinder is scored, polish with a hone. If the scores cannot be removed the cylinder must be replaced. The maximum allowable clearance of the piston within the wheel cylinder is .005 in. As with the master cylinder, all rubber parts are re-

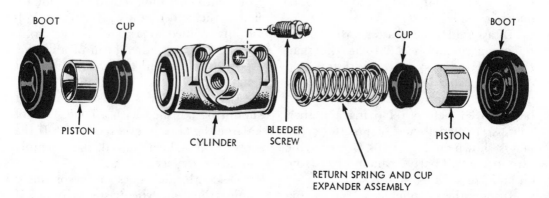

Fig. 3-41. Disassembled wheel cylinder. (*Ford Customer Service Div., Ford Motor Co.*)

placed when overhauling a wheel cylinder. Clean all parts with alcohol before assembly (except rubber parts) and, on assembly, lubricate all parts (rubber parts included) with clean brake fluid. The hydraulic system must be bled after the overhauling of any of the four wheel cylinders.

Brake Disc Service

Brake Disc Inspection

Before the original or replacement brake shoes are returned to the caliper, the brake disc should be visually inspected for the following defects caused by wear and exposure: scoring, rust ridges at the inner and outer circumferences of the disc, and hard spots.

Scoring. A brake disc will become slightly scored under conditions of nor-

mal braking. A slightly scored disc, (say, with scored grooves less than 0.015 in. deep) can be reused without servicing if it is well within the manufacturer's wear tolerances. Heavy scoring will require that the brake disc be machined.

Rust Ridges. Under conditions of normal wear, a ridge of rust will build up on the unused surface of the disc face—at the extreme inner and outer diameters. See Fig. 3-42. If the original shoes are to be re-installed, these rust ridges will not affect brake performance.

If new brake shoes are to be installed, the presence of rust ridges will affect brake performance; the disc will have to be machined to remove the rust ridges. A new disc brake shoe is slightly wider than the old shoe. If the rust ridges on the brake disc are not removed, the new shoe will seat on top of the ridges. A special disc brake grinder, like the one shown in Fig. 3-43, can be used instead of

Fig. 3-42. The disc shown has rust ridges at its inner and outer diameters. The disc must be machined since it is also badly scored. (*Chrysler Div., Chrysler Corp.*)

Fig. 3-43. Brake disc can be ground instead of turned on a lathe to remove light scoring and rust. (*Ammco Tools, Inc.*)

a lathe tool bit to remove slight scoring and the rust ridges.

Hard Spots. The brake discs of a ve-

hicle subjected to hard and frequent braking may develop hard spots. These hard spots are identical to the hard spots formed on brake drums. If the accompanying brake disc wear is such that the disc must be turned on a lathe, the disc will also have to be ground after turning to completely remove all trace of the hard spots. Figure 3-44 shows a grinder attachment on a brake lathe being used to grind down the hard spots.

Additional Brake Disc Test Procedures

In addition to visual checks for the defects described above, two measurements can be made to determine the condition of the disc. Every car manufacturer requires that at least one of these tests be made when new linings are to be installed. Each manufacturer indicates which of the two test procedures should

Fig. 3-44. After the disc is turned on a brake lathe hard spots may still appear on the disc surface. Hard spots can be ground flush using the special brake lathe grinding attachment shown. (*Ammco Tools, Inc.*)

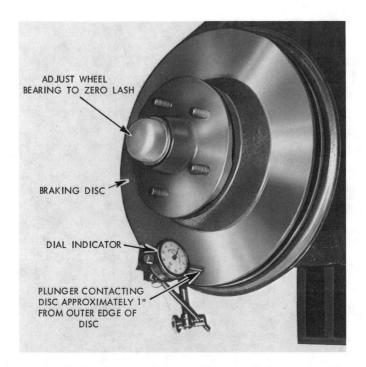

ADJUST WHEEL
BEARING TO ZERO LASH

BRAKING DISC

DIAL INDICATOR

PLUNGER CONTACTING
DISC APPROXIMATELY 1"
FROM OUTER EDGE OF
DISC

Fig. 3-45. Measuring brake disc runout with a dial indicator. (*Chrysler Div., Chrysler Corp.*)

be followed for its particular vehicle. If, for either test, the brake disc exceeds the manufacturer's specifications, the brake disc must be machined or replaced.

Runout. A brake disc should not have excessive lateral runout, or wobble. A dial indicator is used as shown in Fig. 3-45 to check for brake disc runout. The dial indicator is supported by a C-clamp that is clamped to the spindle. The Total Indicated Runout (T.I.R.) should not exceed the manufacturer's specifications as the disc is revolved through one or more revolutions.

Thickness Variation. The thickness of a brake disc should not vary more than 0.0005 to 0.001 in. depending on the vehicle manufacturer's specification. At least three thickness measurements must be made at points approximately 1 in. from the outer edge of the disc to determine if a disc meets the thickness varia-

tion check. A 0-1 in. and a 1-2 in. outside micrometer or vernier caliper can be used to check thickness variation.

Lathe Setup for Turning the Brake Disc

The lathe for machining a brake disc is constructed in two different ways. In most cases an attachment is added to the drum brake lathe, so that both the brake drum and the brake disc can be serviced on a single machine. Fig. 3-46 shows a conventional brake drum lathe, modified by adding a cross feed gear box (at the rear of the machine) and a special tool bar attachment to machine brake discs. The gear box attachment is bolted to the rear of the lathe, either in the field or as a factory installation.

Large service shops, especially those which specialize in brake service, may find it more economical and efficient to

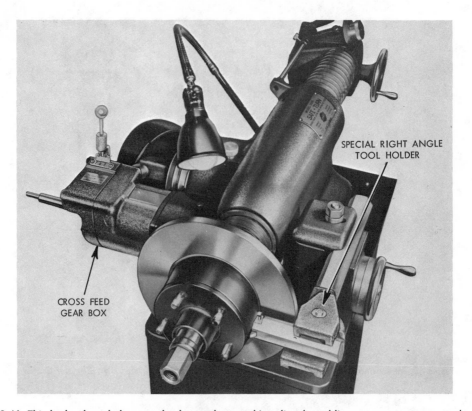

Fig. 3-46. This brake drum lathe can also be used to machine discs by adding as a permanent attachment a power cross feed gear box. The power cross feed attachment moves the cross slide away from the lathe housing. A special tool holder is also necessary, since movement of the cutting tool across the disc face is at a right angle to the normal movement of the lathe tool in turning a brake drum. (*Ammco Tools, Inc.*)

use a special lathe made specifically to turn brake discs, like the one shown in Fig. 3-47.

The discussion which follows on the setup and turning of a brake disc may not apply in every detail to all lathes. Several makes of brake lathes are available. While they are generally similar in construction and operation, differences in design make an all inclusive set of setup and operating procedures impossible. For this reason, *always refer to the manufacturer's operating manual for specific instructions on the setups for and operation of the particular unit.*

The setup for turning a brake disc on a drum lathe with a brake disc attachment consists of correctly mounting the disc and the cutting tool.

Mounting the Disc. Mount the brake disc on a 1 in. diameter lathe arbor, using the appropriate brake disc adaptors to hold the disc securely in place on the arbor. The adaptors seat on the arbor and support the brake disc at its inner and outer bearing cups. An adaptor selector chart, which indicates the correct adaptors for each automobile brake disc, is available from the lathe manufacturer. (The selection and use of adaptors to mount a brake disc on a lathe is similar to the procedure for mounting a front brake drum, which was described earlier in this chapter.)

Fig. 3-47. A lathe specifically designed for brake discs. Both sides of the disc are turned simultaneously on this unit. (*Bear Manufacturing* Co.)

Fig. 3-48. A vibration dampener is attached to the disc face opposite the one being machined. The right angle tool bar is adjusted lengthwise and crosswise to position the cutting tool at the disc face with a minimum of overhang. (*Ammco Tools, Inc.*)

Securely tighten the arbor nut to firmly seat the bearing cups and to rigidly support the disc. Additional 1 in. arbor spacers may be required if both the inner and outer bearing cups are being pressed into the hub.

A vibration dampener is attached to the disc face on the side opposite the one being machined, as shown in Fig. 3-48. The dampener prevents disc vibration during machining which could result in a poor surface finish. The horseshoe-shaped vibration dampener is held to the disc face by four permanent magnets.

Mounting the Cutting Tool. Install the special brake disc tool bar (which holds the lathe tool bit). See Fig. 3-48. Note that the extension or adaptor which inserts into the cross slide swivel block has a clamp at one end. The tool bar (which holds the tool bit) in turn inserts into the clamp of the adaptor.

To avoid deflection under heavy load, the setup should be as rigid as possible. Turn the drum feed handwheel until the disc is brought as close to the housing as the setup will permit. The cross slide should also be brought in as close to the lathe housing as possible, using the cross slide handwheel.

In Fig. 3-48, the adaptor is slid as far back into the cross slide swivel block as possible (until the adaptor clamp rests against the swivel block). Slide the tool bar out of the adaptor clamp until the tool bit is just opposite the inner diameter of the brake disc.

The tool bar should extend from the adaptor clamp only as far as is necessary to machine the entire brake disc friction surface. Ideally, when the tool bit is cutting the inner edge, the outer edge of the disc should just clear the clamp on the adaptor. After adjusting the tool bar, tighten the lock nuts on the cross slide and the adaptor clamp. Figures 3-47 and 3-48 illustrate the proper setup.

Turning the Brake Disc

Ford Motor Company allows their original thickness specification to be reduced 0.100 in. on 1965 through 1967 automobiles. However, only 0.060 in. can be removed from the original thickness of their 1968 automobile brake disc. The usual rule is that not over one-half of the total thickness reduction can be removed from one side of the disc: i.e., an equal amount should be ground from both sides of the disc. Ford manufactures a special tool that determines the amount of stock which has been or can be removed from each face.

Turning the lathe drum feed handwheel (which moves the brake disc toward or away from the cutting tool), bring the point of the tool bit against the disc, either at the extreme inner diameter or outer diameter. Let the tool bit lightly scratch the surface of the disc as the disc revolves. The drum feed handwheel has a micrometer collar. Note the reading; this setting will be used as a reference point to determine the depth-of-cut setting.

Turning the cross slide handwheel, move the cross slide inward across the face of the disc. Stop the cross slide movement when the tool point is directly in front of the deepest score or groove in the disc face. Turn the drum feed handwheel until the tool bit bottoms in the deepest grove. Note on the micrometer collar the number of units that the depth-of-cut dial has moved from its reference setting. This indicates the depth of the deepest groove and the amount of metal which will have to be removed from the face of the disc. Turning the drum feed handwheel, back the tool bit out of the groove. Turn the cross slide handwheel until the tool bit is at the smallest diameter of the disc face. Turn the depth-of-cut (or drum feed) handwheel until the micrometer collar (depth-of-cut dial) reads two units, or 0.004 in. beyond the setting for the deepest groove.

Engage the (cross slide) power feed mechanism by pulling the handle on the disc brake gear box toward the machine, as illustrated in Fig. 3-49. This will machine the disc at the fast feed rate—0.010 in. of travel across the face of the disc for each revolution of the lathe. Pushing the power feed lever away from the machine will turn the disc at a slow feed —0.002 in. of travel per revolution.

The finish of the machined surface of the disc will not be acceptable if the fast feed is used. A disc brake grinder attachment, available as an accessory of the brake lathe, can be used after the turning operation to provide a more acceptable brake disc surface. See Fig. 3-43.

Disc Brake Caliper Service

A disc brake can be removed from the steering knuckle of the vehicle by removing the caliper attaching bolts, identified in Fig. 3-50. Note that in the illustration, the caliper bolts to a splash shield which is in turn bolted to the steering knuckle.

By removing the caliper bolts, the caliper can be removed and disassembled as shown in Fig. 3-51. Care should be taken so that the two O-rings that connect (seal) the two caliper halves together hydraulically are not lost or left out when re-assembling the caliper. Most caliper pistons can be removed from their respective bores by forcing compressed air through the brake fluid inlet, as shown in Fig. 3-52. Note the shop

Fig. 3-49. Machining the brake disc. The cross slide power feed is engaged, which moves the cutting tool outward across the face of the disc. (*Ammco Tools, Inc.*)

BRAKE SERVICE

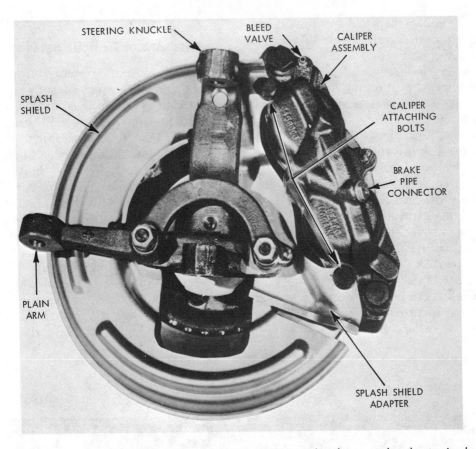

Fig. 3-50. A typical caliper, viewed from the inboard side, is shown indirectly mounted to the steering knuckle. *(Oldsmobile Div., General Motors Corp.)*

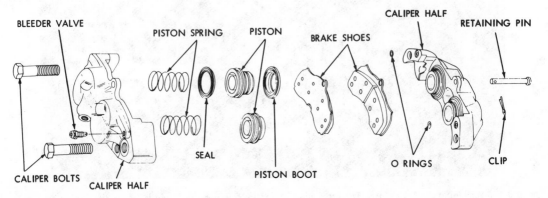

Fig. 3-51. Disassembled four-piston, fixed caliper. *(Oldsmobile Div., General Motors Corp.)*

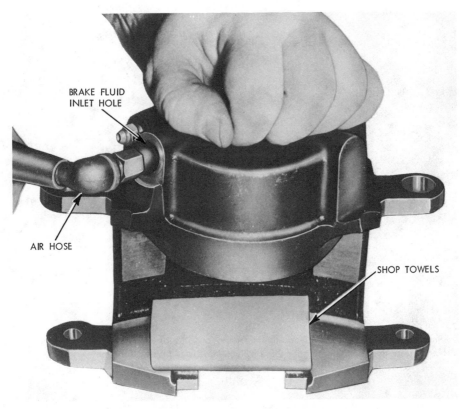

BRAKE FLUID
INLET HOLE

AIR HOSE

SHOP TOWELS

Fig. 3-52. Unless the cylinder wall is badly corroded, the piston can usually be forced from the caliper bore by connecting an air hose to the brake fluid inlet. (*Ford Div., Ford Motor Co.*)

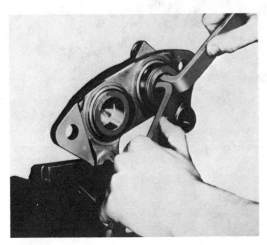

Fig. 3-53. Any tool which expands outward can be used to pull the pistons from their bores. (Most pistons are hollow for a great part of their length.) (*Plymouth Div., Chrysler Corp.*)

towels placed opposite the cylinder bore in Fig. 3-52 to catch and prevent possible damage to the piston. Other caliper designs have a hollow piston in which various tools such as the one shown in Fig. 3-53 may be used to pull out the pistons.

The piston dust boot is pulled out of its mounting grooves as shown in Fig. 3-54. The dust boot may be removed before the piston is removed (Fig. 3-53) or after the piston is removed, depending on the design of the caliper.

Once the piston is removed, the piston seal is removed next. Figure 3-55 shows how a square seal is removed from its groove in the caliper bore. A soft tool is used so that neither the seal will be damaged nor the cylinder wall scratched.

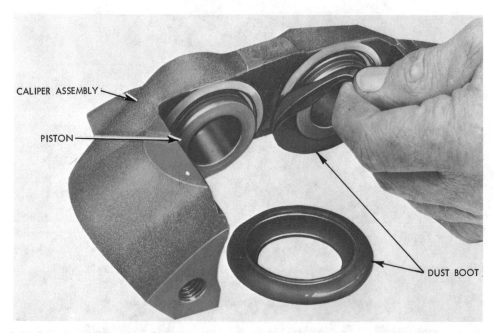

Fig. 3-54. Removing the dust boot from the caliper retainer and the piston groove. In this design the boot is removed before the piston is pulled from the bore. (*Plymouth Div., Chrysler Corp.*)

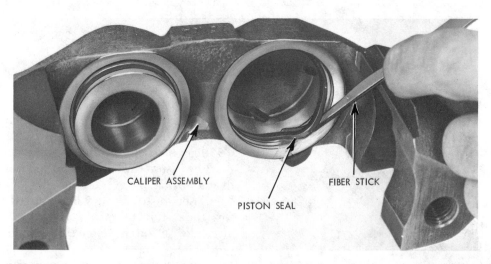

Fig. 3-55. Removing the square piston seal from its groove in the cylinder wall. (*Plymouth Div., Chrysler Corp.*)

The caliper bores are sometimes corroded with rust. If rust is present, a special hone is used to clean the caliper. Figure 3-56 shows a typical hone used to clean the walls of the caliper bores.

Reassemble the caliper using new

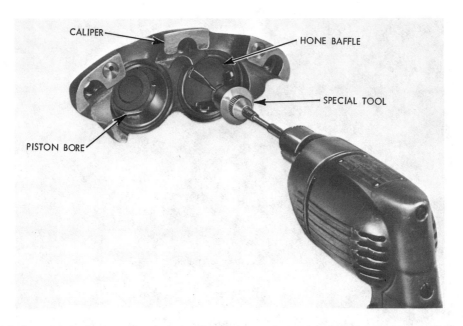

Fig. 3-56. A special disc brake caliper hone can be used to remove rust and corrosion from the cylinder walls. (*Plymouth Div., Chrysler Corp.*)

rubber parts (piston seals and boots). The caliper bolts must be tightened to a specified torque (available from the vehicle manufacturer's shop manual). Figure 3-57 shows the caliper bolts being tightened.

Fig. 3-57. After the caliper is reassembled with new rubber parts, the caliper bolts should be tightened to the specified torque. (*Plymouth Div., Chrysler Corp.*)

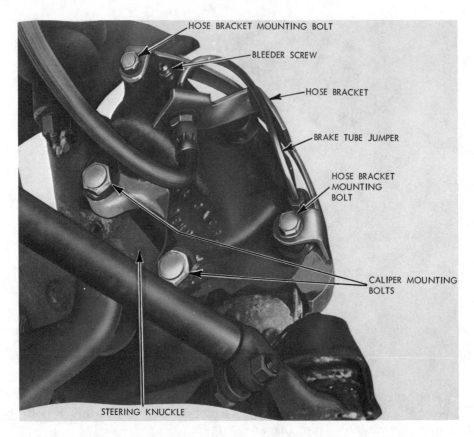

Fig. 3-58. Caliper mounted on steering knuckle. *(Plymouth Div., Chrysler Corp.)*

After the caliper is reassembled, it is remounted on the front wheel steering knuckle. The caliper mounting bolts must also be tightened with a torque wrench to a specified torque. The bolts are shown in Fig. 3-58. Some caliper mounting bolts are safety wired to the spindle after they are tightened to the correct torque. Additional disc brake service procedures are covered in Chapter Four, "Fixed Caliper Disc Brakes" and "Sliding Caliper Disc Brakes."

Diagnosing Poor Brake Performance

An automobile driver brings his car into the repair shop for brake service when he has experienced a change in the operation of his car's brake system. Most brake system failures are due to short cuts and inadequate service procedures when performing a complete brake job. Others are the result of improper or insufficient training of the technician who is performing the brake job.

The following table lists common car owner complaints. Under each general brake operating complaint are some of the brake system malfunctions that could cause the problem. The probable brake system malfunctions are listed in the left hand column. Opposite each of the malfunctions are the repair procedures which will correct that particular malfunction.

TABLE I BRAKE PERFORMANCE CHECK LIST

A. LOW, HARD BRAKE PEDAL

1. POWER BRAKE UNIT NOT OPERATING.

2. EXCESSIVE DRUM TO BRAKE SHOE CLEARANCE.

3. SELF-ADJUSTING BRAKES NOT WORKING.

4. SELF-ADJUSTING BRAKE PARTS CORRODED OR BENT.

5. THIN, GLAZED CRACKED BRAKE LININGS.

6. POLISHED, GLAZED BRAKE DRUM OR DISC.

7. DUAL MASTER CYLINDER SYSTEM HAS LOST THE FLUID IN EITHER THE FRONT OR REAR BRAKES.

8. IMPROPERLY ADJUSTED PARKING BRAKE.

1. BEFORE REPLACING UNIT CHECK VACUUM LINES.

2. MINOR ADJUSTMENT ON BRAKE RELINE IS REQUIRED.

3. INFORM THE CUSTOMER HOW THE SELF-ADJUSTING BRAKE WORKS.

4. LUBRICATE STAR WHEEL. REPLACE BRAKE OPERATING LEVER IF BENT.

5. REPLACE BRAKE LININGS.

6. MACHINE BRAKE DRUM OR DISC ON A LATHE.

7. REPAIR HYDRAULIC SYSTEM. RECENTER WARNING LIGHT (SAFETY) SWITCH.

8. READJUST PARKING BRAKE.

B. LOW, SOFT, SPONGY BRAKE PEDAL

1. AIR IN HYDRAULIC SYSTEM.

2. DEFECTIVE RESIDUAL CHECK VALVE IN MASTER CYLINDER.

3. LOW OR NEARLY EMPTY MASTER CYLINDER.

4. DEFECTIVE BRAKE HOSE.

5. UNGROUND OR IMPROPERLY GROUND BRAKE SHOES.

6. OVERSIZE BRAKE DRUMS.

7. INCORRECT ANCHOR PIN ADJUSTMENT.

1. REFILL MASTER CYLINDER. BLEED SYSTEM. CHECK FOR FLUID LEAKAGE AT MASTER CYLINDER AND WHEELS.

2. REBUILD OR REPLACE CYLINDER.

3. FIND LEAK IN SYSTEM AND BLEED BRAKES.

4. REPLACE BRAKE HOSE AND FLUSH HYDRAULIC SYSTEM.

5. REGRIND BRAKE SHOES TO ANCHOR AND DRUM.

6. REPLACE BRAKE DRUMS.

7. PERFORM ANCHOR PIN ADJUSTMENT.

C, HIGH, HARD BRAKE PEDAL

1. BRAKE PEDAL PUSH ROD TOO LONG.

2. SELF-ADUSTING BRAKES OVERADJUSTING.

3. HARD, GLAZED BRAKE LINING.

4. LOW FRICTION BRAKE LINING.

5. DISC BRAKE CALIPER PISTON FROZEN.

6. POWER BRAKE UNIT NOT WORKING.

1. ADJUST PUSH ROD TO MASTER CYLINDER PISTON CLEARANCE.

2. CONSULT CAR DRIVER AS TO HIS USE OF BRAKES. USE A BRAKE SHOE ADJUSTING TOOL TO CORRECTLY PREADJUST THE SHOE TO DRUM CLEARANCE.

3. REPLACE BRAKE LINING.

4. REPLACE BRAKE LINING.

5. REPLACE OR REBUILD CALIPER.

6. REPLACE POWER UNIT AND READJUST BRAKE SHOE TO DRUM CLEARANCE.

D. BRAKE PEDAL PULSATION

1. DISTORTED DRUM.

2. OUT-OF-ROUND DRUM.

3. NOT CONCENTRIC DRUM, "WOBBLING" DRUM .

1. CORRECTLY INSTALL THE WHEEL TO THE BRAKE DRUM HUB.

2. TURN DRUM ON BRAKE LATHE.

3. TURN DRUM ON BRAKE LATHE WITH CORRECT ADAPTORS.

4. BRAKE DISC HAS EXCESSIVE RUNOUT.

4. TURN DISC ON BRAKE LATHE WITH DISC BRAKE ADAPTORS.

5. BRAKE DISC HAS VARIABLE THICKNESS.

5. TURN DISC ON BRAKE LATHE WITH DISC BRAKE ADAPTORS.

E. POWER BRAKE PEDAL DOES NOT DROP AS ENGINE IS STARTED

1. RESERVE VACUUM WAS NOT DEPLETED FROM TANK.

1. PUMP BRAKE PEDAL 5 TIMES WITH ENGINE "OFF" BEFORE TESTING BRAKES.

2. NO VACUUM TO POWER BRAKE UNIT.

2. DEFECTIVE CHECK VALVE. COLLAPSED VACUUM HOSE.

3. POWER UNIT DEFECTIVE.

3. REPLACE POWER BRAKE UNIT.

F. CAR PULLS TO ONE SIDE AS BRAKES ARE APPLIED

1. FROZEN WHEEL CYLINDER PISTON.

1. REBUILD OR REPLACE WHEEL CYLINDER.

2. RESTRICTED BRAKE TUBE OR HOSE.

2. REPLACE BRAKE TUBE OR HOSE.

3. BRAKE SHOES REVERSED OR BOTH SECONDARY SHOES ARE ON ONE SIDE OF CAR.

3. INSTALL BRAKE SHOES CORRECTLY.

4. GREASE OR BRAKE FLUID ON THE BRAKE LINING.

4. REPLACE OR REBUILD WHEEL CYLINDERS. REPLACE AXLE SEAL.

5. BRAKE SHOE SPRINGS IMPROPERLY INSTALLED.

5. CLEAN SPRINGS AND INSTALL AC-CORDING TO COLOR.

6. BRAKE SHOE SPRINGS STRETCHED OR OVERHEATED.

6. REPLACE SPRINGS ON ALL BRAKE ASSEMBLIES.

7. BRAKE SHOES IMPROPERLY GROUND.

7. CAM GRIND BRAKE SHOE TO MATCH DRUM DIAMETER.

8. LOOSE WHEEL BEARING.

8. ADJUST WHEEL BEARING CORRECTLY.

9. VEHICLE OUT-OF-ALIGNMENT.

9. REALIGN VEHICLE.

10. WORN STEERING PARTS.

10. REPLACE IDLER ARM, TIE ROD, ETC.

11. UNEQUAL TIRE PRESSURE OR TIRE SIZE

11. MATCH TIRE SIZE AND PROPERLY INFLATE TIRES.

G. DRAGGING BRAKES

1. FROZEN WHEEL CYLINDER PISTONS.

1. REPLACE OR REBUILD WHEEL CYLINDER.

2. STRETCHED OR FATIGUED SHOE RETURN SPRINGS.

2. REPLACE SHOE RETURN SPRINGS.

3. MASTER CYLINDER COMPENSATING PORT CLOSED.

3. ADJUST MASTER CYLINDER PUSH ROD CLEARANCE OR FREE PLAY.

4. DISC BRAKE MASTER CYLINDER HAS CHECK VALVE IN LINE TO DISC BRAKES.

4. REBUILD OR REPLACE MASTER CYLINDER WITHOUT A STATIC CHECK VALVE.

5. REAR WHEEL PARKING BRAKE CABLES FROZEN.

5. REPLACE OR LUBRICATE THE PARKING BRAKE CABLES.

6. MINOR BRAKE ADJUSTMENT TOO TIGHT.

6. BACK-OFF STAR WHEEL AT LEAST 10 CLICKS.

H. BRAKE SQUEAK OR SQUEAL

1. DIRT EMBEDDED INTO LINING.

1. REMOVE DIRT FROM BRAKE ASSEMBLY AND DRUM.

2. HARD, GLAZED, CRACKED BRAKE LINING.

2. GRIND BRAKE SHOES OR REPLACE BRAKE.

3. GLAZED, POLISHED BRAKE DRUM.

3. TURN BRAKE DRUMS.

4. FATIGUED, OVERHEATED BRAKE SHOE RETURN SPRINGS.

4. REPLACE SPRINGS.

I. BRAKE CHATTER

1. GREASE OR BRAKE FLUID ON BRAKE LINING.

1. REPLACE BRAKE SHOES.

2. BRAKE SHOES GROUND INCORRECTLY.

2. GROUND BRAKE SHOES SHOULD HAVE .005 TO .008 THOUSANDTHS HEEL AND TOE CLEARANCE.

3. LOOSE BACKING PLATES.

3. TIGHTEN BACKING PLATE BOLTS.

4. EXCESSIVE REAR AXLE ENDPLAY.

4. ADJUST REAR AXLE BEARINGS TO MANUFACTURERS SPECIFICATIONS.

TRADE COMPETENCY TEST

1. How can improper adjustment of the brake pedal linkage cause brake lockup?
2. What causes a brake pedal to have a spongy feel?
3. How can you determine whether or not the brakes need relining?
4. What is the clearance between the shoes and the drum after the brake shoes have been adjusted using a brake shoe adjusting gauge?
5. What should the pressure be in a brake pressure bleeder?
6. What causes tapered drum wear?
7. Is an eccentric drum the same as an out-of-round drum?
8. What supporting devices are used to mount hubbed drums on a lathe arbor?
9. What is a "floating" drum?
10. How does the pressure bleeding operation differ between drum brakes and disc brakes?
11. How do you check the accuracy of the drum setup on the lathe?
12. What are the different parts of the drum brake shoe?
13. How will a standard brake shoe fit into an oversized drum?
14. What should the clearance be between the ends of the lining segment and the drum when the shoe is held firmly against the drum?

15. A brake drum has been turned to a diameter of 11.050 in. What should the brake shoe grinder setting be to cam grind a brake shoe to this drum?
16. Why are brake shoes which are fixed-anchor ground also cam ground in the process?
17. Can mineral oil be used to lubricate the rubber parts of a hydraulic brake system?
18. What is used for the final cleaning of all hydraulic cylinder rubber parts.?
19. What brake disc test requires using a dial indicator?
20. How can caliper pistons be removed from their respective bores when disassembling the caliper?
21. What tool is usually used to clean the walls of the cylinder bores?
22. What are some of the probable causes of a low, hard pedal on a car with self-adjusting brakes?
23. What can cause a disc brake to drag?
24. What is the procedure to use if the brake warning light remains on after bleeding the system?
25. How can you determine the maximum amount of allowable wear permitted on today's drums or discs?

CHAPTER 4

THE COMPLETE BRAKE JOB

This chapter outlines the basic step by step procedures required to restore an automotive brake system to a safe operating condition.

Drum Brakes

This "complete" drum brake job contains all the steps required to service all drum brakes regardless of design.

Test the Master Brake Cylinder

Primary Cup. A defective master cylinder primary cup may be detected by slowly and firmly depressing the brake pedal. If the brake pedal becomes hard, then slowly fades to the floor, brake fluid is bypassing the primary cup or it is leaking from some other part of the system. Usually, by inspecting the master cylinder reservoir for fluid level, an indication is had of whether the primary cup has failed or some other hydraulic part is defective. Asking the car owner if he has had to recently replenish the fluid in the master cylinder often provides an answer. A defective primary cup will cause loss of pedal with no resulting loss of brake fluid. Rebuild or replace the master cylinder to correct a defective primary cup.

Secondary Cup. Loss of brake fluid can be the result of a worn secondary cup. When the inside of the boot at the rear of the master cylinder, Fig. 4-1, is wet with brake fluid, the secondary cup has failed. When the master cylinder is at-

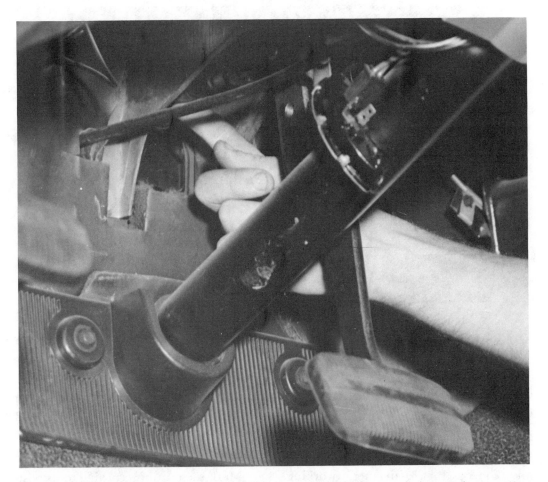

Fig. 4-1. Checking the rear boot of the master cylinder for brake fluid leakage past the secondary cup. (Automotive Parts Rebuilders Assn.)

tached to a vacuum cylinder, power brake unit, check the secondary cup for leakage by removing the vacuum hose at the power unit. Evidence of fluid in the hose indicates a worn secondary cup. Replace or rebuild the master cylinder to correct a worn secondary cup.

Check Stop Lights

While the master cylinder is being checked for operation, the stop lights are observed for proper operation. Inoperative stop lights could be due to: (1) blown fuse in circuit, (2) defective bulbs in tail light sockets, or (3) a defective stop light switch. The stop light check is an important part of the complete brake job. Safety demands that the stop lights always be operating correctly. Repair the stop light before the brake job proper is started; otherwise, it may be forgotten.

Loosen Wheel Nuts

Remove the wheel covers and loosen the wheel nuts. Mark one stud and its corresponding hole in the wheel to maintain dynamic wheel balance (Fig. 4-2). If the vehicle has a tapered, rear-hubbed

Fig. 4-2. Mark the position of the wheel on the hub so that dynamic wheel balance is maintained when the wheel is re-mounted. (*Automotive Parts Rebuilders Assn.*)

drum, remove the cotter key from the axle nut and loosen the nut.

Support Vehicle Off Floor

If a hydraulic lift is at your disposal, raise the car to a convenient working height. If a hydraulic lift is not available for the job, support the vehicle on jack stands under the *body* of the vehicle. Do not support the vehicle under the axle or lower control arm since the stands will get in the way. Many rear wheels are difficult to remove from the rear axle because of low fenders. By placing the stands under the frame of the vehicle, the wheels will hang down on their springs, making for easier removal.

Remove Tires and Wheels

Remove all the wheel nuts and place them in the wheel covers for safe storage, Fig. 4-3. Place the tire next to the brake assembly. Lay the wheel down with the outside, or white sidewall, next to the floor. Place the wheel cover upside-down in the wheel to prevent it from becoming scratched.

Remove All Drums

Mark each drum according to its position on the vehicle, *LF, RF,* etc., so that the drums will be returned to their original positions on completion of the brake job. A few older model vehicles may have left-hand studs and nuts on the left side of the car and right-hand studs and nuts on the right side. Also, the front wheel bearing parts wear into each other; mixing these bearing parts may cause premature failure.

Remove the drums from the front spindles by removing the cotter key from the spindle nut, then the spindle nut itself, safety washer, and outer bearing cone, as shown in Fig. 4-4. Thread the spindle nut onto the spindle. (A few turns is enough.) Grasp the drum firmly with both hands and pull sharply. The

Fig. 4-3. Use the wheel cover, placed face down in the tire well, as a receptacle for brake parts. (*Automotive Parts Rebuilders Assn.*)

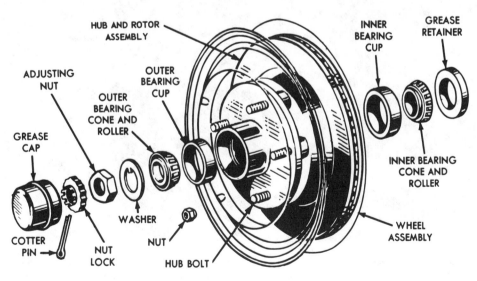

Fig. 4-4. Front wheel assembly, showing the sequence in which the parts are assembled. (*Ford Div., Ford Motor Co.*)

drum will disengage from the spindle, bringing with it the inner bearing cone and seal.

Check Condition of Drums

The brake drums should be turned on a lathe each time the linings are replaced. The drum friction surface may not at first show signs of severe wear (no deep scores, hard spots, etc.). However, a closer inspection will reveal one or more of the common wear problems described in the preceding chapter. A worn drum presents a poor-quality, irregular friction surface to the brake lining. The drum must, therefore, be restored to its original condition if like-new brake performance is to be achieved.

In some cases, the drum may be too worn or distorted to be safely machined and the drum must be replaced.

Check Drum Wear with a Brake Drum Micrometer. Measure all drums with a brake drum micrometer as shown in Fig. 4-5. Determine whether the drums are worn beyond the safety limit. Most drums are worn beyond safety limits if, after the required machining, the

Fig. 4-5. A brake drum micrometer is used to measure drum diameter. The arms are moved outward along the calibrated notches to the basic drum diameter. The micrometer button is then advanced to the drum surface, and the dial reading is added to the notch reading to give drum diameter in thousandths of an inch. (*Automotive Parts Rebuilders Assn.*)

drum diameter would be 0.060 in. greater than its original new car size. Drums which have been worn beyond the safety limit must be replaced.

Check Drums for an Out-of-Round Condition. Measure the drum diameter in more than one location. Variations in the readings indicates an out-of-round drum. A severely out-of-round drum may require machining to the extent that the drum exceeds the safety limit. Such drums must be replaced.

Check for Hard Spots. Excessive hard spots (blue discolorations) showing in the middle of the drum wearing surface are indications that the structure of the metal has been transformed under the heat and pressure of braking. (The friction surface actually changes from cast iron to work-hardened cast iron in spots.)

If the usual amount of metal removal fails to undercut the hard spots, the drum may have to be replaced.

Mount the Most Worn Rear Drum on Brake Drum Lathe

Mount the drum as outlined in the preceding chapter. Check the mounting of the drum on the lathe by making a light scratch on the drum wearing surface while the drum is revolving. If the scratch mark is continuous (through 360°) the drum is properly mounted.

If the scratch mark appears along only a part of the friction surface, either the drum is improperly mounted or the drum is non-concentric. To check the mounting, loosen the lathe arbor nut and revolve the drum one-half turn, Fig. 4-6. Tighten the arbor nut. Make a slight

Fig. 4-6. To check the mounting of the drum, loosen the arbor nut, rotate the drum 180° on the arbor, tighten the arbor nut, and make a second scratch cut on the drum. A comparison of the two scratch cuts will indicate whether the drum is properly mounted. (*Automotive Parts Rebuilders Assn.*)

change in the position of the drum by giving the drum feed handwheel a few turns. Make another trial cut with the tool bit. If the two scratches are side by side, the mounting is correct; the drum is wobbling, or non-concentric. If the two scratches are not side by side, the setup is improper and must be corrected.

A drum that has excessive wobble or lateral runout will cause the brake pedal to pulsate or move up and down as the brakes are applied. These defects usually can be corrected by machining as long as the maximum drum machining limits are not exceeded. If the defects are severe the drum may have to be replaced. Turn the drum, following the procedures given in the preceding chapter.

Clean the Front Wheel Bearings

While a rear drum is being turned on the lathe, the front wheel bearings can be cleaned and inspected (Fig. 4-7).

Clean Inside of Hub. Wash all of the excess grease from the wheel hub with a suitable nonflammable solvent. Figure 4-5 illustrates the dirty grease present on the hub at the time of disassembly. Modern wheel bearing greases need only be packed into the wheel bearing separator cavities.

Check the Bearing Races. Pits or evidence of excessive bearing wear will be noticed on the surface of the bearing cup or races. Whenever the ball or roller assembly (cone) shows any visible irregularities, replace the *entire* bearing assembly even though the other part of the bearing assembly appears re-usable.

A wheel bearing cup (race) is pressed into the hub at the time the vehicle is manufactured. When a cup must be replaced, care must be taken so that the old cup is properly removed from the hub. If the old cup is driven out of the hub in a cocked manner, the hub bore may be enlarged. If this occurs, the new bearing cup may then move or spin inside the hub. Correct wheel bearing adjustment cannot be achieved, nor can the front

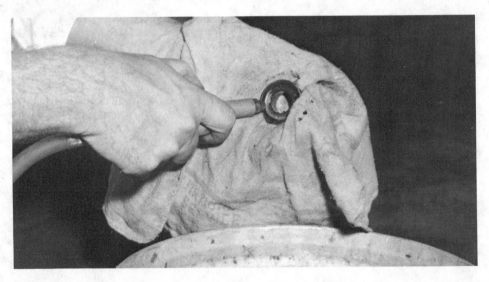

Fig. 4-7. Use an air hose to blow old grease from the front wheel bearings. The bearings can then be inspected for wear. Caution: Do not spin the bearing with air pressure; it may fly apart. (*Automotive Parts Rebuilders Assn.*)

drum be accurately machined on the brake drum lathe, if the bearing cup is loose in the hub. Replace the hub and bearing cups if this condition occurs.

Mount and Turn the Other Rear Drum

Mount and turn the other rear drum. Use the same lathe depth-of-cut setting required to machine the first rear drum.

Inspect Wear Pattern on Old Shoes

While the last of the two rear drums is being machined, inspect the brake assembly of each wheel. Inspect the wear pattern of the brake lining on all four brake assemblies, Fig. 4-8. Normal brake lining wear will leave little or no lining in the center of the shoe. The heel and

Fig. 4-8. Comparing the lining thickness at the heel and toe ends of the secondary shoe. (*Automotive Parts Rebuilders Assn.*)

toe ends of the lining should be of nearly equal thickness. This condition exists because the shoe platform does not bend to conform to the arc of the (slightly larger in diameter) drum. The web of the shoe will resist the tendency of the shoe to flatten out under normal braking forces. Whenever the shoe has more lining worn off one end of the lining segment than the other, the following conditions may be present:

Misplaced Anchor Pin. If the car is an older car, the brake design may include an adjustable anchor. The anchor pin may not have been correctly adjusted at the time of the last brake re-lining. Check for an adjustable anchor pin. Refer to the manufacturer's shop manual for the procedure for correctly positioning the anchor pin.

Worn or Distorted Brake Shoe. The anchor eye of the shoe, with repeated pounding of the shoe against the anchor, may be deformed. The eye of the shoe is sometimes swaged flat, which lets the shoe ride high on the anchor pin. Because

Fig. 4-9. A bearing protector is included in the setup for a front drum in order to shield the inner bearing race in the hub from chips. (*Automotive Parts Rebuilders Assn.*)

of this, the shoe wears off more brake lining at the heel or anchor end than at the toe end of the shoe.

Mount and Turn a Front Drum

Mount the more worn front drum on the arbor of the lathe, using the correct radii adaptors as instructed in the preceding chapter. Place a bearing protector over the hub of the drum to prevent the chips from falling into and scoring the inner race (Fig. 4-9). Check the drum mounting, using the scratch method described earlier. Turn the drum, following the procedure outlined in the preceding chapter.

Remove All Brake Shoes

Remove all the shoes from the backing plates. See Fig. 4-10. Test each spring before storing it in the wheel cover. Either use a spring tester or drop the spring on a cement floor to determine if the spring is still usable. A weak or excessively heated spring will bounce and/or vibrate when it strikes the floor. A good spring will hit the floor with a dull thud.

Observe the color coding of the springs; the springs must be reinstalled in their original positions. Color usually indicates a difference in spring tension. For example, a 1969 Chevrolet uses a gray spring on the primary shoe and a black, heavier spring on the secondary shoe. The stronger, black spring keeps the secondary shoe against the anchor pin at all times, reducing brake noise.

Turn the Other Front Brake Drum

Mount the other front drum, again following the procedure described in the preceding chapter. Use the same machine setting used to turn the first front drum. If hard spots are present on either drum after turning, both drums must be ground to make certain that both are of the same diameter and surface finish.

Fig. 4-10. Use a brake spring tool to unhook the brake shoe retracting springs from the anchor pins. (*Automotive Parts Rebuilders Assn.*)

Fig. 4-11. Clean the backing plates with a wire brush to remove dirt and rust. (*Automotive Parts Rebuilders Assn.*)

Clean the Backing Plates

Wire brush the rust and dirt from the backing plates as illustrated in Fig. 4-11. If the ledges on which the shoes rest show evidence of deep scoring, the ledges should be ground flat. Otherwise, the shoes will hang up as they slide over the grooved ledges.

Inspect the Wheel Cylinders

Loosen the Bleeder Valves. Using a suitable bleeder valve wrench, loosen the bleeder valve on each wheel cylinder. See Fig. 4-12. Note: The bleeder valve is integral with the wheel cylinder; excessive corrosion may cause the complete re-placement of the cylinder because the bleeder valve may twist off while being loosened.

Clear Cylinders Past the Wheel Cylinder Piston Stops. Many cylinders cannot be disassembled while still bolted to the backing plate. Wheel cylinder piston stops, stamped impressions that protrude

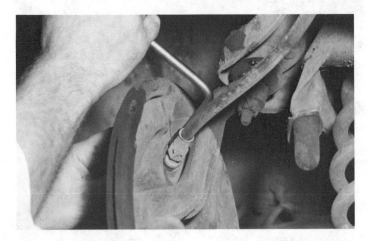

Fig. 4-12. Loosen the bleeder valve with a bleeder valve wrench. Allow the brake fluid to drain from the valve. (*Automotive Parts Rebuilders Assn.*)

Fig. 4-13. The wheel cylinder is shown moved clear of the piston stops on the backing plate. The wheel cylinder can then be disassembled and inspected for wear. (*Automotive Parts Rebuilders Assn.*)

Fig. 4-14. Honing the wheel cylinder. (*Automotive Parts Rebuilders Assn.*)

from the backing plate, are meant to keep the wheel cylinder pistons from coming out too far when the shoes are removed. Where these stops are present, it is necessary that the wheel cylinders be unbolted from the backing plate and pulled out away from the stops so that the cylinders can be disassembled. See Fig. 4-13.

Disassemble the Wheel Cylinders. Disassemble the wheel cylinders as described in the preceding chapter. Observe the condition of the pistons when they are removed from the cylinder.

Minor corrosion can be scraped from the piston head. If the brake fluid appears to be very dirty and dark in color, the brake system should be flushed before the cylinders are rebuilt or new cylinders are installed.

Flushing fluid is usually an alcohol-base compound which dissolves the residue in the lines and hoses. The flushing fluid is usually placed in a pressure bleeder which is connected to the master cylinder. The flushing operation takes place until clear flushing fluid is coming from all four wheel cylinder locations. Brake fluid, usually a green or blue color, is then pumped through the lines with another pressure bleeder until fresh brake fluid is coming from the cylinders.

Honing the Cylinders. A brake cylinder hone is used to clean the walls of the wheel cylinder. Either alcohol or brake fluid may be used as a honing fluid. See Fig. 4-14. After the revolving hone has been moved back and forth through the cylinder a few times, the cylinder should be flushed with alcohol and a clean shop towel pulled through the cylinder. If no defects appear in the cylinder wall, the cylinder may be rebuilt. If, after honing, defects are still evident along the cylinder walls, the cylinder should be replaced.

Rebuild the Wheel Cylinders

After the cylinders have been honed with an inspection hone and found to be free of defects, the cylinders may be re-

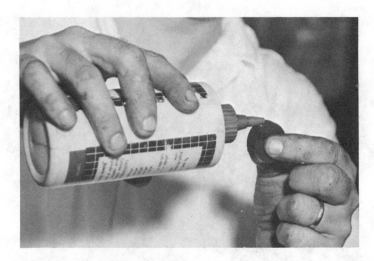

Fig. 4-15. Lubricating the wheel cylinder piston cups. (*Automotive Parts Rebuilders Assn.*)

built. Rebuilding kits are available which contain new metal and rubber parts. Old cups and boots should not be reused.

Remove and clean the passages in the bleeder valves. Then replace and snugly tighten each bleeder valve into its seat.

Coat the wheel cylinder pistons and cups with a light film of assembly fluid (Fig. 4-15). Reassemble in the reverse order of disassembly. Bolt the reassembled cylinder to the backing plate. Install the brake shoe actuating pins inside of the boots.

Fig. 4-16. If a new wheel cylinder is to be installed, the old wheel cylinder is removed from the backing plate and unscrewed from the brake hose. Avoid twisting the brake hose. (*Automotive Parts Rebuilders Assn.*)

Replacement of the Wheel Cylinder

If new replacement wheel cylinders are to be installed, unscrew the front cylinders from the brake hose as illustrated in Fig. 4-16. Be careful that the copper washer between the hose and cylinder is not lost. Disassemble the new cylinders and clean them if required. Reassemble the cylinder with assembly fluid. Replacing the copper washer, screw the new cylinder onto the brake hose firmly. Bolt the cylinder to the backing plate.

If the brake hose has even the slightest twist, the hose clamp on the frame must be disconnected and the twist removed from the hose. A twisted hose will unscrew itself from the wheel cylinder as the car is driven, resulting in loss of all the brake fluid and brake failure.

Disconnect the Rear Parking Brake Cables

Disconnect the parking brake cables as shown in Fig. 4-17. The rear parking brake cables can be maladjusted, which will cause difficulty when installing and adjusting the rear shoes. When the driver complains that the parking brake handle travels too far when he applies the brake, an inexperienced mechanic will often assume that the brake cables have stretched. He will "take up the slack" in the cable by shortening it. Instead, he should have: (1) pulled a rear brake drum and inspected the brake linings for excessive wear; (2) performed a minor adjustment to the rear brakes to bring the shoes closer to the drums; and only then (3) adjusted the cable for slack as required. Shortening the cable without first check-

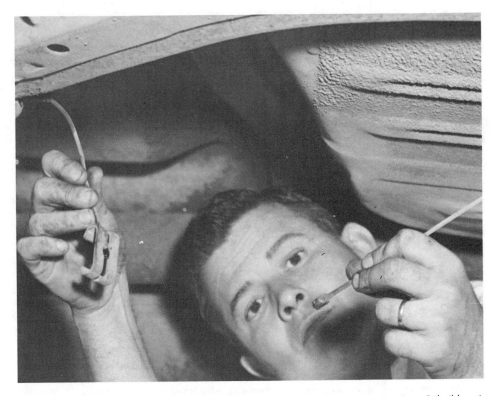

Fig. 4-17. Unhooking the rear parking brake cable from the front cable. (*Automotive Parts Rebuilders Assn.*)

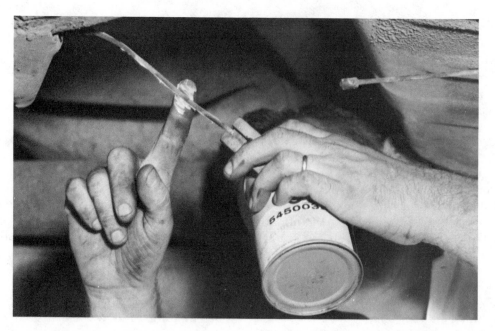

Fig. 4-18. Rubbing brake lubricant on the parking brake cable. (*Automotive Parts Rebuilders Assn.*)

Fig. 4-19. Applying backing plate lubricant to the brake shoe ledges on the backing plates. (*Automotive Parts Rebuilders Assn.*)

ing the rear brake shoe adjustment may cause the rear shoes to be held away from the anchor pin.

Lubricate the Parking Brake Cables

Pull the front cable toward the rear of the vehicle. Coat the exposed cable with brake lubricant, as shown in Fig. 4-18. Pull the rear cable forward through the cable housing. Lubricate the forward section of the cable. Pull the cable in and out until the cable slides easily within its housing. If the cable does not move, it has rusted to the housing. Replace the cable. Note: Do not adjust the parking brake until the rear shoes have been adjusted.

Lubricate the Backing Plate Ledges

Apply a high melting point lubricant to the ledges on the backing plate which support the brake shoes (Fig. 4-19). The lubricant will keep the shoes from causing a "scrunching" noise as they are applied. Apply the lubricant sparingly, otherwise the lubricant will bleed onto the friction material on the shoes and cause erratic brake operation. When the vehicle has a brake design that uses an adjustable anchor pin, the anchor pin should be removed from the backing plate, lubricated, and reinstalled in the backing plate.

Obtain the New Brake Shoes

By using the make and model of the vehicle, find the shoes required for the particular vehicle in a brake shoe catalog or F.M.S.I. (Friction Materials Standards Institute) Brake Shoe Data Book. The first part of the shoe number indicates the F.M.S.I. identification number for the lining segments, which are either bonded or riveted to the core. The digits of the F.M.S.I. number following the hyphen indicate the core number. For example, a 1969 Chevrolet rear brake will require a 2006-228 brake shoe. The number 2006 identifies the proper lining segments, while the number 228 indicates the core number.

If the drums are scored or out-of-round they must be machined oversize, or larger than original size. Correspondingly, the new shoes must have lining segments which are thicker than the lining segments for standard shoes. A general rule to follow is to obtain brake shoes with oversize lining thickness equal to the amount removed from one side of the drum. If twenty thousandths (.020) of an inch of material has been removed from one side of a drum, the brake lining should be at least twenty thousandths of an inch thicker than the original lining.

Most suppliers stock linings which are thirty thousandths (.030) of an inch oversize, which would be the correct lining thickness if the drum has been machined to its maximum safe diameter of sixty thousandths (.060) of an inch greater than original equipment or standard drum size. Usual practice is to cam grind the oversize lining to correspond to the new diameter of the turned drums.

Grind Brake Shoes to Match Drums

As described in the preceding chapter, there are two methods of grinding brake shoes; the standard method and the fixed-anchor method. The first method is used when grinding non-servo brakes. The second method is used when grinding a servo brake with a fixed anchor. Whichever method is used, the shoe is "cam ground" or ground to a diameter 0.030 in. smaller than the turned drum diameter.

The grinder adjustments are calibrated in inches of diameter. The grinder is usually set to the drum diameter *less 0.030 in.* For example, if the turned drum diameter is 11.050 in. or 0.050 in. oversize, then 0.030 in. would be sub-

Fig. 4-20. Fixed-anchor grinding the brake shoe. (*Automotive Parts Rebuilders Assn.*)

Fig. 4-21. Checking clearance at the ends of the just-ground brake shoe. After cam grinding the shoe, there should be .006-.008 in. of clearance at toe and heel when the center of the shoe is held tightly against the drum. (*Automotive Parts Rebuilders Assn.*)

tracted from 11.050 in. which is 11.020 in. The shoes would be correctly ground for the 11.050 in. diameter drum if the grinder is set to 11.020 in. Figure 4-20 illustrates the heel of the shoe in position at the start of the fixed-anchor, cam grinding operation. The grinding is accomplished in several passes across the face of the grinding wheel.

By grinding the brake shoe to a drum size smaller than the actual drum diameter, the shoe will touch the drum in its center. When properly ground the ends of the shoe, or the toe and the heel, will have some clearance. When a shoe is held tightly against the drum in the middle, a 0.006 in. feeler gage should fit between the drum and each end of the lining segment. See Fig. 4-21. If a .006 in. feeler gage will not slide between the end of the shoe and the drum, the abrasive cloth on the grinder should be replaced.

When, as is usually the case, the shoes are being fixed-anchor ground for a vehicle having a duo-servo brake, the anchor pin determines how the secondary shoe fits the drum. Depending on the make and model number of the grinder,

Fig. 4-22. Installing the brake shoe hold-down spring with the proper tool. (*Automotive Parts Rebuilders Assn.*)

gage sleeves or gage plates are provided which are used to position a variable-position anchor pin on the grinder for duplicating the position of the fixed anchor pin on the vehicle. Obtain the correct anchor pin location for the grinder from the chart provided with the grinder. Grind only enough material from the brake lining to insure proper fit of the shoe to the drum and to the anchor pin. Check the fit of the newly-ground shoe in the drum. A .006 in. feeler gage should slide easily between the ends of the shoe and the drum.

Install the Brake Shoes

Correctly install all of the brake shoes onto the backing plates. Be sure the springs are installed correctly. See Fig. 4-22. Usually the primary shoe return spring is installed on the anchor pin first.

Adjust the Anchor Pins

If the brake design has an adjustable anchor pin, adjust the anchor pin to center the shoe to the drum according to the car manufacturer's shop manual.

Adjust the Shoe-to-Drum Clearance

Use a caliper gage to adjust the drum-to-shoe clearance on all brakes. Insert the gage into the drum and adjust the *inside caliper* part of the gage to the drum diameter as shown in Fig. 4-23. Lock the

Fig. 4-23. To establish the correct lining-to-drum clearance, set the lower part of the caliper-type gage to the diameter of the drum. Lock the gage in this position. (*Automotive Parts Rebuilders Assn.*)

Fig. 4-24. Place the upper, or outside caliper part, of the gage across the newly-installed linings. Turn the star wheel until the linings expand and the gage touches the centers of the shoes. The correct shoe-to-drum clearance is now established. (*Automotive Parts Rebuilders Assn.*)

gage. Moving from the drum to the brake shoe assembly, place the outside caliper part of the gage across the centers of the shoes and parallel to the floor as shown in Fig. 4-24. Expand the star wheel by hand until the shoes just touch the gage. The gage is designed to provide a drum-to-brake shoe clearance of .010 in. When the gage is set to the drum diameter, the outside caliper part is thereby opened to a setting .020 in. greater than drum diameter.

Both front drums should have the same diameter. The same gage setting is used, therefore, to adjust the shoe settings on both front wheels. Both rear drums are also the same diameter; but this diameter may not be that for the front drums. The brake shoe setting gage is adjusted to the diameter of the rear drums, and the rear shoes are then adjusted accordingly.

Clean the Drums

Before re-mounting the drums, wipe the drum friction surfaces with a shop towel wetted with clean alcohol to remove any trace of metal dust produced in the turning process. Also, remove any finger marks on the brake lining with clean alcohol.

Pack the Front Wheel Bearings

Pack the front wheel bearings with a good quality, wheel bearing grease. A wheel bearing packer, like the one shown in Fig. 4-25, performs the job quickly and efficiently. The illustration shows both the inner and outer roller bearings in position on the wheel bearing packer. After the retaining plate is screwed onto the threaded shaft, compressed air forces the wheel bearing grease up and through the bearings.

tapered end first. See Fig. 4-26. Place the inner bearing grease retainer in position. Use a seal installer to properly seat the grease seal into the hub. Wipe a light film of grease on the front wheel spindle to allow the inner races of the wheel bearings to spin relative to the spindle. Repeat this procedure for the other front wheel.

Mount the front wheel hub and drum assembly on the front wheel spindle. *Note: Some vehicles have left-hand wheel studs on the left side of the vehicle and*

Fig. 4-25. Using a wheel bearing packer to lubricate the front wheel bearings. (*Automotive Parts Rebuilders Assn.*)

Install Front Wheel Bearings and Mount Drums

Place the inner (larger) bearing in the hub's inner bearing cup, small or

right-hand studs on the right side of the vehicle. Care must be taken to re-mount each front hub on the proper side of the vehicle. Install the outer (smaller) roller bearing, small or tapered end first. Install

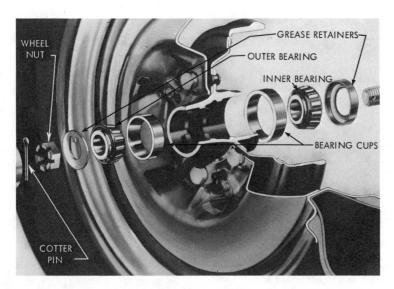

Fig. 4-26. Exploded view of the front wheel mounting assembly, indicating the correct order of reassembly. (*Dodge Div., Chrysler Corp.*)

Fig. 4-27. The wheel nut should be tightened with a torque wrench to pre-load the front wheel bearings to specifications. (*Automotive Parts Rebuilders Assn.*)

the outer grease retainer and then the wheel castle nut. See Fig. 4-26. Use a torque wrench, Fig. 4-27, when tightening the castle nut to adjust the pre-load on the front wheel bearings to the car manufacturer's specifications. Finally, install the cotter pin and grease cap. Repeat the above procedure for the other front wheel.

Bleed the Hydraulic System

Most brake service shops have canister-shaped portable pressure bleeders, which permit the bleeding operation to be done by one man, Fig. 4-28. Open the bleeder and check it to see if it contains enough fluid to perform the job of bleeding the vehicle's brake system. Some bleeder designs, especially those which connect to a tire to obtain the bleeding pressure, must be purged of the air that was inducted into the bleeder when the bleeder was checked for fluid level. To accomplish this, run fluid from the pressure bleeder into the master cylinder reservoir of the car or the bleeder bottle until the air is released (no bubbles of

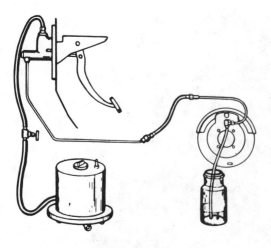

Fig. 4-28. Pressure bleeding the hydraulic system. The pressure bleeder hose is connected to the master cylinder by means of a pressure-tight adaptor. (*Automotive Parts Rebuilders Assn.*)

bleeder to the adaptor. Using a bleeder hose and bottle to catch the escaping fluid, open the bleeder valve of the left front cylinder. Bleed the cylinder until bubbles no longer appear in the fluid entering the bottle. See Fig. 4-29. Then bleed the right front, the left rear, and finally the right rear cylinder.

Disconnect the pressure bleeder hose from the master cylinder adaptor. Remove the adaptor. Add brake fluid, if necessary, to bring the reservoir brake fluid level to the full mark. Replace the master cylinder cap.

Mount the Wheels

Mount and secure each wheel in turn. Install the wheel nuts in a manner that will not distort the brake drums. Tighten

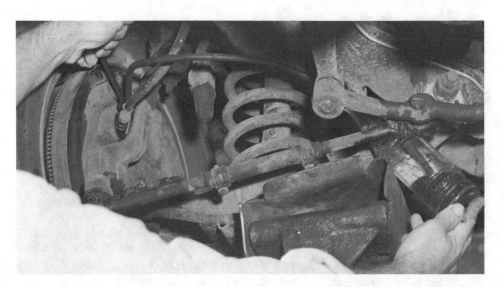

Fig. 4-29. Bleeding a wheel cylinder. A hose is fitted to the bleeder valve and run into a glass or jar partly filled with brake fluid. A special tool (bleeder valve wrench) is used to open the bleeder valve. (*Automotive Parts Rebuilders Assn.*)

air can be seen) and a solid stream of fluid emerges.

Screw the proper adaptor to the top of the master cylinder reservoir. Check all wheel cylinder bleeder valves to make sure that they are closed. Connect the

all of the wheel nuts evenly; do not exceed the car manufacturer's torque specifications. Install the wheel covers.

Check Brake Pedal Height

After a complete brake job, the car,

when returned to the owner, should have a firm pedal with a stroke equal to at least half of the available brake pedal travel. If the pedal is low or spongy, a defect in the brake hydraulic system is indicated. The master cylinder may have to be rebuilt or replaced, probably because of a defective residual check valve.

Connect and Adjust the Parking Brake

Reconnect the parking brake cables. When the parking brake pedal or handle is applied approximately one third of its total travel, both rear wheels should have the same resistance to turning or should be locked. When the brake is released, the rear wheels should turn freely.

Remove Vehicle from Stands or Hoist and Test Brakes

Lower the vehicle from the hoist or stands. Check tire pressure and add air if needed. Test the brakes before moving the car. If the brakes are self-adjusting, operate the car in reverse and bring the car to a stop to provide a final adjustment of the brakes.

Fixed Caliper Disc Brakes

This "complete" disc brake job contains all the basic steps required to service fixed caliper design disc brakes.

Remove the Wheels

Remove the wheel covers and loosen the wheel nuts. Support the car on a hoist or jack stands. Remove the wheel nuts. Mark a hub stud and its corresponding hole in the wheel to retain the wheel balance. Remove all four wheels from their hubs. Place the wheels, with the outer sidewall down, on the floor. Put the wheel covers inside the wheel wells and use the wheel covers to collect the brake parts. Removal of the front wheels ex-poses the front brake discs and their calipers. Mark the brake discs L or R so they will be re-installed properly on the car.

Remove the Left Front Disc Brake Shoes

Remove the two bolts which hold the caliper splash shield—shoe retainer plate to the left front caliper assembly. Lift the retainer plate from the caliper. With the retaining plate removed the brake shoes are exposed to view. (See Fig. 1-38. Chapter 1). Use two pairs of pliers to pull out the disc brake shoes as they may be rusted into the caliper. If necessary, additional clearance to remove the shoes can be obtained by using a water pump pliers (gripping the metal tab of the shoe and the caliper housing) to force the pistons into their bores.

Mark the location of each disc brake shoe on the rear of the shoe as illustrated in Fig. 4-30. A disc brake shoe wears thinner at one end than at the other. The leading edge of the shoe wears more than the trailing edge. If the shoes are to be reused, they must be marked and reinstalled in the same position, otherwise, brake problems may result.

Push the Four Caliper Pistons into the Bottom of Their Cylinders

After the shoes are removed from the caliper, the caliper pistons must be pushed as far as possible into their cylinder bores to provide clearance for the new shoes. The pistons can be bottomed by placing a flat tool across the pistons and prying against the brake disc. The movement of the pistons in their cylinders is a good indication of the condition of the cylinder walls. If the pistons move freely in their cylinders, and if there is no trace of brake fluid leakage past the piston boots, the caliper assembly can be assumed to be functioning properly. New brake shoes can be installed without fur-

Fig. 4-30. After the retainer plate is removed, the shoes are pulled out of the caliper (usually with pliers) and marked for their original location. (*Automotive Service Industry Assn.*)

ther disassembly or rebuilding of the caliper.

If one or more of the pistons are frozen or do not move freely within their cylinders, rust or scoring of the cylinder walls is probably the cause and the caliper must be overhauled. Also, if leakage is apparent the caliper should be overhauled and new piston seals and boots installed.

Push Out Frozen Pistons Hydraulically

Use hydraulic pressure, created by pushing on the brake pedal, to force the sticking or frozen pistons out of their bores. As a precaution, a cover should be placed over the caliper to keep brake fluid from squirting onto the finish of the car in the event that a piston emerges from its cylinder beyond the piston seal. Normally, the piston will not have enough travel to come completely out of its bore unless the disc has been worn beyond factory specifications. Additional brake fluid may have to be added to the

master cylinder reservoir to push the pistons out against the face of the brake disc. The pistons are shown resting against the disc faces in Fig. 4-31.

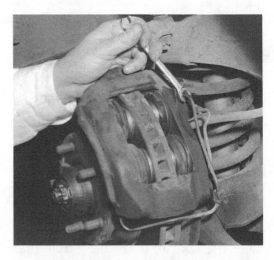

Fig. 4-31. After the shoes are removed, sticking or frozen pistons should be forced as far out of their bores as possible (all the way to the disc face). Before disassembling the caliper the brake fluid transfer tubing is disconnected. (*Automotive Service Industry Assn.*)

**Repeat the Previous Four Steps
for the Right Front Wheel**

Following the procedures outlined above, remove the right front wheel disc brake shoes. Force the piston out of the right front caliper and against the face of the brake disc.

Before proceeding with the disassembly of the disc brake calipers, remove the rear wheel brake drums. Turn the drum having the largest diameter, or the drum most deeply scored, on a drum lathe. Use the procedures outlined earlier in this chapter to restore the rear brakes.

Disassemble the Calipers

Remove the brake fluid cross-over pipe with a tubing wrench, as shown in Fig. 4-31. Then, split the caliper by removing the caliper bridge bolts shown in Fig. 4-32. *Note: The bridge bolts are special heat-treated bolts. Do not substitute other types if the caliper bridge bolts are defective; obtain exact replacement bolts.*

Having removed the bridge bolts and cross-over, lift the outer half of the caliper assembly from the disc. The inner

Fig. 4-32. The caliper halves are separated by removing the caliper bridge bolts. (*Automotive Service Industry Assn.*)

caliper half remains on the car. Allow the brake fluid to drain from the caliper. Clamp the outer part of the caliper in a vise. Care should be taken so that no critical part of the outer caliper half is damaged by the vise jaws.

Check the Brake Disc Wear

Use an outside micrometer to determine if the brake disc has been worn beyond manufacturer's specifications, as illustrated in Fig. 4-33. Check the disc for thickness variation by measuring the disc at three or more places about its circumference, about 1 inch from the rim of the disc.

Fig. 4-33. Use a micrometer to check the brake disc thickness. Check variation in thickness by taking readings at several points along the disc circumference. (*Automotive Service Industry Assn.*)

Check the Brake Discs for Lateral Runout

Install a dial indicator on the spindle. Locate the indicator anvil about 1 inch from the rim of the disc as shown in Fig. 4-34. Rotate the disc slowly. Note the maximum Total Indicated Reading of the indicator. If the T. I. R. is greater than factory specifications allow, the wheel bearing should be loaded to specifications with a torque wrench and a second runout test should be made to elimi-

Fig. 4-34. Use a dial indicator to check the disc for runout. (*Automotive Service Industry Assn.*)

nate the possibility of a runout reading due to loose or damaged bearings. Determine whether the disc should be resurfaced, reconditioned or replaced by the overall appearance of the disc.

Remove the Brake Discs from the Spindles

Remove the grease cap, spindle nut, safety washer, and outer bearing cone. Screw on the spindle nut a few turns. Using the spindle nut as a stop, pull the disc off the spindle sharply. This action will remove the inner bearing and grease seal from the hub.

Bearing Cup Inspection and Replacement

Inspect the hubs' inner and outer bearing races thoroughly for pits and nicks, Fig. 4-35. If a defective bearing cup or race is found, use a punch to drive the cup from the hub.

Do not attempt to drive a new outer race into the hub with a punch, as the outer edge of the new cup may be damaged in the process. Instead drive the bearing cup flush with the hub face using

Fig. 4-35. Check the bearing cups for visual defects. Check the edges of the cups for burrs by running a finger around the edge as shown. (*Automotive Service Industry Assn.*)

a soft brass drift. The lathe arbor and nut can be used to seat the bearing cup completely into the hub as described below.

Lathe Setup for Turning the Brake Disc

After both rear drums have been machined, the setup for machining the front brake discs can be made. (The setup for turning a brake disc is described in detail in Chapter 3 on Service. Only the highlights will be mentioned here.) Remove the tool bar used to turn the brake drums from the lathe cross slide swivel block. Install the brake disc tool bar on the cross slide of the lathe.

Mount the brake disc on the lathe arbor, using the correct adaptors. An adaptor selector chart furnished with the lathe will indicate the correct adaptor to use for the particular brake disc being machined. Tighten the arbor nut to firmly seat the wheel bearing cups in the hub of the brake disc. Attach a vibration dampener to the brake disc; attach it to the face behind the one to be machined first.

Machine the Brake Disc

Adjust the tool bar so that it extends only far enough out of the tool holder to machine the entire friction surface of the disc face. Lock the tool bar in the tool holder. Turn on the lathe. Turning the drum feed handwheel, move the disc so that it just contacts the disc face. Note the reading on the micrometer collar of the depth-of-cut handwheel (the drum feed handwheel in this case). This reading serves as a reference point to determine how much metal is to be removed from the disc face. Set the depth-of-cut control to remove 0.004 inch more than the deepest groove or score mark in the disc face. Move the cutting tool to the extreme inner diameter of the disc face. Turn on the automatic feed.

After the first face of the disc has been machined, switch the vibration dampener to the just-turned face of the disc. Make the necessary changes in the tool setting. Machine the other face of the brake disc, following the procedures mentioned both here and in the preceding chapter.

The finish on the disc face will not be acceptable if a fast feed rate is used. A brake disc grinder attachment is mounted on the lathe and used to make the disc surface nondirectional, or to remove the tool marks. The disc brake grinder also provides an acceptable micro-finish to the disc face. If the disc shows evidence of hard spots, a hard spot drum grinder can be used.

Rebuild the Inner and Outer Caliper Halves

While the disc is being machined, the inner and outer caliper halves can be rebuilt. The inner caliper half can be rebuilt without removing it from the car. The outer caliper half is held in a bench vise as it is being rebuilt.

The brake job illustrated in this section is being performed on a Kelsey-Hayes disc brake design. This design features metal bands, or retainers, which hold the cylinder boots in position. Remove the boots by stretching them and slipping them off their retainers.

Remove the pistons with a piston removing tool (or similar tool with expanding jaws), which grips the piston at its hollowed-out part as shown in Fig. 4-36. After removing the pistons from the cylinder bores, remove the piston seals with a small screwdriver. The screwdriver may be modified to facilitate removal of the seal. Avoid scratching the cylinder wall or the piston seal groove.

Note that in this disc brake caliper design the cylinder bores are not flush with the inner surface of the caliper half. The boot retainer seats on the machined outside surface of the boss, or on that part of the cylinder that extends from the flat inner surface of the caliper. Visually inspect the boot retainers for nicks and burrs. See Fig. 4-37. Remove damaged

Fig. 4-36. Removing a piston from the inner caliper half. (*Automotive Service Industry Assn.*)

Fig. 4-37. A damaged boot retainer is shown removed from the lower cylinder boss. The new retainer (left hand) is being compared to the damaged retainer ring. (*Automotive Service Industry Assn.*)

Fig. 4-38. Seat a new boot retainer with a hard rubber or wooden block to avoid damage to the retainer during installation. (*Automotive Service Industry Assn.*)

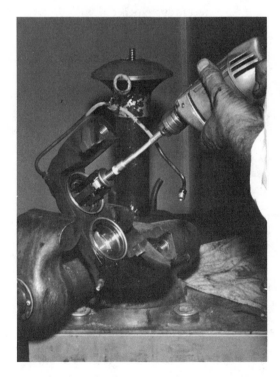

Fig. 4-39. Inspection honing the caliper bores. (*Automotive Service Industry Assn.*)

boot retainers by prying the retainer from the boss of the caliper. Install the new boot retainer by using a special tool or a round hardwood block or mallet head to seat the retainer on the boss, as shown in Fig. 4-38. Later caliper designs have done away with a boot retainer of this type.

Use an inspection hone mounted in an electrical drill to clean the cylinder walls, as shown in Fig. 4-39. Alcohol or brake fluid can be used as a honing fluid. Clean the caliper cylinder bores with a clean shop cloth and alcohol.

Install new piston seals into the grooves of the cylinder bores as illustrated in Fig. 4-40. *Note: Do not reuse old seals or boots.* Lubricate the caliper piston with brake fluid or wheel cylinder assembly fluid. Push the piston into the cylinder bore slowly, being careful not to force the seal out of its groove. See Fig. 4-41.

Install the new caliper piston boots as

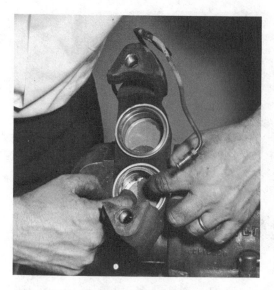

Fig. 4-40. Installing new piston seals. In this design the piston seal seats in a groove machined in the cylinder bore. (*Automotive Service Industry Assn.*)

Fig. 4-42. Installing the new piston boots. The boot is slipped over the retainer and seats in a groove in the piston. (*Automotive Service Industry Assn.*)

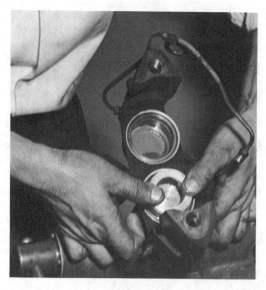

Fig. 4-41. Installing the piston in its caliper bore. Care must be taken not to dislodge the piston seal in the process. (*Automotive Service Industry Assn.*)

shown in Fig. 4-42. The boot fits around the boot retainer, and the inner diameter of the boot fits into a groove in the outer edge of the piston.

Use fine emery cloth or No. 400 wet-or-dry paper to clean the mating surfaces of the caliper halves. *Do not use a file.* The mating surface must be accurate, otherwise the caliper could be distorted when it is bolted together.

Pack the Front Wheel Bearings

Pack the wheel bearings with a good quality wheel bearing grease. Use a wheel bearing packer to insure proper grease distribution throughout the bearings.

Install Wheel Bearings, Mount Disc on Spindle, and Adjust Bearings

The front wheel bearing arrangement for cars with disc brakes is the same as that for a car with front drum brakes. The hub is joined to the brake disc instead of to the brake drum. The inner bearing and seal are installed in the hub as explained in the first part of this chapter.

Mount the disc on the spindle. Install the outer bearing, seal, and spindle nut.

Fig. 4-43. Installing new shoes in the caliper. (*Automotive Service Industry Assn.*)

Use a torque wrench to properly seat the bearing cups and to force any excess of fresh grease out of the bearings. Tighten the spindle nut to a torque of 30 ft lbs. This assures an accurate alignment of the bearings. Then, back off the spindle nut until the disc is loose on the spindle. Tighten the spindle nut finger tight or to the car manufacturer's specifications. Install a new pin and replace the grease cap.

Reassemble Outer Half of Caliper to Inner Half

Bolt the outer section of the caliper to the inner section with the caliper bridge bolts. Refer to the car manufacturer's factory specifications for the torque required to tighten the bolts. Tighten the flare nuts on the cross-over tube with a suitable wrench.

Obtain the correct disc brake shoes by using the F.M.S.I. (Friction Materials Standards Institute) shoe catalog. For ex-ample, the F.M.S.I. number for the shoe shown being installed in Fig. 4-43 is S-728. If the old shoes are to be reused, be sure to install them in their former locations.

After the shoes have been installed, the retainer plate is bolted to the caliper. Install the splash shield-retainer plate correctly or the wheel may scrape on it.

Bleed the Brakes

Install the proper single or dual master cylinder bleeder adaptor if bleeding the brakes with a portable pressure bleeder. Figure 4-44 illustrates a typical bleeder adaptor for a dual master cylinder. Observe the warning on the master cylinder cover relative to the type of brake fluid which must be used.

Connect the pressure bleeder to a front tire to obtain 30 lbs of pressure or inflate the pressure bleeder to 30 lbs of pressure with an air hose. Open the

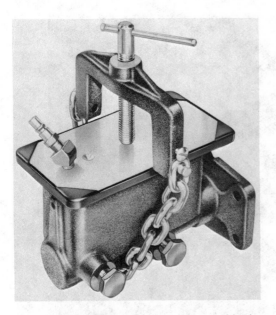

Fig. 4-44. Adaptor for connecting a pressure bleeder to a typical dual master cylinder. (*Automotive Service Industry Assn.*)

bleeder valve on the master cylinder first, then bleed the LF, RF, LR and finally the RR brake assembly as indicated earlier in this chapter. Note: The metering valve bleeder button must be depressed when pressure bleeding the front disc brakes.

Replace Wheels, Remove Car from Hoist and Test Brakes

Install the wheels. Remove car from hoist or jack stands. Apply the brake pedal a few times to insure proper brake operation before the car is moved.

Sliding Caliper Disc Brakes

This "complete" disc brake job contains all the basic steps required to service sliding caliper design disc brakes.

Remove the Wheels

Remove the wheel covers and loosen the wheel nuts. Support the car on a hoist or jack stands. Remove the wheel nuts. Mark a hub stud and its corresponding hole in the wheel to retain the wheel balance. Remove all four wheels from their hubs. Place the wheels, with the outer sidewall down, on the floor. Put the wheel covers inside the wheel wells and use the wheel covers to collect the brake parts. Removal of the front wheels exposes the front brake discs and their calipers. Mark the brake discs L or R so they will be re-installed properly on the car.

Remove the Retaining Pin Clips

Use the blade of a small screwdriver, as shown in Fig. 4-45, to disconnect the clips from the retaining pins. The pins hold the outboard shoe in the caliper.

Retract Brake Shoes

The caliper piston should be bottomed in its bore to allow removal of the caliper from the rotor. The rotor develops a ridge of rust and scale at its outer circumference that makes removal of the caliper difficult if a C-clamp is not used to retract the caliper (Fig. 4-46).

Remove the Locating Pins

The caliper locating or mounting pins hold the caliper to the mounting bracket. The pins are screwed into either a threaded hole in the calipers or the anchor. Use a socket and rachet wrench (see Fig. 4-47) to remove the threaded portion of the pin from the anchor. The pin can now be pulled from the rubber bushings located in the anchor as shown in Fig. 4-48.

The locating pins of the Kelsey-Hayes and Delco Moraine calipers slide through rubber "O" rings in the caliper. Figure

Fig. 4-45. Use a small screwdriver to remove the outboard shoe retaining clips. (*Ammco Tools Inc.*)

Fig. 4-46. Use a C-clamp to bottom piston in caliper bore. (*Kelsey-Hayes* Co.)

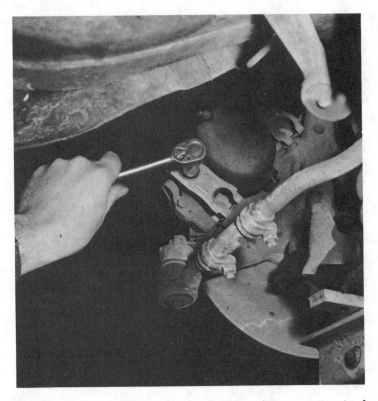

Fig. 4-47. Use a small rachet wrench with a socket to remove the caliper mounting pins from the adaptor. (*Ammco Tools Inc.*)

Fig. 4-48. Removing the locating pins from the anchor bushings. (*Ammco Tools Inc.*)

4-49 shows a pin being removed from a Kelsey-Hayes disc brake caliper.

Remove the Brake Hose

Disconnect the brake hose from the caliper either by removing the bolt that holds it to the caliper (Fig. 4-50) or by turning the threaded end of the hose out of the caliper. Be careful not to lose the seals or washers that are on the hose bolt as shown in Fig. 4-51.

Always re-install the washers in the same way they were originally, or leakage of hydraulic fluid can result.

Remove the Caliper from the Mounting Bracket or Spindle. Rebuild the Caliper

Remove the piston by first placing an old shoe in the caliper to act as a stop.

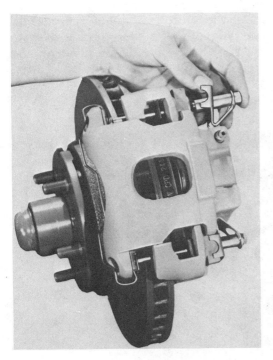

Fig. 4-49. Removing the locating pins from the caliper rubber bushings. (*Kelsey-Hayes Co.*)

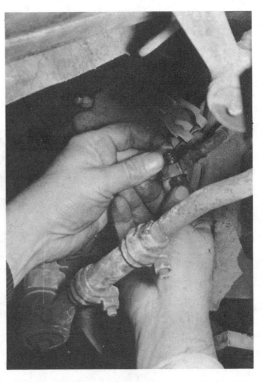

Fig. 4-51. Remove the washers from the brake hose bolt. (*Ammco Tools Inc.*)

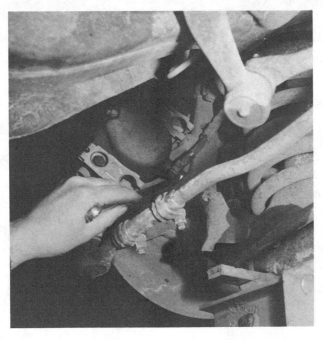

Fig. 4-50. Use an open-end wrench to remove the brake hose bolt from the caliper. (*Ammco Tools Inc.*)

Then, as in Fig. 4-52, blow out the piston by placing a nozzle in the inlet hole at the caliper. Care should be taken to keep the fingers out of the way.

Pry the piston seal out of its groove in the cylinder wall as shown in Fig. 4-53.

With an electric driven hone and alcohol as a lubricant, remove the corro-

Fig. 4-52. Remove the caliper piston with an air nozzle. (*Ammco Tools Inc.*)

Fig. 4-53. Remove the piston seal with a small screwdriver. (*Ammco Tools Inc.*)

Fig. 4-54. Surface the caliper bore. (Ammco Tools Inc.)

Fig. 4-55. Inserting the lubricated piston inside the boot and seal on Ford and Kelsey-Hayes calipers. (Ammco Tools Inc.)

sion from the caliper bore as shown in Fig. 4-54. Wipe the bore with a shop towel dampened in alcohol to clean the caliper before re-assembling it.

Install a new seal in the groove of the caliper bore.

Coat the piston with assembly fluid so it will easily slide inside the caliper boot and seal.

Install the dust boot over the piston and fit the lip of the boot inside the recess in the caliper. Then push the piston down through the boot and seal (Fig. 4-55).

Delco-Moraine calipers use a seal that presses into a recess in the caliper. A special installation tool is used as shown in Fig. 4-56 to install the seal.

Anchor the Outboard Shoe to the Caliper

The outboard shoe is secured to the caliper on Ford products as shown in Figure 4-57. Delco-Moraine shoes are

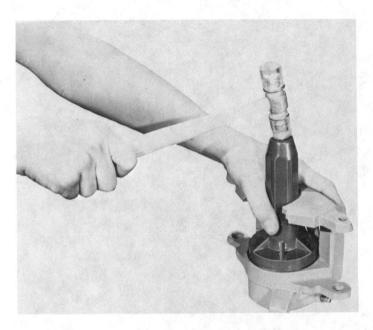

Fig. 4-56. Installing the Delco-Moraine caliper dust boot with a special installation tool. (*Kelsey-Hayes* Co.)

Fig. 4-57. Hold the shoe in the caliper with the retaining pins and secure with the clips. (*Ammco Tools Inc.*)

clamped to the caliper by bending the tabs or ears of the new brake shoes as shown in Fig. 4-58. The C-clamp holds the shoe in place while the tabs are bent.

Determine the Condition of the Rotor

The rotor must be checked for overall thickness to determine whether it may be reconditioned on the lathe. Check

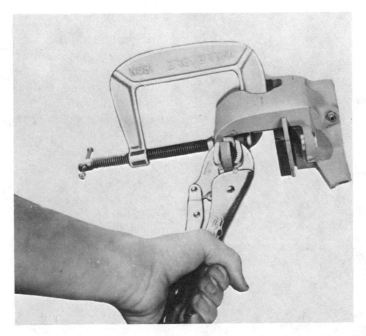

Fig. 4-58. Bend the tabs of the Delco-Moraine brake shoes to secure them to the caliper. (*Kelsey-Hayes* Co.)

Fig. 4-59. Measure the thickness of the rotor with an outside micrometer. (*Ammco Tools Inc.*)

manufacturer's specifications for minimum thickness of the rotor. See Fig. 4-59. Also determine the runout of the rotor. Use a dial indicator as shown in Fig. 4-60 to determine the runout and then mark the results on the rotor.

Fig. 4-60. Determine the run-out or wobble with a dial indicator. (*Ammco Tools Inc.*)

Recondition the Rotor

Recondition the rotor by first mounting it on the arbor of a lathe (Fig. 4-61). A dial indicator is sometimes used to match the rotor's runout on the lathe's arbor to that amount determined when the rotor was on the car's spindle (Fig. 4-60).

Recondition the rotor by removing all the score marks made by the old shoes as shown in Fig. 4-62.

After both faces of the rotor are reconditioned, the micrometer should be used to measure the thickness of the rotor at three or more places about the circumference of the rotor. See Fig. 4-63. A variation of .0005" between readings would mean that the faces of the rotor are not parallel and could cause the brake pedal to hop up and down as the brakes are applied while stopping the car.

Remove the rotor from the lathe.

Remove the Inboard Shoe from the Anchor

Slide the old inboard shoe out of the

Fig. 4-61. Mount the rotor on the disc brake lathe arbor. (*Ammco Tools Inc.*)

Fig. 4-62. Machine the rotor's faces. (*Ammco Tools Inc.*)

Fig. 4-63. Check rotor for thickness variation. (*Ammco Tools Inc.*)

Fig. 4-64. Remove the inboard shoe from the anchor. (*Ammco Tools Inc.*)

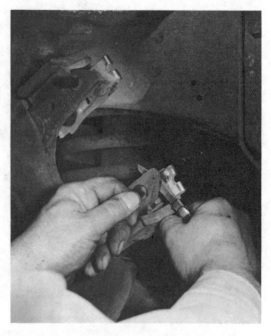

Fig. 4-65. Cut the back off the old bushing with a knife. (*Ammco Tools Inc.*)

anchor of a Ford brake. See Fig. 4-64. The metal clips and stabilizers should be replaced if they are corroded. All of these parts are available in one package called a hardware kit.

Replace the Rubber Locating Pin Bushings

The rubber bushings that are a part of the hardware kit are replaced first by cutting the rear part of the bushing off with a knife. Then pull the bushing out of its hole in the anchor as shown in Fig. 4-65.

The new rubber bushings are coated with water or alcohol and pulled into place with pliers, Fig. 4-66. Install the new inboard shoe under the clips. See Fig. 4-64.

Kelsey-Hayes locating pin bushings or "O" rings are in recess in the caliper. Pry them out with a screwdriver, as shown in Fig. 4-67, and re-install them with water or alcohol as a lubricant.

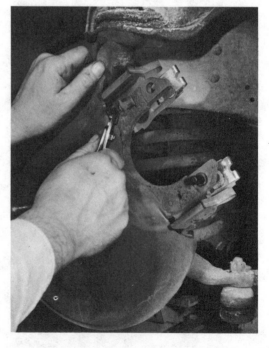

Fig. 4-66. Install the new rubber bushings. (*Ammco Tools Inc.*)

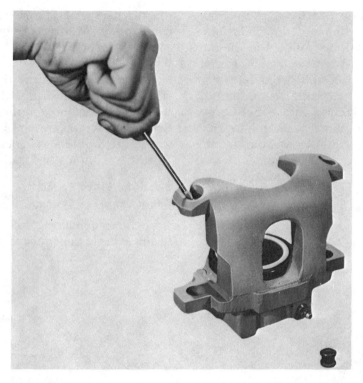

Fig. 4-67. Removing the rubber "O" Rings from a Kelsey-Hayes caliper. (*Kelsey-Hayes* Co.)

Pack the Front Wheel Bearings

Pack the wheel bearings with disc brake wheel bearing grease. Use a wheel bearing packer to insure proper grease distribution throughout the bearings.

Install Wheel Bearings, Mount Disc on Spindle, and Adjust Bearings

The front wheel bearing arrangement for cars with disc brakes is the same as that for a car with front drum brakes.

Fig. 4-68. Tighten the spindle nut with a torque wrench. (*Ammco Tools Inc.*)

The hub is joined to the brake disc instead of to the brake drum. The inner bearing and seal are installed in the hub as explained on page 138 of this chapter.

Mount the disc on the spindle. Install the outer bearing, seal, and spindle nut. Use a torque wrench, Fig. 4-68, to properly seat the bearing cups and to force any excess of fresh grease out of the bearings. Tighten the spindle nut to a torque of 30 ft lbs. This assures an accurate alignment of the bearings. Then, *back off* the spindle nut until the spindle nut is loose on the spindle. Tighten the spindle nut *finger tight* or to the car man-

ufacturer's specifications. Install a new cotter pin and replace the grease cap.

Install the Caliper on the Anchor Bracket

Place the caliper into the caliper anchor and install the caliper locating pins. Use water or alcohol to lubricate the pins to make assembly easier. Use a torque wrench to tighten the locating pins to 35 ft lbs. as shown in Fig. 4-69.

Bleed the Brake System
Check the Brake System

Before delivering the car to the owner, check the brakes for correct op-

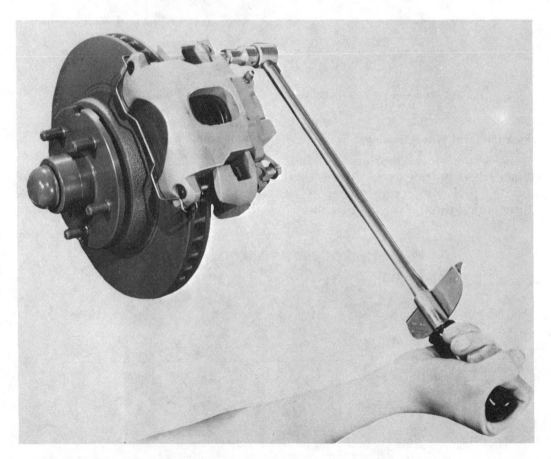

Fig. 4-69. Tighten the locating pins with a torque wrench. (*Kelsey-Hayes* Co.)

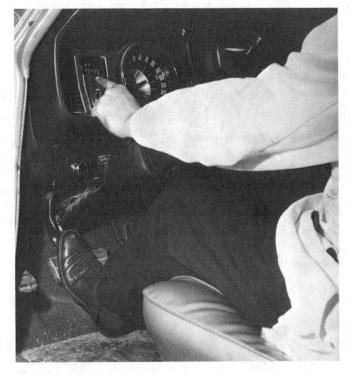

Fig. 4-70. Push the pedal to check if brake warning light is still off. (*Ammco Tools, Inc.*)

eration. Push the brake pedal down hard a few times to seat the disc brake shoes against the rotor. The brake warning light on the instrument panel should remain off. See Fig. 4-70. If it should remain on, follow the procedure outlined below to center the warning light switch.

1. Open a caliper bleeder valve one turn.

2. Push brake pedal down slowly with the engine idling.

3. When the brake light goes out, release the brake pedal.

4. Close the bleeder valve and fill the master cylinder reservoir with brake fluid.

TRADE COMPETENCY TEST

1. How is the operation of the master cylinder affected by a defective master cylinder cup?

2. Why is a wheel mounting stud and its corresponding hole in the wheel marked when doing a brake job?

3. How can a spindle nut be used to pull the inner bearing cone and seal from the hub?

4. Why should the bearing seal be cleaned before the front drum is turned on the lathe?

5. What could cause the lining thickness at the heel or anchor end of the secondary shoe to be thinner than the lining at the toe end of the shoe?

6. How can the condition of a brake spring be tested?

7. What can happen when assembling the rear brake shoes if the parking brakes are maladjusted?

8. What should be used to clean the drums after they have been machined?
9. At what point of the brake job should the parking brake be adjusted?
10. Does the lining of a disc brake shoe wear uniformly?
11. How can frozen pistons be removed from the caliper?
12. What tool is used to check the lateral run-out of a brake disc?
13. What tool is used to determine the thickness variation of a brake disc?
14. Why shouldn't a new bearing cup (race) be driven into the hub with a hard, sharp tool?
15. Why should old piston seals be removed from the cylinder bores carefully?
16. What fluid should be used to clean the calipers?
17. What is used to lubricate new caliper piston seals?
18. How could the caliper be distorted when it is assembled?
19. What torque reading is recommended to properly seat the bearing cups in a disc brake hub?
20. What is the procedure for bleeding a disc brake system?
21. What must be done to the metering valve to bleed disc brake calipers?
22. Why may the procedure for grinding the brake shoe of a fixed-anchor brake assembly differ from that of grinding an adjustable anchor brake shoe assembly?
23. Why is it necessary to grind the brake shoes on a disc brake?
24. Why are the brake shoes of a drum brake cam ground?

INDEX

Numerals in **bold type** refer to illustrations.